AF600289

De Bow's Review

De Bow's Review

The Antebellum Vision of a New South

John F. Kvach

Scholarly publisher for the Commonwealth,
serving Bellarmine University, Berea College, Centre College of Kentucky, Eastern Kentucky University, The Filson Historical Society, Georgetown College, Kentucky Historical Society, Kentucky State University, Morehead State University, Murray State University, Northern Kentucky University, Transylvania University, University of Kentucky, University of Louisville, and Western Kentucky University.

Editorial and Sales Offices: The University Press of Kentucky
663 South Limestone Street, Lexington, Kentucky 40508-4008
www.kentuckypress.com

17 16 15 14 13 5 4 3 2 1

Library of Congress Cataloging-in-Publication Data

Kvach, John F., 1970-
De Bow's review : the antebellum vision of a new South / John F. Kvach.
pages cm
Includes bibliographical references and index.
ISBN 978-0-8131-4420-7 (hardcover : alk. paper) — ISBN 978-0-8131-4422-1 (pdf) — ISBN 978-0-8131-4421-4 (epub)
1. Southern States—Civilization—1775-1865 2. Southern States—Economic conditions—19th century. 3. Southern States—Commerce—History—19th century. 4. Nationalism—Southern States—History—19th century. 5. Slavery—Southern States—Justification. 6. Secession—Southern States. 7. De Bow's review (1853-1880) 8. De Bow, J. D. B. (James Dunwoody Brownson), 1820-1867. 9. De Bow, J. D. B. (James Dunwoody Brownson), 1820-1867—Influence. I. Title.
F213.K83 2013
975—dc23 2013029382

This book is printed on acid-free paper meeting the requirements of the American National Standard for Permanence in Paper for Printed Library Materials.

Manufactured in the United States of America.

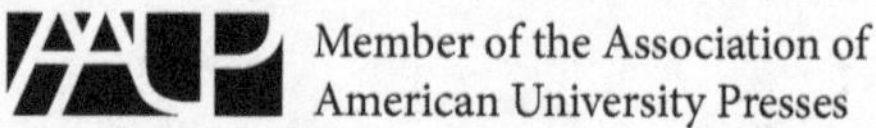
Member of the Association of
American University Presses

To Ann, Ben, and Tom

Contents

Introduction

An Old Foundation for a New South

James Dunwoody Brownson (J. D. B.) De Bow lived a paradoxical life. Born into a middle-class merchant family along the Atlantic coast of South Carolina in 1820, he used his monthly journal, commonly known as *De Bow's Review*, to become the chief spokesman for wealthy planters and entrepreneurs in the Old Southwest. Despite living in an agricultural region dominated by plantations and farms, he used his editorial influence to promote urban development and industrialization as key elements for southern economic growth. Although his peers often wrote in sweeping rhetorical flourishes, De Bow relied on statistical analysis and factual writing to inform his readers. His reputation as a passionate southern fire-eater belied his positive feelings about the Union, which lasted until the early 1850s. He supported secession and the creation of a southern nation but rejected both after the Confederacy's defeat in May 1865. These personal paradoxes have muddled his place in southern history. Ottis C. Skipper, De Bow's only biographer, referred to him as the "magazinist of the Old South," while Paul Gaston believed that he served as the first postwar apostle of the New South Creed.[1] Although both descriptions of him are partially accurate, neither places him properly in the broader context of the nineteenth-century American South. De Bow became the first southerner to recognize and promote a comprehensive regional economic and social vision that blended the South's past with a more diverse future. He foresaw how slavery and plantations could coexist with railroads, factories, and cities. He wanted readers to understand that industrialists, merchants, and planters had similar goals and that they all needed to work together to improve the South's future. His journal succeeded because he introduced new innovations without ever threatening established southern institutions. By being able to blend old practices with new ideas, he created an acceptable framework for southern readers interested in personal profit and community development. De Bow believed that a consolidated regional plan would give the South a competitive economic edge over the North. He articulated a plausible vision of new cities, factories, industries, and farming techniques. His visualization of an evolving South appealed to antebellum readers hoping to find and invest in new opportunities or improve on old ones. That same vision became the foundation for postbellum southerners looking for renewal and redemption after the Civil War. Although the Civil War fundamentally changed the American South, the conflict only disrupted De Bow's efforts to improve the South. He served as a reminder to postwar southern readers that continuity could exist within periods of discontinuity and change.

Although many past and present historians have used *De Bow's Review* as an essential primary source for their own work, few of them have understood De Bow beyond his broad publishing legacy or his role as an angry southern fire-eater. De Bow, the antebellum South's most influential editor and the first proponent of an encompassing regional creed that called for economic and social innovation, spent much of his professional life brokering information, statistics, and opinions to southern readers who wanted to enlarge their worldviews, maximize their profits, and improve the South's future. His greatest trait was his ability to recognize the intrinsic value of disparate plans, schemes, and ideas and then reformulate them into a regional agenda and language that southern readers could accept and understand as their own. He empowered his readers with practical knowledge on commodity prices, market trends, and new inventions, prodding them to think about the region's vast untapped potential beyond cotton, slaves, and land. The *Review* became a place where De Bow and his readers could safely share ideas about urban development, commercial growth, industrial innovation, and new agricultural practices. He channeled valuable information to subscribers who had the ability and capital to elicit regional action, promising them that hard work and personal initiative would yield higher profit margins. He asked subscribers to reinvest their profits in schools, libraries, and other cultural resources as a way of developing a sense of community. De Bow, the information broker, southern promoter, and American idealist, created the foundation of a "New South" by asking antebellum southerners to invest in new machines, processes, and ideas that would enhance the region's commercial and industrial competitiveness. He promised readers that this economic transformation could occur while protecting established southern traditions and institutions. If they did this, he promised, the South would enter into an unparalleled period of economic and social development that would secure southern interests against regional competition from the North and West. His positive editorial tone and promotional flair made him the preeminent spokesman for white southerners who wanted to grab their share of the American dream.

De Bow's legacy as the antebellum South's most prolific regional booster has been obscured by postbellum promoters and historians who have insisted that the "Old South" represented a place frozen in time by languid planters, subservient slaves, and poor white trash. Descriptions of a premodern region that valued only cotton, slavery, and land fail to account for his advocacy of southern urbanization, industrialization, and internal improvements. These limited histories cannot explain the existence of *Review* readers who attempted to develop new southern commercial centers, factories, and railroads. Their monolithic and at times partisan approach to the Old South fail to acknowledge that pre–Civil War southerners lived and worked in a globally oriented region driven by profit-minded planters, merchants, professionals, and factory owners. De Bow's value to these ambitious southerners and to their region lay not in his original ideas but in his ability to recognize, organize, and delineate a regional economic and social agenda that embraced enterprise within the conservative confines of antebellum southern society. De Bow used the *Review* to encourage southern readers to think about new ideas and initiatives that would allow the South to become more competitive in a growing regional rivalry with the North and West. He also reflected the broader aspirations of many nineteenth-century Americans, regardless of region, who looked to expand their mastery of the world around them. He and his readers struggled to establish new traditions in an evolving nation while simultaneously preserving the economic and cultural markers of a slave society. Although they accomplished many of their goals, he, like many antebellum southerners who defied later stereotypes of an "Old South," became lost in a maze of postbellum New South deceptions and in the mawkish remembrances of the Lost Cause.

There was a much darker side to De Bow's agenda, however, one in which information empowered him to manipulate white southern readers as the sectional crisis intensified during the 1850s. De Bow used his words and ideas to dominate southern minds at a time when narrowing viewpoints made readers suspicious of any perceived political, social, economic, or cultural threats. He exploited southerners by publishing inflammatory articles that heightened sectional tension, legitimized proslavery ideology, and encouraged southern nationalism. Information became an important commodity in a region isolated by geography and a willingness to create seclusion through gag rules, mail censorship, and a one-party system that silenced critics and dissenters. De Bow manipulated information and data to create southern paranoia and fear, hoping that such feelings would drive white southerners toward a single regional agenda under the guise of a solid South. His willingness to see different perspectives disappeared as northern attacks against southern institutions intensified, and he refused to compromise with real or perceived enemies of the South. The *Review* stopped being a practical resource for farmers, industrialists, and merchants and instead became an ideological device for regional cranks hoping to drive the South out of the Union. De Bow rejoiced at the news of secession and war because he believed it offered the South an opportunity for a new beginning.

Yet war brought personal misery and maddening isolation to a man accustomed to controlling information and minds. Warring armies and naval blockades destroyed the networks De Bow relied on and the world he loved. Ultimately, military defeat and the collapse of the Confederacy refocused him, and he vowed to use his knowledge to reformulate a regional plan of economic and social redemption. His twenty years of editorial experience meant that he did not have to conjure up new ideas to sell to desperate southern readers. Despite his wrongheaded prewar predictions and his exposed editorial manipulations, thousands of postwar southerners still trusted his advice and opinion. His death in February 1867 limited his postwar influence, and soon a new generation of southern boosters emerged to take his place. This second generation of regional promoters, like De Bow, found it personally and professionally beneficial to gather information and use it to manipulate southern readers with promises that always seemed to lurk just outside their reach. De Bow's true historical legacy likely belongs somewhere between his positive traits as an information broker and his negative qualities as a regional sycophant who manipulated southerners.

Who read *De Bow's Review* was as important as who wrote the articles or published the journal. In order to understand De Bow's editorial legacy, modern readers need to understand the lives and livelihoods of *Review* subscribers as an organic cohort of like-minded antebellum southerners. Partial subscription lists, professional correspondence, and personal letters make it possible to identify thousands of De Bow's followers. The 1860 US Census allowed for the positive identification of almost fifteen hundred subscribers from this larger initial pool of names. Local histories, government records, city directories, archival collections, and family genealogies allowed simple names to become rich personal histories of individuals who subscribed to *De Bow's Review* before the Civil War. These sources allow modern readers to see the interaction between ideology and action and avoid the pitfalls of a simple biography or intellectual history of an individual. *Review* readers are as important to this story as De Bow himself. His ideas can now be placed within the context of their lives and accomplishments and the overall development of the antebellum South. This interplay of individual ideas and collective action created a tangible plan for regional improvement that eventually developed into a creed that would have been recognizable to postwar southerners. Although the extensive scope of the *Review* minimized regional editorial competition, many similar local and state journals developed around De Bow's basic economic principles and editorial tenets. His legacy can now be placed within the context of the accomplishments and failures of his readers and like-minded southerners, who, until recently, have been obscured by stereotypical perceptions of a backward Old South.

The majority of De Bow's support came from urban, middle-class merchants, large planters who lived in cotton and sugar regions, wealthy entrepreneurs, and professional men. The *Review* mirrored their interests. De Bow wanted readers to devote their attention to enterprises that improved the future for all southerners. Many of his subscribers invested in projects that promised to yield personal profits while also benefiting their communities. Although the *Review* became popular among southern readers, De Bow struggled to maintain enough paying subscribers to remain in business. Many subscribers failed to submit their payments on time, limiting the profitably of the *Review.* Despite this hindrance, however, he succeeded where hundreds of other southerners had failed. The *Review* became the antebellum South's most prominent economic journal. Regional, national, and international newspapers and journals regularly borrowed information from it, recognizing De Bow's talents as an editor and pundit. Although it is impossible to gauge how many southerners actually read and followed his advice, enough of them subscribed to the *Review* to make it the most recognizable journal in the antebellum South.

De Bow's intense focus on economic issues made him a relative latecomer as a secessionist fire-eater. Political events and northern attacks on slavery during the early 1850s changed his editorial tone and his personal feelings toward the United States. Early in his career De Bow had shown little interest in discussing slavery. He believed that slavery allowed whites to serve as stewards for inferior blacks. Abolitionist attacks on the South's peculiar institution motivated him to become more active in his defense of slavery. As a devout expansionist when it came to slavery, he worried about the closure of western land to southern slaveholders. This threat to the South's economic future made him question the federal government's role in the abolitionist movement. Before 1854 De Bow had mostly avoided overt political discussions in the *Review,* but the Kansas-Nebraska Act and subsequent violence in Kansas provoked him to become more politically active in the southern nationalist movement. He had balanced his feelings about the nation and the South until this point, but this duality disappeared after the outbreak of violence in Kansas, and his well-known reputation as a moderate economic nationalist evaporated. As a southern fire-eater, De Bow used the *Review* to catalog northern slights, both real and perceived, and to promote a virulent proslavery ideology. His editorial focus shifted to accommodate political as well as economic topics. The *Review* became a public forum for angry southerners who resented northern attacks on slavery and other southern institutions. De Bow led a public campaign for southern independence and assured his readers that the South's economy would benefit from disunion. His economic vision shifted from regional improvement to southern independence.

Unfortunately for De Bow, the Civil War exposed significant weaknesses in the southern economy and in his economic plan. He had assured readers that their productive plantations, modern railroads, large cities, and broad commercial networks would lead to economic independence and growth. By 1860, after all, the South had grown appreciably and ranked as one of the most industrialized regions in the world. Yet too much of the South's economy had been built around King Cotton. Factories produced few goods needed by southern consumers, and merchants still relied on northern suppliers. Railroad companies, meanwhile, failed to standardize their equipment or to create an intraregional transportation network that followed the commercial geography of the South. As a result, many of these structural limitations hampered the Confederacy's war effort and led to internal weaknesses and military defeat.

Hoping to reconstruct the South on its own terms, De Bow urged postwar southerners to rebuild their economy using his prewar tenets. He repudiated his secessionist past in May 1865 and hoped for a quick reconciliation between the North and the South. He tweaked and fine-tuned his economic vision and asked southerners to reinvest in industrial diversification, immigrant labor, new crops, and urban renewal. Although De Bow accepted the military defeat of the South, he carefully avoided criticism of the Confederate government and southern soldiers. Fallen soldiers were to be memorialized as martyrs, and survivors were expected to exhibit the same zeal for reconstruction that they had shown on the battlefield. De Bow hoped to balance the traditions of the past with the necessities of the future. He looked for his readers to lead the economic transformation of the postwar South.

De Bow's vision of postwar economic reconstruction reflected later calls for the development of a New South. Aware that new southern institutions could be built to incorporate past and future traditions, he once again stressed the importance of economic modernization and innovation. This had been his creed since 1846. These ideas later became the basis for New South boosters who hoped to improve the South's economic and social position within the United States. Henry Grady, Henry Watterson, Joel Chandler Harris, Richard Edmonds, and Daniel H. Hill represented a second generation of southern boosters who hoped to change the South. These men garnered widespread public support because they wrote and spoke at a time when southerners had to listen. De Bow attempted to change the direction of the southern economy, still dominated in the minds of many southerners by slavery and cotton. He had the support of thousands of antebellum readers, yet they constituted a small portion of the South's economic capacity. Wartime destruction and the end of slavery made southerners more willing to listen to new ideas. Although circumstances and issues changed over time, the words of De Bow and Grady remained the same. They promised economic prosperity by tempting southerners with new projects and schemes. The continuity of their message is easy to trace—an economically diversified South would become a profitable South, which in turn would lead to a politically independent South. This, they promised, would unite white southerners and allow them to maintain control over their region and unique culture.

De Bow's historical legacy has often been overlooked because his ideas never fit neatly into the artificial compartments created by the terms *Old South* and *New South.* Early Old South scholars such as William Dodd, Ulrich B. Phillips, and Frank L. Owsley engaged his work on cotton production and the South's plantation economy but failed to account for his views on industrialization and urbanization. Eugene Genovese used *De Bow's*

Review extensively as a source but initially saw vestiges of a premodern society emerge rather than an economically diverse region populated by profit-minded southerners. Early New South historians such as Broadus Mitchell and Philip A. Bruce neglected to see De Bow's value because his contributions could be attributed to a prewar mind. C. Vann Woodward used *De Bow's Review* once in *Origins of the New South,* and Paul Gaston focused only on De Bow's postwar commentary as his sole contribution to the New South Creed. Woodward and Gaston failed to acknowledge that De Bow and his readers had articulated the plans and aspirations of men such as Henry Grady and Richard H. Edmonds before these postbellum boosters had been born.[2]

Recent historians have reexamined the antebellum South and have found a much different region than their predecessors had described—and, perhaps, one that De Bow would have found more recognizable as his place and time in history. New people, places, ideas, and motivations emerged as historians scoured the southern landscape away from the lure of plantations and cotton fields. They found ambitious factory owners, merchants, and professionals who lived and worked amid the moonlight and magnolias of the Old South. Jonathan D. Wells identified the existence of a self-aware southern middle class of urban merchants, professionals, and editors who relied heavily on periodicals such as *De Bow's Review* because they reflected their interests and concerns about the South's future. Other historians such as Frank Towers, Tom Downey, and Frank J. Byrne have examined the role of urban merchants and the prominence of commercial centers within the context of the South's plantation economy. They found that city dwellers, town merchants, and a growing middle class of entrepreneurs thrived in a world supposedly dominated by a hegemonic planter class. Rural planters and the South's urban middle class valued *De Bow's Review* because it offered divergent ideas and advice while promoting the systematic accumulation of economic and political capital. Susanna Delfino and Michele Gillespie have shown in numerous anthologies that southerners looked outward for new ideas and hoped to develop new linkages to the outside world. Their research shows that antebellum southerners were neither isolated nor backward in their worldview and that the industrial transformation of the South started long before the Civil War. Recent research by Aaron Marrs and Robert Gudmestad verified that specific individuals, communities, and corporations hoped to propel the South's industrial and commercial development forward by improving the region's transportation system and economic networks. A southern middle class grew as railroads and steamboats created new opportunities for eager southerners. Bruce Eelman's work on entrepreneurs in Spartanburg, South Carolina, explores the interests of middle-class southerners and provides compelling evidence that their desire to modernize was only interrupted by Civil War and not created because of it. This collection of recent research has changed how historians view antebellum southerners and the world they lived in.[3]

This book will challenge current historical and historiographic debates by highlighting De Bow's contributions and his reader's actions within the context of an ever-changing South. Past historians of the antebellum South have failed to provide a broader ideological framework for regional changes and how they fit into a longer history of the South. This study accounts for the development of individual and collective ideas, actions, and outcomes that emerged before and after the Civil War. *De Bow's Review* served as a common denominator that linked Wells's middle-class southern readers, Downey's railroad men, Byrne's merchants, and Eelman's entrepreneurs. Common traits become more evident when individual stories are cast into the wider pool of like-minded men. De Bow provided the intellectual framework for the beginning of the New South Creed, and his readers provided the action needed to put his plan into motion. They, like their postbellum counterparts, ultimately failed because not enough southerners were willing to listen to new ideas. Yet the articulation of an antebellum regional creed and the efforts of thousands of southerners prove that past images of a lazy Old South were as inaccurate as the tales of southern progress being pitched by postbellum New South hucksters. *Review* readers were not afraid of the future, and many of them viewed themselves as shapers of a distinctive southern culture that combined the best of the past and the present. Few feared factories and cities, and in fact they enjoyed them for the material and cultural comforts they provided. These readers were as important to De Bow as he was to them because they needed each other to navigate the South through regional, national, and global changes. Their stories are as important as his in this narrative because they offer evidence that *De Bow's Review* mattered in the practical and intellectual development of the southern mind.

J. D. B. De Bow defies easy periodization because he preceded historical labels created by New South mythmakers and perpetuated by historians. Without knowing the term *New South,* De Bow anticipated the development of a different future for the region. He created a sense of forward momentum and progress for southerners eager to profit from changes in the market economy. By the 1850s the South had entered into a period of intense factory construction, railroad development, and commercial growth but still failed to match northern progress. De Bow worried about southern dependence on northern factories and merchants, and he bemoaned the region's lack of manufacturing and cities. Although he spent fourteen years writing to an antebellum audience, his concerns would have been understandable to postbellum southerners in the late nineteenth century. He borrowed existing ideas about economic development and, for the first time in southern history, successfully consolidated them into a monthly journal. His reverence for past traditions helped legitimize his feelings about the future transformation of the South. Progress and modernity were to be embraced, and he expected regional support for his plan. Postbellum boosters in the 1870s and 1880s used similar techniques to forge a consensus among southerners. Although after the Civil War their creed gave the illusion of being innovative, New South boosters contributed little original material about southern economic diversification and development. As the "magazinist of the Old South," De Bow had created the basic economic tenets for the New South. His editorial contributions suggest that, instead of an Old South or a New South, the nineteenth-century South, like any evolving society, represented the true definition of history—change over time.

1

Learning to Be Southern and American

By the beginning of the nineteenth century, Charleston, South Carolina, stood ready to claim its position alongside New York, Boston, and Philadelphia as one of the great American cities. Since the earliest settlers had founded the small port village on a marshy peninsula between the Ashley and Cooper Rivers in 1670, subsequent generations of Charlestonians had invested capital and labor in their city's economic, social, and cultural development. Wealthy planters and merchants considered the city an important South Atlantic commercial hub in the lucrative triangular trade that developed among North America, Europe, and Africa. Although rice, indigo, and later cotton became the economic foundation of Charleston's export market, slave traders made the city uniquely profitable along the Atlantic coast of the American colonies. Ship captains off-loaded their human cargo and refilled their ships' holds with agricultural products and naval stores bound for Europe. By the time of the American Revolution, city planners had built a sophisticated sewer and drainage system, laid brick sidewalks, and installed gas streetlights despite the loss of commerce during the war. Profit-minded community leaders hoped that these aesthetic and practical amenities might attract new residents and businesses that would add vibrancy to the city. Ambitious planters, slave traders, and merchants benefited from established trade routes and community development, and by 1800 Charleston had grown to become the fifth largest city in the United States. Shipyards, sawmills, grist and rice mills, sugar-refining houses, wagon and wheelwright shops, a rope factory, a barrel factory, an iron foundry, and South Carolina's first textile mill augmented Charleston's thriving commercial sector and employed fifteen hundred workers by the early nineteenth century. Wealthy city residents built lavish single-family homes along the waterfront and constructed elaborate gardens to mark their success. They also invested in cultural institutions such as the Charleston Library Society, the St. Cecelia Music Society, and the College of Charleston. And even though, like most of the United States, the city suffered during the War of 1812, it enjoyed prosperity in the postwar years. Sophisticated Charlestonians eagerly anticipated better days as their city became a global center of commerce and culture in the new republic.[1]

Few observers could have predicted Charleston's sudden economic collapse in 1819. The city had developed into a significant commercial center for the state's low-country planters, upcountry farmers, and merchants. The growth of towns along the fall line that separated South Carolina's coastal and piedmont regions made Charleston an important commercial and financial center. Despite growing competition from nearby cities such as Savannah and regional commercial centers such as Baltimore, Charleston's port remained profitable as high cotton prices and a steady supply of upcountry short staple cotton flowed to the city. Moreover, in 1818 the price of cotton had peaked at just over thirty cents a pound; European demand for southern agricultural commodities had steadily increased since the War of 1812 and brought economic prosperity to much of the United States. The "Era of Good Feelings" had been good to the merchants of Charleston. But unchecked financial speculation and the sudden collapse of European money markets initiated a global economic panic that devastated the American economy. Banks called in loans to remain solvent, escalating the crisis. The lack of hard currency made it difficult for many Americans to pay their debts. And in Charleston the price of cotton dropped to below seventeen cents a pound in 1820 and would continue to fall throughout the decade, averaging nine cents a pound between 1826 and 1832.[2]

The Panic of 1819 damaged the economic foundation of Charleston as stricken planters grew more rice and cotton to compensate for losses but instead flooded the market and lowered prices. Moreover, it created an alarming citywide exodus of residents hoping to escape financial embarrassment and find new opportunities in South Carolina's upcountry and newly opened land in the western territories of the United States. Between 1819 and 1830 more than sixty-nine thousand state residents moved away from South Carolina. Fiscal mistakes and budding rivalries extended the financial depression of the city. Charleston's merchants watched as export revenues dropped from $11 million in 1816 to just under $7.5 million in 1826 and as import revenues decreased from $1.4 million in 1815 to $511,852 in 1821.

The Panic hit American cities especially hard, cutting the incomes of consumers and producers alike. Yet many merchants continued to purchase the same volume of imported merchandise without adjusting to the decrease in consumer spending. And Charleston was not the only city to suffer; the Panic hit other American urban areas just as hard, cutting the incomes of consumers and producers alike. The development of new commercial rivalries also hindered Charleston's economic recovery after 1819. The advent of the steamboat and the construction of new roads and canals shifted existing trade routes away from the city. Merchants in Camden, Columbia, and Hamburg, South Carolina, and Augusta and Savannah, Georgia, challenged Charleston's commercial primacy along the South Atlantic seaboard. The commercial success of Savannah concerned Charlestonians, who worried about losing upcountry trade to Georgian merchants. These commercial rivalries would continue to intensify until the Civil War, threatening the economic future of Charleston. The city had started its long decline toward economic marginalization, cultural isolation, and sectional discord.[3]

The growing political debate over slavery in the United States also limited the collective position of Charleston. Missouri's pending statehood in 1819 ignited discussions over the spread of slavery into western territories, and the ensuing crisis further isolated Charleston from the rest of the nation. Although American sectionalism had existed since the 1770s, the regional debate over Missouri's admission into the Union as a free state or a slave state heightened tension between the North and the South. By 1819 enough northern congressional support existed to challenge the presumption that slavery would become an uncontested part of Missouri statehood. The ensuing debate over Missouri created national anxiety and brought forth murmurs of secession among ardent southern rights advocates. William Smith, a US senator from South Carolina, created the foundation for future proslavery ideologues by arguing that slavery served as a positive good for blacks and whites. Charles Pinckney, a native Charlestonian and signer of the US Constitution, became a leading congressional opponent of any compromise that would restrict the western spread of slavery. In a speech to the House of Representatives in 1820, Pinckney defended slavery and worried about the economic implications for Charleston if any limits on slavery became law. He warned that an eventual civil war would occur if northern politicians continued to agitate against the South's "peculiar institution." Both men's roles in the congressional debates magnified South Carolina's extreme position in the crisis. Pinckney's unmatched intensity set a clear precedent for future sectional disputes over slavery, southern nationalism, and secession. Having served his state and region, the old politician retired to his Charleston mansion to a hero's welcome after Henry Clay's Missouri Compromise seemingly settled the debate in 1821 by prohibiting slavery in most of the unorganized territory obtained from the Louisiana Purchase.[4]

While much of the nation focused on the devastating effects of the Panic of 1819 and the congressional debates over Missouri's entrance into the United States, Charleston residents Garret and Mary Bridget De Bow had more immediate concerns in the summer of 1820. The young couple—Garret, a New York–born descendant of Dutch Huguenots, and Mary, the daughter of a prominent low-country family—had just welcomed James Dunwoody Brownson (J. D. B.) De Bow, their second son, into their family on July 20, 1820. Garret was already struggling to maintain the family grocery store along downtown State Street following the Panic. The birth of James stretched an already tight family budget. Although sectional interests and financial difficulties began pushing the nation apart in 1820, the De Bow family pulled closer together during those difficult times. Garret and Mary raised James in a regionally blended house that valued their respective cultures. It was from this mixture of northern and southern backgrounds and interests that J. D. B. De Bow emerged.[5]

Little is known about Garret De Bow's business career or personal life in Charleston. His father's family had left Amsterdam in the early seventeenth century and moved to New York City. His grandfather, John De Bow, worked as a cordwainer and later married Mary Ellsworth. On May 9, 1774, John and Mary's son Garret was born, before the family moved to New Jersey in the early 1770s. De Bow later served in the New Jersey state militia during the American Revolution. Garret grew up surrounded by a large extended family in New York and New Jersey. Despite his comfortable family situation, however, he eventually decided to move to South Carolina and establish himself in Charleston. Like many Americans in the early republic, he hoped to find new opportunities that would allow him to thrive away from the constraints of family and more familiar surroundings.[6]

Mary Bridget Norton was a family member of South Carolina's planter elite, and her background differed greatly from that of her future husband. Her great-grandfather, John Norton, had been an original settler along South Carolina's Atlantic coast. He purchased 400 acres on St. Helena Island and another 560 acres on what would later become known as Warsaw Island. Norton's death in 1705 meant that his property would be split into nine equal shares and divided among family members. Mary Bridget's grandfather Jonathan inherited land on the southern tip of St. Helena Island and later, in August 1756, deeded two acres for the construction of a chapel and vestry. His son, and Mary Bridget's father, William Norton, continued to farm the family land and live on the isolated island situated between Charleston and Savannah. Mary Bridget, like her future husband, hoped for a more exciting life and often visited Charleston. It was during one of these visits that the two met, and on December 4, 1802, the *Charleston Times* noted that Garret De Bow had married Mary Bridget Norton.[7]

As if economic collapse and political turmoil were not enough to absorb, Denmark Vesey's rumored slave revolt in July 1822 created further hysteria among white Charlestonians. The possibility of more large-scale slave revolts fueled white concerns in a city with the largest urban black population in the nation. The potential for bloodshed led to new slave codes restricting the movement of all blacks, slave and free, in the city. The subsequent arrival of abolitionist reading material at the city post office solidified white suspicions of racial unrest and northern agitation. White Charlestonians' fears caused them to shut their city off from outside influences. The once cosmopolitan city became insular and defensive. Vesey's motives and white reactions created an environment that allowed Charleston to pull further away from rational national debates over slavery and became the basis for South Carolina's hypersensitive response to any perceived threat from the North. Although too young to remember the Panic of 1819, the Missouri Crisis, or Denmark Vesey's failed revolt, James grew up in a city heavily influenced by all three events. As the future editor of *De Bow's Review*, he grew up with a keen sense of being southern and learning how to balance those feelings with being an American. An acute sectional division had started at the time of his birth, and, like the South, De Bow would slowly move toward extremist viewpoints as the North continued to attack slavery and the South's distinctive way of life. He, like his nation, struggled with growing divisions created by internal feelings regarding what it meant to be northern and southern.[8]

The De Bow family initially lived a chaotic life of ever-changing jobs and homes, struggling to find their place in Charleston. In 1807 Garret De Bow was a grocer at 68 East Bay Street, but by 1809 he had become a vendue master, or auctioneer, who lived at 7 East Bay Street. In the following years the family moved from Archdale Street and then back to East Bay Street, before opening a shop at 53 State Street and living at 12 Amen Street. Business prosperity brought newfound luxuries, and by 1820 the De Bows owned three slaves. Yet short-lived success failed to protect the family from outside pressures created by the financial panic; by the early 1820s Garret De Bow had lost his grocery store and declared bankruptcy. Financially ruined, and personally devastated by failure, he tried to regain his business but never rekindled past achievements. On July 14, 1826, Garret died of dyspepsia at age fifty-one, leaving his wife and four children without a provider.[9]

Despite the loss of his father and the economic and sectional turmoil that surrounded him, James De Bow fondly recalled his childhood in overly romantic tones—teasing neighborhood girls, stealing grapes from neighbors, engaging in "fisty wars" with local boys, and enjoying "old Christmas" with his family. As an adult he remembered taking steamboat rides to visit family and friends in nearby Beaufort and Bay Point, South Carolina, and reminisced about his "beautiful past—the youth of hope and joy . . . the light of other days." Years after leaving Charleston, De Bow yearned to "stand again by the banks of the Ashley and the Cooper [Rivers], or hear the waves beating up against the beach of old Sullivan's." In an introspective article for *De Bow's Review* in March 1850, he nostalgically noted that these memories held "everything of life and warmth" for him. He also recalled less flattering memories of a city that had patches of grass growing on previously busy commercial streets, a memory that shaped his later views on commercial progress and civic boosterism in the South.[10]

De Bow's private memories often contradicted his idyllic public musings. In a private journal that he sporadically kept during his childhood, he recorded his personal feelings as they related to his life. His father's death forced him to assume many family responsibilities, and by age ten he had taken a job as a clerk selling liquor at E. and J. B. Delano and Company on East Bay Street. Most of his days consisted of long stretches of inactivity and boredom separated by stocking shelves, helping customers, and taking inventory. He yearned for excitement in his life and grew despondent and restless for change. De Bow lapsed into lengthy periods of depression brought on by the slightest inconvenience or setback. He attempted to lift his spirits by attending parties and dances, taking horseback rides, walking along Charleston's Battery, and swimming in a nearby millpond. At one party he unintentionally insulted a man who took offense and challenged him to duel on the spot. He declined, offering that he "would not disgrace [himself] so much" as to fight at a public gathering but agreed to meet the man later in the evening at a more secluded spot. As De Bow returned to the party, the young man hit him from behind, and a fight broke out. He left the party and returned home after realizing the man had more friends in attendance. Although these activities made life tolerable, he confided in his diary that he suffered from "the want of employment for the body and mind."[11]

There was, however, one escape that offered De Bow respite from his low moods: the downtown Apprentices' Library Society. Charleston's elite had founded and supported a variety of intellectual and cultural institutions by the 1820s, but these institutions often avoided true intellectual debates and instead maintained a nonconfrontational approach that became known as the "Charleston style." This style mirrored the growing political and social homogenization of South Carolina, especially after the Nullification Crisis. Unlike the older, more gentlemanly Charleston Library Society, the Apprentices' Library Society aided young middle- and lower-class men who hoped to improve their lives through practical training and education. The library became De Bow's private refuge from boredom and work. His personal determination to learn and seek answers allowed him to overcome the hindrance of not attending a formal school as a child. In one summer he read Sir Walter Scott's *Ivanhoe*, Henry Fielding's *Tom Jones*, Edward B. Lytton's *Rienzi* and *Last Days of Pompeii*, Barbara Hofland's *The Maid of Moscow*, William Wirt's *Life and Character of Patrick Henry*, Charles Rollin's *Ancient Histories*, and numerous newspapers and periodicals. He attended public lectures as an additional outlet for his growing inquisitiveness and pushed for answers to questions that arose in his mind. These intellectual activities drove him to think about writing, and he studied Parker's *Exercises of Grammar and Composition* to become a better writer. He began to see his city as a writer and hoped to use his newfound interests to aid the development of Charleston.[12]

De Bow witnessed the creation of a southern nationalist movement in Charleston during the early 1830s as debates over slavery and sectionalism continued to plague South Carolina and the United States. Spurred on by what many southerners felt were unfair tariff laws, South Carolinians such as John C. Calhoun, William C. Preston, and Thomas Cooper became leaders of a movement that sought to nullify federal tariffs and protect slavery from attacks by northern abolitionists. Many prominent Charleston merchants opposed these Nullifiers because they threatened the lifestyle that had been built through compromise and tradition. Yet the economic and political decline of the city could not be denied. Timothy Green, a traveler from New York who had previously lived in Charleston, lamented to a friend that the city "appeared to live upon the remnants of its former prosperity—the continued habits which had been formed in better days." Aware of the growing dissatisfaction among southerners, Calhoun became interested in the right of nullification as a way for individual states to reject unjust federal laws. His threat of disunion over the tariffs of 1828 and 1832, and Andrew Jackson's swift presidential response to keep South Carolina in the Union, captured the nation's attention. The tariff debates and subsequent Nullification Crisis changed Calhoun's feelings about economic nationalism and made him a staunch supporter of states' rights. In South Carolina, strong antitariff feelings fused with sectional tendencies and created a growing southern nationalist movement by the early 1830s. Although De Bow was a young boy during the crisis, his interest in southern nationalism and states' rights fused with his lifelong reverence for Calhoun.[13]

Religion became an important part of De Bow's informal philosophical training as he searched for new interests that might lead to a career. He explored different ideas and never limited himself to one church; he often attended two services on Sunday and occasionally attended weekday services. He spent many evenings taking long walks in Charleston and visiting different churches. On June 12, 1836, De Bow attended a lecture by the Reverend Theodore Andrews at the Universalist Church and then walked down to St. Paul's Church to hear a Methodist sermon. After dinner he returned to the Universalist Church and listened to a sermon by the Reverend William Friske. Later that month, he attended another Friske sermon that focused on biblical passages dealing with fire and hell. He personally doubted that the world had been doomed to eternal damnation but enjoyed discussing the concept. Despite this early interest in religion, however, he never embraced a single denomination as his own.[14]

De Bow also spent considerable time exploring Charleston and noting in his short diary special events that interested him. In May 1836, he visited the city's medical college and saw some of the American victims of the "fiendish Santa Anna and his blood thirsty soldiers." Later he went down to the waterfront to see a group of Charleston militia volunteers preparing for war in Florida. He attended a large dinner in their honor and noted that many of the soldiers got drunk and serenaded the city for much of the night. Overcome by feelings of national pride, he celebrated the sixtieth anniversary of American independence with a group of men who vowed "to spill every drop of blood in defense of their liberties."[15]

In September 1836, personal tragedy once again befell De Bow when a cholera outbreak killed his older brother and mother on consecutive days. He confided his emotional pain to his diary and slipped into a prolonged depression. These personal losses, however, eventually sparked a personal and, later, editorial interest in public health. De Bow would later claim that public health served as an extension of the southern economy because clean cities could support more commerce, more industry, and a larger workforce. In Charleston, the cholera outbreak that killed his mother had spread quickly despite the proactive efforts of the city government. Local newspapers published notices from the city's board of health suggesting that citizens spread lime in standing water, clean gutters, eat and drink well, and not become overexcited. Yet, in the week of Mary Bridget's death, thirteen white adults, thirty-seven black adults, and twelve black children died of cholera. The De Bow siblings, now without mother or father, scattered across the city to stay with relatives and friends. Without parents, money, or vocational training, De Bow worried about his future. He contemplated leaving the city and living on a farm, but his uncle, a hardworking planter well acquainted with physical labor, dispelled his nephew's romanticized notion of rural solitude. Unsure of what he wanted to pursue as a vocation, De Bow became increasingly interested in exploring his personal interests before choosing a career.[16]

Personal loss intensified De Bow's desire to become a better person and to attain professional success through hard work. In his diary he wrote in large print: "Laziness is the only cause that I can attribute [to] the suppression of this journal for more than six months and a half. I must be more regular hereafter." De Bow lamented sleeping in too much, noting: "It is with shame that I must admit that I am seldom up earlier—consequently [I] lose the light of the grandest things in nature." Frustrated by unfilled promises to himself, he made a Benjamin Franklin–like list for himself that included keeping less company, adhering to earlier bedtimes, and studying and writing more. After creating his list he listened to the church bells of St. Michael's and to the sound of prostitutes who were "cursing and swearing . . . and were determined to rouse the whole neighborhood and prevent those who had not yet retired from doing so." Both sounds served as reminders of what the future could hold. He woke up the next morning and, as promised, sat down and wrote a factual article on the dangers of unfilled wells in Charleston. This would later become his first published article in the *Charleston Morning Courier*. Yet, within a month, De Bow was once again chiding himself about his undeveloped work ethic, worrying: "Oh idleness, how great an evil are thou? What an impediment in our way under thou influence we remain in sleep."[17]

Unhappy about his position and uncertain future, De Bow quit his clerkship and decided to reevaluate his life and immediate situation during an extended visit to his uncle's plantation on St. Helena Island. On January 8, 1838, he packed his personal belongings and left Charleston. During his two-day journey to the island, he passed many large rice and cotton plantations and, for the first time in his life, saw large gangs of slaves working in fields. He eventually arrived at Robert Norton's plantation and found himself surrounded by happy relatives, good food, and, as he remembered, a young slave who repeatedly yelled: "Marse James come, Marse James come." Norton, the brother of De Bow's mother, agreed to let his nephew stay and think about his future prospects. On the first night of his visit, De Bow found a short proslavery treatise in his uncle's library and eagerly read it. His interest in slavery, piqued by his recent observations and reading, continued to grow into adulthood and became a major influence on his editorial career and on how he viewed the nation.[18]

Despite living in a predominantly rural region of the country, De Bow had spent his entire life in Charleston, rarely venturing outside the city limits. With his stay at Robert Norton's plantation, he now had a chance to explore rural southern society and observe a different way of life. He wandered the fields and roads of St. Helena and observed local customs and attitudes, noting: "The planters are very hospitable but retain many of the aristocratic principles of their ancestors—but little society is kept and comparatively few visits are paid." Unsure of his future, and out of place in a southern society he knew little about, he often retreated to his bedroom to read and reflect on life. He consumed Norton's library, reading Sir Walter Scott, several Shakespearean plays, and Plutarch. His reading habits matched those of other southerners in the late 1830s. Library records suggest that most southern readers preferred romance novels, pedagogy, biography, and history books. De Bow mostly preferred history, philosophy, and biography and, at this early point, showed little interest in science or fiction. As much as he enjoyed spending time in his uncle's library, however, he knew that he needed to make a decision about his future. Norton, worried about his melancholy nephew, confronted De Bow about his moods and urged him to return to Charleston and ask for his old job back. De Bow listened to his uncle's advice and, after staying a month, prepared to return home. Before he left, however, he visited the graves of his great-grandfather and other family members buried on St. Helena. Thoughts of pride flashed through his mind, making him realize that his roots in South Carolina were ancient and strong. These feelings gave him hope as he prepared to return to Charleston in February 1838.[19]

De Bow's new interest in slavery began to emerge in his personal journal and often reflected his upbringing in racially diverse Charleston. Like many antebellum southerners, De Bow believed that God had ordained slavery and that historical precedent in the ancient world had legitimized European superiority over servile Africans. The European Enlightenment further separated the races, according to De Bow, and made slavery "a blessing [for] the African because it is the only condition in which his moral and physical nature can be developed." He believed that Africans had been cursed by slavery because they had ignored "the cultivation and improvement of the mind [as] the noblest gift which man has received from the hands of his Creator." De Bow expressed no inner turmoil or guilt about slavery. At an early age he recognized the economic and social importance of the institution to the South and to southern culture. Thus, although he lived in a society dominated by plantations and slavery, his initial visit to St. Helena gave him direct and immediate access to what was for him a relatively unknown world.[20]

Rather than return to Charleston, De Bow decided to visit another uncle in Robertville, South Carolina, in early 1838 to resolve remaining uncertainties about his future and to delay starting a career. Located in the northwestern corner of the Beaufort District near the Savannah River, John Norton's plantation offered further sanctuary and a chance for De Bow to settle back into a routine of reading, writing, and long walks. He read the Bible, a book about the French Revolution, local and national newspapers, and Robert Hayne's report on the importance and necessity of the Charleston and Cincinnati Railroad. He watched slaves work the fields and marveled at work crews building a nearby railroad. For a moment, as in St. Helena, his concerns and worries seemed secondary to his leisurely existence. All this changed on April 27, 1838, however, when a large fire swept through Charleston and destroyed his personal and family possessions. De Bow returned to Charleston as seven hundred acres of the city lay smoldering. Like disease, fire constantly threatened to disrupt or destroy the social and economic functions of the city. Stunned by personal and civic loss, De Bow would later write about the importance of supporting local fire companies as a way of safeguarding commercial and social interests in all American cities, noting that this advice came from an earlier personal experience. But in April 1838 the fire had a much more immediate influence on De Bow's life, and he returned to Charleston without a home or much money.[21]

Unable to find a job in Charleston, De Bow decided to move to western South Carolina and accept a teaching post at a rural school in Golden Grove. In 1860 he reminisced about teaching at the "Old Field School House," remembering the opportunity as an escape from city life and a chance to enjoy the mountain air. In reality, however, his true feelings were much more negative. In his diary he admitted that what he saw in the upcountry shocked him, particularly the people and their mannerisms. He sneered at how his upcountry brethren used *fellow* as an indiscriminate substitute for *gentleman*, *woman* to describe a "handsome young lady," and *critter* to denote a horse. He noted that in the upcountry being a Charlestonian meant being "looked upon with eyes of envy, particularly should he be well read and be acquainted with books." He suggested that to upcountry residents grammar was a "kind of Hebrew volume, never looked into or studied by teachers or scholars, considered as a pack of contemptible nonsense." Geography was "unknown—Dead! Dead! Dead!" and a schoolmaster was "a fellow that can drink his whiskey and sometimes take a drunken frolic . . . particularly if he would teach cheap and all the time." De Bow could not stand his new job and returned to Charleston after less than a year. By the end of 1838 his life seemed as aimless as his previous year's wanderings.[22]

It was then that De Bow turned to his own education as a possible remedy for this declining situation, enrolling at the Cokesbury Manual Labor School in Cokesbury, South Carolina. The village of Cokesbury, like much of the Abbeville District in South Carolina's upcountry, had benefited from successive cotton booms that produced almost half the state's cotton crop by 1830. The South Carolina Methodist Conference had started the Cokesbury School in 1834 as part of a larger statewide initiative to provide educational opportunities for all white citizens, regardless of background or status in society. The school provided practical agricultural and domestic training to interested young men and women. By 1839, however, De Bow had soured on the realities of manual labor and vocational training, yearning for Charleston and his books. Although he dropped out of the school after less than a year, he had acquired an appreciation for the importance of practical training for poor white southerners. He saw the value of raising the lowest members of society to the point of self-sufficiency, not because he cared about the person, but because that person would not become an economic burden on the rest of society. He later embraced similar feelings about ex-slaves immediately after the Civil War and encouraged white southerners to open vocational schools and allow blacks to become productive members of southern society. He credited his brief time at Cokesbury as being personally fruitful and saw value in the "worthy men who trained us, then, to paths of usefulness and guided our wayward tracks." At the time, however, Cokesbury became another personal failure in a growing list of setbacks.[23]

After being away from the city for so long, De Bow once again found personal solace in the familiar surroundings of Charleston. Friends gave their support, and the Apprentices' Library Society provided ample distraction for the nineteen-year-old. In early 1840 he decided to take classes at the College of Charleston. The college had been chartered by a group of prominent local planters, merchants, and mechanics in 1785 but by the 1830s had fallen onto hard times. In 1836 Charleston's city council provided financial assistance, and, as a ward of the city, the college became the nation's first municipal institution of higher learning. The mission of the school changed from serving wealthy sons of absentee planters to serving any white male with tuition money. De Bow raised the fifty dollars for one year's tuition and began taking classes.[24]

Several professors at the College of Charleston stimulated De Bow's intellect. William T. Brantley, the college's president and professor of moral, intellectual, and political philosophy and of economics and history, awed De Bow with his intelligence and wit. Brantley had attended South Carolina College under the tutelage of the noted southern rights advocate Thomas Cooper and had been classmates with William Harper and William Grayson, well-known proslavery supporters. Brantley became a father figure to De Bow, and years later the student remembered his mentor as "a man of gigantic stature and giant mind." In January 1840 De Bow wrote "Random Thoughts on Slavery" for Brantley and argued that slavery created more problems for slave masters than for slaves. He believed that slavery created a sense of indolence and tyranny because slave owners had no hope for the development of moral character in their slaves. De Bow also credited the scholarship and kindness of Lewis R. Gibbes and William Hawkesworth as guiding forces in his collegiate career. Both men challenged him to understand the importance of language, mathematics, history, and science. Under the nurturing care of these professors, De Bow's personal confidence in his writing and intellectual pursuits grew.[25]

Other students and faculty also observed De Bow's dedication to his education and personal growth. He became a leader in a class that included

William P. Miles, the future mayor of Charleston, and William Henry Trescott, the future diplomat and assistant secretary of state in James Buchanan's administration. A classmate reminisced about De Bow as a student, remembering: "After studying most of the night, he came to college in the morning with that famous black cravat of his tied loosely around his neck, his hair disheveled—his keen black eyes sparkling above that nose—ready for any discussion or intellectual tilt." Fellow students elected him to serve as the vice president of the Cliosophic Literary Society. His debating skills became well-known after he delivered papers on the advantages of formal education, the necessities of mental asylums, the horrors of dueling, and the benefits of Indian removal for economic purposes. He later started a school magazine at the request of the college's administration. These endeavors elevated his reputation on campus and in the city.[26]

The city at large offered De Bow ample opportunity to grow as a writer and be published on a regular basis. The *Charleston Courier*, the *Charleston Mercury*, and the *Southern Patriot* provided daily opportunities, while the *Southern Quarterly Review* offered established writers the opportunity to develop more in-depth analyses. Richard Yeadon, the editor of the *Courier*, published De Bow's first article, one entitled "The Duel's Effect." This fictional but philosophical short story warned readers about the long-term effects of dueling on the participants and their families. He later wrote additional articles about South Carolina's constitution and charter, the political economy of taxation, and the usefulness of science and a memorial for Hugh S. Legare. These articles satisfied his growing ambition as a writer and made him a minor literary name in Charleston. He and his generation of Charlestonians began adding to a cultural landscape that had been muted by earlier economic and social strife.[27]

In De Bow's most personal article, an intimate short story entitled "The Three Philosophers," he assumed the fictional name of Oscar Everett to tell a thinly veiled story about "the neglect of the world, the loss of parents, the unkindness of friends, and the keenest adversity." Like De Bow, Everett attempted to escape his personal pain by rejecting the rational world and the philosophies of Bacon, Locke, and Newton. Instead, he looked for an emotional solution to his suffering and ultimately found solace in the character of Zeno in Aristotle's *Physics*. According to De Bow, Zeno, a minor Greek philosopher and skeptic, dealt with his tragedies by steeling "his bosom against the cares of life, and so master[ing] the emotions and passions of his nature as to be indifferent to pleasure or pain and even to displace them both." Like Zeno, Everett attempted to internalize his feelings and harden himself against future disappointment and rejection. Torn between his past and his future, he unsteadily veered between the realities of hard work and hedonistic pleasures. He eventually retreated to a library, his only sanctuary from pain, and pondered his future. While languishing in the stacks of the library, he concluded that his misery stemmed from his mother's death, and he bitterly denounced her for abandoning him. An unseen voice suddenly emerged, however, and reminded him: "You had a mother and she loved you." Taken aback, Everett broke down and confessed that, "in his childhood, [he] idolized his mother, in her sorrows he had comforted her, and when harm like a barbed arrow had entered her heart, he sought to pluck it forth, and ply some balm to the festering wound." He wailed out loud that "his existence ended with her." As the story closed, Everett accepted his feelings about his loss but wondered aloud why fate had "exiled [him] from that society which he would have richly adorned."[28]

De Bow's short story captured his insecurity, which he admitted arose from the loss of his parents. His father's death forced an otherwise modest middle-class merchant family into financial hardship and, in De Bow's mind, caused him to lose status in a city consumed with social rank. The loss of his mother, meanwhile, created an emotional void in De Bow. His sensitive mind searched for answers. He mourned the loss of his parents but also felt bitterness toward them; Garret De Bow would have had the means to provide his son with a proper education, a chance to learn the family business, and the right to assume eventual control of the grocery store itself. De Bow wondered whether his personal setbacks might have been avoided if his parents had lived. Instead, he had made his own way in life through hard work and experimentation. His feelings of insecurity and concern about the future mirrored those felt by young "southern mugwumps" who grew up in privileged households, received good educations, and traveled extensively. Despite these advantages, young men like De Bow struggled with the changing world around them. His trepidations about his future were as real as his past sense of loss and abandonment.[29]

Thus, it was hard work and perseverance, not privilege or wealth, that marked De Bow's steady rise in Charleston. His commitment to learning allowed him access to other social realms that might have been closed to the son of a merchant and certainly would have been to an uneducated orphan. De Bow's hard work in the classroom and willingness to branch out in new directions earned him the rank of valedictorian of his class at the College of Charleston. On June 28, 1843, a parade of students and various civic groups marched down Archdale Street toward St. John's Lutheran Church to celebrate graduation. The day opened with a prayer and numerous speeches about the importance of self-education, the power of association, the influences of government, the happiness of mankind, and the past and present condition of the United States. De Bow delivered a precommencement speech entitled "Oration—the Religion of Beauty" before William Brantley conferred degrees on eleven students. De Bow than delivered the valedictory speech that capped his college career.[30]

On graduation De Bow decided to pursue a legal career as a means of supporting himself in Charleston. He ventured forward with a new sense of confidence, though later admitting that his legal education consisted of "a single perusal of Blackstone, the work of a few weeks, with some plausibility and address." On May 15, 1844, he passed the bar exam in Columbia, South Carolina, and returned to Charleston, hoping that his new vocation would be "a ready passport to all the privileges, dignities, and immunities, of attorney at law." But he soon became dissatisfied with his work and spent much of his free time at the Charleston Library Society. He also served as secretary for the local Democratic Party, attended the Augusta Baptist Convention, and managed the state Sunday School Union. Slowly, his name became more commonplace in Charleston.[31]

His continued interest in writing led De Bow to seek new literary opportunities with the Charleston-based *Southern Quarterly Review*. In July 1844, his first article exposed him to a larger regional audience, and he soon after became a familiar presence in the *Review*'s editorial office. He learned about publishing, editing, and writing from Daniel K. Whitaker, the *Review*'s editor. Whitaker, a New England–born Harvard graduate, had moved to the South in the 1820s and had served as the editor of the *Southern Literary Journal*, had worked as a cotton planter, and had practiced law before reviving the *Southern Quarterly Review* in 1842. The *Review* originally had been published in New Orleans, but subscription problems and poor editorial decisions to publish political articles damaged its reputation. Whitaker hoped to revive sagging public support by moving to Charleston and starting over. This was a risky proposition for him. His decision proved to be correct, however, and the *Review* once again enjoyed better times. De Bow took note of these struggles and later, in the first issue of his journal in 1846, pledged political neutrality to his readers.[32]

De Bow gained further professional experience as an assistant editor of the *Review* and continued to write articles on a wide variety of topics. The *Charleston Courier* reviewed his article "Oregon and the Oregon Question" and declared it useful and well written despite the author's "natural fervor of youth and of youthful patriotism." But De Bow would later earn heavy criticism from Richard Yeadon, his old editor at the *Courier*, for a partisan article about the Nullification Crisis in South Carolina. Yeadon believed that De Bow had unfairly characterized the Union Party in South Carolina and felt that the article had a flippant tone and a "spirit or prejudice of party." He reminded readers: "The chronicler neither saw nor was part of the great events he has undertaken to narrate." De Bow conceded that he wrote the article without books or references and may have made factual errors. Mindful of past editorial mistakes and their consequences, Daniel Whitaker publicly scolded De Bow for his careless writing. He wrote a retraction distancing himself from De Bow, declaring: "I know of no Junior Editor of the *Review*." De Bow felt betrayed by Whitaker's stance and left the *Review*. Unlike his past disappointments or failures, however, this time De Bow departed feeling satisfied about the valuable experience and training he had received from Whitaker.[33]

Shortly after leaving the *Review*, De Bow received a temporary assignment from the *Southern Patriot* to produce a biweekly newspaper column on his travels around South Carolina. Writing under the name "Swinton," he visited historic sites, small towns, rural plantations, and new factories. He lavished praise on the cultured society of Cowper, South Carolina, but cautioned that too much finery created a "morbid, and if I may be allowed the doctor-like expression, a dyspeptic state of the social system." He celebrated the Fourth of July in Camden, South Carolina, before visiting William Gregg's cotton factory in Graniteville. Gregg was a passionate industrialist and rising public figure who had recently written a series of articles on the necessities of manufacturing in South Carolina for the *Charleston Courier*. Later, these articles became Gregg's *Essays on Domestic Industry* (1845), which critically assessed South Carolina's incorporation laws and attitudes toward industrial development.[34]

Although De Bow and Gregg held similar feelings about industrial development, De Bow criticized Gregg in the *Southern Patriot* for not doing more to help South Carolina and for his negative characterization of state political figures. He overlooked Gregg's efforts to change state incorporation laws. The editors of the *Southern Patriot* publicly distanced themselves from De Bow's harsh comments about Gregg but agreed with his assessment of industrial development, admitting that the region needed "a class whom we have long been anxious to see among us—a cool business-headed class—watchful of facts—of the practical and useful—shrewd in finding out the way, and prompt and energetic in taking possession of it." Perhaps feeling the anxiety of yet another public rebuttal, De Bow left Graniteville without further engaging Gregg. He ended his trip by visiting Vardry McBee's cotton factory and flour mill complex outside Greenville. His last newspaper column highlighted the encouraging gains made by men like Gregg and McBee and applauded the positive steps that had been made in southern industry.[35]

De Bow returned to Charleston in October 1845 and learned that he and twenty-four other local men had been appointed as delegates to a southern commercial convention in Memphis, Tennessee. His growing literary notoriety and his article on South Carolina made him a logical choice, as did his youthful enthusiasm and personal knowledge of Charleston. The convention's organizers had originally asked James Gadsden, a prominent South Carolina politician and resident of Charleston, to promote the meeting. Gadsden reported back that a meeting had been held at city hall in early October and that many of Charleston's finest merchants and entrepreneurs would not attend the Memphis convention because it conflicted with South Carolina's fall legislative sessions. Unworried, however, he believed that interested men would emerge, especially when they found out that similar meetings had been held in the rival city of Augusta, Georgia. Eventually, only seven of the twenty-five chosen actually went to Memphis. Each delegate had previously served the city in some capacity before 1845. William H. Trescott and De Bow, classmates at the College of Charleston, were known because of their recent literary and intellectual pursuits in the city. Ker Boyce, Charles Magwood, and William C. Gatewood were experienced businessmen, and Alexander Black and James Gadsden had been instrumental in developing the South Carolina Railroad Company. These men had invested in banks, railroads, harbor improvements, and public health projects. Although they worked for private profit, they hoped to strengthen the commercial and industrial sectors of the city in order to create a more balanced economy. Like the city's merchants and entrepreneurs, they understood the necessity of linking Charleston to the interests of the Gulf states and the Mississippi River valley. And, like future postbellum boosters, these early promoters suppressed negative stories and embellished positive publicity as a way of attracting new business and outside investments to the city. They hoped to create a new Charleston that embraced and respected past efforts and traditions while simultaneously searching for innovative ideas that would improve the city. De Bow embraced these tactics and later used the *Review* to promote the South as a place where investments grew in a business-friendly environment. Although De Bow continued to search for a vocation in 1845, his avocation as the originator of the New South Creed began in Charleston, ironically, a city often considered to be the bastion of the Old South by postbellum southerners.[36]

An ever-changing Charleston became an early template for southerners who hoped to reinvent the South's economy. Unsatisfied with many aspects of South Carolina's plantation economy, but fully aware of its importance, men such as De Bow believed that past customs and trends could be improved on. Charleston had continually changed to meet new challenges from its settlement in 1670 until the chaotic years of the Panic of 1819, the Missouri Crisis, and the Denmark Vesey conspiracy. Suddenly, however, that spirit of innovation and change slowed, and city residents looked inward for protection and comfort. De Bow accepted what had happened in the past but hoped to improve the city's future by looking beyond agriculture and slavery. He understood that both elements were needed but hoped that capital and energy could be diverted to civic improvements, railroads, factories, and cultural pursuits. And, while future postbellum southerners would claim that they created a New South based on post–Civil War commercial and industrial development in cities like Birmingham, Alabama, and Nashville, Tennessee, these antebellum Charlestonians had already started to look for new solutions to fortify their city's ailing economy in a changing world. The interests of these entrepreneurs and men like them around the South would become the foundation for De Bow's future career as the editor of the region's most important antebellum economic journal. These men, with De Bow's literary contributions, would also create a New South movement while still living in what would later be called the Old South.[37]

None in this group personified the role of antebellum entrepreneur-booster more than Ker Boyce. An upcountry transplant from Newberry, South Carolina, Boyce moved to Charleston in 1817 and became a successful city merchant, banker, and investor. In 1836 he purchased a failing sugar house, reorganized it, and opened the Charleston Sugar Refining Company with $50,000 in capital, thirty-five employees, and modern steam-powered equipment. He later served as the president of the South Carolina Paper Manufacturing Company. In addition to these duties, he sat on the board of directors of the Bank of Charleston, the South Carolina Railroad, the

South Carolina Insurance Company, and the Charleston Gaslight Company, and he was the largest stockholder in William Gregg's Graniteville Manufacturing Company. He also owned significant shares in more than twenty other companies and invested heavily in real estate. De Bow recognized the importance of men like Boyce and began to think of ways to link similar-minded men together. While getting ready for his trip to Memphis, he began to conceptualize a plan that would allow him to do this while simultaneously pursuing his avocation as a writer.[38]

Although the Memphis Commercial Convention would be the first large-scale conference to address southern economic issues, smaller regional cotton planters' conventions had been held in the late 1830s. The Panic of 1837 precipitated a convention in Augusta, Georgia, in 1837 and another one in Charleston a year later. Delegates focused on direct trade with Europe and the promotion of commercial enterprise as solutions for the declining economy of the South Atlantic seaboard states. These early conventions harbored little sectional discord, focusing instead on southern commercial improvement within the larger global context. Yet some delegates, still angry about existing protective tariffs, used the conventions to express their discontent with unjust laws.[39]

De Bow saw merit in the commercial convention movement and parlayed his newfound appointment as a delegate into another writing job. The *Charleston Courier* asked him to write a series of articles promoting the convention's agenda. He began the series by warning southerners about the impending sectional crisis that threatened the nation. He worried that unchecked northern prosperity, unfair tariff laws, attacks on slavery, and southern economic decline created an unbalanced relationship between the North and the South. He saw these issues manifesting themselves in the growing economic contest over western markets and implored southerners to act. A strong relationship between the South and the West served two purposes in his mind: it strengthened the southern economy, and it thwarted northern efforts to expand into western territories. "The South must sympathize with the West, or be alone," De Bow warned. He reminded readers: "The day has passed when a sympathy between the North and the South, or any union of action or of interest has been deemed feasible by the most sanguine." He also highlighted the importance of southern railroad development, agricultural reform, and economic diversification, stressing the importance of a domestic manufacturing sector. He recommended that the South become more like the North: "If the only weapons by which they can be resisted must be fashioned after the models in their own hands . . . we should snatch up those weapons and strike the blow which is to make us free." He reminded southern readers of his sectional loyalty but added: "It is only on this principle that we advocate Southern manufactures. . . . [W]hilst 'agriculture is the blessed employment of man,' manufactures then is the twin sister, treading together with her ever the ways of pleasantness and peace."[40]

With a sense of purpose and a feeling of confidence, De Bow announced his intentions of starting a new business periodical dedicated to southern issues. He had read about New Orleans in Erasmus Fenner's *Southern Medial Journal* and, keenly aware of Charleston's competitive literary market, decided to move to the Crescent City after the Memphis convention. A unique economic and social vibrancy existed in the city, and De Bow wanted to experience it firsthand. Intrigued by the area commonly known at the time as the Southwest (Alabama, Mississippi, Louisiana, Arkansas, and Tennessee), he believed that New Orleans offered him the best chance to succeed as an editor of a monthly journal. He also wanted to better understand the developmental difference between the newer Southwest and the older Southeast.[41]

Growing up in Charleston, a city struggling to reinvent itself and become economically relevant again, influenced De Bow's worldview. His childhood had been altered by the Panic of 1819 and subsequent death of his father, and those circumstances cost him personal opportunities and social standing in a city obsessed with rank and privilege. The Missouri Compromise, the Denmark Vesey conspiracy, and the Nullification Crisis turned a worldly city inward and shaped De Bow's conception of his sectional identity. De Bow became intrigued by what it meant to be a southerner. Yet he had never lived on a farm or a plantation, had no practical experience with slaves, and was the product of a public education. His intellectual curiosity allowed him to seek out and explore new opportunities that placed him increasingly in the public spotlight. His transformation from a struggling wanderer to a city prodigy occurred because he recognized his natural talents and interests in time to craft career goals beyond the life of a clerk or a teacher. Others recognized his newfound passion and natural abilities and aided him in his pursuit of a new life after leaving the College of Charleston. His knack for finding positive publicity and favorable recognition allowed him to deviate from the limited course that seemed to have been set for him after the death of his father and mother. By 1845 he had become a tall, gangly man whose disheveled hair and appearance marked him as something other than a product of a fine plantation or a northern university. His appearance reflected a brooding intellect who spent most of his time reading, writing, and, in general, working to compensate for his past failures and struggles. De Bow emerged from his past with a strong work ethic and a personal drive to succeed. He wanted to fit into southern society by helping his region. Many of his future editorial opinions on agriculture, industry, and commerce can be linked to specific experiences in his youth. Growing up in urban Charleston, a declining city searching for new opportunities, allowed him to see the South in a unique light. Although he was thoroughly and proudly American, his passion to help his region drove him to look for a new South, one that blended past traditions with future innovations.

De Bow's last days in Charleston were bittersweet as he prepared for the Memphis convention and his permanent relocation to New Orleans. He spent days wandering the city and saying good-bye to friends and family. The editors of the *Charleston Courier* asked him to stop in New Orleans on his way to the convention and report on John C. Calhoun's first visit to the Crescent City. They also asked him to travel with Calhoun up the Mississippi River and record the collective mood of South Carolina's delegation. De Bow agreed to do both, eager for the opportunity to spend time with Calhoun. As he left Charleston aboard an ocean steamer bound for New Orleans, he recognized the importance of the moment, and he later commented on its significance: "It was our first trip, from which we did not return, and hence the *Review*."[42]

2

Leaving an Old South, Entering a New South

On his way to Memphis, De Bow stopped in New Orleans for a brief visit to familiarize himself with his new home. He explored the city and became better acquainted with the nation's second busiest port behind only New York City. Thousands of ships crowded the docks and levies, creating a forest of masts and clouds of steam and smoke. De Bow noted that, in the month he visited New Orleans, 81 ships, 22 barks, 33 brigs, 39 schooners, and 220 steamboats arrived or departed from the city. Hundreds of uncounted flatboats from states and territories along the Mississippi River and its tributaries also crowded the docks. He later estimated that by the mid-1840s city merchants annually exported 900,000 bales of cotton, 200,000 hogsheads of sugar, 100,000 hogsheads of molasses, 600,000 barrels of flour, 430,000 sacks of corn, and 135,000 barrels of wheat. At times the pace of the city unsettled De Bow, leaving him nostalgic for the more leisurely life of Charleston. He felt unprepared for New Orleans, and on one occasion he retreated to the tranquility of a cemetery to gather himself and reaffirm his purpose for moving. He emerged from his temporary sanctuary with renewed confidence in his decision to relocate to the Southwest and start a monthly magazine.[1]

The city's social and cultural growth and diversity made it unique in the antebellum South. By 1840 over nineteen thousand free blacks lived and worked in the city as skilled artisans and unskilled laborers. Hundreds of blacks worked as carpenters, masons, shoemakers, mechanics, and painters, while thousands more toiled as stevedores, day laborers, and sailors. In addition to free blacks, the city was home to descendants of French and Spanish settlers and Creoles, all of whom gave it a distinctive feeling in comparison to other southern cities. Visitors to the French Quarter noted its European flair and often commented on the frequency of hearing French spoken. Market day was an important part of the social fabric of the city. A visitor noted that market day became a pageant of "youth and age, beauty and not-so-beautiful, all colors, nations, and tongues . . . [and] one heterogeneous mass of delightful confusion." Unburdened by the oppressive social hegemony found in older southern cities like Charleston, New Orleans retained the vibrant aura of a boomtown. For De Bow it became a cultural and social release for his intellectual and personal curiosities. He worried, however, that it lacked a sense of community and would only develop into "a great depot of merchandise . . . in which every inhabitant is a mere transient adventurer, without any kind of feeling or bond of union."[2]

De Bow's arrival in New Orleans coincided with statewide political changes that threatened to alter Louisiana's economic future. After 1834, Whig candidates swept into office promising better days. They instituted probusiness policies of tariffs, internal improvements, and a banking system. Initially, their agenda created positive changes for many Louisianans, but the Panic of 1837 derailed their economic plans. Democrats took advantage of the situation. By 1845 they had regained enough momentum to call for a constitutional convention with hopes of erasing all Whig tenets from the existing state constitution. They wanted more liberal suffrage laws and stricter residency requirements and promised to forbid the use of public money to fund private transportation projects. For many Louisianans who supported economic growth and broader global linkages, the political interference of Democrats came at an inopportune time. Competition from other markets and commercial centers threatened New Orleans's position as a commercial emporium, and local merchants chafed at the limitation put on public funding of new railroad projects.[3]

John C. Calhoun hoped that his visit to New Orleans would buttress feelings of southern unity between the Southeast and the Southwest. His arrival excited city residents, as did his willingness to preside over the Memphis convention. Local politicians and newspaper editors urged people to put aside their political differences and help decorate city streets, public buildings, and the waterfront in his honor. On the morning of November 7, 1845, cannon fire and music announced Calhoun's arrival in the city. De Bow marveled at the crowds that packed the streets and balconies to catch a glimpse of the famous statesman. The excitement of the day remained a lasting memory for him because of the spectacle he witnessed and because he realized that he would have time to speak to Calhoun about starting a monthly journal. Calhoun had accepted a seat at the Memphis convention because he had a long-standing interest in the economic development of the South. He wanted to use the convention to advocate for federal aid for internal improvement projects. New Orleans's merchants and entrepreneurs initially supported his position because they believed that it would bring them new opportunities. Rather than promote the interests of one city, however, Calhoun advocated for using federal money to build a railroad to forge direct commercial ties between the South Atlantic region and the Southwest. He feared that the economic success of the Southwest would isolate eastern states. Before arriving in New Orleans, he also called for a stronger relationship between the South and the West. De Bow merged Calhoun's positions with his own and eventually developed an editorial style that promoted these ideas as best for the South in general.[4]

Calhoun and De Bow believed that western economic development would have a corresponding positive influence on the South's economy by supplying raw materials to southern merchants. Southerners had watched as northeastern businessmen had transformed the Great Lakes region into a supplier of raw materials and a consumer of finished products created in northern factories. The agricultural and commercial potential of the West intrigued many incoming southern delegates who hoped to benefit from untouched markets beyond the Mississippi River. De Bow believed that access to these areas would stimulate the construction of new railroads, industries, and cities. Many delegates also hoped that a regional partnership would further unify common interests and limit the influence of northern competitors in the Trans-Mississippi region.[5]

The economic plan to connect the South and the West worried planters and merchants in the Lower Mississippi River valley because Calhoun wanted to make Memphis the terminus for western trade. A growing commercial rivalry existed between New Orleans and Memphis, and this changed how many in New Orleans felt about the upcoming convention. While attending a ball held in his honor in New Orleans, Calhoun attempted to soothe local concerns by offering a toast: "The Valley of the Mississippi—Take it all in all, the greatest in the world. Situated as it is, between the two oceans, it will yet command the commerce of the world, and that commerce may be centered in New Orleans." As a southerner, Calhoun understood the need to maintain New Orleans's commercial primacy in the global economy, but, as a South Carolinian, he needed to create direct transportation links between his home state and western markets, and Memphis offered him the best chance at success. James Gadsden, a South Carolina friend and political ally of Calhoun's, reminded him that the South's future strength was dependent on an alliance with the West: "If they do not come to us, we will be overwhelmed by the power that has combined for our ruin. . . . I shall look confidently at your being at Memphis—and if not there, South Carolina will not be heard in the Great Enterprise."[6]

Calhoun's departure from New Orleans was as boisterous as his arrival in the city two days earlier. As the festivities of the last night came to a close, he and many of the delegates from South Carolina and Louisiana made their way to the city's waterfront. Excitement about the convention had risen during Calhoun's visit, and a sizable delegation from New Orleans also boarded the steamer for Memphis. De Bow watched his political idol encourage southerners to look beyond local rivalries and support a broad, pan-southern agenda. He witnessed southerners rally around their political leader. As dusk fell over the city, the *Maria,* a steam packet that normally hauled cotton but now carried convention delegates, pushed upstream toward Memphis.[7]

As the *Maria* steamed up the Mississippi River past large plantations and small port towns, De Bow spoke to any delegate willing to listen to his plan about a southern economic journal. He told them that he hoped to avoid the "strewn wrecks" of past literary failures that had confined themselves "*exclusively* to literature, in its lighter walks of fancy, or its statelier tread of philosophy." He proposed a more practical journal that would appeal to "men struggling with the wilderness, subduing soil into cultivation, opening trade, and creating for it avenues." De Bow wanted his articles to advance the efforts of men who intended to support the economic development of the South, which he called "the physical good," because "the physical want precedes, in order of time, the intellectual." Or, in other words, "ploughshares come before philosophy." Calhoun, Gadsden, their fellow South Carolinian Joel R. Poinsett, and other delegates on board the *Maria* encouraged him to pursue his proposed plan.[8]

Memphis's sudden rise as an inland port for southwestern cotton planters made the city a logical choice for a regional commercial convention. Situated on the high ground above the confluence of the Mississippi and Wolf Rivers, Memphis had by 1845 grown from what one early observer had called a "small town, ugly, dirty, and sickly, with miserable streets" to a fair-sized city. Timber shacks and crude buildings had given way to brick homes and planned neighborhoods. Between 1840 and 1845 the city's population had doubled to four thousand residents. International demand for cotton made

Memphis a key inland port for planters in western Tennessee, northern Mississippi, and eastern Arkansas. In 1826 only three hundred bales of cotton passed through the city; by 1845 that number had increased to seventy-five thousand bales. The demand for cotton energized the local economy and created a new business class of merchants and professional men who oversaw the development of the city. An observer noted that by 1845 the city had seven newspapers, ten churches, three banks, five insurance companies, and seven shipping lines. De Bow later reported: "No place in all the West has greater facilities of trade than Memphis; and the whole appearance of the city is that of activity and enterprise."[9]

City residents had previously supported internal improvement projects that expanded Memphis's commercial development. They formed corporations to build plank roads, turnpikes, and railroads that promised to link Memphis with Cincinnati, Louisville, St. Louis, and New Orleans. New stagecoach lines carried passengers and mail to Nashville, Charlotte, and Jackson, Mississippi. The initial call for a commercial convention in Memphis arose after a dispute over a road into Arkansas. Although many of these early schemes failed because of mismanagement or lack of interest, a group of public-minded middle-class merchants and professionals emerged to support their city's efforts to broaden its commercial network.[10]

By 1845 Charleston and Memphis represented divergent economies and cultures within the South. For many contemporary observers, Charleston represented an older, decaying Southeast, while Memphis reflected a newer, more energetic Southwest. Better situated to capitalize on the region's expanding cotton economy, Memphis found that its commercial status was based overwhelmingly on the wealth of its current generation of business leaders. In Charleston, status was based more on the past, or even lost, wealth of elite merchant families. De Bow noticed these differences and hoped to balance the South's overall economic development by linking the commercial futures of both cities through railroad development.[11]

Excitement grew as hundreds of delegates converged on the Methodist-Episcopal Church for the beginning of the Memphis Commercial Convention on November 12, 1845 (see table 1). Delegates nominated John C. Calhoun to serve as president of the convention, and a nominating committee chose De Bow to serve as one of seven recording secretaries. De Bow's new position gave him unfettered access to convention meetings and reports. He noted with pleasure the harmoniousness of the sessions and sensed a willingness to cooperate among delegates.[12]

Table 1: 1845 Memphis Commercial Convention: Delegates by State and Occupation

		Occupation			
State	**Delegates**	**Agriculture**	**Mercantile**	**Professional**	**Unknown**
Alabama	22	7	2	10	3
Arkansas	20	9	2	4	5
Illinois	21	0	6	9	6
Indiana	7	1	2	3	1
Iowa	4	0	2	0	2
Kentucky	22	4	4	6	8
Louisiana	17	2	2	7	6
Mississippi	178	80	19	37	42
Missouri	36	5	7	8	16
North Carolina	1	1	0	0	0
Ohio	14	0	2	3	9
Pennsylvania	3	0	1	2	0
South Carolina	8	1	3	3	1
Tennessee	197	76	24	59	40
Texas	3	0	0	1	2
Virginia	5	1	1	3	0
Total	**558**	**187**	**77**	**155**	**141**

Source: Journal of the Proceedings of the South-Western Convention, Begun and Held at the City of Memphis on the 12th November, 1845 (Memphis, 1845); US Census Office, *Seventh Census of the United States, 1850* (Washington, DC, 1850).
Note: Of the 558 delegates listed as attending the Memphis Commercial Convention in 1845, I found 460 listed in the 1850 federal census. Missing delegates have been included in the "unknown" column, in addition to those found but with unlisted occupations.

Calhoun's opening speech set the tone of the convention and became influential in De Bow's later views on southern economic development. Calhoun's attempt to encourage private and public funding of internal improvement projects mirrored earlier attempts by the state of Virginia to create a "mixed enterprise" system by blending both private and public funding. Earlier conflicts between liberal and conservative economic forces had by the 1840s created a popular backlash against public works projects, and an open call for federal aid to improve river navigation diverged from the prevailing mood of the nation in 1845. Federally funded internal improvement projects, Calhoun argued, would create new domestic and international markets for southern goods and foster industrial growth. He encouraged private individuals and corporations to take more active roles in expanding the South's railroad system but invited federal participation in river navigation improvements. He justified his position by suggesting that the Mississippi River was an "inland sea . . . on the same footing with the Gulf and Atlantic coast, the Chesapeake and Delaware Bays, and the Lakes, in reference to the superintendence of the General Government over its navigation." Congress had a constitutional obligation to protect interstate commerce. Calhoun avoided previous constitutional debates, deflecting his sectional sentiments by suggesting that these changes would "strengthen the bonds of our Union, and . . . render us the greatest and most prosperous community the world ever held." De Bow agreed with Calhoun's call to action and applauded his nationalistic tone. Like Calhoun, he hoped to maintain the South's political authority by increasing the region's economic power. In 1845 both men worried about the South's growing dependence on northern merchants and industrialists.[13]

Although Calhoun's speech drew loud applause from those at the convention, it later garnered sharp criticism from southerners who felt skeptical of or abandoned by his call for federal support of internal improvement projects. A South Carolina correspondent for the *Young America Magazine* reported that Calhoun's speech alienated many of his constituents. The *Cincinnati Weekly Herald and Philanthropist* wondered how much political support Calhoun had sacrificed in his home state. The editor of the *Southern Quarterly Review*, normally sympathetic to Calhoun, cautioned southerners to invest in agriculture and not worry about the West. The *Knoxville Whig* editor, William Brownlow, suspected political ambition in Calhoun's "coming over to the Whigs," noting that his "grand summersault . . . ought to astonish no one who reflects that Mr. C. wishes to obtain western aid in making him the Presidential nominee of the next [Democratic] national caucus."[14]

In De Bow's mind, constitutional discussions about government funding became secondary when confronted with the loss of western markets to northern interests. De Bow agreed that the South needed to expand its economy and attract western commerce. Although Calhoun foresaw a time when sectional interests would feed into larger political battles, De Bow viewed the dispute in more commercial terms, as "a contest . . . between the North and South, not limited to slavery or no slavery, to abolition or no abolition, nor to the politics of either Whigs or Democrats, as such, but a contest for the wealth and commerce of the great valley of the Mississippi." He worried that states' rights advocates and strict constructionists would halt commercial progress. He believed that Calhoun understood the stakes and recognized the economic consequences of losing the West; projections estimated future commerce along the Mississippi River to exceed $571 million annually. De Bow felt Calhoun's speech galvanized a regional agenda and became the hallmark of the convention.[15]

Convention delegates spent the next three days attempting to create a comprehensive economic plan that integrated the region's agricultural, commercial, and industrial sectors. The committee on railroad development recommended that the Memphis and Charleston line should pass through the cotton-growing regions of Georgia, Alabama, Tennessee, and Mississippi to "bring into intimate connection the ancient cities of Charleston, Savannah, and Augusta, with the more modern cities of Macon, Knoxville, and Nashville; and with Natchez, Grand Gulf, Vicksburg, and the modern Memphis of the American Nile." The committee on manufacturing concluded that the South needed more cotton factories and encouraged southerners to act before northern and European competitors made industrial development difficult. The convention's final report concluded: "Beyond a doubt a new era is fast approaching to the Southern States. . . . [P]eople of the South [need] to economize their capital, erect mills and factories of *all kinds,* bring into use the powers of the present age." De Bow read these reports and later reprinted them in their entirety in his new journal.[16]

The Memphis Commercial Convention became the first large-scale meeting of southerners focused on securing a better economic future for the South. It also became the most formative moment of De Bow's early professional career because it gave him tangible ideas to move forward with and access to southerners interested in improving their region. De Bow hoped to tap into their immediate excitement and parlay their support into a collective long-term commitment to regional improvement. He recognized that he could become the intellectual leader of thousands of influential southerners who up to this point had acted alone or within isolated communities around the South. The unity of cause and excitement it created inspired the first issues of the *Review.* For four days De Bow mingled with men from cities and small hamlets, middle-class merchants and wealthy planters, forward-thinking visionaries and staunch traditionalists. He watched as citizens from the South Atlantic seaboard and the Southwest traded ideas and attempted to create a consensus for future economic development. These feelings of regional unity became part of an editorial style that would make him popular among southern readers. Although no immediate political or economic changes emerged from the proceedings in Memphis, the agenda and tone for future conventions and for De Bow's literary career had been set. He would eventually attend ten subsequent conventions between 1845 and 1859. The commercial convention movement often mirrored De Bow's aspirations and served as a promotional tool for the *Review.*[17]

De Bow returned to New Orleans and began preparing for the initial edition of the *Commercial Review of the South and West.* Although his writing duties would diminish over time, in the journal's inaugural, January 1846 issue he wrote and edited every article. Stressing many of the same points he had used to promote his journal to delegates, De Bow provided practical articles on agriculture, commerce, manufacturing, internal improvements,

Table 2: Subject of Articles in *De Bow's Review,* 1846–1866

Year	Education	Transportation	Promotional	Commerce	Agriculture	Industry	Slavery	Sectionalism
1846	1	1	12	16	12	5	1	0
1847	5	10	33	40	25	6	4	0
1848	2	3	8	10	20	12	1	0
1849	1	10	14	8	10	6	8	0
1850	0	7	22	3	5	14	12	0
1851	0	12	36	9	2	5	9	0
1852	1	7	15	12	8	6	2	0
1853	0	14	32	21	11	3	7	0
1854	4	25	20	14	16	12	8	4
1855	33	29	32	26	29	56	26	5
1856	12	29	18	20	22	13	23	14
1857	13	18	22	19	23	16	27	12
1858	2	23	29	21	30	22	22	18
1859	17	38	52	30	31	26	24	25
1860	4	39	26	28	24	16	20	41
1861	2	1	3	7	3	4	2	11
1866	9	23	36	39	51	30	25	0

Note: The topics of individual articles were collected from the monthly table of contents of *De Bow's Review.* Promotional articles often crossed over into other subject categories yet focused primarily on the endorsement or sponsorship of individual projects, towns and cities, and ideas. Local writers who hoped to increase their city or town's public profile wrote many of these promotional articles.

and southern literature (see table 2). He defended his decision to focus on commerce and his use of a quote from Thomas Carlyle, "Commerce is King," as the journal's masthead motto by reminding readers: "There is no end to the diversities and ramifications of commercial action. . . . [T]ouch agriculture, touch the arts, the professions, fortifications, defenses, transportations, legislation of a country, and the chances are a thousand to one you touch commerce somewhere." He also promised readers that the *Review* would remain free of political rhetoric and party intrigue, a problem that drove readers away from Daniel Whitaker's *Southern Quarterly Review* when De Bow still worked for him in Charleston. Despite his enthusiasm and knowledge of past editorial failures, De Bow understood that starting and maintaining a southern journal was a risky endeavor that required broad support from like-minded readers.[18]

The general content and structure of the January 1846 issue of the *Review* became a template for future editions. De Bow touched on wide-ranging topics to appeal to as many southern readers as possible. He republished the proceedings of the Memphis convention and promoted future conventions. In an article on Oregon and California, he challenged southern readers to look for new markets in the East Indies and Pacific Ocean. He compared the civic fortunes of Charleston and New Orleans, paying close attention to the economic growth of both cities; noting the unrestrained development of New Orleans, he hoped that future prosperity might be better distributed among all southern cities. In addition to full-length articles, De Bow included statistics on and brief summaries of a variety of subjects ranging from commerce on the Ohio River to the military defenses of the Gulf of Mexico. In most articles he focused on regional improvement but within the larger national context. He avoided creating a false sense of progress and chided southerners for opposing railroad construction, not investing in needed technological improvements, and allowing the poor relationship that existed between planters and industrialists. He supported his contentions with statistics from newspapers, government reports, and census records. This reliance on quantitative evidence became a hallmark of the *Review*.[19]

De Bow became an advocate of railroad construction and published monthly reports on the development of key southern railroads. He understood the importance of railroads in the overall development of a regional transportation system. He urged southerners to forgo canal construction and was never an enthusiastic supporter of plank roads. Instead, he hoped that southerners would create a rail system that connected urban commercial centers with regional plantations, factories, and mines. He used the Mississippi and Atlantic Railroad and the Mobile and Ohio Railroad as two early examples of progress. Both lines promised to link interior domestic markets with southern ports. De Bow believed that these railroads would allow southerners to funnel agricultural products and manufactured goods to global markets. He hoped that a developed southern railroad system could be linked to a transcontinental railroad system. The promise of new markets in China, Japan, and Hawaii intrigued him. In June 1847 his efforts were recognized by the directors of the Columbia and Greenville Railroad Company, who applauded his intent to "devote a large portion of the *Commercial Review* to the Railroad interest of the South." More important for De Bow, the directors, led by Joel R. Poinsett, recommended that interested southerners subscribe to the *Review*.[20]

His familiarity with cities gave De Bow a unique perspective on the necessity of fostering urban development in an agricultural region like the South. He often used New Orleans as a reoccurring example of a modern southern city with broad global connections to larger markets. He understood that New Orleans's commercial primacy rested on the agricultural success of farmers and planters in the Mississippi River valley. Cities created new industries, commercial routes, and a sense of progress by allowing the South's business class to develop in concentrated areas. De Bow believed that these developments offered the South its best chance to overtake northern competition and create domestic markets. The creation of stronger internal markets, he implored, "will build up your cities and towns; it will educate your people; it will give you rank, wealth, and importance; it will break the shackles of your dependence upon others, and give influence and prosperity beyond example." St. Louis, Baltimore, Savannah, and Mobile became successful examples of urban development in the *Review*. De Bow published articles that explained the benefits of cities and towns to rural readers.[21]

The development of cities posed new problems for southerners unaccustomed to urban life, and De Bow responded by publishing articles that supported public health initiatives. Although New Orleans had long been an established port, the city struggled to keep up with its growth. As the city's population expanded and its borders encroached on swampy lowlands, the threat of disease became more prevalent. Yellow fever epidemics had ravaged New Orleans every year since 1812, and cholera, typhus, dysentery, tuberculosis, and malaria outbreaks became commonplace. Local hospitals struggled to limit the spread of illness, but the physical location of New Orleans made it difficult to eradicate disease. Many residents fled the city during the summer months, creating an economic void. These daily reminders gave De Bow insight into the connection between public health and commercial development. He initially suggested that New Orleans was healthier than most European and North American cities but retracted his statement after witnessing the deplorable conditions of his city. He believed that cities with less disease attracted more outside investors and created more new opportunities.[22]

De Bow enlisted the help of a small group of southern physicians to discuss the connection between public health initiatives and urban development. He worried about the economic implications of disease, noting: "New Orleans is, unfortunately, almost deserted annually, and all its principal business operations suspended, for at least one-fourth of the year." Dr. W. P. Hort reminded readers that public health affected every citizen of a city: "Upon [it] depends the hope or prospect of advancement, and commerce can exercise no empire when controlled by the adverse and blighting influences of disease and death." Dr. Josiah Nott of Mobile contributed articles on the importance of keeping statistical records to track epidemics. Nott believed that better recordkeeping could save lives by tracking and predicting epidemics. Although these innovations interested De Bow from a commercial point of view, he also recalled the personal toll that disease had taken on his family in Charleston.[23]

De Bow recognized the importance of merchants and professionals to his economic plan and realized that their needs sometimes contradicted those of the agricultural sector. Western migration had created new towns and cities in the Southwest, forcing southwestern planters to use local merchants to sell their cotton crops to commission houses in Mobile and New Orleans. De Bow argued that the South's business class connected rural and urban interests. He advocated a system of cotton warehouses that could be used to store crops during periods of overproduction and low prices. He understood that many planters resisted production control and warehousing but believed that higher profits and better credit ratings would result if merchants could control the flow of cotton to national and international markets. In some cases, he supported tariff protection. Louisiana sugar planters had invested heavily in new machinery and technology and wanted federal trade protection. This position opposed the prevailing attitude among cotton planters, who felt cheated by federal tariff laws that favored the manufacturing sector. De Bow hoped that limited protection for the sugar industry might encourage more innovation and growth. He wanted the South to become more active in the global economy and hoped that southerners would accept some concessions on tariffs for the general betterment of the region.[24]

Industrialization became an important factor in the plan for economic diversification, but De Bow understood that regional apathy and resistance existed. Hoping to encourage southerners to invest in local factories, he asked his fellow South Carolinian William Gregg to write an article for southerners interested in "legitimate home manufactures." Gregg's cotton mills became an early example of how southerners could bring factories closer to cotton fields and produce commercial goods for internal and external markets. De Bow also noted industrial growth among Louisiana's sugar planters and Virginia's iron producers. He wondered why more southerners had failed to embrace industrial development and help end the South's economic dependence on the North. Richard Abbey, a planter from Yazoo City, Mississippi, expressed his frustration with the state of southern manufacturing. Abbey, an innovative cotton planter, complained in the *Review* that economic necessity forced him to buy northern equipment and supplies because southern suppliers failed to meet his demands.[25]

Daniel Pratt wrote to describe his industrial success in Prattville, Alabama. Pratt estimated that his factories produced five hundred cotton gins annually and six thousand yards of cloth on a daily basis. De Bow saw Pratt as a pioneer in southern manufacturing and an exemplar for other southerners. He visited Prattville and applauded its achievement. Prattville's factories had attracted other merchants and businesses, and, at the time of De Bow's visit, the growing town included a gin factory, a sawmill, a foundry, a gristmill, a general store, a horse mill factory, and a tin shop. In addition to these businesses, Pratt had constructed a plank road that connected his town with a nearby landing on the Alabama River.[26]

De Bow's Review became a platform for like-minded men who wished to promote economic diversification. John Pope, a *Review* subscriber and delegate to the Memphis convention, worried that planter apathy and northern competition would soon make it impossible for southerners to recast their economic destiny. Pope blamed planters for failing to invest in other sectors of the economy and insisted: "Men must be spoken to in the language of dollars and cents. . . . [L]et then, the cotton planters of the South arouse from their *criminal* lethargy on this subject and evince to the world that this is their own business; that they have the whole thing in their own hands." He worried that another downturn in the cotton market, as southerners

Table 3: Investment Patterns of Select Readers in Southern Cities and Towns, 1840–1860

City/Town	Readers (*N*)	Railroads	Education	Manufacturing	Banks	Civic
Nashville, TN	10	7	5	4	3	3
Jackson, TN	12	10	5	0	4	4
Memphis, TN	7	6	2	2	6	4
Montgomery, AL	14	13	0	3	5	7
Eutaw, AL	7	6	0	0	0	1
Selma, AL	5	3	0	3	2	1
Mobile, AL	4	4	0	1	1	1
Total	**59**	**49**	**12**	**13**	**21**	**21**

Sources: Composite Census Records, 1850–1860; *Acts of Alabama, 1830–1860* (Catawba: Allen & Brickell); *Acts of Tennessee, Index to Names, 1796–1850*, http://www.tennessee.gov/tsla/history/misc/actsintro.htm.

Note: Numbers in cols. 2–6 represent individual investments. Not every identified reader in each city had a documented investment record. For example, although Nashville had fifty overall readers, investment records exist for only ten of those individuals. Although individual *Review* readers may have invested in more than one project per category, their investment in a particular category counts once. Educational projects included public high schools, private academies, and colleges and universities. Civic projects included public projects such as city gaslights, public art, and urban improvements that benefited entire communities.

had experienced in the late 1830s and early 1840s, or another period of overinvestment in slavery might further limit the South's economy, putting it further behind the North. Pope agreed with De Bow on a plan to control cotton production and encourage industrial development and investment in domestic commercial markets. Indicative of most early articles in the *Review*, Pope's avoided inflammatory sectional discussions or references. Like De Bow, Pope held little personal malice against the North; both men wanted to improve the South but within the confines of the Union.[27]

Like Pope, who worried about the South's economic diversity, James Gadsden urged southerners to expand beyond their overreliance on the agricultural sector because it made the region vulnerable to outside competition from northern manufacturers. What was needed, Gadsden wrote in the *Review*, was a dedicated effort to increase investment in industry and commerce and avoid regional dependence on outside producers (see table 3). He also pushed southerners to think about investing in more schools and libraries as a way of creating better leaders and fostering a sense of community. He believed that the South would meet the challenge and become a great commercial as well as agricultural region.[28]

De Bow made the *Review* a forum for agricultural reform. He encouraged planters to view their plantations as profitable businesses and called for readers to submit practical agricultural articles. Readers responded by offering advice on soil amendment and fertilizers, plantation management, and crop diversification and information on new tools, machinery, and varieties of cotton. De Bow published articles outlining cultivation and harvesting techniques for Indian corn, grain, and rice. Others urged southerners to experiment with exotic crops such as coffee beans, olives, cork trees, and silk. De Bow encouraged southern planters and farmers to join local agricultural groups and share new farming techniques. He published reports from state and local agricultural associations and societies in which readers described subsoil plowing, field drainage, and pest control.[29]

De Bow saw agricultural reform as advancing southern economic strength and independence. New crops might lessen southern dependence on agricultural production from outside the region. Agricultural improvements would create larger profits for planters that could be reinvested in time-saving agricultural devices or other sectors of the southern economy. Better agricultural management would also allow planters to reclaim land originally thought barren in the older parts of the South Atlantic seaboard. De Bow noted: “It is a common complaint, founded, alas, upon too melancholy a truth, that the Southern States have been content to prosecute agriculture with little regard to system, economy, or the dictates of liberal science.”[30]

Sidney Weller, a *Review* subscriber and planter in North Carolina, embodied De Bow’s call for southern agricultural reform. Weller, the largest grape grower and winemaker in the South, had created a diversified plantation on four hundred acres in Brinkleyville, North Carolina. He had experimented with a variety of agricultural schemes in hopes of finding new crops for southern planters and farmers. He eventually settled on growing grapes and wrote extensively on vineyards and winemaking. He wrote numerous articles for De Bow about his experiences and encouraged southern farmers to follow his lead in searching for new agricultural innovations.[31]

Although many readers accepted De Bow’s agricultural contributions, others like Thomas Affleck challenged his vision. A planter and newspaper editor from Mississippi, Affleck proposed that the South remain an exclusively agricultural region and focus on supplying Europe with cotton. De Bow rejected Affleck’s assessment, reminding readers: “The cardinal motive with us, in establishing the *Review,* was the elucidation of ALL THE GREAT

PRINCIPLES OF PROGRESS . . . [and] that all the complicated machinery be understood, and each division brought under distinct observation."[32]

Although De Bow was a nominal Democrat early in his editorial career, his economic vision resembled the Whig Party's probusiness platform, which supported national economic progress through internal improvements, manufacturing, and technological development. He rarely discussed political topics in the *Review.* His strong feelings about Calhoun were more personal than political, and he viewed Henry Clay's ability to create sectional compromises as more important than his American System. De Bow often borrowed rhetoric and ideas from Democrats and Whigs without attributing personal feelings to either party. He understood the editorial importance of political ambiguity to attract the widest variety of southern readers.[33]

Despite his aversion to political topics in the *Review,* De Bow commented on the economic disruption caused by the highly politicized Mexican War. Although a fervent national expansionist who hoped to secure Mexican land, he had misgivings about the Mexican War. Joel R. Poinsett, an ex-envoy to Mexico and noted South Carolina unionist, wrote four articles that opposed the war on political and economic grounds. Poinsett reasoned that republican virtue existed on both sides of the Rio Grande and that war would create unnecessary tension between the two nations. De Bow followed Poinsett's article with skeptical articles by William L. Hodge and Judah Benjamin, members of New Orleans's business class, predicting that any commercial disruptions in southern commerce would benefit northern competitors. Hodge warned: "The great evil that New Orleans has to dread, is a state of war; for even with an inferior power, the injury would be very great." Benjamin supported Hodge's contention and worried that a naval blockade would shut New Orleans off from the rest of the world. De Bow asserted that the Mexican War was an economic issue rather than a political one, and he tried to maintain his promise to avoid political debates.[34]

Although De Bow understood the significance of slavery to the South, he showed little interest in discussing the subject early in his editorial career. He waited eleven months to publish the first full-length article on slavery in the *Review* and six more months to print a follow-up piece on the subject. In the latter article, he offered his first public opinion about the growing national debate over slavery. He seemed puzzled by northern attacks and suggested: "The *argument* for or against the institution . . . so far as the South is concerned, should never more be mooted. . . . [A]s Southerners, as *Americans,* as MEN, we deny the right of being called to account for our institutions." He believed that the moral debate over slavery's existence had been settled and that southerners needed to focus on making the institution more profitable.[35]

De Bow made close personal friendships in New Orleans that broadened his views about the South. Although he maintained close associations with such leading merchants and politicians in New Orleans as James Robb and Pierre Soule, few of his friendships exceeded the depth and closeness of his relationship to Maunsel White. White, an immigrant from Ireland and veteran of the Battle of New Orleans, had by the early 1840s become one of New Orleans's most successful merchants. Despite retiring from active business life in 1845, he continued to invest in factories, real estate, and businesses around the South. He made financial and literary contributions to the *Review.* He wanted to build a state university in New Orleans and wrote articles highlighting the importance of education in the South. De Bow agreed with White's assessment and supported a public university as a civic tool to attract new investment to the city. He also had personal reasons for publicly supporting White's campaign to establish the University of Louisiana (later Tulane University) in New Orleans. White had recommended De Bow for a faculty position, and, as expected, the school's board of administrators hired him to become the first chair of political economy, commerce, and statistics.[36]

Energized by his faculty appointment, De Bow began a public campaign to ensure proper funding for a state university. He implored his readers to support such cultural improvements throughout the South, reminding them that student tuition and fees, not public funds, produced the majority of revenue needed to open and operate a school. He beseeched fellow Louisianans to look at the long-term benefits of education rather than at the short-term inconveniences of opening a state-funded school. De Bow published a curriculum that focused on commerce, agriculture, and manufacturing in the South. He gave public lectures and then published them in the *Review.* The initial excitement, however, eventually gave way to despair. In spite of De Bow's enthusiastic support and White's financial gift, student apathy and financial mismanagement eroded support for the school, ending De Bow's tenure in education.[37]

De Bow became interested in the economic development of his new home city, and readers from New Orleans responded by subscribing to the *Review.* The *Review*'s known readership in New Orleans mirrored De Bow's growing interests in developing the South's economy outward, reflecting a different type of southerner than he had left in Charleston. The average *Review* reader in Charleston was forty-one years old, possessed $15,000 in real estate and $13,750 in personal property, and owned nine slaves. Of the seventy-nine known subscribers, fifty-three of them, or 67 percent, owned slaves. Just over 62 percent of his Charleston readers had been born in South Carolina, with 17 percent coming from northern states or Europe. *Review* subscribers in New Orleans, however, came from a much more diverse background, with fewer direct connections to the region's past. The average reader in New Orleans was forty-five years old, worth $45,000 in real estate and $8,000 in personal property, and owned four slaves. Only fourteen of eighty-five *Review* readers in New Orleans, or 36 percent, owned slaves, and just 17 percent had been born in Louisiana. Fifty-two percent of readers in the city came from a northern state or Europe. In both cities the *Review* appealed mostly to merchants and professionals who had direct interests in the commerce of their region. In New Orleans, however, De Bow found a readership less dependent on past successes and more interested in innovations to make their city better. Although New Orleans had expanded its commercial dominance as a global port, many residents worried that the lack of developed infrastructure would hinder future growth. During the railroad boom of the late 1830s, city boosters attempted to highlight the overall benefits of New Orleans's growth to urban merchants and rural planters. *Review* readers invested in multiple railroad and canal projects that attempted to link the city to western territory. Most of these projects had failed because of funding shortages or competition with other areas of the state. De Bow wanted to renew the excitement that had once gripped the city and cultivate another period of growth that would expand New Orleans's value to the South and the United States.[38]

The shared development of New Orleans and Louisiana became a common theme in the early years of the *Review.* De Bow wanted to help develop the region and attract more readers from his home state. His local reputation increased after the *New Orleans Commercial Times* and the *Concordia Intelligencer* (Vidalia, LA) published positive reviews of his work and expressed hope for more articles on Louisiana. De Bow responded with a historical overview of Louisiana's sugar industry that lauded its growth and the hard work of individual sugar planters but criticized southern manufacturers for not supplying customers with mechanical farm implements. Sugar planters had to import needed machines and parts from northern firms because no local companies could fill orders. He wondered why southerners had not seized this opportunity, noting that the use of steam engines on sugar plantations had increased from 82 engines in 1827 to 408 in 1844. De Bow also examined Louisiana's history and cultural development as a way of highlighting regional communalities. He wanted New Orleans to become the center for all commerce between the Appalachian Highlands and the Rocky Mountains. As a new voice in the city he called for a merchants' association to be created and hold regular meetings, fund a library, offer public lectures, and direct projects that served its constituents. He also began to publish monthly installments highlighting different parishes in the state. He wanted to make sure that all white Louisianans felt tied to his vision of economic and social development, reminding them: "State love is a noble feeling, which we should all inculcate and cherish." He expanded on his feelings on states' rights by concluding: "The existence and preservation of our glorious confederacy depends more than all else upon a strong State feeling and pride, and love, which, prevailing in each of its parts, protects them from all danger of merging in and being lost in the mass."[39]

The cultural development of the South became a regular theme in the *Review*. De Bow received dozens of complimentary books and journals each month and decided to review some of them as a service to his readers. In March 1846 his eclectic interests shone as he reviewed a catalog from the Gallery of Fine Arts in New Orleans, a book on a popular stage actor, two southern agriculture journals, and a collection of poems by William Gilmore Simms. Rather than cast Simms as a southern writer, De Bow portrayed him as a national figure who, in his estimation, transcended time and place. In subsequent issues of the *Review*, he reviewed books by Herman Melville and northern and European journals without mentioning sectional biases. Unlike in later years, when the sectional debate over slavery had hardened his feelings, De Bow's early editorial career remained fairly balanced. He recommended *Chambers' Miscellany* to southern readers despite an article that cast slavery in a negative light, noting that the article failed to diminish the overall value of the journal. De Bow's love of reading and wide range of interests added an element to the *Review* that went beyond his promise of economic salvation.[40]

The *Review*'s reputation continued to grow beyond New Orleans despite hints of De Bow's financial struggles associated with the journal. The Charleston Chamber of Commerce published two public resolutions praising his efforts as an editor, and a writer for the *Semi-Weekly Natchez Courier* suggested that the *Review* benefited southerners "in the practical pursuits of life . . . the planter as well as the merchant . . . the mechanic as well as the professional man." Jesse T. McMahon, the editor of the *Weekly Memphis Enquirer* and a Memphis convention delegate, praised De Bow for his work but reminded him to "see to thy mail books and to thy exchange list."[41]

De Bow's overall vision for economic reform relied heavily on the actions of individuals and communities. In his mind, individual planters and farmers would operate well-managed agricultural units and supply the region with needed produce and cash crops for export. Equally efficient factories would produce needed goods and supplies for southerners and reduce the region's dependence on northern and European manufacturing. Smaller peripheral towns would then become conduits for local trade and funnel commerce to larger international ports, and a system of railroads would link the South together and, ultimately, create a unified region built equally around commerce, manufacturing, and agriculture. This plan, De Bow argued, would allow the South to become independent of northern interests and assume a larger role in national and global affairs.[42]

Much of De Bow's plan coincided with larger developments occurring in the South in the late 1840s. Steady commercial and industrial development had transformed New Orleans, Mobile, Charleston, and Baltimore into important global ports. A growing agricultural market had increased the regional status of Memphis, Vicksburg, Montgomery, Knoxville, and Augusta. A growing transportation system linked these urban centers. Plans for new railroads existed in almost every southern state, with tangible growth in South Carolina, Alabama, Tennessee, and Virginia. Although substantially behind their northern counterparts, southern industrialists and merchants had become increasingly more visible and influential in southern society. More southerners invested in factories and other small manufacturing enterprises.

In the first three years of the *Review*, De Bow expressed a new economic vision to southern readers, and they responded. He collected ideas that had been part of the southern dialogue for generations and published them in a practical, succinct message for like-minded southerners. He recognized themes that interested southern readers and did it within the larger national context of American progress. De Bow's time with Calhoun strengthened both his sense of American nationalism and his southern identity. Most of his personal motivation to create a better South was set within the confines of the Union, not in the nascent ideas of southern nationalists. De Bow had offered the South a comprehensive economic vision for how to compete in a modern world, but he had to wait to see whether southerners would be truly willing to act on his words.

De Bow struggled constantly to keep the *Review* financially viable. Readers failed to make their subscription payments on time, and he compounded the problem by keeping poor records. His agents took money from subscribers but sometimes did not forward the money to him. De Bow neglected to print advertisements that had been paid for, and high printing costs and an ill-advised investment in a printing press further diminished his resources. He had failed to print issues for July and August 1847 and May 1848. Anxious to maintain his business, he borrowed money to keep publishing. In August 1848 he reported that he had lost $8,000. He pleaded with readers to submit their payments: "What have the Editor and Publishers realized from the three years of unremitting toil? Literally nothing! . . . [S]end us the *pittance* that *remains due, even if it must be borrowed from a friendly neighbor.*" He reduced the size of the *Review* and appealed again to readers to pay their subscriptions: "Remember us, we pray you, for our funds are very low, and ought, in all conscience, to be replenished forthwith." Unable to pay his expenses, De Bow closed his office in December 1848.[43]

3

A Busy and Fractured Mind of the South

News of De Bow's failure circulated among affluent southerners who read or contributed to the *Review.* Maunsel White pledged financial support to his friend, and readers from around the South sent subscriptions in to De Bow. R. F. W. Allston of South Carolina delivered eight new paid orders, intending to give them to friends. Miles McGehee of Bolivar, Mississippi, bought ten subscriptions and hoped to resell them to neighbors. James H. Hammond, a former governor of South Carolina, sent money and a public letter that chastised southerners for their literary neglect of such a worthy cause. The *Charleston Mercury* learned: "The subscription list of the *Review* does not exceed 100 in Charleston. Mr. De Bow deserves several hundred names among us for his valuable enterprise." Most southern journals had limited appeal outside the region aside from the *Southern Literary Messenger,* the *Southern Quarterly Review,* and *De Bow's Review,* which were also the most popular among southern readers. A frustrated De Bow estimated that his *Review* had only about five thousand readers compared to the sixty thousand subscribers that *Harper's Weekly* enjoyed. The reading habits of Americans worked doubly against southern editors because northern journals dominated the reading habits of southern readers and most northern readers had little interest in southern journals. De Bow chided southerners for not supporting their homegrown periodicals more and prodded northerners who failed "to sustain or encourage any enterprise south of Mason and Dixon's line." He warned that the suspension of the *Review* might be permanent if readers failed to support his enterprise with paid subscriptions.[1]

Eager to restart the *Review* and find new topics to explore, De Bow took an extended trip to Tennessee, Kentucky, and Indiana in June 1849. He first traveled to Memphis to visit old subscribers and find new readers. He planned to attend a commercial convention in town but learned that an outbreak of cholera had canceled the event. Nevertheless, the visit to Memphis, the place where his editorial career began in 1845, lifted his spirits. He then made his way to Louisville, Kentucky, and spent considerable time with Hamilton Smith, a local cotton factory owner and *Review* subscriber who owned a lavish home near his factory in Cannelton, Indiana. Located along the northern bank of the Ohio River, Cannelton had become the financial centerpiece for a group of northern and southern investors who hoped to develop seven thousand acres of land, mine nearby coal deposits, and operate the cotton factory. Smith believed that his factory's proximity to southern cotton fields would decrease production costs and undercut competitors in New England.[2]

Hamilton Smith served as an excellent model for southern *Review* readers. He had been born in New Hampshire and educated at Dartmouth College before studying law in Washington, DC. In December 1833, he moved to Louisville and began a legal career that served as a catalyst for his commercial and agricultural interests. When Robert Fulton, the inventor of the steamboat, failed to establish an industrial center at Cannelton, Smith organized a group of investors who included Maunsel White and eleven other men from Louisiana and Mississippi. Regional chauvinism had yet to consume southern planters, who saw potential profit in Smith's project. By the time De Bow profiled Smith in July 1851, the cotton mill at Cannelton had 10,800 spindles and 372 looms. In De Bow's mind the large factory embodied the spirit of the Memphis convention because southerners and westerners worked together to improve their collective economic position within the nation. Although Smith's project sat north of the Ohio River, De Bow saw Cannelton as a western enterprise that benefited southern farmers by moving cotton factories closer to cotton fields. Charles T. James, a *Review* reader and industrialist from Rhode Island, believed that Cannelton had the potential to supplant the most profitable factory towns in the North and Europe. Like Daniel Pratt in Prattville, Alabama, and William Gregg in Graniteville, South Carolina, Hamilton Smith made Cannelton a cotton-manufacturing center that promised to boost the South's economic capacity and serve as a practical example of industrial enterprise. Excited by De Bow's visit, the *Cannelton Economist* reported: "Professor De Bow has fully shown himself competent to the preparation and management of such a *Review*—and we feel confident that . . . the people of this valley will insure him their liberal support."[3]

On returning home from his trip, De Bow focused his attention on the *Review*'s problematic business affairs. He had learned from his prior experiences and hoped to avoid further embarrassment by offering timely articles and working with more reliable publishers. Failure had been a steady companion in De Bow's early life, and this setback made him more resolute about recovery. Plagued by poor management and a busy schedule, he needed administrative help and eventually brought in his younger brother, Benjamin F. De Bow, to serve as his business manager. The two would continue to work together until their deaths in 1867. With renewed subscriptions, more borrowed money, and promises of support, the brothers resumed publication of the *Review* in July 1849, but with a warning to readers that they had better be prompt with their payments.[4]

The hard work and constant attention it took to restart the *Review* weighed heavily on De Bow, and during the summer of 1850 he escaped New Orleans and explored the coasts of Louisiana, Mississippi, and Alabama. For many wealthy southerners these trips were common. Urban professionals and rural planters took advantage of better transportation routes and polished resorts to enjoy each other's company. Such a trip also became a social marker used to distinguish between those who could afford such luxuries and those who could not. De Bow's trip served as evidence of his newly found success after his prior difficulties in 1849. He admitted that New Orleans's active city life had exhausted him and that travel would be refreshing before the summer heat descended on the city. Although the trip was supposed to be a pleasurable one, De Bow took time to gather material for new articles and editorial notices. He visited various towns along the Gulf Coast and evaluated their commercial potential and natural resources. In Mobile he enjoyed hearing about new railroad projects and factories that matched the spirit of entrepreneurship he found among the city's merchants. He enjoyed his time at a resort in Point Clear, Alabama, noting the healthy environment it offered. At Mississippi Springs, Mississippi, he spoke about transportation development with N. D. Coleman, a *Review* reader and the president of the Vicksburg, Shreveport, and Texas Railroad. After a visit to Mississippi City, Mississippi, De Bow declared that the town could eclipse New Orleans's future under the right circumstances. He also managed to find enjoyment during his hectic trip and played pool, enjoyed drinks, and smoked cigars with local planters and vacationers. The "hopeful maidens and gay widows," as De Bow remembered his female companions during this trip, provided a welcome respite from work and travel.[5]

De Bow used the newly reconstituted *Review* to feature successful entrepreneurs in other industries, as he had done with Hamilton Smith. No other southern journal offered such insight into the South's growing manufacturing sector, and he wanted to provide models for interested readers. Joseph R. Anderson's Tredegar Iron Works in Richmond earned special distinction for producing raw iron and finished locomotives and railroad axles that were then sold to southern customers. De Bow wrote a lengthy biographical article on John G. Winter, a prominent entrepreneur and industrialist who settled in Alabama after making his fortune in banking and finance in Georgia. Winter used his wealth to fund the Montgomery Iron Works, a flour mill, a paper mill, and a plank road. De Bow lauded his industrial spirit and sense of risk. He hoped that future generations of southerners would become familiar with these early industrial leaders and recognize that, "with the material upon the spot, with an abundance of water power, or with inexhaustible coal and iron fields, provisions without stint, and cheap labor, particularly that of the slave, which is always practicable, it will be strange if the South and West permit much longer their wealth to be drained away by northern manufacturers."[6]

De Bow hoped to stimulate new industrial development in the South by offering articles that provided specific examples and tangible results from factories around the region. He scoured newspapers and relied on readers for information that projected a sense of progress. Daniel Pratt estimated that twelve new factories with almost twenty thousand spindles had been built in Alabama in 1850. Similar reports from other states began to emerge, and De Bow gleefully recorded sixteen factories in South Carolina, thirty-six in Georgia, and thirty in Tennessee in 1850. Southern factories had increased their consumption of cotton from 75,000 bales in September 1848 to 110,000 bales a year later. De Bow saw the capacity for more growth and urged southern readers to stop sending their cotton to northern and European factories and instead create their own industrial sector that could produce finished products. Readers responded with their own ideas about industrial development. Hamilton Smith challenged southerners to become producers as well as consumers of finished goods. Mark R. Cockrill of Nashville proposed the construction of regional cotton factories staffed with slaves from large plantations. Cockrill argued that one-fifth of the total slave population could be redirected to factories without jeopardizing cotton production.

He encouraged planters to build roads and railroads that linked isolated plantations with factories and regional ports. Cockrill's reputation as an innovative planter and stockbreeder—he owned a fifty-five-hundred-acre plantation outside of Nashville and two others in Mississippi—lent credibility to his ideas. De Bow seconded them, rousing his readers to "action, Action, ACTION!!!!—not in the rhetoric of Congress, but in the busy hum of mechanism, and in the thrifty operations of the hammer and the anvil."[7]

As De Bow became more concerned about southern manufacturing, he also became interested in the use of slave labor in the industrial sector. Despite opposition from some planters and detractors who did not want slaves around modern machinery, he supported industrial slavery as the most cost-effective form of labor for southern factories and railroads. He rejected counterarguments that slaves lacked the intelligence or work ethic to operate expensive or complicated machinery. In October 1850 he visited Saluda Factory near Columbia, South Carolina, and watched slaves work under white supervision. A visiting weaver from Lowell, Massachusetts, confirmed De Bow's feelings about the excellent quality of work being done at Saluda. De Bow's observations reaffirmed his belief that slave labor could infuse the South's industrial sector with new energy. He also believed that railroad companies could save money by buying slaves instead of renting them from planters. A *Review* contributor confirmed De Bow's argument after studying the use of slave labor by two railroad companies in Virginia. The reader reported that the James River and Kanawha Railroad Company and the Virginia and Tennessee Railroad Company saved more than half their annual labor costs after buying slaves. De Bow reminded readers that these savings would be passed down to shareholders.[8]

The development of a southern railroad system became paramount to De Bow as interregional economic competition intensified in the United States. Access to new western markets and to existing trade networks made it imperative that the South not fall behind northern competitors. Many southern investors saw railroad construction as an unsafe investment, forcing many state governments to fund projects with a mixture of private money and state-issued bonds and subsidies. Profit-minded southerners looked at these projects with hope but understood that low dividends made them risky ventures. De Bow attempted to instill confidence in the development of a regional network by suggesting that railroads needed to follow the agricultural and commercial patterns of the South rather than just routes created by special interests. Frost lines, harvest patterns, mineral deposits, and towns and cities had to be accounted for when building railroads. He understood the importance of shipping goods along a north-south axis as well as in an east-west direction. He stressed that railroads created a sense of community and cohesiveness. Yet no one plan could be agreed on. At a railroad convention in Memphis in October 1849, promoters suggested four separate southern routes to link the Mississippi River and the Pacific Ocean. De Bow tried to forge a compromise by finding value in each plan but offering Memphis as the best terminus for a southern transcontinental railroad. Ultimately, however, delegates failed to agree on a single solution, leaving De Bow frustrated that local interests sidetracked larger regional goals.[9]

The proposed route of the transcontinental railroad put northern and southern interests directly in competition with each other. De Bow recognized that internal southern bickering made it easier for northern politicians to finalize a route that benefited their constituents. Illinois senator Stephen Douglas had organized political support and purchased public land for the Illinois Central Railroad in anticipation of securing a northern transcontinental route through the Nebraska Territory. De Bow understood Douglas's motives and aligned himself with a group of Louisiana merchants and politicians who supported the Tehuantepec Railroad Company. Led by the *Review* readers Pierre Soule and Judah Benjamin, the railroad would make New Orleans the terminus of a line extending into Mexican territory and ending in San Diego. This route would guarantee the inclusion of southern ports and stop Douglas's proposed project. De Bow increased his editorial campaign to secure a southern route and, dissatisfied with the South's response, called out to his supporters: "Up, up ye men of capital, ye men of influence and enterprise, for it is now common danger that menaces. The hour is now."[10]

In October 1851 De Bow gave a speech to the Tennessee legislature that expanded on his ideas of railroad development and its value to the South. The economic and social potential of railroads and the telegraph seemed limitless to him because they existed "to perform their glorious mission in elevating and perfecting our civilization and our progress." While southern states bickered over routes and funding, he observed, northern states such as New York invested public money in railroads and canals. He worried that narrow views on railroad development threatened to overshadow Tennessee. Industrial progress, he promised, would create cooperation and newfound respect between the North and the South. This would lessen the developing competition between the rival sections and make western markets beneficial for all Americans. He hoped that economic progress would stabilize the political relationship between the North and the South. In a later speech at the Fair of the American Institute in New York City, he admitted to his northern audience: "In my own region I would imitate very much what belongs to your character and career." His reassuring words and moderate tone invoked images of a great southern revolution that would benefit the entire nation. Although his rhetoric would harden in the years leading up to the Civil War, De Bow's balanced message reminded southern readers that they too had a stake in the nation's future.[11]

De Bow helped organize the 1852 New Orleans Commercial Convention so that southerners could further discuss railroad development, and on January 5, 1852, Maunsel White opened it amid the growing excitement of a regional railroad boom. James Robb, a local businessman and railroad promoter, called for increased government funding and the use of public land to encourage railroad development in the South. Robb believed that more southern railroads and factories would attract immigrants who wanted to live in the South. Like De Bow, he saw railroad construction as "a civilizing and conquering power . . . the greatest of all missions." The local attorney and *Review* subscriber Judah Benjamin reaffirmed Robb's suggestions in a separate speech and explained how railroads fostered a sense of community and protected the basic tenets of republicanism. He, like De Bow, saw value in strengthening the bond between the South and the West.[12]

On the second day of the convention, De Bow presented his comprehensive plan to improve and diversify the southern economy. Invoking memories of an Old South that had supplied many of the nation's most prominent politicians, he reminded delegates that southern entrepreneurship had produced the first transatlantic steamship and the longest railroad in the world by the 1830s. He admitted, however, that those days had passed and that northern advances had overtaken southern political and economic dominance. He blamed southerners for this decline, specifically pointing to their overdependence on agricultural production, which limited the South's industrial and commercial development. He proposed a specific plan that linked the interests of planters, merchants, and industrialists. Railroads would open new territory, foster innovation, and expand the commercial network of the South. Factories would stimulate the extraction of raw materials, create new urban centers, and increase the South's global economic status. These changes, De Bow promised, would lead to greater profits for all southerners. He challenged the delegates to become more like their northern counterparts: "You may build rail-roads, erect factories, hold conventions, but you cannot redeem the commercial apathy of the South unless you are content to adopt the same expedients." Despite the rising sectional tension between the North and the South, De Bow saw value in the example set by northern economic progress in early 1852—it provided a model for southern growth and crystallized a regional agenda.[13]

In December 1852 the citizens of Baltimore hosted a similar commercial convention, hoping to address internal improvements and direct trade between the South and the West. Representatives of twelve southern and western states were in attendance. Although De Bow could not make it to Baltimore, he wrote a promotional *Review* article to stir interest in the meeting, noting that Baltimore played an important role in the development of the nation since it lay "nearest the North, nearest the South, nearest the West; so central, in fact, as to be nearest to all." Delegates discussed the need for better communication between the South and the West and how to improve southern shipping. They also recognized the Baltimore and Ohio Railroad and the Chesapeake and Ohio Canal as two outstanding examples of public projects that aided commercial growth. Despite the good intentions of the convention organizers, however, the meeting failed to offer substantive solutions to many of the South's commercial and industrial problems. It also highlighted intraregional differences between southerners because the interests of the Deep South had little bearing on the Upper South. De Bow realized that he had to appease as many readers as possible or risk having them compete against each other, which would weaken the South as a whole and make it more vulnerable to northern competition. Like John C. Calhoun in the 1830s and postbellum New South boosters in the 1880s, De Bow found that forging an actual solid South proved to be more difficult than simply creating the facade of regional unity.[14]

Inevitably, however, political questions complicated De Bow's economic agenda and forced him to discuss topics that he had vowed to avoid in the initial edition of the *Review*. The northern congressman David Wilmot ignited a national debate after he proposed to prevent the extension of slavery into western territory acquired during the Mexican-American War. The discovery of gold in California further exacerbated sectional tensions as lawmakers determined whether the territory would become a free or a slave state. De Bow immediately saw the vast economic potential of western trade for the South, estimating that new commerce could produce $350 million annually. Yet, as politicians quibbled over slavery and western territory, he worried that sectional rivalries might delay the construction of a transcontinental railroad and allow European competitors to gain control of western markets. He also saw the potential wealth of western land and commerce as political tools for the South. It would help create political equality between the sections and protect minority rights. De Bow supported Senator Henry Clay's proposed political compromise, which satisfied many northern and southern moderates by offering concessions to both sides. In June 1850 De Bow attended the Nashville convention, a political meeting called to forge a regional response to any congressional ban on slavery. Although zealous secessionists and states' rights proponents attended the meeting, De Bow found the proceedings tiresome and unproductive. He did, however, admit that the exhibition of southern unity stirred sectional pride within him. Yet, despite his southern leanings and growing political dissatisfaction, he continued to hope that a peaceful solution could be reached between the two sides.[15]

Although Henry Clay's proposed compromise failed to pass Congress in late 1849, Senator Stephen Douglas managed to split Clay's omnibus bill into smaller measures that became known collectively as the Compromise of 1850. The compromise admitted California into the Union as a free state, allowed the New Mexico and Utah territories to use popular sovereignty to determine the status of slavery within their borders, settled boundary disputes in Texas, ended the slave trade in Washington, DC, and enacted a stronger fugitive slave law. Although William Yancey, Robert Rhett, and other southern secessionists—commonly known as fire-eaters—condemned the compromise and the South's submission on key points, De Bow viewed the political concessions as an amicable solution that allowed the nation to move forward to other pressing issues, such as the transcontinental railroad. Like their southern counterparts, northern extremists also felt unsatisfied by the compromise, especially with regard to popular sovereignty and the Fugitive Slave Act. Nevertheless, De Bow applauded the law as essential to southern property rights and accepted popular sovereignty as the way for new territories to decide their place in the Union. Relieved by the political compromise, De Bow hoped: "God grant that the verdict be *peace,* and that some measure shall be devised for the preservation of this glorious Union, in a manner that may cause no section of it to blush." Yet the growing abolitionist movement in the North continued to worry De Bow because its power had started to silence moderates willing to compromise with the South. De Bow was heartened when a group of antiabolitionists in New York City asked him to promote Henry F. James's *Abolitionism Unveiled! Hypocrisy*

Unmasked! and Knavery Scourged! Like De Bow, they resisted the North's growing antislavery movement as a way of minimizing sectional differences.[16]

De Bow attempted to maintain an editorial tone that deemphasized regional extremism on both sides and highlighted national similarities. Although the *Review* attracted southern nationalists and secessionists, he criticized South Carolina's press for framing "an argument for disunion at all hazards, even were the slavery question closed up and amicably settled": "This course is suicidal to the southern cause." In another editorial, he condemned his personal friend and college classmate William H. Trescott for suggesting that free labor and slavery had made the North and South socially and economically incompatible. De Bow countered Trescott's assumption by suggesting that free labor and slave labor worked toward common national goals. Consequently, he took particular note of nonsoutherners who supported slavery as a way of deemphasizing abolitionism. He acknowledged when William Chambers, a British editor, started an extended tour of the South opposed to slavery and ended his trip as a supporter of the institution. Likewise, De Bow seized on the similar transformation of Solon Robinson, a noted northern antislavery agriculturalist who also toured the South and became a proponent of slavery. Robinson admitted that he had ambivalent feelings about the institution until he witnessed its effectiveness. De Bow valued these men because they offered proof that northerners could be rational and willing to compromise on slavery and because their experience suggested that abolitionists were radicals out of touch with their own society.[17]

After the publication of *Uncle Tom's Cabin* by Harriet Beecher Stowe in 1852, De Bow used the *Review* to counter the antislavery theme of the book and to defend southern institutions such as slavery and plantation life. A Georgia reader wondered why such fiction had been written about slavery and questioned the motives of British and American abolitionists since their nations had helped bring slavery to the South. Great Britain soon became a favorite target of southerners who saw hypocrisy in British attitudes toward it. De Bow himself wondered whether Great Britain used abolitionism to drive cotton prices down. John Forsyth, the editor of the *Mobile Register*, concurred with De Bow and argued that slavery had also been the foundation of northern industrial progress, reminding apathetic southerners that slavery, "so far from being the cause of our retardation, is the nursing mother of the prosperity of the North." Yet the cruelty of *Uncle Tom's Cabin* stirred northern readers to confront their feelings about slavery and the recently passed Fugitive Slave Act, which potentially forced them to become complicit in slavery's existence. Stowe's caricature of Simon Legree, a violent master who abused his slaves, reportedly had been patterned after Meredith Calhoun, a *Review* subscriber and planter from Louisiana. De Bow decided that the most effective way to counter Stowe's images of brutality was to highlight slave-management techniques that encouraged their rational and moral treatment. His readers agreed and wrote about their own, more civilized approaches to plantation life. One author believed that locking slaves in small, isolated pens worked better than whipping because it cut them off from their "little weekly dances and chit-chat." Another planter from Mississippi warned that "whipping, when necessary, shall be in moderation, and never done in a passion."[18]

De Bow's own attitudes about slavery stemmed more from the desire to create a profitable institution than from his concern for slaves' well-being. De Bow hoped to transform wasteful plantations into efficient agricultural factories by offering advice on work routines, food rationing, slave housing and clothing, and the general welfare of slaves (see table 4). Using time-management methods from northern factories, a *Review* contributor prescribed strict rules that relied on the use of bells to regulate a slave's day. Although work bells had existed in the South since the 1830s, De Bow encouraged more planters to use time management as a way of maximizing the potential of slave labor. Railroads, telegraphs, and factories had already forced nineteenth-century Americans to focus more on time, and De Bow wanted to make the clock an ally of the southern planter. Mindful of the possibility of abuse and overwork, he urged planters to think about slave happiness to augment the productivity of their workforce. Increased time and labor management meant that masters had to rely more on overseers as the middle managers of their plantations. Caught between the overt power of the plantation master and the covert power of slaves, the overseer needed to earn the loyalty of both parties. De Bow believed that "humanity, on the part of the overseer, and unqualified obedience on the part of the negroes, are, under all circumstances, indispensable." Likewise, he argued, the overseer owed his devotion to the planter because ultimate control lay in his hands. Yet a good master had to assume an active role in the care of his land, slaves, and overseer. De Bow envisioned this complex relationship between a paternalistic planter, a capable overseer, and happy slaves as the key to increasing the profitability and efficiency of a plantation. Of the known *Review* readers, only eight men identified themselves as overseers, and all but one lived in the Deep South. Although many wealthy southerners looked

Table 4: Comparative Slaveholding Levels, 1860

Group	0 Slaves	1–10 Slaves	11–19 Slaves	20–49 Slaves	50–99 Slaves	100+ Slaves
All southern slaveholders	75	72	16	9	2	1
Commercial convention delegates	N.A.	25	17	19	22	17
Confederate congressmen	N.A.	28	20	23	13	16
De Bow's Review readership	6	29	11	26	17	16

Sources: Vicki Vaughn Johnson, *The Men and the Vision of the Southern Commercial Conventions, 1845–1871* (Columbia: University of Missouri Press, 1992), 56; Composite Census Records, 1850–1860; John Niven, *The Coming of the Civil War, 1837–1860* (Arlington Heights, IL: Harlan Davidson, 1990), 34.
Note: N.A. = not available. Figures given are percentages.

down on these men as a necessary evil, they, like De Bow, recognized the importance of good overseers in southern society.[19]

De Bow promoted efficient plantations as part of an increasingly diversified regional economy by attending events that placed southern innovations within the larger national context. His growing national reputation as an authority on the South led to new personal and professional opportunities. Organizers of the 1853 World's Fair in New York City asked De Bow, Maunsel White, and James Robb to serve as committeemen to represent their region. They agreed, and their committee wrote a public letter that supported the theme of the fair—global industrialization and progress—and encouraged southerners to "unite with our fellow-citizens of the North in this great enterprise . . . [and] strengthen the bonds of amity and concord—realize indeed that we are one people, with one hope and one inheritance, one faith and one destiny." The world's fair appealed to De Bow's global curiosity, and he challenged Americans to commingle with other cultures and reduce local and regional prejudices. He pled southerners to take advantage of the opportunity, reminding his readers: "We are Americans yet, taking pride in the achievements of the great republic . . . from the rising to the setting sun."[20]

Heightened awareness of De Bow's reputation as a forward-thinking southerner and expert statistician led President Franklin Pierce to name him the replacement superintendent of the 1850 national census in April 1853. The federal census had become important for many Americans because it figuratively and literally measured their nation's growth and for the first time, many observers noted, counted slaves in a separate statistical schedule. De Bow's natural interest in numbers and his previous experience as the director of Louisiana's state census allowed him to speak expertly on the subject. The use of statistics had also become an iconic part of the *Review.* After Congress appointed Joseph C. G. Kennedy as superintendent of the census in September 1849, De Bow wrote a series of critical articles for the *New Orleans Daily Picayune* offering general advice and direction on the collection of statistics. He viewed accurate recordkeeping as an essential component of the economic and social development of the nation. Kennedy, a Whig from Pennsylvania, had done a commendable job for the first three years but soon became politically vulnerable after the election of Pierce, a Democrat from New Hampshire. As a "doughface," or a northerner with southern sympathies, Pierce removed Kennedy from his position and installed De Bow as his replacement. Although De Bow claimed to have little interest in the position, he accepted Pierce's offer on April 6, 1853, and promptly fired much of the staff as a money-saving gesture and began to work on the nation's numbers. Because of his new job, he announced that he would be moving to Washington, DC, but reassured readers that he would continue to publish the *Review.* Excited by the opportunity and exposure created by his new position, he promised: "The more extended field which is opened, will rather enlarge and diversify the interests of the *Review;* and whilst its distinctive character as a southern work is preserved, will make it, in many senses, a national one."[21]

De Bow's experience in the census office proved to be a difficult one because of his ambition and his shaky relationship with Kennedy. Kennedy had almost finished gathering the statistics for the census when De Bow replaced him. A correspondent for the *New York Daily Tribune* wrote a lengthy article that explored the difficulties between the two men. The article had a sectional tone, referring to Kennedy as kindly and courteous while casting De Bow as impatient and accusatory. A squabble over a desk and personal books became additional fodder for the growing feud. The *Nashville Union and American* published an article that applauded De Bow for firing most of the census staff, streamlining procedures, and generally cleaning up after Kennedy. Despite the political implications of De Bow's appointment, writers from the *New York Times* and the *New Orleans Bulletin,* both Whig newspapers, noted that his appointment had been based on talent and experience. But these positive recommendations did not silence critics. De Bow had made enemies among those who supported Kennedy and among those who opposed his sectional boosterism and support of slavery. For example, in 1857 Hinton Helper used De Bow's statistics to attack slavery as a hindrance to southern agriculture, commerce, and general prosperity. De Bow, meanwhile, had purposely underanalyzed slavery and found Helper's use of statistics unbearable. Later, in a private letter in March 1862 to the then governor of Tennessee, Andrew Johnson, Joseph Kennedy reemerged and encouraged Johnson: "Nab DeBow if he comes in your way. He has not the courage to enter the army while he has been as instrumental as the worst in bringing about the present lamentable state of affairs." Despite these setbacks and personal issues, however, De Bow enjoyed his time in Washington.[22]

In an attempt to capitalize on his newfound fame, De Bow republished many of the *Review*'s most popular articles in a three-volume set entitled *The Industrial Resources, etc., of the Southern and Western States: Embracing a View of Their Commerce, Agriculture, Manufactures, Internal Improvements, Slave and Free Labor, Slave Institutions, Products, etc., of the South.* Later shortened to *De Bow's Industrial Resources,* the eighteen-hundred-page set received high praise from newspapers and magazines around the nation. The *Boston Post* and the *New York Times* applauded his statistical analysis and insight, and a reviewer at *Harper's Weekly* noted: "It is still more important in a national point of view, making the different parts of the Union better acquainted with each other, and increasing the attachment of all to the general interests of their common country." Although De Bow had few northern readers, he hoped that the *Review* would become popular in the North. He reasoned that sectional misunderstandings could be reduced if northern readers better understood southern issues.[23]

Eager to find new or reformulated topics that would connect with more readers, regardless of regional or political background, De Bow focused on the benefits of agricultural reform and scientific farming in the *Review.* By 1853 there were forty-three monthly journals dedicated to agricultural reform in the United States, and he hoped to tap into new markets by offering articles that highlighted successful farming practices. His move to expand the *Review*'s coverage of rural topics corresponded with a growing national movement toward the formation of agricultural organizations. While living in Washington, DC, De Bow became an officer in the US Agricultural Society. Although many southerners viewed the Agricultural Society as a northern-based advocacy group, De Bow encouraged his readers to read its reports and join similar organizations. He wanted the *Review* to become standard reading material for organizations and offered a favorable subscription rate for groups. He provided readers with a variety of articles whose subject matter ranged from cotton and sugar production to the cultivation of grapes, rice, corn, tobacco, livestock, and poultry and the use of guano. *Review* contributors gave detailed reports based on their personal observations. They eventually contributed enough material to make the "Agricultural Department" a standard part of the *Review* for the rest of the decade. Unfortunately for yeoman farmers and small planters, however, De Bow focused most of his material on improving large cotton and sugar plantations because wealthy planters had the capital and interest to embrace innovation. Noting the progress of the sugar cane industry in Louisiana, for example, he enthusiastically reported that state sugar production had grown from 186,000 hogsheads in 1845 to 449,324 in 1853. He congratulated planters for increasing their production despite their willingness to push smaller farmers out of business. This growth reinforced his belief that plantations had to be turned into efficient and profitable agricultural factories.[24]

Southern agricultural associations and conventions became more common as planters and farmers looked to amend wasteful practices that exhausted the land. In December 1853 De Bow attended a six-day planters' convention in Columbia, South Carolina, and delivered a speech on the agricultural, commercial, and political importance of cotton. He also participated in discussions to create a southern agricultural college. Delegates hoped to raise money to start the school and then petition individual states to maintain its existence. The Columbia convention also brought De Bow back into contact with Edmund Ruffin, who promised to write for the *Review*. Ruffin had published books on calcareous manure and the benefits of fertilizer and had conducted an agricultural survey of South Carolina in 1843. These accomplishments made him a well-known expert among southern farmers, but his extreme stance in support of slavery and southern nationalism made him a polarizing national figure. Ruffin feared that any signs of southern weakness might lead to new attacks on slavery, and he had spent years developing a proslavery and secessionist ideology in addition to working in agriculture. De Bow had profiled Ruffin in the *Review* and admired his work, and both men agreed that southern planters needed to improve the management of their plantations and farms. De Bow, however, had yet to embrace Ruffin's extreme sectional rhetoric. Although De Bow and Ruffin maintained a long working relationship, Ruffin strongly disliked De Bow, referring to him as a "crafty & mean Yankee in conduct & principle, though a southerner by birth & residence, & in political philosophy."[25]

Farmers and planters in Alabama listened to agricultural reformers and gradually transformed their southwestern frontier into a cotton kingdom. Between 1850 and 1860 they increased the state's improved acreage by two million acres and raised the total value of all farms by $46 million. The noted Alabama planter and agriculturalist Noah Cloud had traveled to Columbia for the planters' convention and met De Bow while there. Cloud valued De Bow's work, and both men shared a similar vision for the South. Like De Bow, Cloud had been born in South Carolina and later moved to the Southwest to find his vocation. Unlike De Bow, however, Cloud came from a wealthy family that had sent him to medical school in Philadelphia before he moved to Alabama to become a cotton planter. Cloud quickly became a state leader in agricultural reform, and in 1853 he started his own monthly journal dedicated to southern economic development. The *American Cotton Planter* served Alabamians who wanted to learn more about agricultural innovation. Cloud often reprinted articles from *De Bow's Review* because he understood the importance of integrating agriculture and industry, reminding his readers: "Manufactures—yes, this is the true policy for the American cotton planter. . . . [W]e should foster and encourage the introduction of cotton manufacturing in the midst of our fields." The Alabama industrialist and *Review* reader Daniel Pratt supported Cloud's decision to promote economic diversification and used himself as an example: "I am not a cotton planter, notwithstanding I am deeply interested in its cultivation. It is from this plant that I have been enabled to support myself and family, and to give employment to a good number of persons. . . . [T]he most important step towards it [industrialization] is to encourage agricultural improvements." The emergence of Cloud's work corresponded with Alabama's growing agricultural sector. For many planters and farmers, the *American Cotton Planter* and *De Bow's Review* became standard reading.[26]

Much of the positive regional economic momentum and publicity generated by De Bow became partially obscured by Senator Stephen Douglas's Kansas-Nebraska bill in early 1854. Douglas had garnered enough political support to reintroduce his plan to organize the territory immediately west of Iowa and hoped to organize the land for statehood to secure a northern route for an impending transcontinental railroad. On January 4, 1854, he proposed that residents of Kansas and Nebraska use popular sovereignty to choose whether they wanted to be admitted to the Union as free states or slave states. By dismissing the political boundary that had been set by the Missouri Compromise in 1820 and supporting the concept of popular sovereignty, he reignited the national dispute over the western expansion of slavery, especially among northern abolitionists. In April 1854 the Charleston Commercial Convention offered De Bow a public forum to express his disdain for the North's reaction to the Kansas-Nebraska Act. Although De Bow was unable to attend the convention, he sent an open letter that was read and written into the official record. Unlike past articles and speeches, De Bow's letter took a harsher sectional tone that questioned whether the South might prosper outside the Union. He argued that breaking free of northern factories and merchants would allow the southern economy to develop more fully and permit southerners to provide for themselves. He reminded delegates of the importance of building railroads, improving river navigation, and developing a manufacturing sector to compete with northern businessmen. In a more conciliatory tone, De Bow encouraged southerners to "calmly, yet boldly . . . advance in this great work of regeneration . . . without the spirit of recrimination—without sectional bitterness or enmities." His overall tone, however, reflected his growing dissatisfaction. Delegates to the convention fixated on the Kansas-Nebraska bill, the transcontinental railroad, and the growing power of the abolitionist movement. Albert Pike, a *Review* subscriber and prominent southwestern lawyer, accused northerners of seeding the West with sympathetic immigrants. The tenor of the Charleston meeting reflected a far more combative sectional character than had characterized any earlier commercial convention.[27]

National events and rising sectionalism forced De Bow to reevaluate the editorial tone of the *Review*. The steady rise of northern antislavery sentiment in conjunction with the political events of the early 1850s left him frustrated and bitter about real and perceived sectional slights. He became alarmed as northern politicians, writers, and common citizens amplified the tone and frequency of their attacks on slavery. De Bow had been exposed to slavery from his earliest childhood to adulthood and formulated feelings about the institution before becoming a prominent editor. He defended slavery as a social and economic necessity and saw little reason to debate its existence. If agricultural techniques were modernized, slave management improved, and the use of slave labor expanded into the industrial sector, slavery could, he believed, be fully compatible with a modern industrial economy in the South. Consequently, northern attacks on slavery persuaded him to change his view of the Union. These assaults overwhelmed his sense of American nationalism and awakened sectional feelings that had been secondary in his mind and in the pages of the *Review.*[28]

De Bow saw the South's present situation and potential future in more historical terms. He had always been interested in history, believing that progress built on itself and that future generations of readers needed to be exposed to primary sources to understand past successes and failures. He had helped start the Louisiana Historical Society and served as an honorary member of the Wisconsin Historical Society. His friend Charles Gayarré had written the *Histoire de la Louisiane* and the *Romance of the History of Louisiana* using primary sources from Europe and the Americas. Gayarré concluded that, under French and Spanish rule, Louisiana remained trapped by overly romantic, unproductive planters. These early planters constrained regional growth until the American takeover of the territory in 1803. Gayarré argued that southerners had transformed the region into models of commercial efficiency, noting: "Louisiana hardly halted in her march to wealth and power . . . under the luxuriant development of her unbounded resources." His statement about Louisiana's economic development and willingness to shift toward a modern, commercial economy would have resonated with postbellum southerners, who distinguished between a pre–Civil War Old South and a postwar New South. Without knowledge of such terms, De Bow, like Gayarré's early planters and merchants of Louisiana, advocated for a similar shift in practices and ideas that would, he hoped, transform the South into a more modern and profitable region.[29]

De Bow became more sensitive to how historians might interpret history and judge the South. Mindful of northern attacks on slavery and growing sectional biases, he praised southern historians such as Gayarré and Albert J. Pickett who used primary sources to explain the development of the South. In Pickett's case, De Bow found additional reason to applaud his history of Alabama because "the printing, the binding, the illustrations—and they are very numerous—are all the labors of southern hands." Regional biases and attacks on slavery became, in De Bow's mind, too constant a theme in northern-produced history books. His changing attitudes about American history can be best illustrated in two reviews of Richard Hildreth's *The History of the United States.* De Bow provided a brief review that perceived no sectional biases or slights in Hildreth's work. Hildreth, an antislavery proponent from Massachusetts, had questioned the nature of slavery in the United States in an earlier book entitled *Despotism in America.* De Bow seemingly had little problem with his background or work in the first review. Yet, as the nation struggled with the aftereffects of the Compromise of 1850, he recanted his original review and questioned why Hildreth's prejudices against the South seemed so pronounced. De Bow's willingness to accept sectional slights, at least in book reviews, had disappeared.[30]

Over this four-year period, De Bow's professional career had consumed much of his time and thoughts. He began to realize that there was more to life than just work. His friends in New Orleans and Washington, DC, offered welcome diversions, as did his almost constant travel for business and pleasure. A confidential R. G. Dun and Company credit report traced his steady rise back to prosperity after his financial collapse in 1849. In September 1850 a Dun agent recorded De Bow's business failure and the subsequent loan given by Maunsel White to restart the *Review.* By July 1851 the agent guaranteed De Bow as a good credit risk, noting that he "is making money fast, can command what he may at anytime require." By May 1852 De Bow's position had increased enough for a Dun agent to speculate that the editor cleared a modest $12,000 per year and could cover any debts incurred. In April 1853, a Dun agent reported that De Bow's subscription list had finally increased substantially and that the *Review* turned a monthly profit. De Bow had realized his dream of becoming a successful editor and productive member of southern society. Yet there was something still missing in his life. Unwittingly, the Dun agent who wrote the April 1853 report identified that missing element when he reported that De Bow remained unmarried despite his success. De Bow yearned to find someone to share life with and fill that sense of family that had been empty since his mother's death in 1837.[31]

4

Embracing Southern Anger and Southern Nationalism

De Bow's life had changed dramatically since he revived the *Review* in July 1849. His increased involvement in the sectional debate over slavery promised to keep him busy as an editor, speaker, and promoter. He had rescued the *Review* from failure, overseen the completion of the 1850 census, and moved from New Orleans to Washington, DC. His work became more widely and even nationally recognized and his reputation more valued by Americans on both sides of the Mason-Dixon line. He had parlayed his knowledge of the South into new experiences and expected more professional success. Even his personal life, which had long been secondary to an active career, was in full bloom. In early 1854, De Bow met Caroline Poe, the daughter of a Georgetown merchant and a second cousin of Edgar Allan Poe's. And shortly thereafter, on August 5, 1854, the Reverend Clement M. Butler, the rector of St. John's Church in Georgetown, married the young couple. After the wedding they moved into an apartment in Washington, hired a servant, and bought new furniture on an installment plan. Aside from the company of his brother, De Bow had been alone since his mother's death in 1837. But professional and personal happiness had finally found him; his career afforded him the means to pursue his ambitions, and Caroline spurred in him the desire to enjoy life more. From the perspective of his Washington apartment in late 1854, the world likely looked much better than it had in late 1848 when he acknowledged failure and closed his editorial office. In the December 1854 edition of the *Review*, he published an open letter that recalled his past struggles but noted that faith and hard work had allowed him to overcome obstacles and embarrassments. As he entered his tenth year as editor of the *Review*, he promised to work harder, find new authors, explore a greater diversity of topics, and devote more time to his work. Without the foreknowledge of future events that would push the United States closer to war, De Bow closed his letter with a question to readers that was ostensibly about the *Review*'s future but was equally applicable to his and the South's future: "Will our friends stand by us in the movement?"[1]

By 1855 ten years had passed since De Bow had attended the 1845 Memphis convention and relocated to the Crescent City to start the *Review*. During this time the commercial convention movement became an increasingly important part of his life. It offered him direct access to supporters and allowed him to identify new relevant topics. Yet the promising legacy of the 1845 convention, one that had been ordained by John C. Calhoun, now seemed at risk given the administrative morass that characterized the 1855 meeting in New Orleans. In theory, Stephen Douglas's attempt to secure a northern route for a transcontinental railroad should have elicited discussions at the meeting and encourage southerners to agree on a southern route before northern competitors seized the initiative. De Bow even sent a letter of support to the organizers expressing hope that southerners could work together and find a solution that would benefit their region. His confidence in their ability and willingness to work together, however, proved to be misplaced. On the first day, it turned out that the convention president, M. B. Lamar of Texas, had not prepared an opening statement and that no one had brought transcripts from the previous year's convention to read into the official record. Albert Pike, a prominent southwestern lawyer and railroad promoter, failed to produce a report on transportation, offering the excuse that he "lived in a state where there were no internal improvements, and that he had been unable to obtain the necessary information [for a report]." The chairmen for committees on agriculture, education, manufacturing, and mining also did not have their reports ready for delegates. Although Pike later gave an eloquent speech urging southerners to fund a transcontinental railroad without government aid, he also apologized for his earlier lack of preparation. Much to De Bow's regret, the meeting was poorly attended, largely dismissed by critics, and an embarrassment to the city of New Orleans.[2]

Yet, despite this setback, De Bow continued to be committed to enlarging the *Review* and promoting the economic diversification of the South. He also became more interested in the agricultural and educational development of the region. Whereas, in 1845, the first issue of the *Review* had fifteen entitled articles or sections, the January 1855 issue had forty titled submissions.

Despite the additional content, however, De Bow's editorial voice almost disappeared aside from short comments attached to a few articles. Much of his content had been taken from other sources and reprinted without a remark. His editorial column, usually located in the back of the *Review*, vanished for six months; by February 1855 he admitted that he lacked the time to dedicate to his editorial duties. Yet, in spite of his busy schedule, he still found the occasional opportunity to express his opinion, particularly when spurred on by sectional issues. Northern attacks on Muscoe Garnett's pamphlet *The Union, Past and Future: How It Works, and How to Save It*, for example, frustrated De Bow enough to comment because he believed that the Compromise of 1850 and the Kansas-Nebraska Act had solved the debate over western expansion and slavery.[3]

His growing dissatisfaction with the sectional debate over slavery changed how De Bow viewed agricultural reform in the South. Instead of offering practical advice on improving farming techniques or new information on machinery, he began to focus his agricultural articles on what the South needed to do to become more independent of northern influences. He wanted southerners to empower each other with their own practical knowledge and asked them to submit articles about new agricultural processes, local associations and fairs, improvements to machinery, and recent publications that might interest other subscribers. Readers sent him relevant information about cotton, wheat, corn, tobacco, sugar, hemp, rice, and livestock. De Bow, in turn, ask them to plant new crops such as fruit trees, figs, olives, and grapes and new species from Japan and China. He wanted southern farmers to embrace agricultural diversity. *Review* readers responded by sharing personal successes and failures. De Bow applauded J. W. Corey's invention of a seed drill that furrowed and dropped corn seed at regular intervals, especially when the rest of the nation, he reminded readers, focused on "discussing the merits of Minié rifles and Colt revolvers, and similar tools for the trade of death." David Myerle, a *Review* reader from Florida, promoted bear grass as a new form of cordage for naval rigging and hoped that southerners could use it to create a new industry. M. W. Philips, a planter from Mississippi, best captured De Bow's reasoning for agricultural reform when he reminded readers that better farming practices liberated the South from northern dependency and interference.[4]

De Bow understood that only cotton could produce the economic independence he wanted for the South, but, paradoxically, he also understood that cotton created an almost unbreakable connection between southern planters and northern merchants and industrialists. Like many southerners, he believed that good cotton harvests and high market prices would create economic equality between the North and the South. He also believed that agricultural reform would strengthen the South's overall economy and spur regional innovations outside the agricultural sector. Planters needed to think of their plantations as factories so that they could maximize harvest yields and profit margins. Readers responded to De Bow's practical contributions and praised his value to the South. One reader in Tallahassee, Florida, promised: "As long as I live you may consider me a subscriber to your *Review* . . . for never was a laborer more worthy of his hire." Another planter in Perry County, Georgia, apologized for his late payment because he felt "mortified at the idea that after you have imparted to me so much instruction and gratification in your *Review,* I should have requited your labors so poorly as to withhold your dues." The reader then explained how he had attempted to establish a state geological department but failed and hoped that De Bow would write an article "from [his] own pen or from some of [his] able and experienced contributors, upon the application of geology to agriculture."[5]

Education—and with it educational development—was another issue that concerned De Bow, as it had many southerners since the late eighteenth century. Perceived regional slights and indirect attacks on southern culture had inspired generations of southern readers to question the motives of northern writers and publishing houses. De Bow's growing disdain for northern influences emerged in the late 1840s when he began to search for suitable textbooks after reviewing Marcus Wilson's regionally slanted *History of the United States.* His quest to find appropriate texts for southern students emerged in subsequent book reviews. He believed that Charles March's *Reminiscences of Congress* unfairly attacked southern critics of Daniel Webster, found Mary Somerville's *Physical Geography* to be "so warm for abolition and so bitter upon the institutions of the South," and concluded that L. C. Saxton's *Fall of Poland* criticized European slavery too harshly. De Bow wanted textbooks that avoided discussions of slavery because he believed the subject tired and settled. He urged readers to support Walker, Richards, and Company in Charleston and J. W. Randolph of Richmond because these native publishers would help cultivate southern authors and cleanse the region of biased northern books.[6]

The worldview that De Bow sought to promote among southern readers—initially a broad and nonsectional one—had become increasingly narrow and overly sectional by 1855. The Reverend C. K. Marshall of Vicksburg, Mississippi, used the *Review* to urge parents to stop sending southern students to northern universities because it distorted their views on slavery. Drawing from his personal experience as a college professor, De Bow noted Marshall's interest in strengthening southern universities and urged his readers to support educational reform in the South. He demanded that a commission be created to screen textbooks from northern publishers. He also called for southern school administrators to stop hiring northern teachers. The *Review* became a collection point for readers who submitted information about northern and European teaching methods, curriculum changes in southern states, and the existence of model schools in the South. De Bow promoted the University of Virginia and other southern universities because he worried that, "when old Yale sets the tune, all the thousand schools of the abolition states feel not only bound to chime in [about slavery], but do it as a necessary condition of their existence." The fanaticism of northern universities intrigued him because he believed that abolitionism would drive southern students back to the South faster than the merits of southern universities alone.[7]

Even if De Bow had wanted to present a more unbiased critique of the South, the increasingly isolated worldview of conservative southerners made it more difficult for him to be as critical of the South as he had once been in the *Review.* In the past he had tried to offer differing opinions on topics with hopes of widening the intellectual scope of his readers. His commitment to editorial fairness and a lingering sense of American nationalism manifested itself in a willingness to publish articles that deviated from regional standards adopted by less tolerant southerners. That began to change as the sectional debate intensified. In 1853, for example, he had published an article by the northern statistician Dr. Jesse Chickering warning southerners about federal interference if the southern slave population continued to grow at its current pace. Chickering suggested that the recolonization of slaves in Africa offered the best alternative to rapid slave growth. De Bow rejected Chickering's advice and dismissed it as unrealistic and unproductive yet published the article as a service to readers. Many subscribers disagreed with Chickering's assessment and accused De Bow of being an abolitionist for publishing an article by a northern writer. Later in 1855 the *Charleston Courier* criticized him for being overly concerned with northern opinions about slavery. De Bow felt these attacks unfair and noted the importance of understanding contrary opinions and viewpoints. Despite his own unwillingness to compromise with those who had dissenting views on slavery, he lamented that more Americans found it difficult to be impartial on the topic.[8]

Northern opposition to the Kansas-Nebraska Act and the ensuing extralegal violence in the Kansas territory ignited De Bow's career as a southern fire-eater. Since President Franklin Pierce had signed the Kansas-Nebraska Act into law in mid-1854, pro- and antislavery forces had begun to marshal men and supplies to Kansas in anticipation of violence. The use of popular sovereignty to determine the status of slavery in Kansas allowed territorial residents to decide their future but also created the conditions necessary for a proxy war. Antislavery zealots backed the "free-staters" of Kansas, whereas proslavery fanatics supported the "border ruffians" of Missouri. De Bow remained oddly silent when the first elections in Kansas were held and after free-state settlers drafted the Topeka Constitution, which banned slavery from the territory. He eventually broke his silence in early 1856 after joining a group of southerners who supplied money, equipment, and men to sympathizers in Missouri and Kansas. He encouraged southerners to support their right to live and own slaves in western territories. Other proslavery groups used the *Review* as a clearinghouse for information and strategies. Like many southerners, De Bow viewed Kansas as a constitutional test of property rights and civil liberties. Beyond that, however, he saw the issue as restrictive of southern economic development. For ten years he had warned southern readers that they were in competition with northeastern businessmen who also wanted to control western markets. This concerned him because he believed that regional economic development enhanced political power, which in turn protected the South from the tyranny of northern rule. In a fiery speech in New Orleans, he called for vengeance against the "irreconcilable enemies of the southern states." Stirred by this editorial transformation and events in "Bleeding Kansas," a *Review* reader pled with De Bow to "urge us forward; urge us with all of your might; recollect our apathy and aversion to change."[9]

The *Review* began to reflect De Bow's increasingly radical views on secession and states' rights. In the first issue of the *Review* (January 1846), he had promised readers to advocate for their regional interests and defend their rights within the Union. He had remained true to that promise and created a sense of political neutrality that belied an age of partisan party politics. Despite being an extreme advocate of southern issues and institutions, he had never publicly endorsed the secessionist sentiments of fire-eaters such as William Lowndes Yancey and Robert Barnwell Rhett. Although his sympathies lay with them, he tended to view states' rights as protection against constitutional threats to individual liberties and unfair federal policies. De Bow admitted to readers that his crusade to improve the South's economy had diverted his attention away from northern assaults on the region. That changed as events in Kansas escalated. His personal views and editorial stances became less conciliatory and more accusatory of northerners, and he began to question the South's place within the Union. His increasingly pessimistic feelings about the nation's future began to emerge in the *Review*. His editorial tone became exceedingly defensive, and the *Review* became his weapon. In the minds of many northerners and some southern moderates, De Bow's growing reputation as a fire-eater soon overshadowed his years of positive editorial service to the South.[10]

The rise of the antislavery Republican Party in 1854 further contributed to De Bow's growing dissatisfaction with the South's place within the Union. He rejected the newly formed party because he believed it "an active, powerful, unscrupulous organization, vast enough to embrace all of the free states, or nearly all, advancing in solid column in its assaults upon the Constitution of the Union, and upon the rights and liberties of the slaveholding states." Many southerners viewed Republicans as a threat to the Union, claiming that they advocated for nothing more than free labor over slave labor and the special interests of ideologically driven northerners. Although De Bow had previously defended both forms of labor as complementary to the nation's economy, his negative feelings about the Republican Party changed his stance. Unwilling to concede anything to northern opponents, he attacked free labor as a self-serving system that abused free white men because "it drives its own hard bargains with him—uses him, wears him out, and then throws him away." As a comparison between slavery and free labor he published William J. Grayson's epic poem "The Hireling and the Slave." In Grayson's mind slavery was superior to free labor because slaves had their material needs met by concerned masters whereas wage laborers struggled to make a living in the tumultuous contemporary world. Both bond and wage slaves had masters, he argued, but personal interest made the southern planter kinder and more understanding than most northern factory owners. Grayson acknowledged that both labor systems relied on the exploitation of the worker, but bond slaves earned more personal return on their hard work. De Bow agreed with Grayson's general thesis and continued to look for ways to soften the harshness of slavery.[11]

De Bow began to use the *Review* as a proslavery repository for southerners who needed to craft a unified defense against antislavery attacks. In January 1856 he republished what many southerners considered to be the original proslavery treatise—Thomas R. Dew's *Review of the Debate in the Virginia Legislature of 1831–2.* Dew, a professor at William and Mary College, argued that God had created all natural institutions and that sudden changes would disrupt the natural order of society. Using world history to prove that human bondage was an organic institution, he concluded that slavery had become a positive economic and social force in Virginia's history. He rejected slave emancipation or colonization as being unrealistic and contrary to the interests of slaveholders and nonslaveholders. Slave emancipation, Dew argued, would lead to higher taxes, increased crime, economic ruin, and social equality among the races. His claims clarified a distinct proslavery position that incorporated religion, history, social development, and economic growth.[12]

De Bow also reprinted a series of provocative proslavery letters from James Henry Hammond, a prominent planter and politician in South Carolina, to Thomas Clarkson, an English abolitionist. Hammond defended slavery as the cornerstone of southern society by using biblical, historical, and scientific evidence to defend its importance to the South. Later famous for his reference to King Cotton and his "mudsill speech," Hammond explained that slaves earned what they needed through hard work and loyalty to their masters. In return, good masters cared for and satisfied the needs of their naturally subordinate slaves. Another reprint was the 1837 speech of William Harper, a noted South Carolina jurist and politician who defended slavery with biblical and legal arguments. God had created slavery, Harper said, and the legal system ensured that blacks remained in their proper place. He rejected the universal ideals of liberty and equality. He believed that blacks lacked the necessary intellectual skills to understand the self-evident truths of the American Revolution. De Bow later used Harper's arguments to insist that education and moral virtue separated whites and blacks. De Bow and Harper reasoned that unproductive and uneducated slaves had no right to the benefits of the Declaration of Independence or the US Constitution.[13]

These pseudoscientific theories of proslavery ethnologists and physicians became more common in the *Review.* Samuel A. Cartwright, a physician who treated slaves in New Orleans, wrote many *Review* articles justifying slavery as a natural law of science. He believed that blacks were incapable of further development and warned southerners about their inherent laziness and lack of virtue. Cartwright hoped to improve slave productivity by offering cures for *drapetomania,* the slave's ability to avoid responsibility, and *dysaethesia,* the slave's natural lack of a work ethic. In both cases he prescribed frequent whippings and strict oversight as potential cures. Although De Bow rejected brutality as a way of dealing with slaves, his interest in science rendered Cartwright's research credible. Josiah C. Nott marshaled a mixture of anthropology, medical knowledge, and ethnology to establish the inferiority and separate origins of the black race. Nott, a southern physician and surgeon, used cranial and body measurements to argue that blacks and whites came from separate species. De Bow invited Nott to speak at a public lecture on his research and later published the talk as *Two Lectures on the Connection between the Biblical and Physical History of Man.* Nott's conclusions elicited strong feelings among readers who disapproved of his rejection of creationism. And, while De Bow personally disagreed with Nott's polygenist conclusions, he felt that his scientific arguments lent legitimacy to the proslavery position.[14]

De Bow's most prolific contributor on black inferiority was George Fitzhugh, who published ninety-nine articles in the *Review* between 1855 and the start of the Civil War. The eccentric Virginian had shocked northern readers by attacking free society in *Sociology for the South; or, The Failure of Free Society* and *Cannibals All! or, Slaves without Masters.* Unlike other proslavery ideologists, who only defended slavery, he attacked the basic tenets of free society as being inferior to slave society. He rejected the North's adherence to capitalism and competitive commercialism. Fitzhugh claimed that slavery eliminated unemployment and the exploitation of workers in the South. Southern masters provided better standards of living for their workers because free-market competition stripped society of humanity and morality. He used genealogical research to argue that white southerners had engaged in selective reproduction to create a natural "master race." This southern race of natural leaders would eventually dominate northern competition in politics and on the battlefield. Although De Bow often disagreed with Fitzhugh's conclusions, he valued the reaction these arguments got in the northern press. William Lloyd Garrison, the abolitionist editor of *The Liberator,* railed against Fitzhugh's contributions to the slavery debate and likened his work to that of Satan.[15]

The importance of romanticizing slavery and softening the image of the master class became a critical component of the *Review.* Thus, De Bow began to supplement articles on slave management—which provided planters with more humane practices that countered antislavery accusations of mistreatment—with fictional short stories that romanticized the master-slave relationship. William S. White's short story "The African Preacher: An Authentic Narrative," in which a fictional northern visitor witnesses a slave funeral and the raw emotions of the white master, exemplified the supposed fidelity and affection between master and slave. Noting the tenderness of the moment, the northern witness confesses: "It was not the haughty planter, the lordly tyrant, talking of his dead slave as of his dead horse, but the kind-hearted gentleman, lamenting his loss and eulogizing the virtues of his good old friend." The visitor promises: "I shall return to my northern home, deeply impressed with the belief that, dispensing with the name of freedom, the Negroes of the south are the happiest and most contented people on the face of the earth." This literary tactic would later infuse works by such postbellum dialect writers as Thomas Nelson Page and Joel Chandler Harris, whose sentimental images of plantation life punctuated the filial relationship between the benevolent master and his loyal slaves.[16]

A romanticized southern past also lessened the harshness of slavery and helped De Bow use historical precedent to legitimized southern institutions. He reminded readers that slavery had been a natural part of world history and a collective element of the American experience. History, he believed, highlighted the harmoniousness and cohesiveness of a genteel southern society. Although De Bow viewed economic modernity as a positive southern trait, Albert J. Pickett, a *Review* reader and historian from Alabama, lamented the disruption of the South's natural state by "vast fields of cotton, noisy steamers, huge rafts of lumber, towns reared for business, disagreeable corporation laws, harassing courts of justice, mills, factories, and everything else that is calculated to destroy the beauty of a country, and to rob man of his quiet and native independence." Pickett's distress about modern economic forces countered De Bow's feelings about future growth. De Bow, more than most observers in the South, understood that historical precedent could be used to defend slavery as part of a natural southern culture that blended the past with an exciting future.[17]

For some *Review* readers such as James Lyons, the future of the South meant much more than its past. Lyons, a lawyer from Richmond, typified the type of forward-thinking reader that the *Review* initially attracted because of its economic philosophy and later kept as De Bow's editorial support of southern nationalism intensified. Earlier in his career, Lyons had attended conventions that supported railroad development and Henry Clay's American System. As an economic nationalist, he hosted Clay and

Daniel Webster at his Richmond home. He served as chairman of the Richmond and Ohio Railroad and the Richmond and Danville Railroad, and he helped organize the Virginia Central Agricultural Society. He subscribed to the *Review* because it mirrored his interest in integrating Richmond's economy into broader national and international markets. After the Compromise of 1850, however, he became more intolerant of northern attacks on the South. He attended states' rights conventions and in 1850 helped start the Central Southern Rights Association of Richmond. His status as a southern nationalist had been well-known by the time of the 1856 Savannah Commercial Convention, and his election as its president set a new tone for future commercial conventions. That year's convention reaffirmed the South's growing commitment to sectional and economic independence. Convention delegates discussed regional direct trade with Europe, railroad construction, and urban development. The recent defeat of the Republican Party in the 1856 presidential election energized talk of southern independence among some delegates and a sense of triumph in others. Feelings of southern nationalism had crept into the convention's agenda, scaring some moderate delegates away from the event. De Bow encouraged attendees to discuss independence within the context of southern agricultural, industrial, and commercial progress.[18]

Since its inception, the commercial convention movement had served as an opportunity for participants to discuss regional development while simultaneously stoking southern fears of falling hopelessly behind the North. Optimistic participants believed that they could elicit positive changes in the South's economy by offering practical solutions to like-minded southerners willing to work toward a common goal. Less altruistic delegates saw the commercial convention movement as a way of stymieing the northern competition that always seemed to be lurking in the background. De Bow tapped into these feelings and expanded on them in the *Review.* Over time he became the most prolific and well-known figure to emerge from the commercial convention movement. The planning committee for the 1857 Knoxville convention rewarded him for his support by naming him president of the event. At the time, few outside observers understood how far he had moved away from the agenda of the 1845 Memphis convention, one that had inspired him to start the *Review,* or from his call to commercial action at the 1852 New Orleans convention.[19]

On August 10, 1857, De Bow used his opening speech at the Knoxville convention to embrace secession and accept a future for the South outside the United States. He had narrowed his worldview to that of an unapologetic fire-eater and hoped to drag his convention delegates and *Review* readers with him. Appeals for internal improvements and commercial development gave way to proslavery diatribes and disunionist proclamations. Vitriolic speeches by William Lowndes Yancey and Leonidus W. Spratt muted the voices of moderate delegates, as did De Bow, who banned unfriendly newspapers from covering the event. De Bow's gradual transition from American nationalist to southern fire-eater had been a public one, and the Knoxville convention served as reaffirmation of his ideological shift. In his opening presidential remarks, addressed only to southerners, he called for continued economic development to ensure independence. He felt that autonomy would force Europeans to recognize the economic power of the South. He reminded delegates that to secure freedom from the North they had to support regional growth "by stimulating agriculture, by promoting commerce, by steamships, and by steam-mills, and . . . by a system of home education, which shall save our children from the poison which infects the springs from which they have hitherto been in the habit of drinking." He effectively changed the tone of the meeting by pushing political diatribes ahead of economic solutions. This shift toward sectional extremism worried a writer from the *Sacramento Daily Union,* who feared that De Bow would use the *Review* "to exercise a powerful influence upon the minds of those young men among its readers who in a few years must control the destiny of the Southern States."[20]

The economic collapse of international markets and the corresponding Panic of 1857 in the United States provided De Bow with a convenient scapegoat for southern suffering. Although he had rarely shown an editorial interest in banks or financial institutions, he blamed northern mismanagement for the failure of several railroads, low crop prices, overspeculation by investors, and the lack of fluid capital. Southern merchants and planters suffered financially, according to De Bow, because northern bankers and investors failed to follow good practices. The Panic offered him substantive proof that regional economic independence would provide more financial security for southerners. He hoped that the free-trade policies that had been discussed at many commercial conventions would become the true policy of the South. He beckoned northerners to "let us alone" and allow the South to develop away from "the unwise and selfish course pursued by the banks of the North." Eager to reassure southerners about their financial institutions, he provided statistics to highlight the soundness of regional banks and specie reserves. His interest in banking quickly subsided after cotton prices increased.[21]

After the 1857 Knoxville convention, *De Bow's Review* became an outlet for fanatic secessionists. Edmund Ruffin traced northern political aggression back to the Missouri Compromise and concluded that northerners had always dedicated themselves to stealing southern rights. He welcomed open warfare between the North and the South, believing that abolitionists had infiltrated the federal government. He reasoned that independence would end the tyrannical rule of northerners who lacked empathy or understanding of southern society. Boasting of southern manhood, he hoped that the two sides could meet on a battlefield and settle their differences. George Fitzhugh also escalated his attacks on northern society. Critical of progress measured by materialism and greed, he concluded that northern capitalism had made "the poor poorer, the ignorant more ignorant, the vicious and criminal more vile and debased." Fitzhugh criticized the negative influence of urban development, commercial greed, and free trade. These economic forces, he argued, corrupted lives and tainted communities by placing unrestrained greed above all else. De Bow had difficulty accepting Fitzhugh's condemnation of progress and modernity. He had spent the last thirteen years supporting what Fitzhugh wanted to tear down. But his hostility to the North led him to publish Fitzhugh's articles nevertheless.[22]

De Bow's sense of overt sectionalism and willingness to see northern conspiracies against southern interests generated a steady stream of disunionist *Review* articles. In February 1857, John Tyler Jr., a Virginia lawyer writing under the alias of Python, attacked the Republican Party for using simple majority rule as a weapon to attack slavery and potentially overrun the South with hordes of freed slaves and poor northern whites. Northern radicalism, he argued, had already penetrated new territories in Oregon, New Mexico, and Colorado and would continue to spread until abolitionists controlled Congress and seized the federal treasury, military, and judiciary. De Bow endorsed Tyler's article, noting that he regarded "the analysis made as complete, the facts stated indisputable, the positions assumed unanswerable, and the dangers presented as actually existing in every particular." As the sectional crisis became more acute, De Bow asked southerners to organize and become more defensive and unyielding with northerners. He wanted to ensure that a unified South emerged in the event of disunion.[23]

Although many southerners viewed James Buchanan's presidency as a victory against antislavery forces, Edmund Ruffin predicted that an abolitionist president loomed in the nation's immediate future, and De Bow warned of what life would be like in the South if that happened. Ruffin envisioned antislavery politicians using the spoils system to fill government positions with sympathetic northerners. He challenged *Review* readers to resist federal power before an abolitionist president was elected. De Bow agreed with Ruffin's predictions and warned southern readers "to burnish up the weapons . . . and keep them ever ready . . . in case of emergency." His angry tone shocked some readers, and they reprimanded him. He apologized but appealed to their sense of honor, noting: "But, can flesh and blood bear up against injuries so unprovoked and so continuous? Are even saintly virtues adequate to this? Courtesy, dignity, philosophy, may teach the virtues of forbearance, but the instincts of the man will become rebellious at last." De Bow resorted to base racism to suggest that the South would become like Haiti if abolitionists prevailed in their political ambitions. In "The Model Negro Empire of Hayti," he described superstitious and ignorant black leaders who relied on their personal cunning and illegal monopolies to control the nation. He envisioned lazy blacks living off of bananas and fish under the most rudimentary conditions possible. The lack of white oversight meant citizens would have to endure new gender roles, more illegitimate births, and the veneration of Catholic priests. The force of De Bow's prose reflected his growing anger over the possibility of emancipation.[24]

De Bow's readers noticed the editorial shift of the *Review,* and many southerners liked it. A representative subscriber from Columbus, Georgia, reacted positively to De Bow's secessionist rhetoric, happily noting: "I am highly pleased with the strong Southern stand you have taken, and for one, am willing to go with you any length in that direction." Northern observers, meanwhile, were stunned by De Bow's ideological shift. The editor of the *Philadelphia Inquirer* concluded: "Mr. De Bow is one of the most accomplished men of the South. . . . [T]o suppose such a man . . . would become a disunionist is, we repeat, almost incredible, and we can only indulge a hope that the accomplished statistician has been misunderstood or misreported."[25]

His new sectional attitude toward the North made it difficult for De Bow to engage in one personal pleasure that had been a constant throughout his professional life: his frequent trips to the North. He had never hidden this fact from readers, but circumstances after the Knoxville convention made it difficult for him to travel outside the South. Later in his life, when reminiscing about the past, he estimated that he had "visited the vast metropolis [New York City] twenty times before [and] . . . [had] marked its growth each time."

Now, as one of the most public fire-eaters in the South, he realized that he had to confine his travel to southern destinations as a sign of support for the region's growing tourism industry. He took his family, which now included two children, James and Mary, to the Virginia highlands, the mountains of North Carolina, and Charleston, South Carolina. Old Point Comfort, a summer resort town near Hampton, Virginia, became a regular destination for the De Bow family. He hoped that improved railroad transportation, new hotels, and a sense of regional empathy would lead more southern families to stay in the South for their vacations. He warned his readers against traveling to the North and encouraged them to support southern destinations. By the end of the 1850s even travel had become a partisan topic in the *Review.*[26]

In the midst of De Bow's growing involvement in the southern nationalist movement, tragedy struck his personal life after successive epidemics of cholera took Caroline and James in late 1857 and early 1858, respectively. Devastated by these losses, De Bow and Mary left the city for a resort in Berkeley Springs, Virginia. To memorialize his wife, De Bow changed Mary Emma's name to Caroline Mary. His in-laws offered to raise her, but De Bow insisted that she remain with him. He arranged for a private nurse and a tutor, and he relied on the kindness of friends when he traveled on business. His sense of family once again disappeared in the midst of personal tragedy.[27]

In the wake of this tragic loss, De Bow focused even more of his energies on defending the South against literary critics such as Frederick Law Olmsted and Hinton Helper. Olmsted, a correspondent for the *New York Daily Times,* used his book *A Journey in the Seaboard Slave States* to describe the South's poor roads, lack of towns and cities, and untapped economic potential and the evils of slavery. As an active supporter of the free-soilers in Kansas and a dedicated foe of slavery, Olmsted became an especially favorite target of De Bow's. De Bow said that Olmsted's books were "abounding in bitterness and prejudices of every sort." He thought Olmsted had misrepresented himself to southerners who had shown him hospitality, portraying him as a Yankee plunderer stealing from his southern hosts. Hinton Helper's book *The Impending Crisis of the South* provoked De Bow even more, given the author's southern heritage. A native of North Carolina, Helper focused on the negative influence slavery had on free labor and the lives of non-slaveholding whites. Horace Greeley, the editor of the *New York Tribune,* published Helper's critical assessment as proof that an ideological division existed between planters and nonslaveholders. Much to De Bow's chagrin, Helper had used census statistics and material from the *Review* to support his contentions. De Bow insisted that Helper misrepresented facts and suggested that Greeley's financial generosity may have influenced Helper's antisouthern point of view. He warned readers that writers like Olmsted and Helper had to be watched because "the enemy is sleepless and indefatigable in his nefarious work, in bringing up his cohorts to our very doors!" In an attempt to undercut Helper's contention of class rivalries, De Bow published a letter from a nonslaveholding mechanic in Wharton, Texas, who asserted that planters recognized him as an equal and reminded readers that "there are but two classes in the South, white and black."[28]

The sectional crisis convinced De Bow that southerners needed to invest more in the South's industrial development. Despite steady industrial growth during the 1850s, industrial progress in the South still lagged far behind that in the North. In 1858 De Bow reported that only 27,725 of the nation's 131,657 factories were located in the South. Southern foundries produced just a quarter of the nation's pig iron; less than a third of the tanneries were in slave states. And, despite being the only producer of cotton, the South accounted for only 202 of the nation's 1,094 cotton mills. James Martin, a cotton mill owner from Florence, Alabama, wrote an article in the *Review* that challenged southerners to support a wider variety of industries. Martin believed that an educated and trained workforce, employing poor whites instead of slaves, would help the South create a domestic market and generate new consumers of finished products. De Bow agreed with Martin's assessment and provided examples of successful factories in southern cities and towns. Memphis's business sector, for example, had built eighteen steam-powered factories and twelve water-powered mills that produced cotton goods, iron products, carriages, cotton gins, and steam boilers. What De Bow failed to notice, however, was that these factories were linked to cotton production; few factories in the South produced the industrial goods needed by an independent nation.[29]

There were still many southerners who were critical of De Bow's advocacy of industrial modernization. C. K. Marshall urged southerners to reduce cotton production, plant more food crops, raise more livestock, and invest in factories. Marshall wondered why cotton factories could produce raw cloth and yarn but not clothes. Production of finished goods would be essential for southern independence, he reasoned, and he hoped that readers still had time "to correct these evils, and stop these blood-suckers from preying upon our vitals." A *Review* contributor questioned why more southern shipbuilders had failed to materialize, despite the South's abundance of lumber, naval stores, and cotton to transport. A disenchanted reader noted that delegates to the 1858 Vicksburg Commercial Convention had traveled on northern-built railroad cars that rode on iron rails produced in northern foundries. Once they arrived at the convention, delegates used chairs and desks that had been assembled by northern workers and after a long day retired to "lie down to dream of southern independence in a Yankee bed."[30]

Caught up in the excitement of the growing secessionist movement, and feeling the pressure to justify southern independence, De Bow pandered to readers by overlooking or avoiding significant shortfalls in the South's industrial sector. Instead, he promoted new industries that had been neglected in past issues of the *Review.* He saw the opportunity to enlarge the timber industry in the yellow pine forests of Georgia and Florida and in the isolated hardwood tracts of eastern Tennessee and western North Carolina. He published an extract from an agricultural survey from Mississippi that noted high levels of porcelain clay and silica. He suggested that these natural resources could support a glassware factory. He highlighted industrial growth in Mobile and the construction of a resin oil plant and sawmills. City records indicated that these new factories and mills produced 1,798 spars and masts, 2,968 tons of hewn wood, and thousands of barrels of naval stores in 1857. Yet no shipbuilding industry had emerged in Mobile. The South's manufacturing sector produced semifinished goods, creating the illusion of a diversified economy, but in fact the regional industrial economy remained very limited. Too many planters refused to invest in anything but more land and slaves, and this restricted the South's development outside the agricultural sector. Despite De Bow's pleas and the efforts of readers such as William Gregg and Daniel Pratt, the South still lacked the ability to supply many of its own needs.[31]

Cotton production restricted the South, making it difficult for readers to embrace De Bow's ideas about industrial and commercial development. Although De Bow had during the past decade urged readers to embrace agricultural diversity, census records from the late 1850s suggested that many of them failed to heed his advice. Cotton production between 1850 and 1860 had increased by 150 percent. Southerners had worked hard to clear new land, but, rather than diversify their crop production, they decided to plant more cotton. De Bow's call for agricultural diversity had been genuine, but so had his willingness to ignore cotton's increased hold on the South. This duality of purpose ultimately came from a need for more subscribers than from a more altruistic place. De Bow's good intentions had been overwhelmed by personal business needs and an unwillingness to look candidly at the South's shortcomings.[32]

The South's shortage of banks and lending institutions created a system in which planters relied on cotton merchants for long-term credit lines based on their future crops. This system made it difficult to capitalize factories or transportation projects because planters had often reinvested their profits or borrowed money to buy more land and slaves. Many of De Bow's pleas for southern industrialization failed because of cotton's dominance. In 1860 he reprinted an article claiming that industrial investments often yielded 16 percent annually while land and slaves produced only 3 percent yearly. Joseph E. Segar, a lawyer and politician from Virginia, blamed a "half century of apathy and thralldom" on planters who did not support manufacturing enterprises. Segar concluded: "The people of the South, it is notorious, are anti-commercial in spirit—their turn is decidedly agricultural—they incline, accordingly, to invest rather in lands and slaves than in ships and freight; to dig from the soil an ample living rather than to amass princely fortunes by the course of trade." In a brief editorial aside to a larger article in 1860, De Bow wrote: "We have neglected to avail ourselves of the means we have at hand in abundance, to attain the desirable condition of independence."[33]

De Bow saw southerners mainly as producers and exporters and only later came to an understanding of how crucial consumption was to his economic ambitions for the South. His insufficient and inconsistent emphasis on consumption reflected the South's limited economic potential. Workers in southern factories refined raw materials that were then shipped to northern shops for final assembly before being sent back to the South for sale to the workers who had initiated the extractive process. A frustrated De Bow wondered why "the presumption is, so far as our efforts are concerned, the South has nothing to sell!" By the 1850s he realized that the lack of consumer support for southern goods had limited the economic development of the region. Northern manufacturers had cornered many markets and made competition difficult for southerners hoping to open a new factory or store. This meant that the most inexpensive good came from northern business. Southerners, regardless of their personal philosophies, often overlooked the origin of a product in return for a good price or quality craftsmanship. William Gregg, the *Review*'s most experienced industrial contributor, verified these concerns, noting: "The absence of patronage to home industry is an evil that cannot be overcome by political agitation or conventional platforms, but must be worked out by the people themselves."[34]

The prospect of secession prompted De Bow to campaign for more direct southern trade with foreign nations. One Mississippi writer in the *Review* called for his state to build a port along the Gulf of Mexico so as "to place our State in a position in which she will be able, at least, to exert some influence on her own destiny." Virginians urged their state government and individual investors to develop commercial networks to international markets. Ambrose D. Mann helped charter the Atlantic Steam Ferry Company, which, he said, would secure "the future commercial independence of the slaveholding states." Mann and other investors hoped that their steamship line could link southern cotton growers to European ports. William M. Burwell, a Virginia legislator and railroad promoter, planned a railroad system that would funnel southern goods to the South's easternmost deepwater port at Norfolk. Henry A. Wise, the governor of Virginia, supported direct trade with South America and the West Indies. Each of these men understood that the *Review* offered them the best chance to reach southern investors. De Bow continued to hope that the commercial spirit of the South could overcome deficiencies in other economic sectors.[35]

In the early summer of 1859, De Bow traveled around the South to gauge the progress of southern cities and railroads. He commented on the energy of Mobile's businessmen. Local railroad development had helped boost the city's cotton exports from 102,684 bales in 1830 to 503,177 bales in 1857. De Bow took the Mobile and Ohio Railroad from Mobile to Columbus, Mississippi. The growth of Columbus pleased him, and he noted its broad commercial connection to other regions. He left Columbus, traveled to Montgomery, and took the Montgomery and West Point Railroad and other smaller lines to Atlanta, Augusta, and Charleston. After spending time in Charleston, he took a forty-two-hour trip from Charleston to Memphis aboard the Memphis and Charleston and the Western and Atlantic railroads. He noted that the railroads had become an "admirable structure, under the most excellent management." On his way to Memphis, he stopped in Chattanooga, Tennessee, and Huntsville, Alabama, cities he found orderly and handsome. He admired Memphis's progress before leaving for Vicksburg to attend that year's commercial convention.[36]

The Vicksburg Commercial Convention provided De Bow with a public forum to discuss the reopening of the international slave trade. He argued that the importation of Africans would reduce the cost of slaves, making them more affordable for poorer whites. In response to De Bow's interest, delegates elected him to serve as president of the African Labor Supply Association. He worried about the consolidation of the slave population on large plantations. He also hoped that the inflammatory topic would incite northern protests and intensify sectional feelings between the North and the South. His extreme stance on the slave trade put him on the fringe of southern society, even among southern fire-eaters. That stance shocked Edmund Ruffin and Robert Barnwell Rhett, who rejected De Bow's position as untenable and overly divisive within southern society. They believed that questions about the slave trade would frighten moderate southerners away from secession. Ruffin proposed slave colonization as an alternative to reopening the slave trade. Undeterred, De Bow published articles that both supported and rejected his plan, noting: "It is but fair to allow a full discussion of all topics important to the South."[37]

John Brown's raid on the federal arsenal at Harper's Ferry in October 1859 further fueled De Bow's alarmist impulse. Joseph A. Turner of Georgia, a frequent contributor to the *Review,* cautioned southerners to be wary of northerners and pointed to recent arson attacks in Georgia and to Brown's raid as proof that a larger abolitionist plot existed. Another contributor linked the political agenda of the "Black Republicans" to Brown's raid, noting: "His [Brown's] course is the natural result of their teachings." George Fitzhugh argued that "disunion within the Union" would reestablish political balance between the North and the South. Fitzhugh's alternative to secession struck De Bow as a weak response because he believed that only complete separation could protect the South from its enemies.[38]

The growing success of the Republican Party in 1860 offered De Bow the opportunity to rally southern readers against a common foe. He accused abolitionists of building the party on "one single, controlling idea of hostility to negro slavery." Fearful that abolitionists had already taken control of the federal government and that Abraham Lincoln might win the presidential election in 1860, he warned southerners about northern fanaticism. He predicted that abolitionists would disband the federal government within five years and steal the South's constitutional rights. They would do this, he argued, by falsifying the nation's history and declaring that slavery had always been illegal. He implored southerners to defend their property rights from Lincoln and the Republican Party.[39]

The presidential election of 1860 was a pivotal point for De Bow, as it was for many Americans. In July 1860 he dismissed the overall quality of the presidential candidate pool. He characterized Salmon P. Chase as being "eminent for his labors in behalf of the negro stealers and fugitive slaves." He was suspicious of John C. Fremont, a southern-born Republican, and questioned the ability of Andrew Johnson. He warned that William H. Seward qualified as the "most dangerous, and . . . by far the ablest of the Republicans, or what is much the same thing, abolition leaders." His disdain for Lincoln made it "too contemptible to entitle him to a place in the gallery of presidential candidates." Lincoln's election would, however, have the benefit of forcing southerners to "break the ignoble shackles, and proclaim themselves free." He praised John Bell of Tennessee as a man of character and applauded Jefferson Davis for his unconditional support of southern rights. About the Democratic Party, De Bow lamented: "We have a party, hitherto national, but now divided and distracted, and endeavoring to meet the dangers which are upon the country by temporizing expedients, rather than by a bold and intrepid assertion of right, and a manful breasting of the storm."[40]

On November 7, 1860, news of Lincoln's election reached Charleston, setting off celebrations across the city. The dream of southern independence seemed closer than ever as De Bow read the election results posted on the *Charleston Mercury*'s downtown bulletin board. People emerged from their homes and businesses in what one witness called an "intense though quiet excitement." The mood of the crowd slowly escalated as cheers of "*vive la liberta*" rang out and residents unfurled the palmetto flag over the stoops of their homes and shops. Andrew G. Magrath, a federal judge and dedicated *Review* reader, publicly removed his judicial robe and left the bench as a sign of support for the southern cause. Burning effigies of Lincoln and open talk of secession intensified the mood of the crowd. The excitement of the day inspired Mary Boykin Chesnut, the wife of US senator James Chesnut Jr., to start a diary that lasted for the duration of the war. Her private feelings mirrored De Bow's strong public stance on southern nationalism. For years De Bow had made speeches and published articles advocating for southern economic independence and eventual nationhood. His day had arrived. He recognized that Lincoln's impending presidency would drive South Carolina out of the Union, noting with native pride that the "flag of Independence [was] unfurled at Charleston."[41]

After years of sectional debates, party politics, and political compromises over slavery, the collective mood of the nation had soured to the point of possible disunion. South Carolina had become the geographic and philosophical center of proslavery ideologists, southern nationalists, states' rights advocates, and sectional fire-eaters. State leaders such as Robert Barnwell Rhett and Lawrence Keitt warned South Carolinians of northern attacks against southern institutions. Southern newspaper editors inundated readers with editorials that demonized the North and warned of political submission under the Republican Party. Northern editors who had opposed Lincoln because of party affiliation before the election suddenly intensified their attacks on the South as the prospect of disunion increased.[42]

Mistrust and anger became useful tools for De Bow. On November 23, 1860, during a heated secessionist meeting in Charleston, he alluded to a hidden poison in the Constitution that had built up over time and required a treatment. For De Bow the South's political and economic readiness for independence seemed to be that cure. His presence in Charleston on Election Day had been by design. He wanted to witness the city's reaction to Lincoln's victory and to bask in the glory of his cause. Yet, unlike other fire-eaters, who could openly show their disdain for southern unionists and cooperationists, De Bow maintained an editorial balance that reflected more practical business needs because his livelihood depended on it. The extremism that he had directed at northerners could not be redirected at moderate southerners. He had to galvanize a divided southern readership while simultaneously speaking to those who supported secession. The great southern fire-eater, the mouthpiece of the South, continued to worry about the immediate business at hand in November 1860. The *Review* needed readers, and De Bow needed money, regardless of Lincoln's election and the impending crisis that faced the Union. Despite his strong personal feelings about southern independence, he hoped to attract moderate southerners by returning to the same rational editorial tone that had once made the *Review* essential reading for business-minded southerners.[43]

Slave ownership had to be seen as an obtainable goal for all white southerners. If it were not, poor whites would, De Bow feared, lack motivation to fight for its defense. De Bow immediately reached out to southern nonslaveholders because he realized that a new southern confederation needed their support. He feared that internal class divisions about slavery could fracture the South. He gave an impassioned speech directed at nonslaveholders in Tennessee that would be picked up by newspapers around the South. A group of *Review* readers in Charleston known as the "1860 Association" read his speech and offered to publish it as a pamphlet directed at yeoman farmers. The 1860 Association had been created by Robert N. Gourdin, Henry Gourdin, and Andrew G. Magrath as a way of supporting the southern cause by publishing pamphlets. These men symbolized the worldly southerner that De Bow had attracted and cultivated during the 1850s. Robert Gourdin worked as a lawyer before becoming a wealthy partner in the mercantile firm of Gourdin, Mathiesen, and Company. His brother Henry had made a fortune as a cotton merchant in Charleston, and Magrath had become a respected federal judge before removing his judicial robes after Lincoln's election. Each man had benefited from the South's plantation economy and slavery but had separate professional careers beyond agriculture. As leaders of a changing South, they created the 1860 Association as a way of serving their region. Although De Bow's contribution to their worldview cannot be measured, their willingness to take an active role in shaping the South's future matched his stated goal of creating productive citizens. In turn they saw value in De Bow's plea to the nonslaveholders of Tennessee and hoped to widen his appeal with a pamphlet entitled *The Interest in Slavery of the Southern Non-Slaveholder: The Right of Peaceful Secession.*[44]

The Interest in Slavery of the Southern Non-Slaveholder stood out from the dozens of pamphlets that flooded the South in late 1860 precisely because it addressed the concerns of nonslaveholders. De Bow acknowledged that most southerners, himself among them, had never owned a slave. Slavery produced sustenance and profit for all white southerners, he explained, because it protected them from racial equality, economic collapse, and social stagnation. He appealed to his readers' work ethic and place in society, reminding them that the "non-slaveholder of the South preserves the status of the white man, and is not regarded as an inferior or a dependent." He suggested that most nonslaveholders supported slavery and aspired to be masters. Without slavery, he warned, the South would become consumed by class conflict, wage slavery, and racial upheaval, noting: "Yield, and we are forever lost. . . . God never intended us to exchange places with our slaves." His arguments touched on the fears of yeoman farmers and country republicans who worried about racial equality and social standing in a modern world. They had already confronted concerns about their place in a growing market economy and now worried about northern attacks on their mudsill. De Bow assured them that secession would protect their property rights and fortify their privileges as potential slave owners. The promise of social mobility and personal profit became De Bow's device to minimize the differences between slaveholders and nonslaveholders in the South.[45]

Despite the political and social upheaval of 1860 and the prospect of impending secession after Lincoln's election, De Bow continued to balance work with an enjoyable personal life. In the fall of 1860 he married Martha E. Johns, the daughter of a prominent Nashville planter. They had met in

New Orleans in 1859 and started a courtship that culminated in a proposal to her and an agreement to relocate to Nashville from him. It had been two years since his first wife had passed away, and De Bow enjoyed family life on the Johns plantation. The couple traveled to Mammoth Cave, Kentucky, to explore the site and evaluate the newly finished Louisville and Nashville (L&N) Railroad. Constructed under the leadership of the *Review* subscriber James Guthrie, the L&N promised to quicken travel between Nashville and Louisville and to increase the flow of commerce between the two cities. Although De Bow enjoyed his initial trip on the new line, he worried that the "rocking, and dancing, and jumping of the cars [did little] to allay the feeling of averaging almost forty miles per hour." He left convinced that the new railroad and the natural attraction would create new jobs in Kentucky. Even the threat of war failed to diminish his boosterism. Although he did not know it at the time, this short trip would be a relaxing anomaly in his increasingly busy schedule. Despite his promise to spend more time in Nashville, he continued to work from his editorial office in New Orleans's French Quarter.[46]

De Bow stood ready to help the South in any manner he could in the winter of 1860. His personal and professional transformation from southern booster to fire-eater had been stark. His economic ambitions shifted away from bringing the South in line with national developments and moved instead toward economic self-sufficiency in preparation for a split from—and perhaps a war with—the United States. He enabled the secessionists' usurpation of the commercial convention movement. His commitment to the improvement of education was turned into a paranoid preoccupation with abolitionists' alleged infiltration of schools and textbooks. He closed himself off from northern literary influences. By the mid-1850s he had become the primary source of proslavery rhetoric. The emergence of the Republican Party intensified his reaction to perceived threats to the South. He demonized and vilified the North by linking all events to abolitionism and northern greed. With the election of Abraham Lincoln, he warned that for Republicans abolition was a religion, "the Negro their God" and "its preachers . . . the Sewards and Garrisons, [and] Sumners." Convinced that war was inevitable, he dedicated himself to the future of the new southern nation and proudly boasted to his readers: "The active part which is now being taken by the Editor in the movements of the South are [*sic*] having their fruits." He would now have to wait and see if other southerners were as willing as he was to accept the bitter fruit of secession and war.[47]

5

Reading and Investing in De Bow's Ideas

After fourteen years in business, De Bow had cultivated a healthy subscription list by offering practical articles to southern readers interested in commercial growth, urban development, industrialization, agricultural reform, and railroad construction. In more recent years he had also earned the respect of southern nationalists, states' rights advocates, and secessionists who valued his willingness to support their cause. To his readers, regardless of their motivations for subscribing to the *Review,* the journal represented an important southern resource. To De Bow, however, it represented that and his primary means of supporting himself and his family. He did not have the luxury of alienating southerners by becoming something that he was not. He was a businessman as well as a southern patriot. If William Lowndes Yancey insulted a crowd with his sectional rhetoric, he might lose a vote of support, whereas, if De Bow offended a reader, he might lose a paid subscription or a future subscriber. De Bow had spent fourteen years cultivating support for the *Review,* and he understood his targeted audience. Although he needed broad support from southern readers, he had directed much of his editorial content toward a small but growing cohort of middle- to upper-class southern merchants, professionals, entrepreneurs, and planters. He became their public advocate. He wanted to avoid editorial mistakes that had shuttered hundreds of previous southern journals and magazines by offering relevant articles to individuals interested in the southern economy. As much as southern readers came to rely on the *Review,* De Bow needed their unwavering support to remain in business. Without that support, his message of regional economic growth and personal self-improvement might have gone unnoticed by disinterested or complacent southerners. He spoke to his readers directly through the *Review*, and they often responded with letters and articles that embraced his ideas. Not all southern readers supported his efforts or agreed with his general themes, but enough did to make the *Review* the preeminent southern journal by 1860.

De Bow's Review attracted southerners with similar feelings about regional economic development. Its readers shared many traits but none as distinctive as their regional identity. De Bow wrote for southerners, and they responded by reading the *Review*. His desire to integrate the region's commercial, industrial, and agricultural sectors attracted a wide variety of subscribers. Many of his readers lived in towns and cities or on large plantations. He had less appeal among yeoman farmers and poor white laborers. He often wrote and published articles that focused on regional problems or innovations that required large amounts of capital. This editorial decision excluded many poor southerners. Enough middle- to upper-class southerners, however, read the *Review* to make it a popular and influential magazine. De Bow's readership reflected his vision of a diversified southern economy. Many urban subscribers worked to improve their cities and towns, and rural planters experimented with ideas they read about in the *Review*. A significant number of readers accepted the primacy of cotton but hoped to redirect agricultural profits to fund transportation projects, civic improvements, and new factory construction. Many readers displayed a willingness to embrace changes that benefited individuals and communities. De Bow hoped to appeal to subscribers motivated by profit and civic responsibility. Before he could engender a sense of change, however, he needed to attract and maintain readers. Who read the *Review* mattered, and he understood the necessity of appealing to readers who could effect change in their communities.

The lax reading habits of southerners had ended many editorial careers by 1860, and De Bow understood that his chosen career path was a risky one. But he also understood how to avoid common mistakes associated with owning and editing a regional journal. Between 1792 and 1860 in the South almost 850 separate periodicals had been started and, for the most part, had ended. Southern readers notoriously failed to pay subscriptions, leaving desperate editors unprotected from creditors and northern competition. Most journals focused on specific themes or genres such as agriculture, religion, literature, or current events. These monthly magazines also provided southern writers with a public forum in which to discuss topics and issues that interested them. Periodicals became the primary intellectual stimulation for many southern readers. Prominent southerners had attempted to start journals, but few sustained enough paying readers to last for more than a couple of years. William Gilmore Simms, the South's most prolific and popular writer, failed four times as an editor. De Bow understood the literary climate he entered and proceeded cautiously by offering broad articles and practical advice to readers. He avoided discussions of party politics, unless, of course, the politics were those of the Republican Party. These basic tenets allowed him to develop the *Review* into a journal that met the needs of many different types of readers.[1]

Many southerners embraced reading as an important part of their daily lives. In 1850 there were eighty-seven newspapers and magazines being printed in Virginia. Alabama had more periodicals than seven northeastern states. Libraries existed in the South, but distance and isolation made it difficult to encourage regional reading habits outside towns and cities. Many southern communities sought cultural and social refinement through the construction of libraries. By 1850 fifty-seven southern libraries had more than one thousand volumes, although only five ranked among the top twenty largest libraries in the United States. Subscription libraries, college libraries, mercantile libraries, and private libraries provided interested southerners with books, periodicals, and newspapers. Southerners mimicked their northern counterparts' literary habits, and reading became a common activity shared by the nation's growing middle class. Southerners read northern journals for enjoyment and to keep up with current national events, and many northerners, weary of rapid societal change, enjoyed the nostalgic stories and articles often found in southern literary magazines.[2]

The *Southern Review,* the *Southern Literary Messenger,* and the *Southern Quarterly Review* offered De Bow successful editorial templates for his own project. Although dwarfed in size by northern competitors such as *Harper's Monthly Magazine* and the *North American Review,* all three southern journals sustained a sizable readership for many years. De Bow estimated that the *Southern Quarterly Review* had 3,000 readers in 1845. In comparison, *Harper's Monthly Magazine* claimed 7,500 subscribers in 1850, and its European counterpart, *Blackwood's Magazine,* boasted 5,750 readers in 1849. In 1848 De Bow had 825 subscribers—but almost two-thirds of those readers had not paid their subscriptions. Although by the mid-1850s thousands of southerners subscribed annually to the *Review,* poor recordkeeping and time have erased many of their identities. Enough partial subscription lists, personal letters, and business correspondence exist, however, to re-create a list

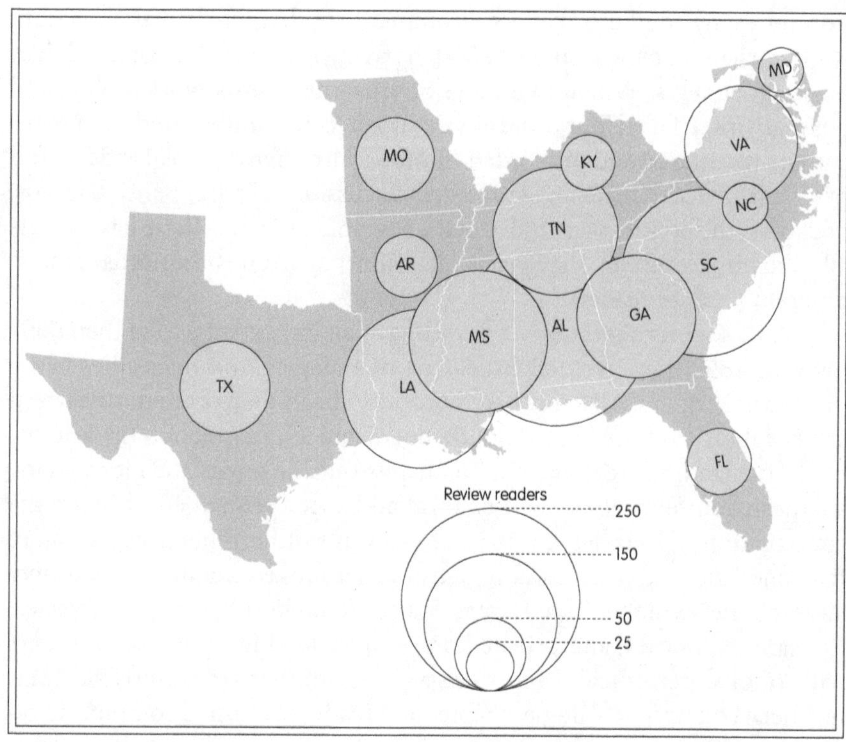

Known *Review* subscribers per southern state. (Map by Dick Gilbreath)

of 1,496 identifiable readers. These known subscribers provide insight into who read the *Review* and how they interacted with the world around them.[3]

De Bow wrote specifically for southern readers interested in economic and regional topics, and his audience reflected this editorial choice. Aside from a small number of northern merchants in Cincinnati and New York City who subscribed to the *Review* for business purposes, more than 90 percent of De Bow's identified readers lived in the South (see map). Within the region, 74 percent lived in the Lower South, which stretched westward from South Carolina to Texas, and 25 percent lived in the Upper South and border states. De Bow understood that intraregional nuances existed in the South. Already aware of the older South's economic situation, he had relocated to New Orleans to be closer to new markets and communities in the Southwest and Mississippi River valley. Just over 58 percent of his known readers lived in Tennessee, Alabama, Mississippi, Louisiana, Arkansas, and Texas, while only

33 percent lived along the South Atlantic seaboard. The geographic diversity of these readers encouraged editorial balance between the interests of well-established areas in the east and more recently developed regions in the west.[4]

De Bow's known readers reflected the rapid development of the Southwest. Inexpensive land in Mississippi, Arkansas, western Tennessee, and Alabama lured planters and merchants away from the Atlantic coast. This sudden shift defined the values of new communities and redefined the status of older ones. Fifty-four percent of De Bow's readers had been born in South Atlantic states; only 16 percent were native to the Southwest. Of Alabama's 264 known subscribers, 55 had been born in Alabama, 48 in Georgia, 30 in Virginia, 51 in South Carolina, 9 in Europe, and 16 in various northern states. Conversely, of South Carolina's 213 readers, only 31 had been born outside the Palmetto State, and none came from the Southwest. Although De Bow had to take these changes into account, he benefited from the cultural persistence created by interregional emigration.[5]

De Bow's message of integrated economic development resonated among readers who lived in the Southwest's Black Belt region, which stretched from central Alabama, through much of northern Mississippi, and into parts of Arkansas, Louisiana, and western Tennessee. The development of new communities, commercial networks, and transportation routes appealed to De Bow. His vision of economic development corresponded with systems being created by wealthy planters and urban merchants. The absence of southwestern readers who owned or worked at banks is an indicator of how the agricultural and commercial sectors worked together to market the region's cotton crop. Isolated from coastal cities, southwestern planters and merchants created interior markets and sufficient transportation routes that connected small towns to international ports such as Mobile or New Orleans. Planters consigned their crop to local cotton merchants, more commonly known as *factors,* who extended credit on the future sale of what planters produced. Factors in small interior towns then shipped the cotton to associates in port cities, where the commodity could be sold on the international market. The linkage between small-town cotton factors and large coastal factorage houses reduced the region's dependency on banking but increased planters' dependency on credit. Many of De Bow's readers in these areas, regardless of background or occupation, invested in projects that expanded the commercial profile of their community. The preservation of plantation culture and slavery relied on the successful commercial integration of the Southwest's planters and business class with global markets.[6]

The *Review* became popular in Alabama's Black Belt region because it offered planters and merchants a template and advice for economic development. Seventy percent of Alabama's readers lived in Black Belt counties in central and western parts of the state. Relatively unburdened by natural hindrances, these readers worked to integrate themselves and their plantations or businesses into larger markets. Planters and merchants created a network of interior commercial centers linked by roads and railroads. The towns of Cahaba, Selma, Eutaw, and Marion became prosperous cotton centers with substantial numbers of *Review* subscribers—fourteen readers lived in Cahaba, thirteen in Selma, twelve in Eutaw, and seventeen in Marion. Although not large or well-developed towns, these urban centers became important to the economy of Alabama's Black Belt region. Cooperation between market-oriented planters and local merchants typified the economic relationships between *Review* readers in Dallas County. Located in west-central Alabama, this Black Belt county had rich farmland and access to the Alabama River. De Bow's readers in Selma, the largest town in the county, hoped to expand their community's profile by investing in railroad projects and other civic improvements. The development of Selma served as an example of the growth De Bow promised when private and public motives intermingled. Citizens lobbied for and received state support for a bank and a $190,000 loan to connect the town with the Alabama and Tennessee Rivers Railroad. De Bow's readers in Selma, regardless of occupation, supported transportation and commercial improvements. Thornton Boykin Goldsby, a *Review* subscriber and planter who lived near Selma, invested in five railroad projects, a plank road corporation, and a telegraph company. John W. Lapsley, a prominent lawyer and merchant, also hoped to connect his town with larger markets and solidify Selma's commercial prominence. He invested in the same railroads and plank road as Goldsby and also bought stock in a gaslight company, a coal mine, and a lime works. Both men worked as individuals and within a community of like-minded southerners who read the *Review*. Selma continued to expand, and during the Civil War its industrial capacity, railroad connections, and proximity to Montgomery made it an important munitions center for the Confederacy.[7]

The popularity of the *Review* extended into the Black Belt region of western Tennessee. Almost 49 percent of De Bow's known readers in Tennessee lived in the far southwestern corner of the state. As did his Alabama readers, these readers lived in small towns or on large plantations. By 1860 the top 5 percent of planters owned 46 percent of the wealth in western Tennessee. Their interests corresponded with market forces generated by cotton. Hiram S. Bradford, a *Review* subscriber and planter from Haywood County, owned almost $50,000 in real estate and had amassed a personal fortune of $72,000. Despite his success as a cotton planter, he invested in the Big Hatchee Turnpike and Bridge Company. He also followed De Bow's general advice and invested in less tangible but equally important social institutions such as the Brownsville Academy, Union University, and the Brownsville Female Institute. His son later told De Bow about his father's admiration for the *Review,* noting: "Your work is Herculean and all we say is keep your shoulder to the wheel, it will begin to move at first by inches [and] after a while it will come out of the mire and that's what a country we will have."[8]

De Bow's popularity in Alabama and Tennessee diminished outside each state's Black Belt region. His focus on large plantations and well-connected urban centers made the *Review* less applicable to yeoman farmers living in mountainous, isolated regions in the South's upcountry. In eastern Tennessee, where small farmers produced wheat crops with little slave labor, his readership was almost nonexistent. In northern Alabama, few readers lived outside Huntsville. De Bow spent little time exploring these regions or writing about possible economic innovations that might link them to the larger southern economy. This lack of understanding or interest in mountainous areas extended to western North Carolina, where De Bow had no readers west of Alamance, a town slightly east of Winston-Salem. Later in the 1850s he would begin to take interest in the mineral and lumber resources of these regions.[9]

Readers in the Southeast's plantation belt had characteristics similar to those of the readers who lived in the Southwest's Black Belt. The eastern Cotton Belt extended from south-central North Carolina, through the Piedmont and part of the upcountry of South Carolina, and into south-central and parts of western Georgia. Large concentrations of *Review* subscribers lived on large plantations and in commercial towns linked to the cotton industry. In Georgia De Bow had five readers in Atlanta, twenty in Augusta, seven in Macon, and eight in Rome, and in South Carolina readers clustered in and around Camden, Edgefield, and Columbia. Unlike in the Southwest, in the eastern Cotton Belt rural planters and urban merchants initially had a contentious relationship. Planters resisted railroad development and opposed the creation of town culture. Undeterred by this resistance, South Carolina merchants altered state incorporation laws and perceptions about private profit to become more acceptable to area planters. In Georgia, politicians

Table 5: Population Growth in Southern Cities and Towns, 1850–1860

City	1850 (*N*)	1860 (*N*)	+/– (%)
Augusta, GA	11,753	12,493	+6.3
Baltimore, MD	169,054	212,418	+25.6
Charleston, SC	42,985	40,578	–5.6
Mobile, AL	20,515	29,258	+42.0
Montgomery, AL	4,935	8,843	+79.1
Memphis, TN	8,839	22,623	+155.9
Nashville, TN	10,478	16,988	+62.1
New Orleans, LA	116,375	168,675	+44.9
Natchez, MS	4,434	6,612	+49.1
Petersburg, VA	14,010	18,266	+30.3
Richmond, VA	27,570	37,910	+37.5
Savannah, GA	15,312	22,292	+45.5
Vicksburg, MS	3,678	4,591	+24.8
Total	**437,196**	**601,547**	**+37.6**

Source: Joseph C. G. Kennedy, *Preliminary Report on the Eighth Census, 1860* (Washington, DC: US Government Printing Office, 1862), 242–44.

overcame planter interference by partially funding a state railroad system. By 1850 four separate railroads linked Georgia's interior cotton towns to coastal ports. De Bow's readership reflected the commercial network created by cotton and railroad development. Almost half De Bow's known readers in Georgia lived in Atlanta, Augusta, Macon, and Savannah (see table 5). The gradual commercial transformation of the Southeast encouraged De Bow to believe that older parts of the South could once again become competitive in global markets.[10]

The growth of the urban South provided De Bow with a natural audience for his ideas. The South's urban population had more than tripled between 1790 and 1860, creating new linkages and opportunities for profit-minded southerners. When integrated into the regional railroad system, which was quadrupling in size during this same period, these urban centers became incubators for southern economic development. Sixty-two percent of De Bow's known readers resided in southern cities and towns (see table 6). The geographic location of these urban centers had little influence on who

Table 6: Distribution of *Review* Readers in Urban Centers

City	Known Readers	City	Known Readers
New Orleans, LA	81	Mobile, AL	17
Charleston, SC	78	Alexandria, LA	16
St. Louis, MO	56	Baton Rouge, LA	16
Richmond, VA	48	Atlanta, GA	16
Nashville, TN	38	Vicksburg, MS	15
Montgomery, AL	36	Wharton, TX	14
Tallahassee, FL	29	Georgetown, SC	14
Savannah, GA	26	Cahaba, AL	14
Louisville, KY	24	Selma, AL	13
Baltimore, MD	22	Camden, SC	13
Augusta, GA	20	Natchez, MS	13
Edgefield, SC	19	Eutaw, AL	12
Jacksonport, AR	19	Memphis, TN	12
Jackson, TN	19	Halltown, VA	11
Jackson, MS	18	Somerville, TN	11
Marion, AL	17	Huntsville, AL	10

Source: Composite Census Records, 1850–1860; US Census Office, *Eighth Census of the United States, 1860* (Washington, DC: US Government Printing Office, 1864).
Note: Figures given are numbers of readers.

subscribed to the *Review.* Combined, Charleston and New Orleans, the two largest cities in the Lower South, had thirty-two more readers than St. Louis, Louisville, and Richmond. The size of the municipality also had little influence on subscription numbers. Wharton, Texas, and Halltown, Virginia, had more individual readers than Petersburg or Mobile. Overall, thirty-nine separate communities had more than ten individual subscribers to the *Review.* De Bow's urban readership increased as his focus on the necessity of cities and towns expanded.[11]

De Bow's readership in Richmond, Virginia, exemplified the support he had among the business elite in many southern cities. Forty-eight subscribers lived in the South's most industrialized city. Hugh W. Fry and Joseph R. Anderson each owned large iron foundries and produced finished goods that ranged from nails to railroad locomotives. Fry embodied the entrepreneurial

Table 7: Value of Manufactured Goods in the Southern States, 1850–1860

Industry	1850 ($)	1860 ($)	Regional Growth (%)	National Growth (%)
Agricultural implements	784,452	1,582,483	101.7	160.1
Steam engines	833,284	4,060,803	387.3	68.2
Iron founding	1,587,930	2,504,362	57.7	42.0
Sawed lumber	8,846,476	17,941,162	102.3	63.9
Flour and meal	16,581,817	30,767,457	85.5	64.2
Cotton goods	5,665,362	7,172,293	26.6	75.7
Woolen goods	1,108,811	2,303,303	107.7	N.A.
Leather	3,577,599	4,074,406	13.8	66.9
Boots and shoes	1,491,944	2,729,327	80.3	67.8
Soap and candles	394,778	489,913	24.0	66.0

Source: Joseph C. G. Kennedy, *Preliminary Report of the Eighth Census, 1860* (Washington, DC: US Government Printing Office, 1862), 169–85.

spirit that De Bow hoped to cultivate in other middle-class southerners (see table 7). He had opened a small commission house and wholesale grocery in the late 1840s. By 1854 he had become successful enough to start the Belle Isle Manufacturing Company and produce iron products. Eager to expand production, he funded construction of a railroad bridge that linked his factory to nearby coal pits. Fry and Charles Wortham, another *Review* subscriber, later purchased the Old Dominion Iron and Nails Company. They used slave labor and became wealthy industrialists in the city. Likewise by 1860, Joseph R. Anderson's Tredegar Iron Works had become the largest iron foundry and rolling mill in the South, employing almost nine hundred free and slave laborers on a five-acre complex. Lewis D. Crenshaw and Richard B. Haxall, both *Review* readers, leased land from Anderson and built the largest flour mill in the nation. Crenshaw and Haxall used profits from the mill to invest in a woolen factory and in the James River and Kanawha Canal Company. Other subscribers such as James Lyons became involved in the commercial development of the city by helping raise money for railroad projects. Lyons chaired a committee for the Richmond and Danville Railroad that raised $600,000 from private investors to supplement the $900,000 donation from the state. He also became involved with the Virginia Central Agricultural

Society and helped build a statue of George Washington. These were the type of men that De Bow hoped to attract to the *Review.* They had the capital and spirit to change their communities and would become more important as the promise of southern independence loomed in 1860.[12]

The diversified economic development of Nashville attracted similar business leaders to the *Review.* The growing city had thirty-nine readers who

Table 8: Investment Patterns of Individual *Review* Subscribers in Alabama and Tennessee, 1830–1860

Name	Town	Railroad	Turnpike/ Plank Road	College/ University	Factory/ Mining	Civic	Bank/ Insurance
Francis Gilmer Jr.	Montgomery, AL	2	1	0	0	1	1
Charles Pollard	Montgomery, AL	4	1	0	0	1	2
Joseph H. Winter	Montgomery, AL	0	3	0	2	1	1
John H. Murphy	Montgomery, AL	2	1	0	0	1	0
Charles Crommelin	Montgomery, AL	2	2	0	0	1	0
Thomas H. Watts	Montgomery, AL	3	0	0	1	0	0
William H. Taylor	Montgomery, AL	1	1	0	0	1	1
Bolling Hall Jr.	Prattville, AL	3	0	0	0	0	1
Daniel Pratt	Prattville, AL	2	1	0	2	1	2
John W. Lapsley	Selma, AL	4	1	0	4	1	1
Thornton Goldsby	Selma, AL	6	1	0	0	0	0
Robert Jemison Jr.	Tuscaloosa, AL	1	1	0	3	1	0
George Shortridge	Montevallo, AL	3	0	0	2	0	0
James L. Price	Perry County, AL	6	2	0	0	0	0
David B. Scott	Scottsville, AL	1	0	0	2	0	0
Vernon K. Stevenson	Nashville, TN	3	1	1	1	1	1
Edward East	Nashville, TN	0	1	1	0	1	1
James Woods	Nashville, TN	0	0	0	1	1	4
Alexander Allison	Nashville, TN	2	0	1	2	0	0
William G. Harding	Nashville, TN	0	3	0	1	1	0
Milton Brown	Jackson, TN	1	0	1	0	1	0
Samuel Lancaster	Jackson, TN	4	3	1	0	0	2
James Elrod	Jackson, TN	4	2	0	0	0	1
Samuel Rhea	Blountsville, TN	3	3	0	0	0	1
Hiram S. Bradford	Brownsville, TN	0	1	3	0	0	1
Joshua Elder	Clarksville, TN	2	1	0	0	0	1
Austin Miller	Bolivar, TN	2	2	0	0	1	1
Paulding Anderson	Lebanon, TN	2	4	1	0	0	1

Sources: Composite Census Records, 1850–1860; *Acts of Alabama, 1830–1860* (Catawba: Allen & Brickell); *Acts of Tennessee, Index to Names, 1796–1850*, http://www.tennessee.gov/tsla/history/misc/actsintro.htm.

Note: Each number represents a separate investment in a public corporation.

represented each sector of the southern economy (see table 8). William W. Berry owned the largest drug store in the city and was estimated to be worth over $500,000 in 1860. He later became a founder and benefactor of the Bolivar Female Academy. James Woods began as a city merchant and eventually created a profitable iron works in the city. He later partnered with Thomas Yeatman, another *Review* reader, and opened Woods, Yeatman, and Company and created the Cumberland Iron Works. The foundry produced annual revenues that exceeded $300,000. Later in his career, Woods partnered with John Beaty, a *Review* reader, and started a soap factory in Nashville. In addition, Woods served as a commissioner for the Bank of Tennessee, the Tennessee Marine and Fire Insurance Company, and the New Orleans and Ohio Telegraph Company. The potential of Nashville's future economic growth thrilled southern nationalists as much as the city's active business class excited De Bow.[13]

Immigrants had become increasingly common in southern cities, and De Bow's readership reflected this demographic change (see table 9). Over

Table 9: *De Bow's Review* Readers, by Place of Birth

Place of Birth	**Readers (*N*)**	**Place of Birth**	**Readers (*N*)**
Alabama	82	Massachusetts	34
Arkansas	2	Michigan	1
Canada	3	Minnesota	1
Connecticut	13	Mississippi	47
Delaware	1	Missouri	11
England	16	New Hampshire	2
Florida	4	New Jersey	6
France	9	New York	28
Georgia	155	North Carolina	119
Germany	22	Ohio	9
Illinois	3	Pennsylvania	17
Indiana	3	Rhode Island	1
Ireland	39	Scotland	12
Italy	3	South Carolina	283
Kentucky	59	Tennessee	110
Louisiana	63	Vermont	5
Maine	9	Virginia	226
Maryland	37		

Sources: Composite Census Records, 1850–1860; US Census Office, *Eighth Census of the United States, 1860* (Washington, DC: US Government Printing Office, 1864).

7 percent of the *Review's* known subscribers came from Europe. De Bow encouraged southerners to accept immigrants as a way of bolstering the South's white population. Although many European immigrants worked as common laborers, some became prominent business owners. Maunsel White had left Ireland as a young boy and became a wealthy merchant-planter in Louisiana. John Bones emigrated from Ireland to Augusta, Georgia, where he opened a successful hardware store. He later became a director of the National Bank of Augusta and opened a new store across the Savannah River in Hamburg, South Carolina. Despite the rise of anti-immigrant rhetoric in the South in the mid-1850s, residents in Charleston accepted, for example, John C. Gravely. An anonymous agent for R. G. Dun and Company, the nation's largest credit bureau, reported that Gravely, a *Review* subscriber and immigrant from England, did "moderate business with planters and mechanics, [was] safe and respectable, and accepted by the city." De Bow's willingness to accept immigrants made him popular among Europeans moving to the South.[14]

Transplanted northerners accounted for almost 10 percent of De Bow's known readers. Many of these northern-born southerners made significant contributions to their communities and to the South. Daniel Pratt had been born in New Hampshire and moved to Alabama in 1833. He developed a model factory complex in Prattville and became an example of industrial success in the *Review.* Despite his success, however, some of Pratt's neighbors remained skeptical of his allegiance to the South. In 1853 an agent from R. G. Dun and Company noted that Pratt had donated $100,000 in charitable contributions to local schools and churches yet remained unpopular with nearby residents because he insisted on having "things his own way and monopoliz[ing] everything." For some southerners the pursuit of excessive profits or aggressive business practices became traits associated with northern society. Doubts about Pratt's motives continued to linger even after he declared his loyalty to the Confederacy in 1861. Like Pratt, Oren Metcalfe left New England and purchased a large cotton plantation outside Natchez, Mississippi, becoming a respected member of his community. Aside from operating his plantation, Metcalfe opened a general store, worked as a physician, sold insurance, and served as the county sheriff for thirty years. He invested in local transportation projects and served on the Jefferson College board of directors—Mississippi's first institution of higher learning. Pratt and Metcalfe balanced their private ambitions with public service. Both men characterized the influence northerners had in developing their communities. De Bow took little notice of Pratt's northern lineage, perhaps thinking about his own family ties to New Jersey and New York. By 1860 De Bow recognized that the South needed to be unified, minimizing as many potential internal divisions as possible.[15]

De Bow's interest in commercial development attracted southern merchants who lived in towns and cities around the South. Of the 1,468 *Review* subscribers with known occupations, 328, or 22 percent, identified themselves as merchants in the 1860 federal census (see table 10). The growth of

Table 10: *De Bow's Review* Readers per Occupation Sector, 1860 (*N* [%])

State	Readers	Professional	Agricultural	Commercial	Industrial
Alabama	264	80 (31)	110 (42)	45 (17)	12 (5)
Arkansas	39	17 (44)	10 (26)	8 (21)	0
Florida	42	17 (40)	14 (33)	7 (17)	3 (7)
Georgia	124	24 (20)	37 (30)	44 (36)	10 (8)
Kentucky	31	4 (13)	4 (13)	19 (61)	3 (10)
Louisiana	195	42 (22)	82 (43)	63 (33)	7 (4)
Maryland	22	2 (9)	0	16 (73)	3 (14)
Mississippi	160	46 (29)	83 (53)	17 (11)	1 (1)
Missouri	58	7 (12)	3 (5)	38 (66)	7 (12)
North Carolina	23	4 (17)	8 (35)	6 (26)	1 (4)
South Carolina	213	64 (30)	76 (36)	50 (24)	8 (3)
Tennessee	134	38 (29)	38 (29)	35 (27)	11 (8)
Texas	77	17 (22)	33 (43)	17 (22)	2 (2)
Virginia	112	33 (29)	22 (19)	36 (31)	11 (10)
Total	**1,494**	**395** **(27)**	**520** **(35)**	**401** **(27)**	**79** **(5)**

Sources: Composite Census Records, 1850–1860; US Census Office, *Eighth Census of the United States, 1860* (Washington, DC: US Government Printing Office, 1864).

cities and new commercial networks in the Southwest increased the profile of the South's merchant class. By 1860 over thirty-eight thousand merchants lived in the region, yet they remained overshadowed by the hegemonic power of wealthy planters and the sheer numbers of rural nonslaveholding whites. The South's business community became increasingly influential in southern society by shielding rural planters and farmers from direct interaction with outside market forces. De Bow saw the merchant class as an essential link to local, state, national, and international markets. He described the role of the merchant as "the promoter of enterprise, the encourager of agriculture, the friend of peace." He viewed commerce as the motivation behind industrial development and reminded his agricultural readers that "in vain does the farmer labor in the finest climate, on the most fertile soil, if he is beyond the reach of that mercantile agency without which his products are worthless."[16]

The merchants of Charleston had supported the literary efforts of their native son since 1846, and they now applauded him for his extreme regional stance in 1860. Seventy-eight *Review* subscribers lived in the city, constituting 37 percent of all known South Carolina readers. Of those living in Charleston, 44 percent identified themselves as merchants. De Bow's familiar name made the *Review* popular among the city's business class. A new generation of commercial leaders had emerged by the early 1850s. They attempted to increase the city's shrinking market share, business having been lost to Savannah, Augusta, and the Southwest. Unlike past generations of merchants, who had benefited from Charleston's early commercial primacy, younger merchants were often self-made and profit oriented. Bernard O'Neill exemplified the type of reader De Bow attracted. An immigrant from Ireland, O'Neill moved to Charleston and worked as a grocery clerk. Within five years he opened his own wholesale grocery business. His success as a business owner provided him status in the community, and he became the vice president of the South Carolina Loan and Trust Company, the president of the Hibernia Bank, and a director of the South Carolina Railroad Bank. He later served as a city alderman. An agent from R. G. Dun and Company noted that O'Neill had started with "a few barrels of potatoes and apples" in 1847 and, by 1860, owned nine slaves and a carriage. O'Neill needed the commercial information provided in the *Review*, and De Bow needed readers like O'Neill who encouraged and supported commercial development as the presidential election and possible sectional strife approached in 1860.[17]

Merchants in Mobile, Alabama, had a similar influence on the development of their community during much of the 1850s. For many years the city had languished in relative obscurity as transient merchants flooded Mobile during harvest time but then left the city for the remainder of the year. The development of the city stagnated and its commercial position was threatened until a permanent merchant class assumed control of its future. Albert Stein and Charles Le Baron, both *Review* readers and city merchants, symbolized the commercial ascent of Alabama's largest city. Stein, a transplanted German civil engineer, developed and built the city's waterworks and improved the freight capacity of Mobile Bay. Le Baron, a commission merchant from Pensacola, Florida, moved to Mobile in 1840 and promised to "leave politics and politicians alone, and devote myself entirely to business pursuits, and to the development in every way of the resources of our Southern country." Le Baron understood the importance of linking the South's interior with Mobile and became a major investor in the Mobile and Ohio Railroad Company. He also helped expand Mobile Bay's commercial capacity. As the owner of a large commission house that dealt with clients in Europe and South America, Le Baron needed unfettered access to domestic and international markets. By 1851 De Bow claimed that Le Baron had "identified heart and soul with his adopted city of Mobile and her prosperity." Although Mobile competed with New Orleans for regional cotton, De Bow recognized that a possible southern confederacy needed secondary commercial ports to maintain regional trade. Southern economic independence would create enough profit for all white southerners, he speculated, allowing Mobile to grow accordingly.[18]

Outside large coastal cities, merchants became important to the development of small towns throughout the South. The merchant class often invested in a variety of private and public projects that would increase the profile of their community. Their interaction with outside market forces provided broad insight into transportation and commercial innovations. Samuel Lancaster, a *Review* subscriber and merchant in Jackson, Tennessee, owned a successful dry goods store. Between 1831 and 1849 Lancaster invested in ten different transportation projects that promised to connect Jackson with larger markets. The commercial success of the western Tennessee town pleased Lancaster, and he later became involved with civic projects that improved the quality of life in Jackson. Lancaster's commitment to commercial and civic development typified the role of merchants in many southern towns. Likewise in southwestern Virginia, Thomas Boyd, a hotel owner in Wytheville, embodied many of the same traits as Lancaster. Boyd had furnished the Virginia and Tennessee Railroad Company with needed capital when eastern tidewater planters threatened to block state appropriations. He understood the importance of a rail connection to Wytheville's commercial future. He also understood the necessity of civic improvements to attract new growth, and he invested in public works projects. This type of diversified, entrepreneurial spirit in Jackson and Wytheville embodied De Bow's economic vision for a more commercially integrated South.[19]

De Bow hoped that merchants would help integrate the agricultural, industrial, and commercial sectors of the South and serve as intermediaries between urban and rural areas. Like many early nineteenth-century Americans, southerners had been conditioned to question the motives of merchants and to fear urban space. De Bow hoped to change those perceptions. Southern merchants became increasingly independent of planter hegemony. They shaped the interests of rural planters to meet their own needs. Past fears gave way to excitement as commercial development provided new opportunities. Merchants often invested in their communities' development as a way of expanding commercial interest. Urban space became important because it allowed the South's business community to grow more organically without interference from planters and farmers fearful of market forces.[20]

Many of De Bow's readers worked in professional positions that supported commercial and industrial development in southern towns and cities. Of De Bow's readers with known occupations, 22 percent worked as lawyers, doctors, or bankers or in insurance offices. They often provided the capital and leadership needed to fund large projects and became promoters for their growing communities. De Bow became aware of such men and the importance of town boosterism after his visit to Memphis in 1845. At the Memphis convention, he had become acquainted with Robertson Topp and Robert C. Brinkley. Topp, a lawyer by training, lived in Memphis and looked for new ways to promote his adopted hometown. Born in Nashville to a prominent family, he had moved to Memphis in 1831. He invested in early railroads and helped improve the city's waterfront. He also developed neighborhoods in South Memphis and built the Gayoso House, the city's largest hotel. He served two terms in the Tennessee House of Representatives as a Whig before returning to the private sector. He later became the president of the Memphis and Charleston Railroad Company and an early subscriber to *De Bow's Review.* Impressed with De Bow's work, Topp pledged to find ten new subscribers as proof of his support. De Bow, speculating on the possible loss of readers in the event of war, hoped that all southerners would follow Topp's example and support the *Review.*[21]

Robert C. Brinkley exhibited the same passion and willingness as Topp to blend personal motivation with public interest. De Bow noted in a brief biography of Brinkley that he had "set the example himself in improvements, and constantly kept it up by the construction of extensive and substantial buildings in the city, realizing thus an almost princely income from property at first unproductive." Brinkley served as president of the Little Rock and Memphis Railroad Company and the Planters Bank of Memphis. He later built the Peabody Hotel in downtown Memphis as a symbol of his city's prosperity. Despite these personal gains, however, De Bow noted: "Mr. Brinkley encourages, with a most liberal hand, every public enterprise, the intent and effect of which are to promote the prosperity and growth of Memphis." Topp and Brinkley supported De Bow's work because he supported their personal and public economic ambitions.[22]

In Huntsville, Alabama, Thomas Fearn helped make the city into an important commercial and industrial center in the northern part of the state. Fearn had been born in Virginia and spent time studying medicine in the North and Europe before moving to Huntsville in 1820. Although trained in medicine, he became a leading member of the city's business community by investing in local canals, railroads, turnpikes, and banks. He also served in the state legislature, was a trustee of the University of Alabama, and helped fund the construction of the city's waterworks. His commitment to Huntsville was absolute, yet others found his efforts self-serving and manipulative. The local Democratic newspaper suggested that he belonged to a "Royal Party" of prominent merchants and ridiculed public projects that yielded private profits. Local opponents worried that greed and mismanagement of public funds might create a privileged aristocracy that would corrupt the republican values of the community. Although opposition to commercial progress continued, the city's commitment to growth created commercial and industrial momentum in northern Alabama. Thomas Fearn represented the influence and power of urban boosters in the Southwest. As a staunch unionist in 1860, he watched national events unfold and, like many *Review* readers, wondered what would happen next.[23]

De Bow's interest in the South's railroad system made him popular among like-minded southerners who saw economic and social benefits in railroad construction. Railroad promoters such as James Robb and Judah Benjamin used the *Review* to encourage general transportation development in the South. Others like Samuel Tate, Milton Brown, and Vernon K. Stevenson benefited from De Bow's willingness to endorse individual railroads. Tate, the president of the Memphis and Charleston Railroad Company, alerted De Bow to possible connections between his rail line and mineral deposits in northern Alabama and western Tennessee. Tate later moved to Alabama and helped develop Birmingham's postwar railroad and iron industry. Milton Brown, the president of the Mississippi Central and Tennessee Railroad Company and, later, the Mobile and Ohio Railroad Company, linked Jackson, Tennessee, to markets in the Ohio River valley and the Lower Mississippi River valley. Vernon K. Stevenson, another *Review* reader and the president of the Nashville and Chattanooga Railroad and the Nashville and Northwestern Railroad Companies, began his career as the owner of a dry goods store and eventually became Tennessee's foremost railroad promoter. He understood the necessity of linking Nashville to markets in the North and the South and raised money to build railroads and promote towns. De Bow relied on individual investors and railroad executives to encourage transportation development. Between 1850 and 1860 more railroad mileage was constructed in the South than in any other part of the nation.[24]

De Bow's readership reflected the steady growth of industry in the antebellum South. Some of the South's largest industrialists—Daniel Pratt, William Gregg, and Joseph R. Anderson—subscribed to the *Review*. Other, less prominent industrialists helped their communities become more economically diversified. Robert Jemison, a reader in Tuscaloosa, Alabama, owned a sawmill, flour mill, toll bridge, and stagecoach line. He also served as president of the Northeast and Southwest Alabama Railroad and on the board of the Warrior Manufacturing Company. Just east of Tuscaloosa in Bibb County, David Scott built a large cotton factory in 1834 and continued to manufacture cloth goods until his factory was burned by James Wilson's raiders in 1865. In Clover Hill, Virginia, James H. Cox symbolized the successful integration of industrial and transportation development in the South. In 1840 he purchased land outside Richmond and started the Clover Hill Mining Company. Rich coal deposits produced high profits, and by 1853 he had built a twenty-one-mile railroad spur that connected his coal pits to the Richmond and Petersburg Railroad. Eager to build on his coal and railroad empire, he constructed a large hotel on his property and transported city tourists on trains that had supplied coal to Richmond's factories. De Bow hoped that successful examples of industrialization would encourage other southerners to think about factories and mills.[25]

The diversified economic growth of Montgomery, Alabama, served as an example of how a group of *Review* subscribers collectively influenced the direction of an individual community. In 1848 De Bow noted that "the music of the saw, hammer, and trowel is heard in almost every street" of Montgomery. The city had benefited from strong political support by a group of transplanted Georgians who moved from the Broad River area to Alabama's Black Belt. They chose to build a town along the Alabama River. Montgomery steadily grew as local cotton planters and merchants made the town their regional hub for commercial and industrial activity. De Bow's readership reflected the diversified development of the city. Of Montgomery's thirty-seven identified readers, eleven were planters, nine worked as merchants, twelve maintained professional careers, and three worked in manufacturing. Many of these readers invested in transportation and public works projects that expanded the commercial influence of the city. Of the sixteen readers with known investment records, twelve owned shares in local railroads, five owned shares in plank road companies, seven helped establish gas lighting in the city, and seven more served on the boards of directors of manufacturing firms. Revisiting the city in the pages of the *Review* in 1858, De Bow claimed: "Montgomery is destined . . . to rank first among Southern inland towns."[26]

No resident of Montgomery or perhaps the South represented the entrepreneurial spirit of De Bow better than Charles Teed Pollard. Pollard understood the necessity of linking agriculture, commerce, and industry to create an integrated economic system. He had been born in Virginia and worked as a clerk and bookkeeper before moving to Alabama in 1828. He settled in Montgomery and married the daughter of John B. Scott, an original Broad River land speculator and settler in Alabama's Black Belt. He invested in a merchandizing firm and partnered with Francis Meriwether Gilmer Jr., another *Review* subscriber, to open a cotton storage warehouse. Pollard invested heavily in railroads and mining companies. He later became president of the Montgomery and West Point Railroad Company and other regional lines. In addition to his railroad investments, he also served on the boards of the Bank of Mobile, the Montgomery and Tuscaloosa Plank Road Company, the Exchange Hotel, the Montgomery Gas Light Company, the city's first ice factory, and the Montgomery Copper Mining Company in Talladega, Alabama. Understanding the importance of social and cultural development, he helped start the Alabama Bible Society and the University of the South and served as chairman of the building committee that oversaw construction of the new state capitol building. He continued to wield local and regional influence on urban development and railroad growth until his death in 1888.[27]

Other *Review* readers benefited from Montgomery's diverse development and helped support the city's growth. Thomas Hill Watts, a wealthy lawyer and successful politician, invested heavily in railroad companies and in the Pine Barren Manufacturing Company. William Taylor and Joseph Winters partnered to fund railroad and plank road construction and helped pay for gas lighting in the city. Winters also commanded the local militia unit known as the Metropolitan Guards. Enough general readers lived in Montgomery to support Armand Pfister's bookstore. In 1846 four *Review* readers—Charles Pollard, Francis M. Gilmer Jr., Charles Crommelin, and William Taylor—partnered to construct the Exchange Hotel. By 1860 city merchants handled over a million bales of cotton, manufacturers had started thirteen factories, and four railroads connected or would soon connect Montgomery to other parts of the nation. Frederick Law Olmsted, the northern traveler who rarely complimented southern institutions, described Montgomery as "a prosperous town, with very pleasant suburbs, and a remarkably enterpris-

Table 11: Average *De Bow's Review* Reader per Category per State, 1860

State	**Readers (*N*)**	**Age**	**Real Estate ($)**	**Personal Estate ($)**	**Slaves (*N*)**
Alabama	264	44	40,329	69,456	46.3
Arkansas	39	37	24,694	18,890	14
Florida	42	46	18,530	30,714	40.3
Georgia	124	44	24,009	47,145	28.3
Kentucky	31	41	41,905	53,337	5.91
Louisiana	195	44	96,861	53,523	53.8
Maryland	22	43	47,462	28,281	3
Mississippi	160	43	62,556	63,122	45.5
Missouri	58	40	54,036	32,180	6
North Carolina	23	44	33,230	48,445	46.1
South Carolina	213	43	40,399	55,558	56.5
Tennessee	134	42	55,894	42,717	21.8
Texas	77	43	34,373	22,114	16.7
Virginia	112	46	62,269	39,127	26.7
Average		**42.71**	**45,468**	**43,186**	**27.48**

Sources: Composite Census Records, 1850–1860; US Census Office, *Eighth Census of the United States, 1860* (Washington, DC: US Government Printing Office, 1864).

ing population among which there is a considerable portion of Northern and foreign-born business-men and mechanics." Despite Olmsted's claim of northern influence on the city's business leaders, only seven of De Bow's thirty-seven readers had been born in the North or Europe. Each reader in Montgomery came from a different background and held a wide variety of interests, yet De Bow's ideas resonated with them. Like thousands of other southern planters, merchants, and industrialists, these men read the *Review* because it represented how they felt about the South's future (see table 11).[28]

Despite living in a predominantly rural region, only 35 percent of De Bow's known readers identified themselves as planters or farmers in census records. Many more subscribers in all likelihood owned and farmed land but recognized a different occupation as their primary source of income or interest. Most of these planters lived in the eastern Cotton Belt in South Carolina and Georgia and the Black Belt of central Alabama, northern Mississippi, and southwestern Tennessee. These areas had become the foundation of the South's plantation economy, and De Bow understood his readers' reliance on cotton and slavery (see table 12). He focused on improvements to large plantations, and his readership reflected this decision. Of the 511 known planters and farmers who subscribed to the *Review*, 166, or 33 percent, owned more than $100,000 in real estate and 199, or 39 percent, had more than that amount in personal property (see table 13). Wealthy cotton and sugar planters clearly found value in De Bow's ideas. Yet this did not mean that the *Review* served only their interests. Interestingly, of the six readers who owned more than $1 million worth of real estate, only three identified themselves as planters, the other three identifying themselves in the 1860 federal census as a lawyer, a doctor, and a railroad president. And, of the six readers who owned more than $500,000 in personal property, only two listed themselves in the census as planters. The economic diversity that De Bow craved for southerners seemed to play a part in the overall wealth of these readers, and he hoped that they could continue to thrive in a new southern nation. For example, although Charles Pollard thrived as a railroad president and real estate developer in Montgomery, he owned as many improved acres of farmland and more livestock than Charles Gunter, a devoted cotton planter who lived outside town.[29]

The *Review* appealed to slave owners who had expanded beyond the small family farm. Sixty-three percent of all known *Review* readers owned slaves at a time when only one-third of all white families could afford to buy even a single a slave (see table 14). In 1860, 46 percent of all white slave

Table 12: Median Real Property Holdings of Southern Legislatures and *De Bow's Review* Readers, 1860 ($)

State	Southern House Members	Southern Senate Members	*Review* Subscribers
Alabama	6,000	18,000	20,000
Florida	2,000	10,000	15,000
Georgia	4,000	8,000	14,000
Louisiana	10,000	11,000	40,000
Mississippi	7,000	7,500	22,700
South Carolina	8,000	25,000	15,000
Texas	8,600	10,000	10,000

Sources: Composite Census Records, 1850–1860; US Census Office, *Eighth Census of the United States, 1860* (Washington, DC: US Government Printing Office, 1864); Ralph A. Wooster, *The Secession Conventions of the South* (Princeton, NJ: Princeton University Press, 1962).

Table 13: Median Personal Property Holdings of Southern Legislatures and *De Bow's Review* Readers, 1860 ($)

State	Southern House Members	Southern Senate Members	*Review* Subscribers
Alabama	15,00	40,500	47,000
Florida	7,000	42,000	30,000
Georgia	9,000	13,000	35,000
Louisiana	8,000	24,835	12,000
Mississippi	15,000	20,000	38,000
South Carolina	24,000	45,000	30,000
Texas	10,000	15,000	10,000

Sources: Composite Census Records, 1850–1860; US Census Office, *Eighth Census of the United States, 1860* (Washington, DC: US Government Printing Office, 1864); Ralph A. Wooster, *The Secession Conventions of the South* (Princeton, NJ: Princeton University Press, 1962).

owners owned between one and four slaves; only 15 percent of De Bow readers fit that criterion. *Review* readers, on average, tended to own larger plantations and more slaves: 46 percent owned between five and nineteen slaves, 21 percent owned between twenty and forty-nine slaves, and 16 percent owned between fifty and ninety-nine slaves. Finally, and perhaps most tellingly of De Bow's editorial focus, *Review* readers made up 4 percent

Table 14: Total Slave Owners in the South and among *De Bow's Review* Readers, 1860 (*N* [%])

State	Total Slave Owners	1–4 Slaves	5–19 Slaves	20–49 Slaves	50–99 Slaves	100+ Slaves
All Alabama	33,730	14,404	13,295	4,344	1,341	346
	(11)	(43)	(39)	(13)	(4)	(1)
Alabama *Review* readers	195	26	60	39	42	29
	(21)	(13)	(31)	(20)	(22)	(15)
All Arkansas	1,149	659	424	56	10	0
	(<1)	(57)	(37)	(5)	(1)	
Arkansas *Review* readers	21	9	8	2	2	0
	(2)	(43)	(38)	(10)	(10)	
All Florida	5,152	2,233	2,111	603	158	47
	(2)	(43)	(41)	(12)	(3)	(<1)
Florida *Review* readers	29	5	8	9	3	4
	(3)	(17)	(28)	(31)	(10)	(14)
All Georgia	41,084	17,534	17,187	5,049	1,102	212
	(13)	(43)	(42)	(12)	(3)	(<1)
Georgia *Review* readers	79	10	32	21	13	3
	(8)	(13)	(41)	(27)	(16)	(4)
All Louisiana	22,033	10,235	7,873	2,349	1,029	547
	(7)	(47)	(36)	(11)	(5)	(<1)
Louisiana *Review* readers	106	22	30	20	19	15
	(11)	(21)	(28)	(19)	(17)	(14)
All Mississippi	30,943	12,689	12,359	4,220	1,359	316
	(10)	(41)	(40)	(14)	(4)	(<1)
Mississippi *Review* readers	122	14	3	28	31	16
	(13)	(11)	(27)	(23)	(25)	(13)
All North Carolina	34,658	16,071	14,522	3,321	611	13
	(11)	(46)	(42)	(10)	(2)	(<1)
North Carolina *Review* readers	14	3	5	3	1	2
	(1)	(21)	(36)	(21)	(7)	(14)
All South Carolina	26,701	10,017	11,392	3,646	1,197	449
	(9)	(38)	(43)	(14)	(5)	(2)
South Carolina *Review* readers	151	21	54	31	21	19
	(16)	(14)	(36)	(21)	(14)	(13)
All Tennessee	36,844	19,179	14,553	2,550	335	47
	(12)	(52)	(40)	(7)	(1)	(<1)
Tennessee *Review* readers	76	14	29	1	10	2
	(8)	(18)	(38)	(25)	(13)	(3)
All Texas	21,878	11,345	8,373	1,827	282	54
	(7)	(52)	(38)	(8)	(1)	(<1)
Texas *Review* readers	47	8	23	1	2	2
	(5)	(17)	(49)	(23)	(4)	(4)
All Virginia	52,128	25,355	20,996	4,917	746	114
	(17)	(49)	(40)	(10)	(1)	(<1)
Virginia *Review* readers	67	11	34	12	8	2
	(7)	(16)	(51)	(18)	(12)	(3)
Total southern slave owners	307,205	139,853	123,378	33,044	7,053	2,358
	(100)	(46)	(40)	(11)	(3)	(<1)
Total slave owner *Review* readers	932	143	432	194	152	94
	(100)	(15)	(46)	(21)	(16)	(910)

Source: Composite Census Records, 1850–1860; US Census Office, *Eighth Census of the United States, 1860* (Washington, DC: US Government Printing Office, 1864).

of the South's 2,358 planters who owned more than one hundred slaves in 1860. In Alabama, 8 percent of the 346 largest owners subscribed to the *Review.* At a time when only 2.5 percent of all southerners possessed more than fifty slaves and the average slaveholder owned ten slaves, the average *Review* reader possessed forty-one slaves, and almost 27 percent of its readers owned more than fifty slaves. Articles on slave management, the role of overseers, and commercial growth appealed to the largest plantation owners in the South. Joshua and Mayham Ward of Georgetown, South Carolina, inherited five rice plantations with over eleven hundred slaves from their father, Joshua John Ward. The Wards attempted to operate their rice empire using strict business practices as prescribed by De Bow but admitted that it was difficult to control the hourly routines of slaves. Despite these problems, the five plantations produced 4.4 million pounds of rice in 1860. Another reader, Meredith Calhoun, a sugar planter from Rapides Parish, Louisiana, purchased fourteen thousand acres from his father-in-law in 1836 and divided the land into four plantations. With the help of hundreds of slaves, he built a large plantation complex and one of the state's most modern sugar mills. He also developed an inland port near Colfax, Louisiana, to ship sugar directly to buyers. Calhoun purchased a newspaper and supported the Democratic Party. He was reputed to be the model for the character Simon Legree in Harriet Beecher Stowe's *Uncle Tom's Cabin.*[30]

De Bow's political ambiguity during the 1840s and part of the 1850s made the *Review* appealing to a wide spectrum of southern readers. Before the collapse of the two-party system in the mid-1850s, *Review* readers with known political affiliations were divided equally among the Democrat and the Whig Parties. As a nominal Democrat with Whig proclivities, De Bow understood how to appeal to both groups. His political education had come from following John C. Calhoun's career, and, much like his idol, he understood the importance of building broad support among southerners. His political vagueness disappeared after the collapse of the Whig Party and the creation of the Republican Party. By 1860 his editorial support of the Democratic Party mirrored the political consolidation occurring among his readers and in the South. Despite the political upheaval caused by slavery and secession, however, he rarely touched on party politics beyond attacking the Republican Party.[31]

De Bow balanced his personal political views with the editorial necessities of the *Review,* and the political diversity of his readers reflected this decision. Unwilling and unable to alienate possible southern readers, he often discussed political topics within the context of economic reform. He made few assumptions about the collective political feelings of his subscribers. Many of his readers assumed probusiness characteristics normally associated with the Whig Party. Although Daniel Pratt and Joseph R. Anderson were prominent Whigs and industrialists, others factory owners such as James H. Cox and Malcolm E. Smith were staunch Democrats. In the agricultural sector, *Review* readers who owned highly mechanized sugar plantations differed politically from cotton planters in Alabama's Black Belt. De Bow understood the economic position of both groups. Some readers like Nathaniel Greene Foster of Madison, Georgia, and Thomas H. Watts of Montgomery, Alabama, began reading the *Review* as Whigs, switched to the American Party in the mid-1850s, and became Democrats by the time of the Civil War. Despite these political changes, both Foster and Watts continued to subscribe to the *Review.* De Bow's editorial vision often transcended political feelings because he embraced prosouthern ideas that both parties advocated and supported.[32]

Aside from common traits such as geographic location and regional identity, many of De Bow's readers shared an inability to pay their subscriptions on time. Despite De Bow's reputation as a successful editor, the lack of paying customers hindered the business affairs of the *Review.* De Bow pleaded with subscribers to pay their bills, reminding them: "The first necessity of such a journal is money, . . . [and] the experience of ten years has enabled the editor to acquire facilities possessed by few, if any others." His readers responded occasionally to his requests, but poor bookkeeping made it difficult to track readers. One Alabama subscriber admitted personal embarrassment for neglecting his bill and enclosed ten dollars and a note praising De Bow. Aaron V. Brown, an ex-governor of Tennessee, wrote De Bow a personal apology and included money for two unpaid years. In frustration, De Bow reprinted an article by the *New York Mirror* that blamed southerners for neglecting their own writers and periodicals. The prosouthern editor of the *Mirror* noted that he often received "an unremitting shower of public and private praise from the South, accompanied with an unremitting neglect to subscribe and pay for the paper." De Bow felt proud of his work and reminded readers of its uniqueness in the South. Reader apathy bothered him because he felt that it reflected on the *Review.* In late 1854 he asked: "Should the planter or the manufacturer, the merchant or the railroad advocate, or shareholder deriving benefit, direct or even indirect, from the labors which have been performed, not cheerfully appropriate a modicum of that benefit to the support of those labors?" Subscription problems plagued De Bow throughout the *Review*'s run, and, although he overcame these issues, they marked the South's continued inability to support internal literary projects.[33]

As southerners waited for political events to unfold in 1860, De Bow continued to inform and manipulate them with the *Review.* His years of service to the economic growth of the South had shifted to include a rabid distrust and dislike of the North and an almost complete loyalty to southern institutions. As had happened many times in the past, his readers responded favorably to shifts in his editorial tone. A reader in Raleigh, North Carolina, claimed: "There is no man who deserves more of the gratitude of the whole South than you do." Another reader likened the *Review* to the Holy Gospel because it provided "life and light to the rights and institutions of the South." But perhaps the most insightful and prophetic feedback De Bow received came from a reader in Columbus, Georgia, who rightly saw looming sectional conflict in the nation's immediate future and promised De Bow: "I am highly pleased with the strong Southern stand you have taken, and for one, am willing to go with you *any length in that direction.* Your *Review* is by far the most thorough expounder and defender of our political rights, and as a Southerner, I feel grateful to you." De Bow hoped that many more of his readers would be willing to make similar vows of loyalty to the South and to the *Review* as the presidential election approached in 1860.[34]

6

War Tests De Bow's Theories and Patience

On December 20, 1860, the recording secretary of the Convention of the People of South Carolina marked 169 ayes for secession and nary a nay against disunion. Although there had been moderate opposition to immediate secession in the state, the lack of a single dissenting vote proved that the issue of slavery had narrowed regional interests and hardened personal viewpoints in South Carolina. De Bow felt great pride in his home state's unity as he watched the proceedings in downtown Charleston. Forty years before, and a few blocks away from Institute Hall, where delegates gathered to sign the secession ordinance, Garret and Mary Bridget De Bow had given birth to James in the midst of a financial panic and a sectional crisis that divided the nation and isolated Charleston. De Bow's attachment to the city never waned, and his triumphant return as a leading fire-eater sparked personal memories of past successes and failures. He hoped that others understood his sacrifice for the southern cause and that new readers would support the *Review* as a patriotic gesture. His personal life and professional career were now inextricably linked to the existence of a southern nation.[1]

The editorial tone of the *Review* began to shift in early 1861 in hopes of swaying moderate southerners who might otherwise block immediate secessionists from forcing their states out of the Union. Antisecession demonstrations in Richmond, western Virginia, Florida, and Georgia's Cotton Belt made De Bow anxious to find sympathetic voices that resonated in these areas. He directed exclusively at southerners articles that highlighted the positive qualities of regional independence and the negative ramifications of remaining in the Union. Robert M. T. Hunter, an ex-senator from Virginia, warned readers that they would become an oppressed minority if they failed to leave the Union. Henry A. Wise, an ex-governor of Virginia and a staunch fire-eater since the creation of the Republican Party, reminded readers in the Upper South that the Underground Railroad had cost them millions of dollars in lost property and then listed twenty-eight additional acts of northern aggression against southern interests. Major W. H. Chase, a railroad agent and an officer in the Florida militia, examined the commercial advantages of secession and believed that southern independence could be achieved without bloodshed because the South had the constitutional right to leave the Union. The *New York Times* republished Chase's *Review* article, noting that it came from "one of the most respectable and widely-known gentlemen in the southern country."[2]

De Bow also used the specter of racial equality as a tool to solidify regional unity. Edmund Ruffin warned that northern abolitionists would descend on the South and enslave poor whites. Another *Review* contributor believed that northerners wanted to conquer the South by "elevating the negro slave to an equality with the white man." De Bow used racial fear to galvanize white supporters and to mend, or at least obscure, internal divisions that existed among southerners. Racial equality strengthened the collective identity of white southerners because it went beyond simple discussions of slavery—an antislavery southerner could harbor racist feelings despite opposing human bondage. De Bow reminded readers that a new southern nation would become a racial sanctuary that protected their rights and natural cultural superiority. He wanted to forge the facade of a unified South using slavery and race as its foundation. The North represented a direct threat to southern institutions, and De Bow reminded subscribers: "Never was the South so nearly united as at present, and the day of her deliverance from an insolent and vexatious sectional tyranny is evidently at hand." The appearance of a cohesive South intrigued De Bow as much as it would future postbellum New South boosters. Yet, like theirs, his vision of regional unity existed only in the minds of those unwilling to see and accept internal dissent in the South.[3]

The feelings of *Review* readers reflected larger internal divisions about secession and disagreement over De Bow's role as a fire-eater. In January 1861 he inexplicitly published three letters that highlighted internal dissension among southerners. A subscriber in Travis, Texas, lauded De Bow for his work and sent him extra money as a contribution to the southern cause. Another reader in Uniontown, Alabama, felt that disunion hurt the South and asked De Bow to cancel his subscription until the threat of war passed.

A third reader in Memphis, Tennessee, chastised De Bow for publishing "articles so inveterately inimical to our Union—and that at a crisis so perilous—that every true patriot should stand by it": "I cannot but feel disinclined any longer to continue my subscription." Despite publishing these letters, De Bow worried that such conflicting emotions would hamper the southern cause, and he worked harder to ensure great unity among his readers.[4]

As Mississippians prepared to hold their own secession convention in January 1861, De Bow became worried about vocal unionists and cooperationists who opposed immediate secession. Although few knowledgeable observers believed that unionists could block Mississippi from leaving the United States, De Bow visited the state's convention and presented delegates with a palmetto flag and a promise of a "new confederation, [that] shall bring us in safety and honor from the crumbling materials of the old one." He wanted to ensure that Mississippi would be a complete victory for southern nationalists. Despite measurable opposition in the northern part of the state, on January 9, 1861, Mississippi's delegates voted 85–15 to secede from the Union. Ethelbert Barksdale, a *Review* reader and the editor of the *Jackson Mississippian,* rejoiced that his state had followed South Carolina. As a vocal fire-eater himself, he had often taken advantage of De Bow's willingness to share information and ideas by borrowing articles from the *Review* to sway his state's newspaper readers and promote their shared interest in the creation of a southern nation.[5]

Residents of Alabama also began preparing for their convention in January with similar internal divisions about secession. The typical "straight-out" delegate who supported immediate secession and the typical Alabama *Review* reader had much in common. They mostly lived in the Black Belt counties of southern and central Alabama, invested heavily in land and slaves, and lived near railroads. These areas had supported the Whig Party during the 1840s, investing heavily in internal improvements, commerce, and many of De Bow's other basic economic tenets. In comparison to cooperationists and unionists in northern Alabama, "straight-out" delegates had similar economic profiles with all known *Review* readers from the state. The average secessionist delegate possessed $26,270 in real property and $60,523 in personal property and owned 32.5 slaves, whereas the typical cooperationist held $16,388 in real property and $26,304 in personal property and owned 15.9 slaves. The average *Review* reader from Alabama held $40,329 in real property and $69,456 in personal property and owned 46.3 slaves. By the late 1850s De Bow had directed much of his editorial content at wealthy planters and professionals who supported southern institutions because they had benefited most from them. He offered them ways of improving their personal portfolios, and they responded by supporting the *Review*.[6]

Although De Bow did not attend Alabama's convention in early January 1861, the conflict over secession pitted *Review* readers there against one another, despite their similar backgrounds and interests. Thomas Hill Watts, a wealthy lawyer and planter who had invested heavily in factories and railroads in his native Montgomery, emerged as a leading immediate secessionist at the convention. Watts and William L. Yancey worked together in the hopes of ensuring victory at the state convention. Unsure of immediate secession, Robert S. Jemison Jr., another planter and industrialist who read the *Review*, opposed Watts and Yancey as the leading cooperationist in the state. Watts and Jemison were the wealthiest delegates at the convention and the type of reader that De Bow coveted. Both men had diversified portfolios that included large plantations, hundreds of slaves, and investments outside the agricultural sector. Their personal feelings about secession mirrored larger divisions among *Review* readers. Watts helped Yancey attack cooperationists by questioning their loyalty, while Jemison wondered aloud whether they planned to have a bloody statewide purge of anyone who opposed immediate secession. Despite Jemison's objections and significant opposition from residents in northern Alabama, on January 11, 1861, convention delegates voted 61–39 to leave the Union. A defeated Jemison returned home to his plantation in rural Tuscaloosa, while Watts remained in Montgomery and prepared for war.[7]

In late January 1861 De Bow traveled to Louisiana's convention because he now understood that each southern state had a sizable contingent of men who opposed secession. Sugar planters who benefited from protective federal tariffs and merchants in New Orleans who thrived on northern connections along the Mississippi River posed the most likely risk to immediate secession because it threatened to disrupt their lives and livelihoods. De Bow attended the convention ready to use his personal connections from his many years of living in New Orleans to ensure a certain victory. Lincoln's election, however, had done much to solidify disunionist feelings in the state, and delegates voted 113–17 to join the southern confederacy. Furthermore, any worries that secession would damage the pace of commerce in the state seemed far-fetched as ships from every nation but the United States lay docked along New Orleans's lower levee in late 1861. Proud of her husband's accomplishments in Louisiana, Martha De Bow wrote him: "I have no ambition so great as that to see my husband become the acknowledged prince of the world."[8]

Strong resistance to secession in eastern Tennessee worried De Bow because the state represented the geographic center of a possible southern nation. Spurred on by charismatic unionist leaders such as William G. "Parson" Brownlow, the editor of the *Knoxville Whig* and a prominent Methodist preacher, many residents in eastern Tennessee felt as strongly about blocking secession as planters in western Tennessee felt about supporting the disunionist cause. De Bow had met Brownlow at the 1857 Knoxville Commercial Convention and knew not to underestimate his opponent. Like De Bow, Brownlow supported slavery and diversified regional economic development, but, unlike De Bow, he believed that regional reform could be done within the confines of the United States. Brownlow had sparred with John Mitchel, the Irish-born editor of the *Southern Citizen* and a *Review* subscriber, when Mitchel drew parallels between the Irish independence movement and the South's secessionist cause. Brownlow's nativist and unionist tendencies created enough of a backlash to force Mitchel to leave the state. De Bow feared that Brownlow could divide Tennessee and make the creation of a southern confederation more difficult. In February 1861 it seemed as if that scenario had come true when unionists and cooperationists in eastern and middle Tennessee won a legitimate statewide referendum against secession. Eventually, it took a second rigged vote under the supervision of Governor Isham Harris to guarantee Tennessee's future in the Confederacy. That day became doubly special for De Bow when he learned that Martha had given birth to James Jr. in Nashville. Excited by the news, De Bow wrote a friend about the birth, expressing hope that "the young De Bow in recompense perhaps of his father's long service in the cause is a born citizen of the Southern Republic, upon whose escutcheon God willing he will make his mark."[9]

On February 4, 1861, when the Provisional Confederate Congress met for the first time in Montgomery, Alabama, De Bow's vision of a southern nation had finally come to fruition. Though he had joined the movement late in comparison to other fire-eaters such as William Yancey, De Bow had quickly become a key supporter. Now he wanted to help his new nation in any way he could. The tone in Montgomery, however, quickly turned against many of the fire-eaters who had helped the South get to nationhood. It was recognized by many southern leaders that moderate political choices could entice the Upper South to join the Confederacy. De Bow, for one, was unfazed by this political shift toward the center because the *Review* had taught him how to balance his sectional rhetoric with the political reality of a divided South. Yancey, Rhett, and other fire-eaters had never cared enough to develop a similarly nuanced approach, and they quickly lost status in the Confederacy. De Bow approved of the political choices made in Montgomery. He believed that the Confederate Constitution adequately protected slavery and secured the personal rights of white southerners. Many of his readers and personal friends accepted high-level positions in the Confederate government. He had worked with the newly elected Confederate president, Jefferson Davis, during Franklin Pierce's administration and believed that "President Davis is endowed by nature with many heroic qualities which fit him for the great position now assigned to him by history as the second father of his Country." Alexander Stephens, the vice president of the Confederacy, had been De Bow's first paying subscriber in 1846, and the newly appointed Attorney General Judah Benjamin, Secretary of the Treasury Christopher G. Memminger, and Secretary of War LeRoy Pope Walker had been loyal subscribers to the *Review* since the 1850s. De Bow left Montgomery satisfied with his new nation and used the *Review* to reprint "Old King Cotton" and the "Ballad for the Young South" as the poetic axis for a new southern nation that embraced the best of its past and its future.[10]

Unfortunately, the excitement of Montgomery and the subsequent birth of the Confederacy quickly became overshadowed by events in Charleston Bay in March 1861. After South Carolina left the Union in December 1860, Union major Robert Anderson evacuated less-secure Fort Moultrie for the more isolated Fort Sumter, an unfinished fortress in the middle of Charleston Bay. South Carolina troops occupied Fort Moultrie and later turned away a federal supply ship en route to Fort Sumter. De Bow had recently published a *Review* article about Charleston Bay and understood the strategic and tactical value of Fort Sumter. In April 1861 Lincoln ordered that more supplies be sent to federal troops, recognizing that this action might elicit a southern reaction. On April 12, 1861, four *Review* readers started the chain of events that led to the beginning of the Civil War: President Jefferson Davis ordered Secretary of War LeRoy Pope Walker to command Confederate general P. G. T. Beauregard to give permission to Edmund Ruffin to fire the first cannon at Fort Sumter. De Bow enjoyed watching southern troops bombard and capture Fort Sumter within a day. He confidently worried that a quick southern victory might hurt the South because "old channels of trade would revive, agents of northern manufactures would infest our cities . . . and forever prostrate those incipient manufacturers which are now under the impulse of patriotism and the public want, springing up in every part of the South." Ironically, when later recalling these early days of the war, De Bow admitted "how little preparation had been made by her [the South] for such event."[11]

The northern writer Charles G. Leland, upset about De Bow's role in the secession crisis, wrote a damning article that highlighted how he felt about the fire-eater and the *Review*. The editors of the *Continental Monthly*, a journal dedicated to literature and national affairs, published the harsh three-page tirade, in which Leland accused De Bow of being biased and boastful. He thought that the *Review's* editorial tone had the "heavy, clumsy ring of the great cracked bell of De Bow." He pointed out what he saw as the *Review* editor's intellectual dishonesty: "Unfortunately the character of De Bow as a deliberate and accomplished liar, and the exposure of his infamous falsification of statistics, have somewhat sunk the character of his 'Review, Industrial Resources, etc,' out of Dixie, where, only, due honor is paid to those who are like him." And he went on to criticize the *Review* itself and, through it, southerners generally: "The magazine is, however, as a whole both curious and characteristic. It shows, as in a mirror, the enormous ambition, the uneasy vanity, the varnished vulgarity of the Southerner, his claims to scrupulous honor, outflanked and contradicted at every turn by an innate tendency to exaggerate and misrepresent, and his imperfect knowledge employed as a basis for the most weighty conclusions." In Leland's mind De Bow had ceased being a clear-thinking observer of the South and had devolved into an apologist who supported southern institutions, regardless of merit or function. Although De Bow would have denied such accusations in 1861, he later admitted that at the time his editorial vision had been clouded by southern nationalism.[12]

Indeed, because De Bow had overconfidently lulled readers into believing in the power of cotton, few southerners had weighed the economic implications of independence in April 1861. When in July 1860 William Gregg had used the *Review* to question the South's preparedness for true economic independence beyond cotton production, De Bow dismissed his concerns. Later, in November 1860, the *Charleston Mercury* captured the South's collective hubris when it noted that cotton served as the best way to control the North and Europe. Cotton had created thousands of fortunes in the South, and few white southerners had reason to doubt that southern independence would change their condition. De Bow felt confident that war would force southerners to harvest natural resources, build factories, and tap into an entrepreneurial spirit that had been corrupted by northerners. Southerners, he argued, could use cotton profits to replace northern capital and continue to diversify the South's economy. This had been his creed since 1846, and he now saw an opportunity to reap the profits of his editorial work. No longer, in his mind, would an estimated $100 million a year in capital flow north. He boasted that southern cotton factories could produce 400,000 yards of cloth per day and fund new projects for the Confederacy. Like many southerners, he also assumed that cotton would produce needed diplomatic recognition for the Confederacy. He mocked Lincoln's expressed doubts that Europeans would support a proslavery regime and the loss of cotton and wondered: "Is there any man . . . insane enough to suppose Great Britain will tolerate such a prohibition [on cotton] for a moment."[13]

De Bow's relentless use of statistics and rhetoric to highlight the South's economic progress obscured inherent weaknesses in the region's industrial and transportation sectors. He failed to acknowledge that in 1840 the South had accounted for 20 percent of the capital invested in the American industrial sector but that by 1860 that figure had dropped to below 16 percent. Certainly, the South had enjoyed substantive growth in manufacturing when compared to the rest of the world, but it still lagged behind the North. By the start of the Civil War, southern factories could produce only 233 of the 631 items known to have been fabricated by American manufacturers. And, although thousands of miles of railroad track had been laid in the 1850s, the South's share of the nation's overall mileage had shrunk from 44 percent in 1844 to 35 percent in 1860. Individual state governments had liberalized incorporation laws to encourage railroad development but rarely funded private companies. Southern lawmakers often failed to support projects that crossed state lines. Southern railroads became a fractured, disconnected system without long intraregional trunk lines connecting cities and towns.[14]

An early wartime manufacturing survey in Virginia highlighted modest industrial development in the state and provided De Bow with favorable, yet limited, examples of southern mobilization. Residents in Norfolk and Lexington prepared for war and economic independence by building new factories and encouraging the production of yarn and cloth from home. In the port city of Norfolk the state survey recorded thirteen new factories that produced brass items, leather goods, musical instruments, and cannons. City mills produced an estimated 120 bushels of flour every ten hours, and local millers vowed that they could increase production as demand rose. Norfolk businesses managed to adapt to military demands while continuing to fill basic civilian needs. Likewise, in Lexington, a small town nestled in the Shenandoah Valley, local millers on Buffalo Creek produced enough flour to rename a local road "Sack Road" because of the volume of wagon traffic created by wartime demands. Iron foundries that had existed since the early nineteenth century suddenly increased production to meet the military demands of the Confederacy. Also in Lexington "the family spinning-wheel and loom have been resurrected from their hidden corners, brushed up, and set to work again." De Bow saw these optimistic reports as proof that southerners could meet the challenge of possible wartime shortages. He had never doubted their talent or potential, reminding readers: "Our people . . . have all the energy, industry, and ingenuity which is necessary to success, and are now showing it."[15]

De Bow also used the *Review* as a propaganda tool to laud southern sacrifice and disparage the northern war effort. Early Confederate victories in Kentucky, Missouri, and Virginia inflated his sense of confidence in the South's superior fighting skills. He encouraged patriotic citizens to let their unselfish acts become the "war cry for the whole of the Confederacy." Negative or counterproductive stories needed to be suppressed to maintain southern morale, he believed. Yet his unwillingness to publish critical stories ignored growing problems concerning the value of Confederate treasury notes and the use of counterfeit money. Instead, like many southerners in mid-1861, he believed that sacrifice and perseverance could overcome most obstacles, including the North's numerical advantage in men and materiel. He harped on internal divisions in the North, promising that northern armies would "again and again be scattered as chaff before the wind!" His natural talents as a regional promoter created positive stories for the Confederacy, but his uncritical approach distorted information for unwitting readers who had been isolated by war.[16]

In July 1861 hundreds of southern delegates met at the Convention of the Cotton Planters in Macon, Georgia, to discuss the financial well-being and economic future of the Confederacy. Earlier, in mid-May, the Confederate Congress had passed the Produce Loan Act, which authorized the government to purchase cotton with the intent of making it the fiscal foundation of the Confederacy. De Bow promoted the event and encouraged southerners to think about selling their cotton harvests in exchange for government bonds that yielded 8 percent. At the convention, the prominent industrial promoter and *Review* subscriber Duff Green urged the Confederate government to issue treasury notes backed by cotton and to secure new lines of credit from European lenders. He hoped that new sources of revenue would allow the South to invest in needed railroads and factories. He promised that new markets for southern cotton in Asia, India, and Africa would replenish public and private coffers. Thomas J. Hudson, president of the Macon convention, reminded *Review* readers: "To make the triumph of Southern arms more valuable to the present and future generations, it is necessary that all our efforts should be directed to the development of our great resources." Later, in a letter to De Bow, the Confederate congressman John Perkins of Louisiana linked political freedom to commercial independence and hoped that the South could create a new economic foundation that would reflect its new, distinctive national character. These men, like De Bow, believed that the Confederacy's economy could produce wartime revenue and still fund civilian projects that enhanced the nation's commercial future.[17]

In August 1861 De Bow became an agent for the Produce Loan Office and began to raise money for the Confederacy. The office had been created after the Confederate Congress failed to pass a direct tax bill to fund the war. Christopher G. Memminger, the Confederate secretary of the treasury, predicted that issuing government bonds based on future cotton crops could raise an estimated $150 million annually if agents could entice southern planters to loan their cotton to the government. Memminger hoped that loan agents could then sell the cotton to European buyers and infuse the government with needed revenue. De Bow supported the plan and used the *Review* to endorse it. The *Nashville Union and American* found: "It is gratifying to hear of the appointment to office of such a zealous, uncompromising, thorough-going Southerner as Mr. De Bow." The editors of the *Memphis Daily Appeal* published a similar recommendation of De Bow's talents and estimated that the Produce Loan Office had already generated $30 million by September 1861. Yet this early excitement proved to be premature as rampant inflation and resistant planters who worried about their investments doomed the office's ability to generate revenue. By November 1861 *The Times* of London reported: "As to the produce loan, we suppose every man in the Confederacy, except the Secretary of the Treasury and Mr. De Bow, is conscious of its utter failure." Frustrated by the lack of public support and dwindling resources, De Bow watched northern armies capture immense amounts of cotton while desperate planters smuggled their remaining supply to Europe. He later admitted that he spent more time burning cotton than selling it during the war.[18]

De Bow's conduct as a loan agent came under scrutiny as speculation about his poor performance emerged. Rumors swirled that his management style upset President Davis. The *Nashville Daily Union* speculated that many planters felt pressured to sell their crops to De Bow for fear that he would order "that the torch be applied to [their] crop." John B. Jones, a government employee in Richmond and the future author of *A Rebel War Clerk's Diary at the Confederate States Capital*, accused De Bow of favoritism and mismanagement while in office. Jones hinted that De Bow eventually lost his government position for "alleged irregularities, the nature of which is not clearly stated by the new Secretary of the Treasury." De Bow denied any scandal and continued to travel as a loan agent while still fulfilling his editorial duties. His difficulties with the Produce Loan Office lessened the quality and consistency of the *Review*, however, and, as one newspaper writer observed, it became increasingly difficult to find the *Review* on newsstands.[19]

De Bow's long hours and the constant travel associated with the Produce Loan Office and the *Review* worried his family. Martha kindly blamed the postal system rather than her husband for the lack of letters she received. She became worried when only his traveling trunk and blanket arrived at their Nashville home. He had been detained by supporters and neglected to stop his luggage. Robert Norton, De Bow's uncle in South Carolina, also worried and counseled his nephew about his health and career. One of De Bow's nephews pled with him to reduce his workload, warning: "I think it is time, Uncle James, for you to settle down in some place, for you have been a wanderer all your life." A love of travel and a busy schedule had been hallmarks of De Bow's life since he left Charleston in 1845. War made his life only busier, but he enjoyed the lifestyle and continued to work hard for the Confederacy.[20]

Definitive military victories and high civilian morale reaffirmed De Bow's confidence in the Confederacy after the first year of war. He reminded *Review* readers in Virginia and Kentucky that their sacrifice and gallantry had helped repel invading northern armies. He recognized that the South had only to exist to remain independent and felt confident that southerners could adequately defend their territory from northern troops. He speculated that northern armies would push further into the South and be cut off from their supply lines. Despite recognizing the South's natural defensive position, however, he also hoped that southern troops would invade the North because "its population is a spiritless rabble, who have few arms and know little of their use, and who are endowed with no sense of personal or national honor." Such extreme rhetoric was out of touch with reality.[21]

Because De Bow had spent years reducing northern foes into easily digestible caricatures, he could not accept that the North had the stamina to mobilize and fight a war to defend the Union. He had never contemplated defeat because he believed that God had sanctioned the southern cause and that slavery had been an extension of his will. In De Bow's mind, the South fought to preserve slavery as a southern institution. Lincoln, however, had sidestepped the issue of slavery and used the preservation of the Union as a way to mobilize northern troops and civilians. Wedged between De Bow's belief in the southern cause and his editorial hubris lay doubt—and, perhaps, the truth. Early in 1862 he admitted to his readers: "We cannot conquer the North except by exhausting it, or by stirring up dissension between the northeast, east, and northwest."[22]

The intrusion of northern troops in the Deep South and Union victories in Tennessee and Kentucky in early 1862 further tested De Bow's confidence in the Confederacy. Invading northern armies threatened to disrupt life and business in western Tennessee, northern Mississippi, and coastal Louisiana. One overconfident writer for the *New York Herald* reported: "We have the rebel armies so completely invested that when our heavy blows begin to fall they cannot escape." Southerners became more alarmed when Union general Ulysses S. Grant captured Fort Henry and Fort Donelson in Tennessee and threatened to push further south. De Bow tried to track the movements of both armies but rarely found rumors accurate enough to trust. In one instance, while he was sitting in the lobby of the St. Charles Hotel in New Orleans, cheering soldiers and civilians signaled to him a great southern victory at Pittsburg Landing, Tennessee. Additional rumors indicated that Confederate general P. G. T. Beauregard had been victorious at the Battle of Shiloh and that southern forces stood ready to invade the Ohio River valley. De Bow's initial excitement soon turned to despair, however, when official news sources reported that the Battle of Shiloh had been a Confederate defeat punctuated by high causalities and the death of the popular Confederate general Albert S. Johnston. In the coming days new reports indicated that Union troops had also captured key fortifications along the Mississippi River and the important railroad cities of Huntsville and Decatur, Alabama. De Bow understood that the loss of northern Alabama's two largest towns meant that the enemy now controlled vital junctions of the Memphis and Ohio, Memphis and Charleston, and the Mobile and Ohio railroads. He also recognized that New Orleans's security had been compromised, and he nervously toured the city's defensive works while waiting for more news.[23]

De Bow nevertheless felt confident enough in New Orleans's defensive works to travel to Jackson, Mississippi, to visit wounded troops in city hospitals. He left his personal library and editorial office in the care of a friend during his trip, intending to return in a few days. Yet, while in Jackson, he noticed an influx of refugees streaming into the city. He became further alarmed when a special train carrying the financial assets of New Orleans's banks and financial institutions arrived in Jackson. Although he worried about the accuracy of their information, he nevertheless asked fleeing refugees about the condition of New Orleans. They reported that federal gunboats had breached the city's defensive works and had captured it with little resistance. He continued to question travelers until he felt confident that the city had fallen without a fight. De Bow's frustration and anger over losing the South's most valuable commercial port increased when he realized that his personal and professional belongings had also been lost, signaling, as he later remembered, "the darkest hour of our trials and our peril."[24]

The fall of New Orleans in April 1862 highlighted major deficiencies in the Confederacy's railroad system. Federal troops under General Grant had purposely attacked busy junctions in Tennessee, Mississippi, and Alabama. The Confederacy did not have enough troops to defend its transportation routes or enough supplies to repair any damage inflicted by the enemy. The prewar primacy of cotton in the Deep South meant that most railroads followed commercial routes from inland plantations out to coastal cities. The surrender of New Orleans isolated interior commercial centers and made it difficult to connect with other cities. Half-finished lines, underfunded projects, and civic rivalries hindered the flow of southern transportation. Increased traffic and the lack of repair shops resulted in more accidents, equipment shortages, and crowded cars. These setbacks made it difficult to move troops and supplies. A frustrated De Bow watched southern factories such as the Charlottesville Factory Company in Virginia lie dormant because of "the difficulty in procuring wool and cotton in the transportation from Texas and the South, where both articles are believed to be abundant." De Bow's prewar optimism about the South's railroad system gave way to wartime frustration and anger. On a trip from South Carolina to Mississippi he encountered several overturned railroad cars that had derailed because "track, engines, and cars are all dilapidated, and no time for repairs, and no material to repair with." Unwilling to admit failure in public, he privately confided that soldiers in the field were safer than southern train passengers.[25]

In June 1862 De Bow visited Charleston and became concerned as federal troops under General David Hunter threatened the city. Although Charleston served as an important commercial and transportation hub along the South Atlantic coast, the city also represented the ideological birthplace of the Confederacy and made a tempting target for an image-conscious man such as Hunter. Aware of Charleston's intrinsic political value, and with fresh memories of New Orleans in his mind, De Bow toured the city's defensive works with trepidation and concern. He found that most residents had already fled the city, and he counted seventy shuttered businesses in its busiest commercial district. Food shortages and a growing black market also frustrated him. The federal naval blockade had damaged Charleston's economy and would continue to do so throughout the war. Fears of easy capture, however, disappeared after Confederate troops repulsed Hunter's small army at the Battle of James Island, securing the city until late in the war.[26]

De Bow left Charleston and traveled to Vicksburg, Mississippi, to survey the growing military threat to another important southern commercial center. Unlike Charleston, which had only been threatened by federal troops, Vicksburg had endured direct assaults and cannonades that left many buildings damaged or destroyed. De Bow noticed that only a few stores, homes, and churches remained untouched by the fighting and that most residents, except for soldiers and male slaves, had left the city. As in New Orleans and Charleston, De Bow toured the defensive works around the city and visited the CSS *Arkansas,* a large ironclad ram that had recently attacked and defeated a federal naval squadron on the Mississippi River. He hoped that shipbuilders in Vicksburg could continue building more ironclads and launch a Confederate counterattack to retake occupied river cities. The memory of the surrender of New Orleans and the impending problems of Charleston and Vicksburg prompted De Bow to admit: "The Sea God and the River God have never been our ally in this fight."[27]

Although traveling gave De Bow firsthand knowledge of the South's immediate situation, the disruption of reliable information networks frustrated him because it narrowed his broad worldview. He had spent decades reading the daily newspapers, monthly journals, government reports, and books that shaped his personal and professional persona. The war brought maddening silence. Southern newspapers and journals began to disappear because of the lack of supplies and subscribers. Union troops targeted telegraph wires that had previously tapped out fresh news and dispatches to southern towns and rural areas. De Bow found the persistence of unreliable rumors frustrating. In the early summer of 1862, while on a train to Richmond, he heard a rumor that Confederate general Joseph E. Johnston had won a great victory over General George McClellan's Army of the Potomac on the outskirts of the city. On reaching Richmond, however, he learned that the rumor had been incorrect. Johnston had been wounded in the field, and General Robert E. Lee, a *Review* reader, had assumed command of the Army of Northern Virginia and a dire situation. De Bow spent his time in the city touring military hospitals and visiting with troops. He learned that many government offices had prepared for immediate evacuation as federal troops crept closer to the city. A disheartened De Bow left Richmond fully expecting to hear of the Confederate capital's surrender. When his train pulled into Charlotte, North Carolina, however, he learned that a British fleet had steamed into the Chesapeake Bay and driven the federal army away on behalf of the Confederacy. De Bow left Charlotte overjoyed that Confederate victory had been secured through British intervention. Yet he quickly found out that no British fleet existed and that the story had been false. Frustrated by such inaccurate information, he wondered whether the enemy purposely used misinformation as a weapon against southern morale.[28]

Despite his criticism of possible misinformation campaigns against the South, De Bow used similar scare tactics to remind southern readers of the atrocities that they had narrowly missed by leaving the United States. Early in the war, Lincoln had made it easy for him by enacting martial law and suspending civil liberties as a way of coercing Maryland to remain in the Union. In August 1861 the US Congress passed the First Confiscation Act, which allowed federal troops to seize southern property used to support the Confederacy. De Bow correctly saw this as an attack on slavery and believed that, if enforced properly, the directive could "doom every southern man to pauperism." He reminded readers that they had left the Union to guard against such blatant attacks on property rights. Lincoln's more inflammatory Emancipation Proclamation yielded an even more dire warning from De Bow, who felt that it added a racial element to the conflict and warned: "Henceforth the war assumes a new aspect, and mankind will be shocked by the atrocities which it invites. Nothing in history will furnish a parallel. We have indeed fallen upon fearful times." De Bow urged readers to support the growing northern antiwar movement led by Democrats unhappy with Lincoln's policies. He promised southerners that Clement Vallandigham, a leader of the Ohio Democratic Party and a vocal northern opponent of the war, had the support of 75 percent of all citizens in the Northwest. In De Bow's isolated world such accuracy seemed problematic, but he wanted to give readers positive information, whether it was true or not.[29]

In the condensed May/August 1862 issue of the *Review,* De Bow exhibited a strange sense of confidence that contradicted even his usual level of boosterism. He dismissed the effectiveness of the federal naval blockade and insisted that southern commerce had increased since the war started. He urged southerners to use the defense of Vicksburg as inspiration, not because its residents had successfully resisted northern attacks, but because the city had emerged from federal bombardments unscathed. This information, however, contradicted his earlier reports of the city's almost complete physical destruction. De Bow confidently hoped that more southerners would subscribe to the *Review:* "Money is not scarce. It is plentiful all over the Confederacy." Yet his own finances had become strained after moving his editorial office to Columbia, South Carolina, following the fall of New Orleans. He also found it difficult to reach readers as federal troops occupied increasingly larger amounts of the South. His sense of external confidence belied a great deal of personal apprehension about the future.[30]

De Bow's Review became an early casualty of the war. By August 1862 only 417 of approximately 3,900 readers had paid their subscriptions. Wartime disruptions and the cost of supplies made publishing the *Review* difficult. De Bow could no longer provide information to his readers and still make a profit. Thus burdened by personal debt and consumed with other obligations, he decided in late 1862 to close his editorial office for the duration of the war, with the exception of one issue in 1864. De Bow's adult life had been dedicated to informing southern readers, and now, in their moment of crisis, one that he helped create, his editorial voice went silent. Invading armies made it difficult to get settled in one area long enough to work. The De Bow family shuttled from one safe haven to another. After fleeing Nashville and New Orleans in 1862, Martha and the children moved to Winnsboro, South Carolina, then to Jackson, Mississippi, and then Selma, Mobile, and Uniontown, Alabama, before settling in Columbus, Mississippi, at the home of a friendly planter. Late in the war the family moved back to Winnsboro, where they lived until April 1865.[31]

As De Bow toured the South in late 1862 his personal feelings about wartime suffering became more acute. Upset about the lack of foreign intervention on behalf of the Confederacy, and worried by a noticeable drop in southern morale, he shared his concerns with Mississippi governor John J. Pettus. While the two men stood on the steps of the statehouse in Jackson, a nearby city arsenal blew up, killing dozens of civilians and soldiers. De Bow ran to the scene of the explosion and witnessed a "shocking sight [of] . . . arms, legs, heads, and mutilated bodies of men, women, and children scattered in every direction." The ensuing fire destroyed the railroad depot, multiple stores, and the warehouses of the Vicksburg Railroad. This disaster depressed De Bow, as did the city's shortage of coats and blankets as winter approached. A month later he visited Selma, Alabama, and, although he found it alive with industry and business, he recognized that much of the South still suffered from wartime shortages. Although De Bow enjoyed his brief visit to Selma, he lamented: "Santa Claus makes but sparing visits to the children, and is gingerly of his offerings. Pleasant and joyous faces are rare, and boys must be content with very sober frolicking. We are not like the enemy, to fiddle while Rome burns." Even news of a Confederate victory at Fredericksburg, Virginia, could not shake De Bow from his personal despair. He had been one of the most vocal fire-eaters to call for war, and in early 1863 he still heartily supported the southern cause, but in two years he had lost his Nashville home, his personal library and editorial office in New Orleans, the security of his family, and the *Review*.[32]

The plight of displaced southerners and wartime refugees also tormented De Bow throughout the war. Thousands of white southerners lost their homes and property as invading Union troops occupied new territory. De Bow admitted in a postwar article that he had never thought about the personal sacrifice created by war. He watched as friends and family fled their homes and lost their property. He helped arrange transportation and housing for displaced residents after Union troops occupied Jackson in May 1863. Remaining city residents learned that federal troops had burned most of the major buildings, factories, and bridges in the area. This set in motion another large-scale migration of southerners searching for solace and safety. De Bow watched helplessly as they suffered, conceding: "Depression is wide-spread. . . . [T]he country is overrun with refugees from Mississippi, but where will they go and how be entertained?" These negative reports had a corresponding negative influence on soldiers and civilians alike. Desertion rates in the Confederate armies increased as soldiers worried about their homes and families, and, for civilians like De Bow, the personal suffering erased any romantic notions that they had about life in a new southern nation.[33]

The federal naval blockade increased the suffering of southern civilians as the war progressed. Early in the war Union general Winfield Scott, a Virginian who rejected secession, implemented the Anaconda Plan, which called for the Union navy to blockade the South's sea and river ports, preventing commercial dealings with the outside world, and thus slowly strangling the Confederacy. De Bow had failed to anticipate this possibility when he promised prewar readers that cotton would guarantee the South's future as an independent nation. Additionally, he did not predict that foreign factory owners had stockpiled substantial cotton reserves after successive bumper crops and low prices in the late 1850s; nor did he anticipate the emergence of Indian and Egyptian cotton. In his haste to build a southern nation, he became a reductionist who saw only what he wanted to see. As recently as August 1861, for example, he had estimated that British factories consumed fifty-one thousand bales of cotton per week and believed that "a persistence in blockading the Southern ports, so as to prevent the egress of cotton, will involve the Lincoln Administration in a war with Great Britain." Like most southerners, he believed that Great Britain, France, or Russia would intercede on behalf of the Confederacy because of economic or humanitarian reasons. Frustrated by international politics and the realization that no relief was coming, De Bow lashed out at Europe, oddly hoping: "If a reunion with the North ever takes place, the South would be heartily prepared to join in a war that might be undertaken against these powers." By mid-1863 it became clear to him that King Cotton existed only on paper and that "our cotton was not indispensably necessary to [foreign] nations, and it did not confer on us the power to dictate relations and policy."[34]

Even more devastating, the South's prewar fixation on cotton production limited the development of other crops that could feed a hungry nation. Although De Bow had during much of the 1850s called for agricultural diversity, he continued to pander to cotton planters, who had limited interest in staple crops such as wheat or corn. The states of the Deep South had become overly reliant on commercial farms in the Upper South, the border states, and the Northwest for their food supply. This reliance on outside food production created an acute food shortage for many soldiers and citizens of the Confederacy. As the war progressed and fighting limited the Upper South's crop production, southern military planners became increasingly interested in the relatively untouched fields of Alabama. De Bow had assessed Alabama's agricultural potential, and it sparked hope in him, as was evident in his description of what he saw on the way to Selma: "Crops on the route everywhere beyond parallel; equaling the fair valley of the Nile. This portion of Alabama will alone feed the army of the Confederacy. Our greatest apprehension is now at rest." He began to tour the state's Black Belt region, but he also worried that its bountiful fields would tempt enemy troops.[35]

On April 24, 1863, after a day of surveying crops in Marengo County, Alabama, De Bow received word that enemy troops had been spotted nearby. He made his way to the relative safety of Selma to escape them but missed an outbound train to Mississippi that was later captured by federal cavalry. On a later train back to Mississippi he saw burned bridges, destroyed trains, and torn-up railroad tracks. This raid made him more frustrated that the South did not have enough troops to defend its fields, railroads, and towns. He questioned why so many southerners had been made exempt from military service, estimating that 800,000 men between the ages of twenty-one and forty-five remained civilians. He seemed to ignore that, at age forty-three, he could have easily picked up a rifle and fought for the cause he so believed in. De Bow returned to Alabama and continued to wage his personal war against the North as a civilian observer of the southern home front. He hoped that Alabama's relatively untouched farmland could infuse the Confederacy with needed supplies and a corresponding boost in southern morale. The war was beginning to affect more than just the soldiers in the field.[36]

Women helped stabilize the South's home front by assuming meaningful roles as military service pulled more men away from their families. As a man who remained a civilian for the duration of the war, De Bow recognized and applauded their service to the southern cause. He reminded male readers that women had quietly sacrificed for the Confederacy: "Woman performs her mission still. Her smiles are for the brave, her scorn for the timid. In tears, but with prayers and blessings, she sends forth son, lover or husband, and glories in the part they are to take in maintaining the liberties and honor of their country." Southern women spun cloth on old looms, molded soap from animal fat, and sacrificed their finest dresses for bandages. They did this, De Bow reminded readers, while maintaining their family's business or farm. He marveled that, despite wartime shortages, women kept their children neatly dressed and clean and could make a bonnet last longer with a simple twist or turn. The lack of food and supplies made southern women expert barterers too, and De Bow applauded them for reusing old items rather than craving new ones. Women also became victims of displacement and harsh treatment as northern troops moved deeper into the southern interior. De Bow believed that these sacrifices made women on the home front as important as soldiers in the field. Mrs. C. M. Jordon of Lynchburg, Virginia, sent De Bow two patriotic odes promising that women would continue to fight and not let future generations forget about the martyred heroes of the Confederacy. Struck by Jordan's sentiments, De Bow later remarked that the odes reflected "the spirit and fire which glow in them [southerners], and which distinguish our Southern women everywhere."[37]

The news of Confederate troops in Maryland and Pennsylvania and the successful defense of Vicksburg in June 1863 inspired De Bow to think optimistically about the future of the South. In his mind southerners had endured years of fighting, shortages, and sacrifice while northerners watched the war from afar. With the war now heading north, he wanted Confederate general Robert E. Lee to "repay with interest the injuries done in Mississippi and Louisiana." He gleefully noted northern panic when southern troops made their way toward Washington, DC, and Philadelphia. De Bow believed that a good harvest, a developing industrial sector, and staunch civilian support ensured ultimate victory for the Confederacy. But then news of Confederate defeats at Gettysburg and Vicksburg reached him in mid-July 1863. Especially disheartened by the surrender of Vicksburg, he lamented: "We have lost the Gibraltar of the Southwest, and the enemy will derive a moral strength from the conquest which will be equivalent to a dozen victories." He recognized that federal troops had divided the Confederacy. On July 17, 1863, he witnessed thousands of people leaving Mississippi and privately conceded that the state had been lost to the enemy. For the first time, in either private or public correspondence, De Bow acknowledged that the South had misjudged the North's will to fight and that he dreaded the idea of total defeat.[38]

De Bow managed to cobble together enough paper, ink, and articles to release a combined July/August 1864 edition of the *Review.* John Tyler Jr., a regular prewar contributor, wrote a scathing article blaming Confederate politicians for failing to connect the interests of southern and western farmers. He wondered why westerners had chosen to ally themselves with northeastern factory owners instead of southern planters. For years De Bow had warned readers of this potential alliance, but in 1864 he proclaimed: "If there ever was a good and sufficient reason for reconstruction with the North-west, there are now a thousand reasons otherwise. *It is too late!*" The loss of western support frustrated him because he recognized the potential strength of a regional alliance against northern interests. Although in 1864 he considered western markets forever lost to the South, postbellum southerners would again find themselves divided by the forked road of northern industrialism and western agriculture. Unlike De Bow, however, the next generation of southern boosters would guide their fellow citizens toward the special interests of northern industrialists.[39]

In the same 1864 issue of the *Review*, De Bow wrote a series of articles that attempted to rally southern feelings about the war. He pled with southern writers and orators to galvanize support for the Confederacy: "War is not an affair entirely of the sword. . . . [T]he pen is sometimes mightier." He lamented that southern writers had not produced a single song or book of lasting quality during the war. He then spoke directly to *Review* readers and asked them not to hoard money or supplies. Military failure, he promised, would lead to northern atrocities and a type of tainted reunification that he equated to a father shaking the hand of his murdered child and then becoming friends with his son's killer. De Bow's blind hatred of the North made him incapable of even contemplating southern defeat, despite growing evidence to the contrary.[40]

Critics of De Bow's editorial biases and sectional prejudices reminded readers of his past mistakes and what they had cost the South. J. M. Shackleford of the *Nashville Daily Union* accused him of promoting a monarchical ruling class in the South and issued a stern warning that he should be "rammed down a big cannon": "Should [he] be executed without the benefit of a clergy [*sic*], he could not object upon his theological doctrines. To catch and punish the scoundrel, would, I have no doubt, be agreeable to God, and all good men. But there is catching before shooting and hanging." A writer for the *Daily National Republican* in Washington, DC, wondered why King Cotton had disappeared during the war and jokingly asked readers to note that cotton "is not by any means the king we were so industriously taught to believe by the false figures and lying assertions of the De Bows of the South." In early 1864 false reports emerged in the North that Jefferson Davis had ordered De Bow arrested for rejecting the political power of cotton in an article. A writer for the *Union County Star and Lewisburg Chronicle* confessed that, if indeed De Bow had become critical of the South in an article, then it reflected his honesty on the subject. The *Western Reserve Chronicle* in Warren, Ohio, published an article that compared De Bow to Galileo for his willingness to be honest about the South's collapsing fortunes, adding: "The defection of the strongest and most rabid partisan of Southern theories, was a mutinous ebullition not dreamed of, by either friend or foe of the rotten cotton Confederacy." The power of De Bow's public image still resonated among northern observers, who continued to use him as an easily recognizable measurement of southern extremism.[41]

As the war wore on, De Bow's southern chauvinism turned to bitter criticism about regional economic failure. He condemned state governments that had failed to develop their own economies. He criticized Charleston's business elite for not expanding the city's commercial and industrial realm. He realized that too much emphasis had been placed on cotton production and manufacturing. Aware that the Confederate government had been forced to establish new factories and mills in the midst of fighting, he later confessed that if the Confederacy had already had an "established diversified industry . . . the contest would have been brief and our independence would have been achieved." He blamed this deficiency on southerners "who have croaked against Southern enterprise, and manufacturing at the South, who are constantly setting forth the idea that our young men will not make merchants . . . or try to become business men": "We repeat, let us beg that class of men to cease their croaking." De Bow did not, however, own up to how much his own sectional croaking had diverted him from promoting a diversified and modern economy in the late antebellum years. He understood that his vision of economic development had been partially flawed because it had devolved too narrowly to a focus on cotton manufacturing, commerce in large commercial ports, and the success of wealthy planters. His interest in reaching out to cotton planters and the wealthy had come at the expense of yeoman farmers and small producers. These mistakes would have to be rectified if the *Review* was to resume publication and regain its status as the South's most prominent economic journal.[42]

By the beginning of 1865, De Bow recognized that southern independence had failed. Although he had promised readers that the southern interior could never be taken by Union troops, he later admitted: "The sad delusion vanished, when in a territory a thousand miles in length, and as much in breadth, armed bands of blue-coats were everywhere discovered, sweeping from the mountain to the sea, from river to river, sacking and plundering and devastating, burning villages and ravaging estates." The surrenders of Wilmington, North Carolina, and Charleston, South Carolina, in February 1865 meant that the South no longer controlled any major Atlantic ports and was isolated from the rest of the world. These losses forced De Bow to look back at the earlier surrenders of New Orleans, Mobile, and Savannah and the South's conduct of the war. In hindsight he believed that the surrender of Vicksburg had "struck a damper to the hearts of thousands, and shook, for the first time, the faith that the success of the cause was predestined." The commercial weaknesses of the South had been exposed by the North's military superiority. The federal naval blockade had caused massive inflation and suffering in the region. The reality of defeat overwhelmed De Bow. Yet thousands of Confederate soldiers continued to march, fight, and die for a doomed cause. Like millions of exhausted southerners, De Bow waited for the end to come and mercifully stop the suffering.[43]

After the military collapse of the Confederacy and the ensuing capture of Jefferson Davis in the late spring of 1865, De Bow returned home to Nashville and began to think about his future. Almost immediately he conceptualized a history of the war from the South's perspective. He believed that such a history would earn him an income, reinsert his name in the public's consciousness, and allow him to "furnish the future historian with material which might otherwise be lost." He desired to shape how Americans viewed and judged the South. The rough outline of the war in his personal notes had a decidedly southern theme that started with an image of a Confederate soldier in full uniform holding a slightly furled flag with a caption that read: "Furl that banner, it is best; For there's not a man to wave it, and there's not one left to love it." He hoped that his sympathetic rendering of the sectional crisis and subsequent war would rehabilitate feelings by creating a common national past of sacrifice and suffering. He urged acceptance on readers: "The struggle is now over, but its deeds belong to the American name. They cannot be obliterated. Let us read of it as of the events of a hundred years ago." Within months of the end of the war, De Bow had already pushed away from an ideological past that threatened to hinder the future of the South.[44]

The wartime loss of the *Review* had taken from De Bow his most prized possession, and after two years of editorial silence he wanted it back. It defined him more than any other accomplishment in his life. As a brand, *De Bow's Review* had become one of the most recognizable names in southern culture. Northerners and southerners had strong and often contradictory feelings about it. That had served him well in the years before the war, but now, after the war, his name had become synonymous with failure, and his current condition seemed to validate that connection. Like the lives of his readers, his life was in disarray. Although he had lost his library, his papers, and the *Review*, thousands of his subscribers had been displaced, ruined, or killed during the war. In Somerville, Tennessee, a brief survey of *Review* readers found that, of eleven prewar subscribers, five had been killed in fighting and one had moved to Memphis. This type of disruption happened in hundreds of towns and cities across the South. Readers struggled to regain a sense of normalcy after four years of fighting, and De Bow wanted to help them. He believed that his ideas—which had been around since 1846—could be recast and reused to guide the South toward regional salvation. Yet, without proper funds, supplies, or readers, the prospect of reopening the *Review* seemed distant. Still, the ideas were there, and they were his. He simply needed to look back at his old ideas to create a New South. As anxious in 1865 as he was in 1845, De Bow returned to New Orleans and began to work on a regional economic journal dedicated to helping southerners embrace industrial development, urban growth, agricultural diversity, and commercial prominence. He hoped that the *Review* would once again become standard reading for southerners interested in improving their region's position within the United States. His future relied on it.[45]

7

The Reformulation of De Bow's Old New South

Like many white southerners in the late spring of 1865, De Bow had to reconcile his feelings about the Confederate defeat with the prospect of rebuilding the South and rejoining the United States. Burned-out cities, wrecked railroads, untended fields, and disconnected commercial routes confronted millions of southerners, both black and white. Hundreds of thousands of southern men had been killed in battle or died of disease, leaving behind displaced widows to tend to their children and family farms or businesses. The reality of slave emancipation and federal occupation proved to be equally daunting for many white southerners. Thousands of ex-slaves stopped working and moved around the South in search of loved ones who had been sold to distant plantations. Like their ex-masters, they remained unsure of the future. Abraham Lincoln's assassination meant that a southerner, Andrew Johnson of Tennessee, assumed the presidency, stoking some hope in the South for a lenient reconstruction of the Union. Eager to restart his postwar life, De Bow swore an oath of allegiance to the United States on July 15, 1865, and filed for a presidential pardon two days later. Although he despised Johnson, De Bow believed that he would offer generous terms that would once again allow the South to reap the "golden fruits of industry, enterprise, prosperity, and cheerful allegiance." On August 29, 1865, President Johnson granted De Bow a full pardon despite objections from those northerners who considered him a traitor. An unnamed editor of the *Washington Standard* hoped that De Bow might be handed over to ex-slaves so that they could "hang up 'de fiddle' . . . at the same time 'hang up De Bow.'"[1]

Many of De Bow's readers also had to reclaim their lives, regardless of social rank or economic position. Like De Bow, they had to move past bitter feelings to begin the rebuilding process. For readers in Richmond, Virginia, a year-long siege by federal troops and a citywide fire in April 1865 left many of their homes and businesses devastated. The city's industrial district had been severely damaged, and warehouses, factories, and mills were left idle. Many of Richmond's business elite were *Review* readers who suffered from the effects of this destruction. In 1860 the average reader in Richmond owned $70,000 in real property and $33,500 in personal property. In comparison, readers in New Orleans possessed $20,000 in real property and $8,000 in personal property, whereas the average *Review* reader held $19,000 in real property and $24,000 in personal property. These men had made Richmond the most industrialized city in the South, and war had destroyed or damaged much of what they had created. John L. Bacon's large grocery warehouse had been confiscated by Confederate officials in 1862 and then destroyed by fire in April 1865. The loss of northern clients during the war closed Joseph Brummel's expansive distillery and mill complex on Seventeenth Street. Lewis Crenshaw had supplied Confederate troops with thousands of blankets and uniforms before fire destroyed the Crenshaw Woolen Mill in 1863. Joseph R. Anderson, perhaps the *Review*'s most successful prewar industrialist, had been wounded in battle and then had his Tredegar Iron Works temporarily confiscated by Union troops. For Roger Pryor, a prominent Richmond editor, the war cost him his freedom when federal troops captured him in 1864. After the war he realized that his future lay elsewhere, and he moved to New York City to start a long legal career. Like De Bow, Pryor had staked his editorial reputation on secession and the defense of slavery, and, like De Bow, he suffered consequences for his role in the war.[2]

Although some subscribers failed to recover from the war, others began to rebuild their lives almost as soon as the *Review* reader James T. Lyons helped surrender Richmond to federal troops on April 3, 1865. Wartime profits allowed Hugh W. Fry to rebuild damaged machinery at the Old Dominion Iron and Nails Company. Despite the loss of slave labor and damage to his equipment, Fry rebuilt a larger factory than he had had before the war. In May 1865 Wellington Goddin used his lucrative career as a real estate agent and auctioneer to open the First National Bank of Richmond, the first bank to operate in the city after the war. Richard B. Haxall quickly reopened his flour mills along the James River and began to hire local residents. Likewise, Abraham and William Warwick invested $50,000 in upgrades to their Gallego Mills Manufacturing Company and reentered the national flour trade as leaders in the field. These *Review* readers, along with hundreds of other merchants, industrialists, and bankers, revived Richmond by simply doing what they had done before the war—investing in the city's commercial and industrial growth for personal and civic gain. Many of these business leaders also helped transition the city back into the Union. In late August 1865 the businessmen of Richmond held a meeting to reaffirm their loyalty to the United States. Attendees chose seven prominent local business leaders to speak on their behalf, and among that elite group were *Review* readers William Macfarland, Richard Haxall, Abraham Warwick, James Lyons, and John S. Caskie. This select group of urban activists had relied on De Bow's commitment to the diversified economic growth of the South, and, like De Bow, they had helped stimulate the prewar development of Richmond. They now took it on themselves to aid in the postwar rebirth of the city. In September 1865 De Bow visited the city and left impressed with the level of activity and progress.[3]

In Alabama, far removed from the devastation of Richmond, *Review* readers relied on similar prewar habits and practices to recover from war. Nathaniel H. R. Dawson, a respected lawyer and politician in Selma, had owned two large plantations, two general stores, and seventy slaves and had served as the president of the Selma Gas Light Company before the war. But slave emancipation and the devastation of war forced Dawson to declare bankruptcy in 1865. Within a few years, however, he had used his legal career as a catalyst for new opportunities and became involved in educational reform, serving on the University of Alabama's board of trustees and as President Grover Cleveland's commissioner of education. For James H. Houston, a middling physician from Woodville, the war created new statewide opportunities that had not existed before the war. His service as an assistant surgeon in the Confederate army broadened his worldview, and after the war he became a founding member of the Alabama State Medical Society and later served as the superintendent of education for Perry County. Despite joining the Republican Party after the war, Houston earned the respect of his community because of his sober professionalism. For Sewall Jones Leach, a New York native who moved to Tuscaloosa in the 1830s, the war added to a lifetime of challenges. After working as a dentist and a jeweler, Leach opened a cotton factory in 1846 and an iron foundry and plow factory in 1852. His businesses thrived until a fire destroyed them in 1859. He opened a cannon foundry during the war and supplied the South with artillery until federal troops destroyed his business in 1864. Undaunted by past setbacks and the war, he then built a factory that produced sorghum mills and castings before selling out and becoming part owner of the Tuscaloosa Cotton Mills. Readers such as Dawson, Houston, and Leach used their prewar skills and knowledge to reinvent themselves after the war. De Bow hoped that these types of readers would continue to subscribe to the *Review* because Alabama had lost many of its young leaders during the war.[4]

The war claimed the lives of subscribers who might have helped guide Alabama beyond its immediate troubles in 1865. Stephen F. Hale, a lawyer and planter from Greene County, Alabama, had left Kentucky in 1837 to become a teacher but eventually entered into law in 1841. Later, Hale fought in the Mexican-American War, served in the Alabama legislature, and represented his congressional district in the Confederate Provisional Congress in February 1861. His success as a lawyer and planter allowed him to build one of the finest homes in Eutaw, purchase twelve slaves, and be appointed to the board of the Carrolton and Eutaw Railroad Company. He served in the Confederate army as a lieutenant colonel of the Eleventh Alabama Infantry Regiment until his death during the Battle of Gaines's Mill outside Richmond on July 18, 1862. As recognition of his service to his community and his sacrifice on the battlefield, the legislature renamed the eastern half of Greene County after Hale in 1867. George C. Whatley, another transplanted Alabamian, used his legal career to invest in a modest plantation and nine slaves in Calhoun County. Like Hale, Whatley served as a representative in the state legislature and invested in local railroads. His status as a planter, lawyer, and businessman made him a natural choice to represent his community at the Alabama secession convention in January 1861. He then served as the captain of Company G in the Tenth Alabama Infantry Regiment until his death during the Battle of Antietam in September 1862. Both Hale and Whatley had become productive citizens in their respective communities by successfully balancing their personal and civic obligations. Their diversified economic portfolios and interests in developing southern institutions would have made them natural leaders in the postwar South.[5]

De Bow toured the South in late 1865 because he wanted to gauge the progress of regional recovery and meet with readers who survived the war. He took a second trip to Richmond and left impressed by the constant sound of construction, an indication to his mind that white southerners wanted to restore what they had lost during the war. And, while he found the railroad connection between Richmond and Columbia, South Carolina, difficult and slow, he refused to blame fellow southerners for his delays. Instead, he accused northern capitalists and the federal government for failing to invest in the South's transportation system. In Charleston he proudly noted that all classes of white citizens worked hard to rebuild their city. He then traveled to Alabama and became excited by progress in Huntsville, Montgomery, and Mobile. During his trip he encountered enthusiastic northern investors with ready money searching for inexpensive land, though he objected to their overconfident manner and rude behavior. This extended trip gave him enough insight into the plight of southerners to inspire him to work harder to reopen the editorial office of the *Review.* It also made him believe that the military occupation of the South hindered regional recovery. Southerners wanted to rebuild their lives, homes, and businesses and be left alone. De Bow had to find a way of assuring southern readers that his economic recovery plan would help them while reassuring northern observers that his ideas were part of a broader national plan.[6]

De Bow needed data to begin the process of understanding what had happened in the past and what needed to be done in the future. Previously unpublished federal reports and census data highlighted inherent shortcomings in the South's economy, which had fallen considerably behind northern industrial innovations despite being technologically advanced in comparison to most nations. De Bow might have refrained from declaring regional economic independence in 1861 after reviewing the industrial returns from the 1860 federal census. At the time he intuitively believed that southern factories had adequately prepared for war and independence, and this sense of regional development lulled him into believing that southern manufacturers could replace items produced by northern suppliers. But what he found in the postwar compilation of industrial statistics shocked him. In comparison with the rest of the nation, the South had actually declined in cotton manufacturing during the 1850s. The number of cotton mills there had remained the same from 1850 to 1860 and accounted for only 15 percent of all mills in the United States in 1860. During the 1850s, New England cotton mills had increased capital investments by 30 percent, spindles by 40 percent, and overall production by 44 percent. By contrast, during the same period, the South had increased its spindle count by 5 percent and accounted for only 6.7 percent of the aggregate value of all cotton goods produced in the United States in 1860. De Bow recognized that war had only exacerbated these regional inadequacies, making true industrial recovery more difficult.

The South had to move quickly to reinsert itself into the national economy or risk becoming a de facto colony of the North.[7]

Other sectors of the South's economy had similar shortcomings in 1860. Only 20 percent of the 398 woolen mills in the United States were located in the South. And, while Rhode Island alone had 57 mills that produced 3,168,500 pounds of wool, all eleven southern states combined had 78 woolen mills that processed 3,590,184 pounds of wool. Between 1850 and 1860 the number of clothing factories decreased in all southern states except for Louisiana, Arkansas, and Florida. Louisiana's 402 percent increase in cloth production accounted for two-thirds of all new southern production in 1860. Only 41 of the nation's 239 firearm factories and 6 of 99 nail forges were located in the South. The South had 24 of the nation's 555 paper plants and produced just 18 percent of the available paper stock in 1860. Likewise, southern coal mining accounted for little of the nation's production despite having an estimated twenty-five million acres in untouched coalfields. The production of southern railroad iron also lagged behind northern competitors by a significant margin. No southern factory could build railroad car wheels, only one produced steel railroad springs, and the South had only one locomotive factory in 1860. Southerners had managed to create a railroad boom during the 1850s without having the means to build their own equipment or mine regional fuel. De Bow failed his readers before the war by allowing them to invest in the most innovative technology of their time but without any corresponding infrastructure to support a modern transportation system. He hoped to rectify that mistake in the postwar years.[8]

Likewise, the political economy of cotton had failed to sustain southern independence or generate foreign recognition for the Confederacy, and De Bow understood that he needed to confront these issues while simultaneously encouraging southerners to plant more cotton. The production of cotton, more than any other crop, offered southern farmers the fastest way to attain needed capital for personal and regional recovery. The war had devastated the South's cotton plantations, commercial networks, and international connections with factory owners. Further, the region had fallen from being the largest global producer of cotton in 1861 to the fifth largest in 1866. English manufacturers had purchased 1.2 billion pounds of southern cotton in 1861, but by 1863 that figure had dropped to 85 million pounds. The wartime naval blockade of the South had allowed India, China, and Egypt to fill European orders and gain a significant share of the global cotton market. De Bow initially estimated that the South's cotton harvest for

1866 would be close to 5 million bales despite the loss of slave labor. He later amended his estimate to 1.5 million bales, a fourth of the 1861 output. But he had woefully underestimated the labor issue and how it would influence cotton production. His sources in southern Alabama reported that a third of all black laborers had deserted cotton plantations around harvest time and that Georgia planters struggled with similar labor shortages. These economic shortcomings translated into racial tension and fear. Fred A. Conkling, a *Review* contributor who presented a paper on cotton and labor at the Statistical Society of New York, warned southern readers that they had to remove ex-slaves from the South and reinvigorate the work ethic of poor whites for cotton to become king once again. He blamed the arrogance of planters who used flawed logic to doom an entire region. De Bow pled with cotton planters to send him information that might help improve future harvests through the better use of technology or the improved management of labor.[9]

Joseph C. G. Kennedy, De Bow's old census nemesis, compiled statistics showing that between 1850 and 1860 southern farmers had essentially ignored De Bow's pleas for agricultural diversity and scientific farming. Much of the South remained underdeveloped and had been unproductive during those years. For every two acres of improved land there remained three acres of unimproved soil. Virginia farmers had cultivated only eleven million of the state's thirty million total acres of potential farmland. While southern wheat production had increased from 2.5 bushels per inhabitant in 1850 to 3.5 bushels in 1860, this growth still fell short of the national average, which had increased from 4.33 bushels per inhabitant to 5.5 bushels. And, even though southern corn production had increased from 184 million bushels in 1840 to 282 million bushels in 1860, the western states had increased yields from 145 to 470 million bushels during the same period. Average southern crop yields had also fallen short of the national average in oats, peas, beans, potatoes, and butter. Although southerners still owned more swine per capita than the rest of the nation, the region's total number of pigs dropped from 215 per inhabitant in 1850 to 175 in 1860. During this same period, southern livestock production increased by 86 percent while that in the rest of the nation rose by 100 percent. Each new acre of cotton, meanwhile, robbed the South of new crops. De Bow's insistence on developing better regional agricultural diversity had been real, but so too had his willingness to enable cotton planters to continue their cycle of producing more cotton so that they could buy more land and slaves. The practices of southern farmers would have to change if they hoped to compete with northern and western farmers, who had fed a nation and an army with food to spare.[10]

Past mistakes and widespread suffering motivated De Bow to prepare the first postwar issue of the *Review* in late 1865. He hoped to reintroduce his basic economic tenets—industrialization, urbanization, commercial development, and agricultural reform—but in a way that resonated among readers in the postwar South. He now hoped to lead the South back into the Union. He collected past payments that were due to him and reestablished old connections with contributors and readers. He hoped that his "After the War Series" would reinsert his ideas in the minds of southerners. Surprisingly, the national press responded favorably to De Bow's return. The *Rochester Republican* remembered his unmatched devotion to economic matters. The *New York Times* believed that he could offer leadership and hoped that he might constitute "a very favorable token of the progress of sound opinion and right purpose in the South." The editor of the *Canton Daily Mail* thought that he could rekindle feelings of progress among southerners. Northerners wanted to put the war behind them, and, regardless of his prior reputation, De Bow offered them a chance to embrace native leadership that southerners might follow. This public support fueled his efforts to restart the *Review*, and he sent out inquiries to postmasters around the South asking about the status of readers. Although many readers had died or been displaced by war, he located enough of them to re-create a short subscription list. He reopened editorial offices in New Orleans and Nashville, with future plans to open new offices in New York; Boston; Washington, DC; Cincinnati; and Charleston. He wanted his ambitious new *Review* to become a journal that touted the economic development of a reunified nation and a healthy South.[11]

In January 1866 De Bow published the first postwar issue of the *Review*. In the first article, "Future of the United States," he conceded the South's complete defeat and rejected the doctrine of secession. The strength of the Union had been tested and had survived. He encouraged southerners to look forward and "put their shoulder to the wheel, intellectually and physically, to redeem—such is the vastness of our resources and the flexibility of our institutions—what has been lost, and remove all traces of the recent calamitous times." Sensing the growing political power of the Radical Republicans in Congress, he pled for sectional harmony and a moderate plan of reconstruction. He reminded southern readers that slavery's destruction had been complete and hoped that "the people of the South, universally, are willing to give a fair and honest trial to the experiment of Negro emancipation, which has been forced upon them." He believed that southerners, more than any other Americans, had "intimate knowledge of negro character, and sympathy with him and his fortunes, which is but the natural result of long and close association."[12]

De Bow went so far as to reject his secessionist past as a political misunderstanding. He claimed that "the political teachers of his youth and early manhood . . . Jefferson, Calhoun, Madison, and McDuffie" had taught him to support states' rights as a logical defense against federal abuses. He explained that states' rights and secession had been used as a threat to create "new understandings and new compacts, in which the rights of all sections would be observed and respected." He denied ever wanting war with the North and saw the conflict as a spontaneous act of political aggression. His reversal shocked the many readers who remembered him as a prominent agitator for war. Yet, for his reformulated economic plan to work and be accepted by readers, past mistakes had to be accounted for and dismissed. He claimed that military defeat had awoken southerners to new feelings of loyalty to the United States despite acknowledging that a year earlier "ninety-nine in the hundred of the Southern people were devoted to the Confederacy, gloried in its achievements, doubted not an instant of its just cause and its eventual triumph." This new passion for reunion had to be rewarded, he argued, because the South wanted to erase the stains of disunion. He promised worried northern readers that southerners understood that "their work was done—the cause had failed—hopelessly, and they acquiesced!"[13]

The demise of the Confederacy had to be explained in a manner that southern readers could accept and understand as truthful and sensitive to their loss. De Bow had contributed to many of the problems that had led the South to war and had later plagued the Confederacy. He decided to clarify his past positions on many topics and explain the causes that led to the South's ruin. This meant that he had to spin negatives into positives and highlight good acts that symbolized a moral yet defeated cause. The shortages created by the federal blockade became the impetus for southern creativity, according to De Bow. He recalled how every scrap of paper from old books and ledgers became new writing paper, and he applauded the use of goose quill pens. Instead of repairing damaged or lost goods, people simply did without them as a patriotic sacrifice. In his overly romantic memories of the war, De Bow forgot the negative aspects of trying days and instead recalled: "The people of the Confederacy kept up a cheerful and hopeful spirit, and felt the utmost confidence of eventual triumph." Eager to remind postwar southerners of wartime camaraderie, he published an article by George Fitzhugh that urged southerners to forgo past rivalries and embrace the common cause of regional improvement.[14]

Looking back at the weaknesses and failures of the Confederacy, De Bow recognized that a leadership void had made it difficult to overcome economic and military shortages. President Jefferson Davis's stubbornness, imperial bearing, overconfidence, and contempt for others, according to De Bow, made it difficult to work with him. Vice President Alexander Stephens, perhaps the ablest man in the South in De Bow's mind, proved to be too frail to fulfill his duties. De Bow believed that the Confederate Congress had little talent, wasted too much time, and had no power to legislate. He saved special criticism for C. G. Memminger, who he claimed had mismanaged the financial needs of the Confederacy and lacked the background to have been the secretary of the treasury. His feelings about Memminger, however, likely stemmed from his failed experiences as a treasury agent. He did commend Secretary of the Navy Stephen Mallory and Postmaster John H. Regan for their abilities to create functioning departments out of nothing. Looking back at those who led the South to war, and comparing them to those leaders who actually served during the war, De Bow lamented that "pigmies" had been in charge of the Confederacy. He held special contempt for talented southerners who failed to serve the cause and remained in private life but who often "exercised a baleful influence by venturing Cassandra prophecies." These self-absorbed men, he felt, "did a great deal to secure the ultimate ruin of the cause." Similar criticisms about inept Confederate leadership emerged in the postwar South as white southerners, led by Edward A. Pollard and Jubal A. Early, searched for explanations for the "Lost Cause." Like many defeated southerners, De Bow had difficulty accepting that he had simply been wrong about the strength of southern nationalism and the reality of a divided South.[15]

De Bow also confronted the issue of southern manhood in light of the Confederacy's defeat. He believed that southerners underestimated their northern opponents because they had tried to avoid war. In comparison, southern troops immediately exhibited their natural talents on the battlefield and enjoyed early success in the war. These troops, however, could not fight on equal footing when they lacked proper tents, uniforms, or arms and were facing a well-supplied foe. Despite these shortcomings, De Bow reminded readers, the brave Confederate soldier never complained about the lack of food or ammunition. As if to add an element of sectional fairness to his reasoning, he also reminded southern readers: "Let us at least do the army of the North the justice to say, that although it had thousands of base and bad men in its ranks, it had thousands of noble and true ones, and that although it robbed and plundered and burnt and desolated at times, it yet often protected and saved."[16]

Many prominent southerners began to leave the South rather than live under the possibilities of federal occupation, and this postwar emigration of southern leadership to Europe and South America concerned De Bow. Judah Benjamin had escaped to England, and Matthew F. Maury had moved to Mexico, rather than live under northern occupation. De Bow felt that these men, and others like them, should have stayed to help lead the South after the war. Robert E. Lee noted De Bow's willingness to remain in the South and sent a letter of support to the *Review.* Among De Bow's lesser-known readers, Charles G. Gunter, a wealthy planter and politician from Montgomery, moved to Brazil after the war and bought enough land and slaves to re-create the plantation he left behind in Alabama. A frustrated De Bow reminded readers: "Agreeing with some of the leaders of the South . . . that it is the duty of her sons to remain in the country, and abide by its fortunes for weal or for woe, we have discouraged all schemes of emigration."[17]

In May 1866 the Joint Committee on Reconstruction summoned De Bow to testify on the condition of the postwar South. He used the public forum to create an image of a peaceful and remorseful region. According to him, southerners rejected secession and accepted northern victory; they had become tired of political strife. He questioned the need for military occupation and reassured listeners that secessionists held little animosity toward ex-slaves or unionists. Concerned congressmen queried him about violence in Louisiana and wondered what could be done to improve the situation. He explained that violence was rare and that most southerners welcomed the new opportunities created by northern investments. He hoped that the Freedmen's Bureau would be dissolved and that local communities would be put in charge of education for ex-slaves. He opposed the granting of citizenship to blacks who could not read or write. Ex-slaves could earn their citizenship through education and proper vocational training and then be granted the right to vote, he argued. He questioned the motives of Republicans who hoped to punish the South and overthrow Andrew Johnson's administration.[18]

Despite his optimism, De Bow accommodated the realities of the postwar South. He renounced his secessionist past and regained his US citizenship. He encouraged readers to embrace reconciliation and new ideas as ways of speeding up economic recovery. His reverence for the past became secondary to the immediate needs of the region. He assumed that his readers—the prewar economic and political elite in many southern communities—would help lead southern recovery efforts. He understood that resistance to northern occupation and violence against blacks would only provoke northerners to impose harsher limitations on the South. He counseled readers to forget about past defeats and accept that "brave and true men never waste time over the inevitable and the irretrievable." He confidently predicted that southerners would "perform all the duties [of citizenship] . . . quietly, soberly, orderly, without ostentation or parade, and if the Federal authorities and the people of the North will act with a liberal and enlarged spirit, and with the generosity which the conqueror can well afford, the South may yet be restored and a great future open upon it."[19]

Slave emancipation was one of these realities that De Bow had to confront after the war. Although his views about racial inferiority remained unchanged, he reminded readers: "The ties of sympathy between the Negro and the white man, his former master, are not dissolved because slavery has ceased." The sudden migration of thousands of ex-slaves in search of new homes and lost family members, however, concerned him. He worried about the productivity of free labor and the relationship between ex-masters and ex-slaves, and he thought that blacks had no real choice but to go back to work. They could become productive members of society, leave the United States, or "like the Indians submit to annihilation." This meant that white southerners needed to convince northerners that they knew how to best control the situation. Many concerned northerners wanted southerners to find a solution for their race problem because thousands of ex-slaves had already moved north looking for new lives and jobs. For De Bow and *Review* contributors such as Josiah C. Nott, ex-slaves had to return to their plantations and accept a racial hierarchy that always placed white over black.[20]

The freedom and productivity of ex-slaves became De Bow's main concern in the immediate aftermath of the war because liberty destabilized the South's labor pool and empowered freed blacks at a time when white southerners needed help reclaiming untended fields and harvesting summer crops. De Bow watched as they escaped from their plantations and moved to urban centers or small plots of rural farmland. In response, he advocated for fixed contracts that would keep ex-slaves accountable and productive in a free society. He believed that productive ex-slaves would stimulate positive feelings among white southerners. This meant that any black person who refused to work needed to be dealt with severely or deported. As if to punctuate his advice with practical warnings, he published cautionary dispatches that highlighted lazy ex-slaves and problematic work contracts. Few *Review* contributors mentioned the availability of ex-slaves as an effective labor force. One subscriber warned readers that he had hired ex-slaves to work but watched them descend into drunken stupors. Yet, mindful that white southerners also needed to be productive, De Bow published an article by W. Archer that blamed whites for creating the South's labor problem by not working enough. Archer challenged readers to forget about slavery and the role of ex-slaves in the postwar South and instead learn to "work successfully in the open fields, beneath a burning sun, and accomplish feats of industry surpassing anything in the history of negro slavery."[21]

The federal government responded to the South's growing social and labor problem by creating the Bureau of Refugees, Freedmen, and Abandoned Lands, more commonly known as the Freedmen's Bureau. De Bow took an immediate interest, and in January 1866 he met with General Oliver O. Howard, the commissioner of the bureau, to express his concern about the agency's future. He found Howard to be a capable gentleman but wondered why "the kindness of Uncle Sam has instituted for the Freedman associations and regulations which he has not yet been inclined to vouchsafe to their white brethren of *American* descent." He supported free education for ex-slaves because he wanted to create a class of productive workers and responsible citizens who understood their rights in and obligations to a free society. He asked southern readers to accept black schools as a way of avoiding unproductive freedmen, who added little to the South's economy. Noting the unruly behavior of free blacks in Jamaica and the West Indies, he worried that American ex-slaves would become lazy and insolent. William H. Trescott confirmed De Bow's fears after reporting that the Freedmen's Bureau in South Carolina's Sea Islands harbored criminals and vagrants. De Bow believed that the bureau fostered "the poison of discontent, and the feelings of envy, of jealousy, of insubordination and of turbulence" toward their old masters among ex-slaves. He published a brief poem modeled after Edgar Allan Poe's "The Raven." In it, the unknown writer wondered: "On your honor, as a Negro, will you labor as before? Quoth the Negro: 'Nevermore.'"[22]

De Bow encouraged the use of immigrants to supplement the South's unsettled workforce. In the 1840s and 1850s many southern factories and railroad companies had converted from free labor to slave labor. In the minds of many southerners, slavery had made European immigration an unwelcome institution supported by northern factory owners who espoused a free labor ideology. To underscore his point, De Bow published statistics from the first ten months of 1865 showing that 110,000 immigrants moved to New York, Pennsylvania, and Illinois while fewer than 20 immigrants apiece moved to Arkansas, Alabama, Florida, Georgia, and North Carolina. Tennessee and Virginia, the two most popular southern destinations for immigrants in 1865, had just 350 and 465 arrivals, respectively. De Bow worried that postwar southerners would continue to ignore the "constant stream of hardy and industrious immigrants" while their mines, factories, and plantations lay untouched or understaffed. He implored readers to accept European immigrants and Chinese laborers as part of a dependable workforce, preferring German immigrants to all others because "they love the soil they cultivate, love freedom and independence, hate aristocracy, and are not only good farmers, but mechanics and artisans." A *Review* contributor supported De Bow's assertion and suggested that southern promotional material be printed in German. Another reader studied the cultural habits of Chinese coolies and concluded that they worked hard and usually returned to China within five years, making them optimal choices for an expendable workforce. De Bow understood that a sense of stability and calm had to emanate from the South to attract immigrants. He used his promotional skills to downplay growing racial violence and economic problems, bragging: "When the era of good feeling is restored [in Tennessee], and angry passions which rule the hour have subsided . . . Nashville and Memphis will then take place among the proudest emporiums of the country, and will attract a dense and wealthy population."[23]

Aside from the merits of attracting an outside labor force, De Bow also promoted northern and European investment in the postwar South. Early in his editorial career, he had encouraged northern investors to build cotton factories and railroads in the South. He had borrowed ideas about factory construction and investment strategies from Charles T. James, a prominent Rhode Island entrepreneur, and published them for the general benefit of his readers. Later, in the mid-1850s, after the *Review* became more sectional, he rejected northern investment as a hindrance to the profit-minded businessmen who were emerging in the South. In mid-1857 he published two articles that warned readers about Yankees in Virginia and the "Yankee colonization of the South." But after the war that view disappeared, and he openly courted outside investors. With nearly all native southern capital destroyed in the war, he welcomed outside investment. He applauded a French consortium for purchasing coalfields and large tracts of land in Virginia. He encouraged northerners to become cotton planters. The *Review* published extensive listings of plantations for sale and promoted investment companies such as the American Land Company in New York City. He helped William T. Withers, a real estate broker from Jackson, Mississippi, list eighty-one plantations in Mississippi and noted that "northern capitalists may feel safe in his hands." He hoped that northerners might create new opportunities for southerners, who in time could regain control of their land.[24]

De Bow responded to the needs of outsiders who wanted to buy and farm southern land by publishing practical agricultural articles in the *Review.* These basic articles also allowed him to remind old readers that they too needed to think about agricultural diversity and scientific farming. He wanted to regain his reputation as an agricultural reformer by inviting top agriculturalists and *Review* readers to submit articles that would help southerners reformulate their farms. Contributors offered advice on farming techniques and on new crops such as sugar beets, Indian corn, and exotic grains. The use of agricultural machinery became especially important after the loss of slave labor. De Bow provided detailed instructions for farmers who wanted to grow enough cotton to make a profit and enough food to feed their families. He estimated that a 1,250-acre farm needed 1,000 acres of cotton and only 250 acres of corn to maintain a healthy balance between profit and productivity. For smaller farmers, however, he suggested a much more diversified spread of land, estimating that a 40-acre farm should include the following: 10 acres of cotton; 10 acres of corn, potatoes, and fruit; and 15 acres of woodland. Although De Bow still catered his advice to large cotton planters and interested outsiders, his practical agricultural advice provided a general resource for the many southerners not involved in cotton production.[25]

Percy Roberts, a planter from Hernando, Mississippi, responded to De Bow's public call for regional information on postwar cotton production. He reported that, although Panola County had escaped the direct disruption of war, cotton planters had been able to cultivate only half the available land in the county because of labor shortages and poor weather. Despite these setbacks, however, Roberts approvingly noted: "Many of our young men, whom the fortunes of war have reduced from wealth to poverty, have doffed their gray jackets, and are wielding the plow-handle with an energy which does not solace Thad Steven's philosophy of our incapacity for work." De

Bow supplemented Roberts's general observations with statistics that verified a large drop in Mississippi cotton production. Yet he also saw innovative possibilities emerging in the state and wrote about the advent of new cotton factories in Mississippi. Local developers in Meridian had overcome formidable swamps and postwar setbacks to build a factory for planters who wanted to sell their cotton locally. De Bow hoped that the positive news of new factories might offset Roberts's report about Mississippi cotton.[26]

De Bow hoped to convince postwar readers that they needed to invest in a more diversified industrial sector because the South's prewar focus on cotton factories had been a mistake. He now republished newspaper articles, essays, and reports that offered practical advice on manufacturing, hoping to create regional momentum for "new furnaces, mills, factories, tanneries; new mines of iron, coal, copper, lead, and zinc; new railroads, countless oil wells; . . . the multiplication of machinery and the establishment of new industries." The timber industry, which he had neglected before the war, became a special focus in the *Review* as investors bought large timber stands and sawmills in western North Carolina, eastern Tennessee, western Georgia, northern Florida, and parts of Louisiana. His interest in timber brought his attention to the upcountry and mountainous areas of the South, which he had virtually ignored before the war. A lumber boom in Georgia and Florida resulted in dozens of new sawmills in Augusta immediately after the war. An influx of Alabama timber revitalized Mobile and made it a successful lumber port. De Bow encouraged southerners to harvest southern forests and supply domestic and national markets with needed lumber. Existing towns and railroads could be converted to accommodate the South's lumber industry while continuing to meet the needs of local farmers. De Bow envisioned new sawmills, furniture factories, paper mills, turpentine stores, and railroads being built to help support the lumber industry.[27]

De Bow also imagined the benefits of building a southern petroleum industry. The wartime development of northern petroleum fields surprised the many southerners who had been isolated by the war. Northern production had increased from 600,000 barrels in 1860 to 2.3 million barrels in 1865. Still unsure of the uses and value of oil, De Bow reprinted northern articles that explained the new industry. The presence of large coal deposits in the South's mountainous areas led to hope that large oil reserves also existed. De Bow urged southerners to invest in oil extraction and develop new oil fields. He compared the excitement of the petroleum industry to that of the California Gold Rush.[28]

Articles about mining and mineral extraction became more common in the postwar *Review.* De Bow explored different mining enterprises and concluded that enough mineral resources existed to supply new southern iron foundries and factories. Contributors wrote about coal, iron, and gold reserves that could benefit the South's economy. Aware of northern Alabama's coal- and ironfields before the war, De Bow hoped that these deposits could expand the postwar South's industrial capacity. Albert Stein, a longtime contributor from Mobile, urged his city to extend its commercial resources to industrialists and miners in northern Alabama before regional competition isolated the port city. De Bow agreed with Stein's assessment and reminded readers of the importance of linking commerce and industry to create a more diversified economy.[29]

Prewar knowledge of rich coalfields in northern and central Alabama helped Daniel Pratt expand his status as the South's preeminent industrialist and fulfill De Bow's personal interest in developing the region. As one of the most vocal prewar supporters of southern industrialization, Pratt had agreed with De Bow on most issues concerning the future of the South. By 1860 the well-managed Prattville Manufacturing Company supported 140 workers and the company town of Prattville. Although far removed from the fighting for most of the war, Pratt found it difficult to upgrade and repair machinery or sell new cotton gins to southerners unable to market cotton. The financial loss created by the war nearly drove him out of business, and he later lamented: "Before the war I think I was doing more gin business than any two establishments in the world. If we had escaped this war I think I would have run the Northern gins out of the market." After the war he recovered most of his prewar customers and began to produce cotton gins for southern planters. But he wanted to expand his portfolio and began to buy and develop thousands of acres of coalfields in Alabama with the help of his son-in-law Henry F. DeBardeleben. He also purchased the Red Mountain Iron and Coal Company, which later became the Pratt Coal and Coke Corporation, a future subsidiary of the United States Steel Corporation. His postwar investments in factories and mines became the foundation for the creation of Birmingham, Alabama, which was developed under the direction of the Elyton Land Company, owned in part by Samuel Tate, Bolling Hall, and James Gilmer, three prewar *Review* readers who had long subscribed to De Bow's economic creed of urban development and industrial growth.[30]

De Bow promoted the economic potential of southern cities. He celebrated the commercial revival of New Orleans and Memphis as river traffic increased after the war. After a trip to Virginia he noted the industrial and commercial reemergence of Richmond and the continued potential of Norfolk as an international port. He lauded Nashville's fortuitous commercial proximity to Memphis, St. Louis, Cincinnati, and Knoxville. With minimal wartime damage and good commercial connections to the North, Nashville stood poised to assume a new level of economic importance.[31]

De Bow asked southern newspaper editors to publish favorable articles about the South. He also encouraged city governments to create the statistical reports that would add legitimacy to his claims of progress. Monthly and annual reports from Memphis, Savannah, New Orleans, and Mobile became regular parts of the *Review.* These statistical overviews had been common before the war but became important postwar indicators of regional recovery. De Bow assumed that export levels indicated broader activity among planters, manufacturers, and merchants. Although Charleston had incomplete numbers in early 1866, De Bow used projections of warehoused cotton to forecast "the revival of a commerce, which we confidently anticipate will increase and multiply until Charleston shall rank first among the cities of the South."[32]

In June 1866 De Bow gave a speech in Cincinnati on the importance of regional harmony and railroad development. He hoped to create a sense of sectional reconciliation that would link the commercial future of Cincinnati to the resources of the South. He noted that the North had the capital to fix the South's railroad system and that the South had the natural resources to fuel northern economic growth. Still proud of southern achievements, he wrote: "The South sleeps; she is not dead." He reassured his audience that southerners wanted to end sectional hostility and promote national economic recovery. After he finished his speech, James W. Sloss, the president of the Nashville and Decatur Railroad, reaffirmed his friend's appeal for northern capital and intersectional cooperation. Like De Bow, he believed that a direct railroad connection between Nashville and Cincinnati would create new agricultural and industrial opportunities for southerners and benefit northern merchants. Sloss later joined Daniel Pratt and the other promoters in developing the city of Birmingham in 1871. With the aid of northern capital, Sloss's furnaces produced pig iron for factories in Cincinnati, Cleveland, and Chicago.[33]

In October 1866 De Bow became president of the Tennessee Central and Pacific Railroad Company. The state of Tennessee had charted the new railroad in March 1866, and investors hoped that it would provide better access to eastern Tennessee and the Cumberland Plateau. De Bow first mentioned the railroad in August 1866 and believed that it could link Knoxville and Nashville to Jackson, Mississippi, which served as a hub for larger western railroads. After accepting the presidency of the new railroad, De Bow addressed a letter to the people of Tennessee in the *Review.* He reminded readers of his long commitment to internal improvement projects, noting that railroads had created "a system which has built up our cities and developed our interior; adding indefinitely to the value of our lands and to our physical, moral, and other comforts." But he also added: "We are but in the middle, and not at the end of our labors." The Tennessee Central became the tangible outcome of De Bow's personal crusade for railroad development. His knowledge of railroad matters and what had worked and failed became the basis of his presidency. Unfortunately for De Bow and Tennessee investors, financial problems delayed construction until 1869, and in 1877 the Nashville, Chattanooga, and St. Louis Railroad consolidated the debt-plagued Tennessee Central and assumed control of twenty-nine miles of track and a northern-built steam engine named the "J. D. B. De Bow."[34]

In the period after the war, De Bow transformed the *Review* to match the needs of the postwar South. He created a sense of regional progress, both real and imagined, that encouraged reinvestment in the South and avoided sectional animosity. He focused on regional betterment and community development by embracing national unity when it benefited the South. He suggested that southerners remove themselves from political debates and focus on economic development. For his vision of recovery to work, a sense of progress and excitement had to outweigh reports of violence and strife. He recognized his mistakes, attempted to correct them, and reintroduced his revamped ideas to southern readers as a way of attaining economic salvation. He had started his editorial career as an American nationalist, had become an ardent southern secessionist, and then had returned to his original faith in national progress within the span of twenty years. This fluidity of thought arose in a mind that understood most modern economic principles and how they shaped society. De Bow's successes lay in his ability to recognize practical ideas and bring them together into a coherent economic plan. The past mattered to him because it provided structure and precedent for the future. He had promoted the idea of an industrialized economy in the antebellum South, and other promoters of economic diversification would later popularize the notion. He promised readers that they would benefit from successive waves of development if they followed his advice and helped reestablish the South, guaranteeing them: "Such a turn in the tide can only be in one direction, *and that is to the southward.*"[35]

In January 1867 De Bow wrote an article that condemned his prewar vision of industrialization and overreliance on cotton factories. He promised readers that diversified industrialization would erase the errors of the past that had been revealed by the war. He urged southerners to act on his words and allow him to advise them on "how to begin the Reformation." The *Review* had always given ample space to articles on factories and manufacturing, he noted, but he promised now to provide articles and sketches of machinery, factories, and tools that would be useful for entrepreneurs interested in starting new enterprises. Believing that he understood his readers' needs, he prepared to print the first installment of this new industrial section in the February 1867 issue of the *Review.*[36]

As he had done many times before in his professional life, De Bow decided to take an extended trip through the North and the South to witness progress firsthand. He visited factories and stores in Louisville, Cincinnati, and New York. He complained about the safety of railroads and hoped that state governments would regulate construction to ensure the well-being of passengers. He noted the level of progress and reconstruction in towns and cities between Washington, DC, and Charleston. Yet, when he arrived in Charleston, he became melancholy. In what would be his final visit to "dear old Charleston," he was reminded of the work that still needed to be done in the postwar South. Burned homes, destroyed businesses, and grass-filled streets evoked sad childhood memories of the city he had grown up in. Instead of dwelling on the past, however, he saw economic potential amid the rubble. He foresaw a new era of commercial greatness in his old city. Writing directly to the merchants of Charleston in his last article before his death, he implored them: "Never say FAIL—brothers in this hour of common disaster, Awake! Awake! There is a future before us, perhaps more brilliant than the past, if we are to be true to that past."[37]

The January 1867 issue of the *Review* proved to be his last, and it is not clear whether De Bow saw it in print. In early February 1867 he traveled to Elizabeth, New Jersey, to attend to his sick younger brother. On arrival at Benjamin De Bow's side, the elder De Bow complained of feeling ill himself. His symptoms became worse, and on February 27, 1867, he died of acute peritonitis. Unsure of what to do with the body, local residents put his corpse on a southbound train without a clear destination. De Bow's remains never reached Nashville or any other known burial spot. His family failed to erect a headstone or monument in his memory. It was an ignominious end to a long, high-profile public life.[38]

The southern press mourned De Bow's passing. One southern obituary writer noted that his contributions to the South had been unmatched and that De Bow would be memorialized in death by the articles, statistics, and opinions of the *Review*. Even northern newspapers commented on his death. The *Boston Daily Advertiser* recalled that he had "warmly espoused the cause of secession . . . but since the war his personal views on politics and slavery were considerably modified." The editor of the *North American and United States Gazette* recalled that De Bow had "constantly kept in the public eye for a number of years, sometimes by his merits, sometimes by his faults."[39]

De Bow's ideas became the lasting foundation for a second generation of New South boosters who had little reason to attribute their plan to past writers and promoters. These men would claim that their vision of the South's future was unique. But long before Edward Atkinson lauded the importance of southern industry, Richard H. Edmonds dazzled readers with weekly statistical reports of progress in the *Manufacturers' Record*, Daniel H. Hill promoted agricultural reform in *The Land We Live In*, and Francis W. Dawson, Henry Watterson, and Henry W. Grady used their newspapers as regional pulpits to preach about a New South, De Bow had made all the same arguments. He was, of course, responsible in part for the fact that he did not receive credit for his prescience. His ultimate inability to see beyond the defense of southern institutions minimized his national reputation and historical legacy, while his reputation as a militant southern sectionalist overrode his views on economic development and regional improvement.[40]

There was very little new in the regional message of salvation espoused by second-generation boosters such as Henry W. Grady who claimed to have solutions for what ailed the South. Grady, perhaps the most infamous postwar promoter of the New South Creed, had made a career of reminding white southerners that their romantic past included more moonlight and magnolias than railroads and factories. In his most famous speech, delivered in 1886, he promised a New York audience that southerners wanted to invest in industry, promote agricultural diversity, solve their race problem, and remain good citizens of the United States. As the editor of the *Atlanta Constitution*, he promoted a sense of regional harmony because he wanted northern investors to feel safe when dealing with southerners and investing in the South. Yet De Bow had already done this before and after the war. In 1866, twenty years before Grady's famous speech, De Bow published "The

Future of the United States," which made the same promises and predictions as Grady would in New York. Even Grady's hometown was not new to De Bow. Although many postwar observers believed that Atlanta epitomized the positive changes associated with new southern economic development, De Bow had already published articles on the economic possibilities of the small railroad junction (in June 1847) and had described the importance of the Atlanta Rolling Mill and Western and Atlantic Railroad (in October 1858). Grady's city had grown partly because of the prewar support and investments of *Review* readers such as Alexander H. Stephens, G. G. Hull, and J. H. Steele. De Bow's prewar interest in regional economic development extended even to analyzing what was, in 1860, the ninety-ninth largest town in the United States. By the start of the Civil War, De Bow would have considered the growth of Atlanta to be old news, not a new beginning.[41]

A similar type of collective forgetfulness about the past seemed to plague second-generation New South boosters in Charleston too. Francis Dawson, the owner and editor of the *Charleston News and Courier*, became a vocal supporter of postwar industrialism and commerce, especially in relation to moving cotton factories closer to cotton fields. He believed that southern factories could elevate the lives of poor whites by improving their social and economic status. Like De Bow had done countless times before and after the war, he encouraged northerners to invest in cotton mills and urged southerners to do likewise. Dawson also called for the Charleston Chamber of Commerce to help young merchants instill a sense of commercial spirit in the city. He, and many downtown merchants, believed that a new hotel would attract visitors to the city. Eager to start construction on the hotel in 1888, Dawson and his followers asked George W. Williams to make the first large donation toward their goal. Before the war Williams had opened a wholesale grocery store and eventually became one of the largest merchants in the South. War had not interrupted his upward trajectory, and in the postbellum years he chartered the First National Bank of Charleston while maintaining his original wholesale business. Williams, a prewar *Review* reader and acquaintance of De Bow's, had been part of the group that had sent De Bow to Memphis in 1845. The idea of Charleston's civic rejuvenation was not new to Williams or De Bow. In fact, De Bow had filed dozens of reports and dispatches on the commercial development of the city and wished for nothing more than his hometown to thrive as it had when his father was still alive.[42]

De Bow and his *Review* quickly faded from the public memory as southerners continued to reclaim their lives while enduring the turmoil of Reconstruction and the violence of white redemption. Southern newspapers in the late nineteenth century and the early twentieth occasionally mentioned him in the context of southern economic development. In March 1899 the *Atlanta Constitution,* Henry Grady's primary tool for spreading his version of a postbellum New South Creed, published an article about Robert Barnwell, a subscription agent for *De Bow's Review* who became its editor after De Bow's death. In the flawed piece, the newspaper writer attributed the success of the *Review* to Barnwell, mentioning De Bow only in passing as "a brilliant and wealthy naturalized Frenchman, who exerted a strong influence on the politics of the state at that time, and who operated a magazine for the promulgation of slavery doctrines." In incorrectly introducing Barnwell as the *Review*'s editor, the newspaper author more accurately described De Bow, noting: "His name and his memory are factors which will perhaps count for little in these bustling, modern days of perfect reunion and reconciliation, but fifty years ago he was known throughout the United States as one of the most powerful and effective pro-slavery editorial writers, and is at present recalled as one who left an indelible impress on the history page of that revolutionary era." This certainly described De Bow better than one of his assistants. In November 1903, an unknown writer from the *Nashville American* attributed the South's industrial growth to De Bow, claiming: "Some of James D. B. de Bow's prophecies are being strikingly verified." A year later in the same newspaper, another article traced the industrial development of the South from the antebellum period to the twentieth century. Although much of the postwar South's growth was attributed to modern innovations, the article commended De Bow for his farsightedness and admitted "that Mr. DeBow was a true prophet and . . . that the reasoning employed by him is just as fresh and even more forceful now, under changed conditions, than it was then." Despite De Bow's having lived in Nashville during the last years of his life and perhaps even been buried in an unmarked grave within the city limits, his name had been incorrectly spelled in both articles, and both authors failed to connect his accomplishments to their cities. De Bow's legacy had by the turn of the twentieth century been relegated to historians.[43]

Perhaps the most fitting tribute to De Bow's legacy came at the 1900 Southern Industrial Convention in New Orleans, when delegates gathered to discuss the South's economic future. As had southerners at the 1845 Memphis Commercial Convention, twentieth-century southerners gloried in their region's untapped agricultural, industrial, and commercial potential.

Likely unaware that dozens of similar meetings had been held before the Civil War, the convention's vice president, Sidney Story, opened the first session by congratulating "the South and the City of New Orleans, on the great industrial awakening which this Convention indicates." A correspondent at the meeting who wanted to capture the seemingly historic moment attempted to put it into perspective for southern readers. He knew, however, not to start his historical foray with the popular boosters who had filled newspaper columns or made flowery speeches to enthusiastic postwar audiences. Writing in De Bow's adopted city about economic and social topics that had been as relevant in 1845 as they were in 1900, he correctly posited:

> History can be graphically shown as an ever-widening circle. How many of the 1,200 delegates that attended [the convention] have even an inkling that they were simply treading in the tracks of their forefathers? The spirit of De Bow must have hovered over the scene with philosophical satire, to see the children of his generation going the same round that his contemporaries tramped, the process to be enthusiastically revived after nearly half a century. Certainly if lessons are to be learned from the past, nothing wiser could be done by the managers than to have at every meeting some competent hand to draw warning and inspiration from those efforts of our grandfathers; thus mistakes could be avoided, suggestions could be gathered and ideals cherished.[44]

De Bow's ultimate legacy to the South proved to be his ability to construct and gather ideas that resonated with southern readers interested in improving their region. De Bow took individual schemes, community plans, and regional hopes and wove them into a distinctive sectional creed that publicly promised a better future for the South. Readers supported him because they believed in his values, intellect, and ideas. Although their political and social outlooks tended to be narrow and conservative, they valued new innovations that promised better days. Early in his editorial career De Bow fostered intellectual curiosity and challenged subscribers to think beyond their immediate needs. He encouraged them to invest in new factories, railroads, libraries, schools, and cultural institutions as essential parts of a diversified South. He hoped that planters saw the value of industry and cities and that city dwellers and factory owners would embrace the necessity of plantations. It went unsaid that slavery served as the social and economic foundation for all white southerners. The *Review* mirrored the South and reflected the interests of enough southerners to make it one of the few profitable southern journals before the Civil War. De Bow promised readers that new industries and commercial centers would limit outside influences and create a more balanced political relationship between the North and South. The fear of unchecked northern advances and perceived southern shortcomings worried him and, ultimately, changed his editorial tone. The sectional crisis, driven by slavery and western expansion, distracted him and made him bitter and vengeful. During the late 1850s the *Review* reflected his souring mood. His message of regional salvation changed to sectional hatred, and his articles became less about economic and social improvements and more about fortifying the South against the outside world. Unfortunately, the Civil War exposed the South's weaknesses and highlighted De Bow's inability to convince enough southerners to make his regional creed effective. Fortunately for him, however, his personal and professional reputation had become synonymous with progress and action, and postwar southerners wanted his editorial guidance once again. He stood poised to reclaim his position in southern society and began to collect new articles on urban development, industrial and commercial growth, and agricultural reform. His postwar message of redemption came from the prewar pages of the *Review*. De Bow had only to borrow from himself to establish a postbellum New South Creed. His readers—the ones who survived the war—embraced his reemergence and worked to reestablish their lives within the context of political and social reconstruction. His death in 1867 meant that his ideas never resonated with younger southerners eager to move the South in new directions. That generation, however, would have their own spokesmen who would make their own promises and, like De Bow before them, would ultimately fail the South.

Acknowledgments

When I conceived of the idea that J. D. B. De Bow would make a good topic for my dissertation I did not realize that he would become an almost constant companion in my life for the next eight years. Although my friends and family might have tired of him long ago, I have enjoyed my time with De Bow and his readers. Yet I did not get to this point without the aid and support of others, and now I can thank those who have helped me along the way. I will begin with Robert J. Norrell, Stephen Ash, and Dan Feller, who oversaw my dissertation and helped me become a better historian. I would also like to thank Will Bolt, Fashion Bowers, Travis Hardy, and especially Aaron Crawford for their companionship and their willingness to read anything I put in front of them. Likewise, Chris Paysinger and Tom Reidy have logged many hours reading drafts of chapters and listening to my ideas. My colleagues at the University of Alabama in Huntsville have also made this process easier with their support, as have many of my students who have taken an interest in southern history. Diana LaChance spent hours picking out my grammatical mistakes and challenging me to be a better storyteller. My Huntsville friends kept my stress levels low with long summer nights on top of Monte Sano and B&G days that usually meant more fun than work for me. Thanks to all of you. I also want to express my special gratitude to Michele Gillespie, Anne Dean Watkins, Bailey Johnson, and the anonymous readers at the University Press of Kentucky. Michele has been overly kind to me, and I hope to pay that same kindness forward to someone else in the future. They have made this a wonderful experience.

Finally, I want to thank my family for all they have done to help me along the way. I have been blessed with great parents who have supported me throughout my life. Jim and Kathy Kvach have never waivered as my beacons of love and happiness. My sister, Jenny, has always believed in me regardless of how much I have teased her. She and her family have provided me with much love and laughter. I have also been lucky enough to have in-laws who made me part of their family without hesitation. Gib and Kate

Verkamp have meant the world to me, and, although my mother-in-law did not live to see my book on a shelf, she never doubted me and always reminded me that I had the luck of the Irish on my side. I would also like to thank Max and his family for their love and support. Most importantly, I want to thank my two sons, Ben and Tom, for bringing me so much joy in life. The "Three Club" has meant a lot to me, and I look forward to new adventures with my two best friends. They have changed my life and made me a better person. And, finally, I want to thank my wife Ann because her support has been essential to everything that I have accomplished since the day that I sat next to her on an airplane and realized that my future was with her. Some joke that she has earned early sainthood for being married to me, but for me she is the earthly embodiment of grace and beauty. Thank you to the three most important people in my life. The debt I owe each of you cannot be repaid, so instead I will just try to be the best father, husband, and person that I can be and hope that is enough.

Appendix

The Identified Readership of *De Bow's Review*

Last Name	First Name	County	State	Age	Occupation	Real Estate ($)	Personal Estate ($)	Slaves (*N*)
Agee	N. A.	Monroe	AL	33	Lawyer	4,000	30,000	
Aiken	John G.	Mobile	AL	60	Gentleman		60,000	40
Alexander	Abram Franklin	Greene	AL	58	Physician	80,000	134,000	105
Allen	William W.	Mobile	AL	55	Merchant	40,000	160,000	29
Armsted	William B.	Montgomery	AL	30	Physician	3,000	33,000	23
Babcock	Joseph	Dallas	AL	29	Merchant	700	15,000	20
Bailey	James Francis	Perry	AL	49	Judge	10,000	25,190	17
Banks	James J.	Macon	AL	50	Farmer	11,200	25,600	12
Banks	S. P.	Macon	AL	34	Physician	2,240		
Barclay	Thomas C.	Marshall	AL	41	Lawyer			3
Barnett	T. M.	Butler	AL	62	Farmer	1,350	700	7
Barrow	John T.	Lauderdale	AL	23	Farmer	800	1,000	1
Barton	Absalom A.	Macon	AL	42	Farmer	19,200	40,000	26
Battle	Cullen Andrews	Macon	AL	41	Farmer			8
Berry	John R.	Macon	AL	30	Farmer	16,000	92,000	91
Bibb	William C.	Montgomery	AL	40	Planter	75,000	37,000	10
Boyle	John C.	Sumter	AL	48	Merchant	1,500	4,000	
Brazelton	Andrew J.	Perry	AL	45	Merchant	19,000	50,000	18
Brooks	William McLin	Perry	AL	45	Lawyer	26,000	50,000	11
Broughton	W. D.	Randolph	AL	21	Shoemaker			13
Brown	Thomas B.	Montgomery	AL	51	Planter	40,000	150,000	6
Bryant	E. N.	Sumter	AL	47	Farmer	8,000	52,563	129
Buford	M.	Macon	AL	35	Farmer	900	100	
Burns	J. H.	Dallas	AL	50	Merchant	20,000	90,450	43
Burt	P.	Greene	AL	50	Planter	43,000	84,000	
Caldwell	John Henry	St. Clair	AL	33	Lawyer	1,000	1,000	
Carlisle	E. K.	Perry	AL	47	Merchant			
Chambliss	N. R.	Dallas	AL		Professor			
Chilton	W. P.	Montgomery	AL	49	Lawyer			8
Clark	Richard	Perry	AL	45	Physician	2,000	40,000	4
Clay	Clement C., Jr.	Madison	AL	42	US senator	10,000	35,000	3
Clay	Clement C., Sr.	Madison	AL	70	Lawyer	60,000	85,000	89
Clements	Luther M.	Tuscaloosa	AL	38	Physician	50,000	100,000	36
Cloud	Noah	Montgomery	AL	50	Planter	12,000	14,000	9
Cobb	B. E.	Dallas	AL	45	Physician	12,760	65,000	45
Cobb	M. E.	Shelby	AL		Teacher			
Cocke	N. W.	Bibb	AL	37	Farmer	1,200	3,500	2
Coleman	Radford E.	Greene	AL	41		6,000	14,500	9
Collier	John J.	Greene	AL	49	Planter	8,000		93
Cook	N. L.	Montgomery	AL	22	Printer			
Cooper	A. B.	Wilcox	AL	59	Farmer	35,250	105,082	91
Copeland	Mack M.	Montgomery	AL	31	Broker	8,000	6,000	6
Costley	Warrenton	Chambers	AL	38	Physician	2,700	10,000	
Crawford	Joel T.	Macon	AL	48	Farmer	28,000	41,000	50
Crawford	M. A.	Greene	AL	30	Merchant			
Creswell	Samuel L.	Greene	AL	40	Planter	20,000	113,000	129
Crommelin	Charles	Montgomery	AL		Lawyer			
Curry	Jabez Lamar	Perry	AL	35	Farmer	140,000	200,000	146
Davidson	John Howard	Marengo	AL	43	Planter	1,500	375	58
Davis	A. R.	Greene	AL	53	Planter	20,000	57,880	61
Davis	William L.	Dallas	AL	28	Planter	28,000	48,000	47
Dawson	Nathaniel Henry	Dallas	AL	31	Lawyer	40,000	120,000	31
Deas	James	Dallas	AL	52	Merchant		8,600	
Deyampert	L. Q. C.	Perry	AL	67	Farmer	85,600	307,900	57
Drummond	W. F.	Marengo	AL	33	Physician	3,500	7,000	5
DuBose	John	Marengo	AL	23	Planter	8,000	19,790	15
DuBose	Kim C.	Marengo	AL	50	Planter	83,700	142,840	129

Last Name	First Name	County	State	Age	Occupation	Real Estate ($)	Personal Estate ($)	Slaves (*N*)
Dudley	John, Jr.	Lowndes	AL	68	Farmer	20,000	57,880	107
Dumas	Albert A.	Wilcox	AL	30	Merchant	5,700	14,285	10
Dunklin	D. G.	Butler	AL	36	Merchant	28,000	37,000	36
Dunn	William D.	Mobile	AL	50	Railroad president	100,000	50,000	15
Edwards	Charles Alva	Autauga	AL	35	Physician	1,500	6,000	9
Ellerbee	A. W.	Dallas	AL	44	Farmer	63,750	140,000	132
Evans	James L.	Dallas	AL	43	Lawyer	5,000	9,000	28
Fackler	John J.	Madison	AL	58	Merchant	14,000	150,000	20
Farley	Charles K.	Dallas	AL	37	Physician	9,360	10,310	10
Farmer	Joel H.	Calhoun	AL	35	Farmer	2,000	6,000	2
Fearn	Thomas	Madison	AL	70	Physician	46,000	128,000	37
Forsyth	John	Mobile	AL	46	Editor	12,000	35,000	2
Forward	Samuel	Clarke	AL	60	Farmer	20,000	80,000	54
Fowler	William B.	Calhoun	AL	63	Mechanic	250	300	
Fox	D. J.	Wilcox	AL	48	Physician	15,000	70,000	50
Fulton	William Frierson	Sumter	AL	20	Farmer	40,000	90,000	73
Gafford	A. W.	Butler	AL	50	Farmer	3,000	15,000	5
Gardner	Virgil H.	Dallas	AL	51	Planter	96,000	105,000	60
Gates	Joseph R.	Mobile	AL	45	Merchant	15,000		
Geiger	Alexander	Sumter	AL	42		40,000	82,000	80
Gilmer	Francis M., Jr.	Montgomery	AL	50	Merchant	83,500	563,500	42
Gilmer	James J.	Tallapoosa	AL	52	Farmer	60,000	140,000	13
Glover	Benjamin	Marengo	AL	50	Planter	20,000	78,000	101
Glover	W. A.	Greene	AL	56	Planter	91,200	193,000	148
Goldsby	G.	Talladega	AL	25	Farmer			
Goldsby	Thornton Boykin	Dallas	AL	64	Planter	639,500	273,400	6
Goldthwaite	George	Montgomery	AL	51	Lawyer	101,500	310,000	99
Gooch	Nathaniel M.	Madison	AL	38	Farmer	1,000	1,000	10
Goodwyn	Albert Gallatin	Autauga	AL	52	Physician	25,000	40,000	20
Gorce	Robert T.	Perry	AL		Farmer	10,000		
Gordon	A. W.	Mobile	AL	62		300,000	50,000	2
Gould	W. P.	Greene	AL	60	Planter	116,000	64,320	52
Graham	J. P.	Perry	AL	65	Lawyer	32,000	60,000	15
Grant	William A.	Montgomery	AL		Broker			
Griffin	G. G.	Marengo	AL	59	Planter	83,000	404,000	230
Griffin	William H.	Dallas	AL	46	Farmer	6,000	12,000	3
Gullett	John Eades	Wilcox	AL	44	Farmer	201,916	81,341	46
Gunter	Charles G.	Montgomery	AL	54	Planter	200,000	125,000	116
Hadley	J. D.	Russell	AL	38	Farmer		2,000	2
Hadley	John L.	Sumter	AL	58	Physician	24,180	83,165	
Haile	C.	Dallas	AL	40	Farmer	32,800	100,000	72
Hale	Stephen Fowler	Greene	AL	44	Lawyer	8,000	47,000	12
Hall	Bolling	Autauga	AL	47	Lawyer	54,000	90,000	65
Haralson	A. L.	Autauga	AL	35	Planter	11,000	25,000	19
Harrison	Edmund	Montgomery	AL	55	Planter	44,100	19,000	5
Harrison	T.	Russell	AL	76	Farmer	4,000	11,000	10
Hart	B. T.	Marengo	AL	26	Planter	12,000	16,000	12
Hayley	Jesse J.	Dale	AL	44	Physician	1,500	1,500	
Hemphill	F. F.	Baldwin	AL	47	Turpentine distiller	70,000	30,000	52
Henry	James	Pickens	AL		Physician	13,000	2,200	
Hibbler	William H.	Sumter	AL	56	Farmer	80,000	150,000	73
Hill	G. F.	Chambers	AL	52	Farmer	6,000	25,000	16
Holman	W. P.	Perry	AL	26	Physician	3,900	78,000	6
Hopkins	A. F.	Mobile	AL	64	Lawyer	200,000	25,000	9
Houston	James H.	Perry	AL	17	Physician	2,500	12,000	9
Huey	James G. L.	Talladega	AL	61	Merchant	20,000	37,000	45
Huggins	W. D.	Dallas	AL	27	Merchant			

Last Name	First Name	County	State	Age	Occupation	Real Estate ($)	Personal Estate ($)	Slaves (*N*)
Hunter	Charles	Dallas	AL	67	Farmer	40,000	50,000	23
Hunter	John Starke	Dallas	AL	64	Lawyer	150,000	215,380	138
Jackson	A. B.	Montgomery	AL	63	Farmer	1,320	16,820	16
Jackson	P. M.	Montgomery	AL		Manufacturer		3,600	3
Jemison	Robert S.	Tuscaloosa	AL	58	Farmer	30,000	26,250	110
Jermigan	C. H.	Macon	AL	31	Physician	3,500	17,000	
Johnson	William R.	Colbert	AL		Physician			
King	H. R.	Franklin	AL	40	Farmer	20,000	20,000	25
King	Porter	Perry	AL	35	Judge	80,000	100,000	90
Knapp	A. R.	Montgomery	AL	53	Butcher	500	1,000	1
Laird	W. H.	Coffee	AL	42	Merchant		6,000	1
Lang	W. W.	Dallas	AL	69	Farmer	28,000	126,000	133
Lanier	Thomas C.	Pickens	AL	37	Farmer	15,000	67,000	55
Lapsley	John W.	Dallas	AL	53	Merchant	7,500	17,000	5
Lawson	P. B.	Perry	AL	59	Collector	11,500	15,200	
Leach	Sewall Jones	Tuscaloosa	AL	48	Merchant			17
LeBaron	Charles Leonard	Mobile	AL	56	Merchant	10,000	4,000	
Lee	F. A.	Dallas	AL	43	Farmer	14,000	47,000	42
Lee	J. M.	Dallas	AL	49	Physician	20,000	107,414	3
Lewis	B. B.	Shelby	AL	21	Lawyer	2,000	3,300	4
Lewis	H. M.	Montgomery	AL		Agent	1,500		3
Lide	C. M.	Dallas	AL	35	Farmer	20,800	41,770	36
Lightfoot	Philip L.	Greene	AL	50	Physician	45,000	122,000	117
Lockett	Napoleon	Perry	AL	47	Lawyer	45,000	202,600	126
Malone	John Lewis	Franklin	AL	33	Farmer	40,000	40,000	49
Martin	Abram	Montgomery	AL	62	Lawyer	38,000	17,000	26
Martin	James	Lauderdale	AL	61	Manufacturer		10,920	10
Mathews	Thomas M.	Dallas	AL	46	Farmer	150,000	335,000	143
May	James T.	Talladega	AL	38	Farmer	2,000	300	
McAlister	William T.	Perry	AL	31	Physician		2,000	
McCalley	Charles W.	Madison	AL	38	Merchant		2,500	2
McCalley	William J.	Madison	AL	37	Farmer	40,000	65,000	11
McDow	William L.	Sumter	AL	29	Farmer	32,400	76,000	85
McDowell	J. A.	Wilcox	AL	45	Planter	26,050	50,350	
McLelland	George G.	Montgomery	AL	30	Carpenter	2,000	18,000	
McMillan	A.	Marengo	AL	78	Planter	250	100	
McMillan	N. A.	Choctaw	AL		Hotel keeper		2,000	
McNab	John	Barbour	AL	53	Merchant	80,000	116,000	74
Means	David J.	Greene	AL		Physician	21,000		110
Meek	H. J.	Lowndes	AL	46	Farmer		311	
Meeks	L. B.	Jefferson	AL	44	Farmer		175	
Merriwether	James B.	Montgomery	AL	21	Planter	36,000	115,561	118
Miller	Thomas R.	Mobile	AL	48	Broker	40,000	120,000	7
Minge	George W.	Perry	AL	55	Farmer	63,600	99,980	125
Miree	William S.	Perry	AL		Farmer	12,000	70,545	29
Mitchell	R. V.	Montgomery	AL	26	Physician	15,000	5,895	3
Moody	Washington W.	Tuscaloosa	AL	54	Lawyer	6,600		38
Moore	David L.	Madison	AL	22	Planter	137,000	180,000	56
Morgan	J.	Dallas	AL	50	Physician	50,000	6,000	3
Morgan	John Tyler	Dallas	AL	36	Lawyer	6,500	10,000	
Moulton	C. H.	Montgomery	AL	34	Planter	84,000	212,340	
Murphy	John H.	Montgomery	AL	27	Merchant	75,000		
Myers	Robert C.	Montgomery	AL		Planter	20,000		
Myers	William P.	Sumter	AL	47	Farmer			
Myrick	Richard J.	Montgomery	AL	22	Physician			
Nash	James M.	Montgomery	AL	44	Broker		50,000	
Neal	Absalom D.	Pickens	AL	41	Farmer	15,000	40,000	27

Last Name	First Name	County	State	Age	Occupation	Real Estate ($)	Personal Estate ($)	Slaves (*N*)
Noble	John O.	Madison	AL	35	Merchant			
Norris	William Jefferson	Dallas	AL	52	Bank president		35,000	9
Northington	W. H.	Autauga	AL	38	Lawyer	5,000	30,000	11
Nott	Josiah Clark	Mobile	AL	56	Physician	40,000	10,000	16
Oliver	T. M.	Mobile	AL	45	Clerk			
Ormond	John J.	Tuscaloosa	AL	65	Lawyer	122,800	190,850	137
Patton	J. L.	Perry	AL	29	Farmer	12,000	50,000	47
Pearce	S. H.	Autauga	AL	37	Farmer	13,000	48,210	40
Pearson	James M.	Tallapoosa	AL	42	Planter	11,500	60,000	26
Peden	Warren W.	Franklin	AL	60	Farmer	26,000	60,000	51
Peebles	Howell W.	Clarke	AL		Farmer	5,000		
Pegues	Eliza H.	Dallas	AL		Widow	31,000	84,000	94
Pegues	S. W.	Dallas	AL	26	Planter			94
Petty	John F.	Mobile	AL	36	Jailor			
Pfister	Arnand P.	Montgomery	AL	58	Merchant			
Pickens	E. H.	Butler	AL	60	Clerk	7,000	30,000	
Pickens	James	Lawrence	AL	45	Farmer	1,000	500	
Pickett	Albert James	Montgomery	AL		Planter			68
Pitts	David W.	Perry	AL	39	Planter	30,000	40,000	50
Plaut	G. H.	Dallas	AL		Tinner	2,500		
Poellnitz	B. B.	Marengo	AL	38	Planter	15,000	38,000	54
Pollard	Charles Teed	Montgomery	AL	55	Railroad	215,000	350,000	116
Pratt	Daniel	Autauga	AL	61	Manufacturer	92,319	250,000	107
Price	James L.	Perry	AL	20	Planter	70,000	100,000	95
Pride	H. J.	Franklin	AL	55	Farmer	20,000	80,000	71
Pritchard	William	Marengo	AL	39	Overseer	8,000		
Redwood	George E.	Mobile	AL	47	Physician			
Reese	A. J.	Dallas	AL	33	Physician	18,000	150,000	139
Reese	J. S.	Autauga	AL	39	Planter	40,000	50,000	35
Reid	John Coleman	Perry	AL	36	Lawyer	1,500	10,970	8
Reid	Rufus J.	Perry	AL		Lawyer	3,500	25,375	8
Ridgeway	Bradley H.	Greene	AL	49	Planter	98,200	130,000	93
Rives	Thomas	Dallas	AL	74	Farmer	14,390	53,800	71
Roberts	J. W.	Montgomery	AL	48	Merchant	167,000	125,000	
Robinson	J. N.	Dallas	AL		Merchant			
Rogers	W. A.	Greene	AL	58	Physician	40,000	120,000	74
Root	Robert P.	Marshall	AL	29	Clerk			
Royston	L. Y.	Perry	AL	30	Lawyer			32
Rudulph	John B.	Butler	AL	57	Planter	14,468	67,890	12
Rumph	William M.	Dallas	AL	48	Farmer	25,000	80,000	17
Rutland	John W.	Franklin	AL	40	Farmer	40,000	65,000	15
Samford	William James	Lee	AL	43	Lawyer	15,000	39,000	
Saunders	G. B.	Sumter	AL	44	Law clerk	3,500	800	
Sayre	P. T.	Montgomery	AL	38	Lawyer	27,000	76,740	63
Scott	David B.	Bibb	AL	57	Manufacturer	4,000	50,000	8
Scruggs	James H.	Madison	AL	40	Judge	6,000	9,000	32
Seawell	J. H.	Bibb	AL	58	Physician	300	2,500	1
Sellers	Daniel C.	Wilcox	AL	40	Planter	29,000	108,700	116
Shegog	George	Lawrence	AL	35	Physician	200	14,000	12
Shephard	Alexander K.	Perry	AL		Planter	25,000	5,000	
Shortridge	George David	Shelby	AL	45	Lawyer	5,000	10,500	11
Sibley	Origen	Baldwin	AL	20	Timberman			130
Sledge	Leven A.	Marengo	AL	37	Planter	30,000	60,000	54
Sledge	William Henry	Sumter	AL	37	Physician	40,000	53,250	48
Smith	Etheldred L.	Lauderdale	AL	50	Farmer	15,000	21,000	17
Smith	J. B. R.	Barbour	AL	52	Farmer	1,500	5,000	3
Smith	Malcolm B.	Autauga	AL	60			134,000	

Last Name	First Name	County	State	Age	Occupation	Real Estate ($)	Personal Estate ($)	Slaves (*N*)
Smith	Washington M.	Dallas	AL		Farmer	45,000	80,000	83
Smyly	Daniel C.	Dallas	AL	41	Planter	35,000	78,000	78
Spencer	J. M.	Greene	AL	45	Physician	40,000	32,520	36
Stein	Albert	Mobile	AL	58	Engineer	10,000	2,500	6
Stone	John M.	Butler	AL	25	Brick mason	600	125	
Stone	Lewis Maxwell	Pickens	AL	41	Lawyer	12,000	34,595	4
Stradman	F. W.	Dallas	AL	38	Merchant	3,000	1,000	
Strother	G. H.	Wilcox	AL	40	Farmer	21,400	46,194	36
Strother	J. P.	Dallas	AL	54	Farmer	106,500	139,000	75
Suggs	Calvin A.	Greene	AL		Merchant			
Taylor	Solomon S.	Mobile	AL	42	Turpentine distiller	5,500	2,500	1
Taylor	William Henry	Montgomery	AL	62	Merchant	187,000	210,900	54
Terrell	A. J.	Montgomery	AL	44	Planter	15,000	57,500	
Thomas	C. E.	Dallas	AL	34	Merchant	12,000	25,000	12
Tompkins	Charles C.	Barbour	AL	39	Carriagemaker	2,500	2,500	1
Troy	D. S.	Dallas	AL	27	Lawyer	800	15,000	8
Vasser	Rebecca	Autauga	AL	20				
Walker	G. J. S.	Dallas	AL	17				73
Walker	LeRoy Pope	Madison	AL	40	Lawyer	128,000	155,000	6
Walker	Percy	Mobile	AL	45	Lawyer			3
Waller	W. W.	Montgomery	AL	45	Banker			7
Walthall	J. N.	Perry	AL	21	Farmer	49,560	90,000	107
Watts	Thomas Hill	Montgomery	AL	41	Lawyer	190,000	300,000	179
Weissinger	Leonard A.	Perry	AL	58	Farmer			
Whatley	George Craghn	Calhoun	AL	39	Lawyer	7,000	20,000	9
White	J. D.	Marion	AL	22	Merchant			
Whitfield	Gaius, Sr.	Marengo	AL	55	Planter	102,000	300,000	283
Williams	Price	Mobile	AL	49	Merchant	24,000	110,000	10
Winston	Thomas G.	Chambers	AL	46	Farmer	6,500	35,000	19
Winter	John G.	Russell	AL	61	Manufacturer	3,000	2,000	20
Winter	Joseph Samuel	Montgomery	AL	39	Lawyer	40,000		
Womack	John W.	Greene	AL	52	Lawyer	401,500	337,500	35
Woodfin	E. B.	Perry	AL	40	Farmer	45,000	88,000	5
Wray	Albert G.	Montgomery	AL	58	Farmer	6,600	34,570	18
Wren	J. K.	Lauderdale	AL	36	Manufacturer		6,000	
Wyatt	W. B. R.	Autauga	AL	38	Planter	26,000	40,000	43
Yancey	William L.	Montgomery	AL	46	Lawyer	27,000	60,000	
Alexander	C. B.	Drew	AR	40	Physician	8,000	2,000	1
Allen	A. A.	Drew	AR	41	Merchant	6,000	10,000	3
Anderson	Robert S.	Jackson	AR	33	Lawyer	18,920	900	
Bell	M. L.	Jefferson	AR	30	Lawyer	44,000	24,000	3
Board	C. W.	Jackson	AR	41	Merchant	4,000	1,000	
Bowen	John L.	Jackson	AR	44	Farmer			
Brown	W. D.	Jackson	AR	28	Speculator	2,000	2,000	
Burton	Robert A.	Phillips	AR	38	Physician	5,000	5,000	4
Clay	L. R.	Jackson	AR	38	Farmer	10,000	8,000	12
Dawson	L. E.	Ouachita	AR	29	Farmer	10,000	32,421	32
Dodd	William	Jackson	AR		Physician			
Gordon	Anderson	Conway	AR	40	Merchant	12,000	23,000	4
Gossett	L. C.	Jackson	AR	41	Carpenter	750	100	
Govan	William H.	Phillips	AR	28	Farmer	9,600	32,000	16
Hanly	Thomas Burton	Phillips	AR	46	Lawyer	100,000	20,000	13
Harris	J. L.	Clark	AR		Physician	3,800	5,000	
Henderson	J.	Jackson	AR	20	Gambler			
Henry	James A.	Pulaski	AR	42	Merchant	5,000	15,000	1
Hilliard	Isaac H.	Chicot	AR	49	Planter			81
Hubbard	James M.	Phillips	AR	50	Farmer	75,000	80,000	50

Last Name	First Name	County	State	Age	Occupation	Real Estate ($)	Personal Estate ($)	Slaves (*N*)
Jackson	Mead H.	Independence	AR	31	Physician	2,000	4,000	
Jones	H. M.	Jackson	AR	31	Physician	4,000	10,000	11
Jugo	W. H.	Jackson	AR	27	Bookkeeper		300	
Kellogg	R. R.	Jackson	AR	37	Law clerk	10,000	2,000	
King	Charles	Phillips	AR	28	Merchant	5,000	50,000	1
Main	John H. F.	Sebastian	AR		Physician	39,040	30,000	
Moore	James H.	Arkansas	AR		Planter	80,000	32,200	26
Patterson	W. K.	Jackson	AR	37	Lawyer	10,580	15,080	10
Pickett	W. H.	Jackson	AR	45	Physician	54,000	60,000	
Pike	Albert	Pulaski	AR	50	Lawyer	200,000	40,000	6
Priston	Walter	Phillips	AR	40	Farmer	50,000	100,000	
Redman	C.	Jackson	AR	37	Clerk	1,500	300	
Selvey	Garland	Jackson	AR	42		1,250		
Simmons	J. B.	Jackson	AR	25	Physician	1,000	2,500	1
Smith	W. R.	Jackson	AR		Merchant		5,000	
Thompson	Arthur	Phillips	AR	34	Gentleman	35,000	18,000	11
Ward	T. R.	Jackson	AR	40	Farmer	5,600	6,400	7
Watkins	F.	Jackson	AR	40	Physician	2,500	5,000	
Williams	R. P.	Hempstead	AR	21	Farmer	600	1,058	1
Anderson	James E.	Leon	FL	21	Physician			
Batchelder	George F. C.	Santa Rosa	FL	56	Merchant	40,000	10,000	8
Berry	Robert H.	Leon	FL	51	Merchant	4,000	7,000	2
Bloxham	William D.	Leon	FL	54	Farmer		25,000	31
Bond	J. S.	Leon	FL	27	Physician	4,000	10,000	12
Bradford	Edward	Leon	FL	30	Planter	29,000	74,000	130
Brevard	T. W.	Leon	FL	50	Lawyer	15,500	25,000	34
Brown	Thomas	Leon	FL		Farmer	30,000	2,000	
Bryan	C. A.	Leon	FL	30	Law clerk		300	
Call	Richard K.	Leon	FL	67	Planter	31,000	81,000	121
Campbell	Robert P.	Monroe	FL	50	Merchant	25,000	10,000	
Carr	William A.	Leon	FL	58	Farmer	31,000	56,000	67
Chain	John	Santa Rosa	FL	58	Lawyer	200	1,000	
Chaires	C. P.	Leon	FL	34	Farmer	18,000	58,000	93
Craig	W. P.	Leon	FL	52	Planter	13,000	37,000	35
Croom	George A.	Leon	FL	38	Planter	15,000	40,000	48
Davis	William W.	Leon	FL	48	Lawyer	5,000	20,000	20
Dupont	Charles H.	Gadsden	FL	55	Judge	55,000	75,000	64
Ewart	David	Marion	FL	74	Author		6,000	6
Fisher	A. A.	Leon	FL		Farmer	16,000	47,230	45
Flagg	F. H.	Leon	FL		Railroad treasurer	4,000	2,000	5
Gamble	John G.	Leon	FL		Physician			
Gamble	Robert	Leon	FL	45	Planter	8,000	15,000	4
Harrison	Richard	Madison	FL		Farmer	10,000		
Holland	D. P.	Franklin	FL	38	Lawyer		8,000	7
Joiner	J. W.	Marion	FL	38	Mechanic	1,200	200	
Long	Medicus A.	Leon	FL		Lawyer	20,000		
Maxwell	E. A.	Escambia	FL	41	Lawyer	7,000	8,000	2
Maxwell	G. T.	Leon	FL	32	Physician		25,000	14
Milton	John	Jackson	FL	52	Lawyer	40,000	40,000	36
Palmer	David L.	Duval	FL	65	Farmer	7,000	30,000	39
Parkhill	G. W.	Leon	FL	35	Physician	36,000	133,000	172
Perkins	Thomas J.	Leon	FL	43	Merchant	4,000	40,000	5
Randolph	J. L.	Leon	FL	40	Engineer		400	
Raney	David G.	Franklin	FL		Merchant			
Rutgers	H. L.	Leon	FL	55	Merchant			1
Sanders	Richard	Leon	FL		Sheriff		8,000	
Spencer	Samuel W.	Franklin	FL	40	Physician			14

Last Name	First Name	County	State	Age	Occupation	Real Estate ($)	Personal Estate ($)	Slaves (*N*)
Walker	David S.	Leon	FL		Judge	6,000	13,000	4
Ward	George Taliaferro	Leon	FL	50	Planter	70,000	130,650	115
Williams	James M.	Leon	FL		Merchant	5,000		
Williams	R. W.	Leon	FL	52	Planter	6,000	6,500	37
Alexander	A. L.	Wilkes	GA	57	Farmer	20,000	224,000	46
Allen	A. M.	Columbia	GA	44	Planter	5,000	2,769	20
Berrien	John M.	Floyd	GA	18	Clerk			
Bones	John	Richmond	GA	67	Merchant	35,000	200,000	11
Brigham	Henry	Chatham	GA	48	Merchant	32,000	35,000	7
Briscoe	Lucilius H.	Baldwin	GA	31	Lawyer	1,700	9,800	2
Broome	James J.	Richmond	GA	19	Merchant		700	
Brown	A. E. W.	Hancock	GA	56	Planter	20,000	50,000	25
Bruce	A. N.	Sumter	GA	34	Merchant	12,000	11,050	5
Bunn	Henry	Houston	GA	64	Manufacturer	42,300	93,650	113
Butt	John D.	Richmond	GA	34	Merchant	3,500	9,000	
Church	Alonzo	Clarke	GA	77	Minister	2,500	25,000	13
Clarke	Robert C.	Fulton	GA		Merchant			
Clarke	Thomas M.	Fulton	GA	31	Merchant			
Cohen	Moses S.	Chatham	GA	40	Merchant	7,000	10,000	
Crump	George H.	Richmond	GA	33	Merchant		150	
Cunningham	Alexander F.	Chatham	GA	75	Physician		3,000	
Dawson	James C.	Richmond	GA	38	Merchant			1
Denmead	Edward	Cobb	GA	47	Farmer	65,000	20,000	25
Dennis	Michael	Putnam	GA	58	Farmer	42,200	100,000	114
Dickens	Ephraim	DeKalb	GA	55	Farmer	200		
Erwin	Robert	Chatham	GA	28	Merchant	3,000	96,000	8
Farmer	John Jackson	Morgan	GA	35	Farmer	1,000	1,000	
Fleming	Porter	Richmond	GA	51	Merchant	33,000	35,000	24
Flewellen	A. C.	Muscogee	GA	35	Physician	10,000	28,000	7
Flournoy	Josiah A.	Macon	GA	31	Farmer	14,000	23,100	21
Foster	Nathaniel Greene	Morgan	GA	51	Lawyer	20,000	50,000	57
Gardner	James T., Jr.	Richmond	GA	36	Merchant		9,000	
Glover	J. H.	Cobb	GA	20		26,000	100,000	29
Goodrich	William H.	Richmond	GA	52	Builder	80,000	135,000	
Gowdy	Hill	Chatham	GA	41	Merchant	1,000	10,000	7
Guerard	John M.	Chatham	GA	32	Lawyer	1,500	5,000	
Hamilton	Luke M.	Chatham	GA	24	Railroad		20,000	1
Hammond	M. C. M.	Clarke	GA	45	Planter	30,000	80,000	17
Hanson	J. H.	Hall	GA	80	Lawyer	550	70	
Hardee	Noble A.	Chatham	GA	55	Merchant	50,000	100,000	9
Harris	Miles G.	Hancock	GA	56	Planter	25,000	54,000	70
Hartridge	Algernon S.	Chatham	GA	29	Merchant	13,400	147,000	6
Heard	Isaac T.	Richmond	GA	21	Merchant			
Hertz	Edwin E.	Chatham	GA	39	Merchant		25,000	
Hill	Benjamin H.	Troup	GA	37	Lawyer	30,000	40,000	59
Hill	R. G.	Decatur	GA	36	Farmer	10,000	20,500	40
Holcombe	Thomas	Chatham	GA	44	Merchant	27,000	10,000	12
Huff	William A.	Bibb	GA	26	Merchant	4,500	10,000	1
Hulbert	Edward C.	Fulton	GA	20	Railroad			
Hull	G. G.	Fulton	GA	31	Railroad president			15
Hurt	Joel E.	Muscogee	GA	40	Farmer	16,000	91,800	
Jackson	William E.	Richmond	GA	43	Manufacturer	72,200	46,000	14
Jones	Elijah E.	Morgan	GA	65	Physician	24,000	121,000	116
Jones	Seaborn	Muscogee	GA	65	Lawyer	125,500	54,000	67
Jossey	William J.	Spalding	GA	31	Railroad treasurer	7,000	7,000	
Lachlison	James	Chatham	GA	45	Manufacturer	7,300	15,400	2
Lathrop	James W.	Chatham	GA	44	Merchant	28,000	75,000	11

Last Name	First Name	County	State	Age	Occupation	Real Estate ($)	Personal Estate ($)	Slaves (*N*)
Lumpkin	Joseph Henry	Floyd	GA	61	Judge	9,000	48,000	6
Marshall	B. S.	Richmond	GA		Printer			
McCord	Zachariah	Richmond	GA	39	Merchant	4,000	54,600	8
Moore	J. B.	Decatur	GA	44	Farmer	10,000	120,000	
Moremen	John S.	Dougherty	GA	35	Farmer	6,000	29,200	
Nelson	John	Richmond	GA	44	Merchant	16,000	20,000	6
O'Neill	Hugh	Morgan	GA		Physician	15,000	60,325	70
Ormond	James	Fulton	GA	45	Merchant	21,000	20,000	18
Palmer	John T.	Burke	GA	37	Physician	10,000	6,248	6
Phillips	William	Cobb	GA		Lawyer	16,000	16,000	14
Pledger	W. H.	Elbert	GA	30	Farmer	2,000	2,700	
Porter	John W.	Morgan	GA	63	Farmer	13,600	32,700	53
Pow	Lewis W.	Jasper	GA		Farmer	7,750		
Printup	Daniel S.	DeKalb	GA		Railroad			4
Rasdal	Leander W.	Bibb	GA	21	Student			
Reid	Francis W.	Chatham	GA	29	Merchant	6,500	1,000	
Riley	A. Hamilton	Sumter	GA	39	Farmer	7,000	48,540	24
Ross	John B.	Bibb	GA	52	Merchant	120,000	332,000	16
Saffold	Thomas P.	Morgan	GA	38	Farmer	25,000	50,590	73
Saffold	William O.	Morgan	GA	47	Farmer	60,000	156,000	21
Shorter	Alfred	Floyd	GA	56	Farmer	125,000	232,000	64
Sims	Frederick W.	Chatham	GA	33	Publisher	2,400	20,500	1
Smith	W. R.	Floyd	GA	69	Farmer	100,000	72,000	19
Spallock	James M.	Floyd	GA	43	Farmer	12,000	18,000	24
Stephens	Alexander H.	Taliaferro	GA	48	Lawyer	18,000	35,000	30
Stovall	Pleasant	Clarke	GA	67	Merchant	80,000	80,000	
Sullivan	A. J.	Floyd	GA	18	Clerk			
Thompson	James F.	Richmond	GA		Printer			
Tison	John M.	Glynn	GA	41	Merchant	8,000	40,000	76
Tison	William H.	Chatham	GA	47	Merchant	14,000	45,000	8
Tunno	William M.	Chatham	GA	54	Merchant			
Walker	E. J.	Richmond	GA		Lawyer		3,500	
Walker	William W.	Richmond	GA	35	Railroad clerk		500	
White	Samuel G.	Baldwin	GA		Physician	18,900	45,350	45
Wilcox	Albert	Chatham	GA	50	Dentist		500	
Williams	William T.	Chatham	GA	75	Merchant	7,050	38,000	
Willis	Richard J.	Greene	GA	70	Farmer	30,000	86,000	92
Adams	Asbury Arnold	Sumter	GA	32	Farmer	23,000	40,000	37
Adams	William B.	Chatham	GA	35	Bookkeeper		1,500	
Alexander	John William R.	Floyd	GA	41	Lawyer	4,000		8
Alexander	William F.	Floyd	GA	27	Farmer	300	150	
Ansley	Jesse A.	Richmond	GA	34	Merchant	19,000	5,000	
Arnett	F. G.	Decatur	GA	50	Farmer	80,000	40,000	10
Ayres	Asher	Bibb	GA	46	Merchant	50,000	59,000	5
Baker	Boling	Fulton	GA	40	Lawyer			5
Barry	Edward	Richmond	GA	42	Druggist		20,000	
Bashlor	James H.	Chatham	GA	50	Merchant	1,500		1
Batty	Thomas A.	Columbia	GA		Druggist			
Beall	Albert A.	Richmond	GA	30	Merchant		6,000	
Beard	George R.	Orleans	GA	36	Warehouses	14,000	2,000	13
Bloom	Thurston R.	Bibb	GA	36	Merchant	77,500	59,000	48
Boston	John	Chatham	GA	59	Port collector	6,000	70,000	8
Cheever	William W.	Chatham	GA	36	Merchant		500	
Cheeves	Isaac G.	Macon	GA	49	Farmer	15,000	55,800	49
Cuyler	Richard R.	Chatham	GA	62	Banker	20,000	50,000	3
Cuyler	William H.	Chatham	GA	65	Judge	33,000	44,000	22
French	Hiram L.	Schley	GA	41	Farmer	3,000	1,000	

Last Name	First Name	County	State	Age	Occupation	Real Estate ($)	Personal Estate ($)	Slaves (*N*)
Graves	J. P.	Houston	GA		Farmer	8,000	8,000	
Gresham	John J.	Bibb	GA		Lawyer	50,000	100,000	8
Lathrop	Harvey W.	Chatham	GA	40	Merchant	10,000	45,000	
Lewis	Daviet W.	Hancock	GA	43	Planter	20,000	50,000	75
Lincoln	William W.	Chatham	GA	46	Druggist	8,000	25,000	4
Linton	John Sankey	Clarke	GA	47	Manufacturer	10,000	55,000	45
McGehee	Edmund J.	Houston	GA	46	Planter	35,000	38,000	57
Ponce	Demos	Hancock	GA	77	Planter	5,000	14,700	21
Powell	N. B.	Decatur	GA		Farmer	3,000	1,500	15
Winmberly	E. A.	Houston	GA	36	Farmer	11,000	22,500	33
Wooding	Robert E.	Columbia	GA		Planter	3,000		
Woolfolk	James H.	Bibb	GA		Merchant	18,000	23,000	68
Word	R. H.	Greene	GA	46	Farmer	9,000	37,000	40
Abney	Lucien B.	Fleming	KY	25	Physician			
Ainslie	George	Jefferson	KY	46	Iron founder			
Archer	James	Jefferson	KY	69	Farmer		450	
Baird	Robert F.	Jefferson	KY	44	Lawyer	10,000	25,000	4
Baxter	John G.	Jefferson	KY	35	Manufacturer	8,000	3,000	
Bell	John	Jefferson	KY	41	Merchant	7,000	100,000	7
Bremaker	Charles	Jefferson	KY	28	Merchant	6,000	3,000	1
Bruce	Eli Metcalfe	Kenton	KY	52	Farmer	2,800	8,400	14
Buchanan	George C.	Jefferson	KY	26	Fisherman	300	30	
Cochran	Archibald P.	Jefferson	KY	36	Manufacturer	50,000	28,000	
Fisher	J. W.	Jefferson	KY	26	Merchant		700	
Fox	William H.	Jefferson	KY		Merchant	25,000	69,000	
Gardner	Edward A.	Jefferson	KY	47	Merchant	27,000	74,000	
Garvin	William	Jefferson	KY	64	Merchant	100,000	400,000	13
Gibson	Hart	Fayette	KY	25	Lawyer			
Harbison	Alexander	Jefferson	KY	66	Merchant	39,000	22,000	3
Hutchings	D. B.	Logan	KY	26	Farmer	20,000	15,000	14
Lambert	Robert B.	Nelson	KY	46	Clergy			
Macklin	George B.	Franklin	KY	29	Pork merchant		2,000	
Monks	Joseph	Jefferson	KY	49	Merchant	145,000	65,500	
Moore	John	Jefferson	KY	32	Merchant			1
Newcomb	H. D.	Jefferson	KY	50	Merchant	200,000	250,000	1
Slevin	Thomas	Jefferson	KY		Merchant			
Speed	James	Jefferson	KY	48	Lawyer	50,000	10,000	4
Tompkins	Samuel D.	Jefferson	KY	35	Merchant	5,000	15,000	
Warren	Levi L.	Jefferson	KY	51	Merchant	100,000	75,000	
Watson	John	Jefferson	KY	36	Merchant	25,000	25,000	
Welby	George	Jefferson	KY	45	Merchant		15,000	
Weller	Jacob F.	Jefferson	KY	28	Merchant			
Wicks	George W.	Jefferson	KY	35	Merchant	8,000	14,000	
Wilder	J. B.	Jefferson	KY	46	Druggist	10,000	60,000	3
Aime	Valcour	St. James	LA	63	Sugar refiner	160,000	229,300	
Augustin	Numa	Orleans	LA	48	Merchant		3,000	4
Bach	J. M.	Jefferson	LA	60	Merchant	10,000	6,000	
Bagley	Anderson	Carroll	LA	37	Physician	69,000	94,465	60
Baker	John H.	Orleans	LA	44	Clerk		2,000	1
Barand	A.	Orleans	LA	55	Teacher	1,800		
Barnett	Felix	Bossier	LA	36	Planter	5,700	6,190	
Barrow	David	West Feliciana	LA	54	Planter	446,800	871,165	103
Barrow	R. H.	West Feliciana	LA	36	Planter	126,000	326,000	144
Barrow	W. R.	West Feliciana	LA	28	Planter	8,000	50,000	108
Beard	William W.	Morehouse	LA	33	Teacher	2,300	4,600	
Beatty	William J.	Rapides	LA	36	Farmer	81,600	7,880	50
Bellier	J. B.	Rapides	LA	47	Minister			

Last Name	First Name	County	State	Age	Occupation	Real Estate ($)	Personal Estate ($)	Slaves (*N*)
Benjamin	Judah P.	Orleans	LA	49	Lawyer			
Black	Charles	Orleans	LA	45	Merchant			
Blanchard	C. H.	Rapides	LA	54	Farmer	12,500	6,400	19
Bonzeno	M. F.	Orleans	LA	45	Physician			
Bringier	L. A.	Ascension	LA	32	Planter	80,000	90,000	147
Briscal	Claiborne C.	Madison	LA	30	Lawyer	3,000	25,000	
Briscoe	J. W.	Tensas	LA	41	Planter	160,000	170,000	10
Brousseau	A.	Orleans	LA	45	Merchant		60,000	8
Brown	J. C.	Caddo	LA	37	Farmer	2,500	250	
Brown	Shepherd	Orleans	LA	55	Merchant	107,500	300,000	10
Brunot	Felix R.	Baton Rouge	LA	25	Lawyer			4
Burnley	Harden	Assumption	LA	56	Planter	25,000	45,000	41
Bush	Louis	Lafourche	LA	40	Lawyer	70,000	70,000	16
Cain	Sylvester H.	Caddo	LA			5,000		18
Caldwell	Lafayette	Baton Rouge	LA	35		50,000	39,000	61
Calhoun	Meredith	Rapides	LA	55	Farmer	1,079,900	50,000	709
Cammack	C. W.	Orleans	LA	45	Merchant	20,000	4,000	1
Campbell	J. B.	Orleans	LA		Cooper			
Carriere	A.	Orleans	LA	58	Merchant	40,000	56,000	2
Catlin	John D.	Carroll	LA	31	Planter	38,400	45,425	
Chambers	Josiah	Rapides	LA	40	Farmer	458,500	28,000	335
Cheney	Oscar	Rapides	LA	31	Farmer	14,200	975	22
Choppin	Vor	St. James	LA	43	Farmer	109,000	100,000	
Clarke	J. G.	Orleans	LA	56	Physician			
Coffin	John D.	Orleans	LA	54	Sawman			2
Coleman	N. D.	Madison	LA	60	Planter	57,000	270,000	18
Collins	T. W.	Orleans	LA	48	Lawyer	12,000	1,000	
Colombe	D.	Point Coupee	LA	50	Planter	4,000	50	
Compton	L. G.	Rapides	LA	35	Farmer	592,400	41,780	51
Conrad	Charles Magill	Orleans	LA	56	Merchant	100,000	3,000	
Conrad	F. D.	Baton Rouge	LA	61	Farmer	150,000	282,000	237
Crawford	W.	Orleans	LA	54	Broker	15,000	10,000	
Creighton	J. R.	Attakapas	LA	44	Planter	11,700	29,850	37
Cunningham	Michael	Orleans	LA	29	Merchant			
Cushman	Ralph	Avoyelles	LA	60	Judge	6,000		
Daunis	M. H.	Terrebonne	LA	40	Planter	75,000	123,000	25
Denegre	James D.	Orleans	LA	48	Merchant	250,000	550,000	6
Desbrest	L.	St. Landry	LA	27	Merchant		3,000	
Desmare	Alphonse	Orleans	LA	34	Merchant		1,000	
Dimitry	M. D.	Orleans	LA	50	Teacher	20,000	1,000	1
Dugue	F.	Jefferson	LA	45	Farmer	340,000	125,000	80
Dunbar	G. W.	Orleans	LA	40	Merchant	20,000	8,000	
Dupre	L. J.	Opelousas	LA	36	Lawyer	10,000	60,000	
Dupuy	Gustave O.	St. John	LA	30	Merchant		5,000	
Dyer	D. H.	Claiborne	LA	45	Farmer	5,000	15,000	10
Eastin	R. F.	St. Martin	LA	35	Judge	15,000	2,000	11
Elder	D. J.	Caddo	LA	32	Merchant	12,000	25,000	2
Fellows	Cornelius	Orleans	LA	50	Merchant	200,000	100,000	6
Fergusson	H. B.	Rapides	LA	35	Farmer	38,500	2,800	31
Field	Spencer	Orleans	LA	50	Merchant	9,000	3,000	3
Flournoy	J. H.	Ouachita	LA	32	Merchant			
Ford	J. M. P.	Caddo	LA	51	Farmer	42,000	5,000	4
Forstall	E. J.	Orleans	LA	65	Merchant	50,000	25,000	14
Freret	George A.	Orleans	LA	43	Banker	12,000	10,000	
Gaines	C. C.	Orleans	LA	30	Bookkeeper			
Gayarré	Charles	St. Helena	LA	55	Politician			7
Gazza	Jean B. C.	Lafourche	LA	41	Physician	6,000	2,000	2

Last Name	First Name	County	State	Age	Occupation	Real Estate ($)	Personal Estate ($)	Slaves (*N*)
Gerand	P. A.	Orleans	LA	50	Merchant	50,000	2,500	3
Gerard	M. E.	Orleans	LA	31	Lawyer	3,100	12,500	
Gibson	Tobias	Terrebonne	LA	59	Planter	300,000	234,000	29
Glass	T. A.	Claiborne	LA	38	Farmer	20,000	34,000	27
Goldenbow	William	Orleans	LA	36	Shipping agent	20,000	5,000	
Goodwin	D. C.	Rapides	LA	49	Farmer	40,550	5,800	
Graham	George Mason	Rapides	LA	53	Farmer	206,000	14,970	
Gray	A. M.	Avoyelles	LA	49	Farmer	90,000	5,000	33
Grima	Felix	Orleans	LA	62	Lawyer	23,000	5,050	6
Gunther	Louis	Orleans	LA		Merchant			
Hagan	John	Iberville	LA		Planter	203,500	8,000	38
Hamilton	W. S.	West Feliciana	LA	90	Planter	80,000	169,800	154
Haralson	H. B.	Baton Rouge	LA	50	Farmer	10,000	52,000	47
Harper	F. A. F	Franklin	LA	42	Lawyer	4,200	1,000	
Hart	S. M.	Baton Rouge	LA	44	Merchant	27,700	10,000	1
Herron	August F.	Orleans	LA	25	Merchant			
Herron	Francis J.	Orleans	LA	23	Merchant			
Higgins	J. T.	Orleans	LA	25	Merchant	12,000	9,000	
Hooper	C. A.	Catahoula	LA	39	Planter	180,000	10,000	69
Hopkins	H.	Orleans	LA	32	Clerk			
Hopkins	Harvey	Attakapas	LA	52	Planter	100,000	10,000	72
Huger	J. M.	Orleans	LA	50	Merchant	63,500	500	17
Hyams	S. M.	Natchitoches	LA	47	Planter	107,000	77000	25
Hynson	Robert C.	Rapides	LA	64	Farmer	148,250	69,000	
Ivy	William N.	Assumption	LA	70	Planter	83,500	74,000	
James	John	Rapides	LA	35	Teamster			
Janvier	H. P.	Jefferson	LA	25	Insurance	13,000	10,000	
Jenkins	W.	Madison	LA	41	Planter	65,000	2,500	26
Jennings	N. R.	St. Helena	LA	50	Farmer	12,000	21,980	14
Johnson	William A.	Orleans	LA	33	Merchant			
Kennedy	R. B.	East Feliciana	LA	40	Planter	15,000	35,000	30
Kenner	Duncan F.	Ascension	LA	47	Planter	90,000	250,000	473
Kleinpeter	Josiah	Baton Rouge	LA	31	Farmer	9,000	21,750	17
Kohn	J.	Orleans	LA	30	Tailor			
Lapeze	J. M.	St. John	LA	44	Merchant	9,000	3,000	
Lea	J. N.	Orleans	LA	45	Lawyer	7,000	4,000	
Lebourgeois	Louis S.	St. James	LA	39	Farmer	135,000	143,200	
Lesparre	Auguste	Orleans	LA	35	Shipping agent			
Lesseps	Charles	Lafourche	LA	38	Farmer	40,000	25,000	
Levy	E. L.	Orleans	LA	49	Merchant	15,000	20,000	2
Levy	H. J.	Orleans	LA	33	Merchant		2,500	4
Levy	S. L.	Orleans	LA	51	Merchant	150,000	30,000	
Lewis	A. D.	Bossier	LA	27	Clerk			
Lewis	J. L.	Claiborne	LA	52	Farmer	100,000	100,000	9
Logan	Daniel P.	Orleans	LA	47	Merchant	20,000	40,000	2
Luckett	Robert C.	Rapides	LA	22	Physician			
Lyall	John	Lafourche	LA	55	Farmer	105,000	81,000	34
Lyman	Joseph B.	Orleans	LA	31	Lawyer		250	
Maddox	Thomas H.	Rapides	LA	66	Farmer	270,500	8,870	186
Magruder	Leonard	Rapides	LA	24	Farmer	88,800	6,880	51
Maher	Philip	Madison	LA	49	Planter	300,000	5,000	81
Mandeville	H. D.	Catahoula	LA	48	Planter	180,000	10,000	
Martin	James	Carroll	LA		Merchant		1,800	
Martin	W. C.	Claiborne	LA	47	Merchant	2,500	3,000	
Martyn	S. Craig	Orleans	LA	52	Physician		17,000	
Mayer	John F.	Orleans	LA	54	Trader		350	
McCall	Duncan	Tensas	LA	33	Planter	58,400	34,000	78

Last Name	**First Name**	**County**	**State**	**Age**	**Occupation**	**Real Estate ($)**	**Personal Estate ($)**	**Slaves (*N*)**
McCarty	J. C.	Orleans	LA	30	Tailor			
McChristy	John	Baton Rouge	LA	32	Farmer	2,000	12,000	9
McCord	David	Orleans	LA	48	Clerk		500	
McHatton	James A.	Baton Rouge	LA	45	Farmer	100,000	130,000	107
Miles	William M.	Orleans	LA	40	Lawyer	200,000	120,000	
Mitchell	J. J.	Orleans	LA	38	Merchant	2,000	3,000	
Mittenburger	C. A.	Orleans	LA	45	Merchant			
Moise	E. M.	Jefferson	LA	49	Lawyer	12,000	12,000	5
Moore	John	St. Martin	LA	72	Planter	25,000	10,000	
Moore	Thomas Overton	Rapides	LA	56	Planter	320,000	24,300	226
Mount	William S.	Orleans	LA	48	Cashier	3,000	4,000	
Musgrove	R. G.	Orleans	LA	37	Broker	18,000	40,000	1
Mussina	Jacob	Orleans	LA	35	Merchant			
Newton	Cincinnatus W.	Orleans	LA	37	Merchant		5000	
Noland	Joseph	Madison	LA	37	Planter	150,000	5,000	66
Osborne	M. S.	Franklin	LA	47	Farmer	30,000	6,000	58
Palmer	Benjamin Morgan	Orleans	LA	43	Minister		3,000	5
Patrick	Jesse C.	Baton Rouge	LA	60	Planter	1,075,000	45,000	57
Pemberton	John	Orleans	LA	41	Insurance president	45,000	25,000	5
Phillips	H.	Claiborne	LA	54	Gentleman	2,000	8,000	7
Pierce	G. M.	Baton Rouge	LA	35	Farmer	12,000	60,500	15
Pohlhaus	John H.	Orleans	LA		Accountant			
Porche	E.	Terrebonne	LA	60	Planter	30,000	81,600	39
Prescott	Aaron	Rapides	LA	53	Farmer	125,000	18,880	59
Prudhome	Emile S.	Natchitoches	LA	27	Planter	16,000	48,805	41
Ranney	H. J.	Orleans	LA	48	Railroad president	250,000	100,000	17
Reed	James	Plaquemines	LA	55	Farmer	10,000	1,300	2
Richard	A. R.	Orleans	LA		Merchant			
Richards	Newton	Orleans	LA	45	Stone cutter		3,000	
Richardson	F. D.	St. Mary	LA	47	Planter	60,000	60,000	24
Riddle	J. L.	Orleans	LA	53	Professor	145,000	30,000	
Robb	James	Orleans	LA	46	Railroad president			4
Robertson	Edward White	Baton Rouge	LA	37	State auditor	5,000	11,200	
Roselius	Christian	Jefferson	LA	56	Lawyer	150,000	30,000	
Ross	James	Orleans	LA	50	Flour inspector	10,000	5,500	7
Rost	P. A.	St. Charles	LA	60	Judge		600,000	83
Scarborough	Thomas C.	Carroll	LA	43	Engineer	2,500	5,700	
Seger	Augustin B.	Orleans	LA	42	Railroad officer	4,000	2,000	5
Short	Hugh	Carroll	LA	45	Lawyer	50,000	30,000	13
Shute	T. L.	Orleans	LA	52	Merchant		10,000	
Simms	B. B.	St. Landry	LA	38	Farmer	5,000	17,600	30
Slawson	J. B.	Orleans	LA	45	Omnibus owner	150,000	5,000	
Soule	Pierre	New Orleans	LA	55	Lawyer			
Sparrow	Edward	Carroll	LA	49	Lawyer	665,550	582,000	138
Starke	W. H.	Orleans	LA	35	Clerk			
Stern	Henry	Orleans	LA	27	Merchant			
Stokes	J. A.	Baton Rouge	LA	39	Farmer	15,000	20,000	28
Stone	Harry B.	Orleans	LA		Harborman			
Thibodaux	Bannon Goforth	Lafourche	LA	48	Planter	63,300	110,000	29
Thompson	Edward	Orleans	LA		Merchant			
Thompson	W. E.	Orleans	LA	60	Merchant	100,000	40,000	7
Thornton	Charles A.	Rapides	LA	47	Farmer	100,000	4,900	89
Tilton	Frederick W.	Orleans	LA	40	Merchant	54,000	10,000	2
Tucker	George W.	Lafourche	LA		Farmer	20,000	20,000	71
Tully	A. J.	Orleans	LA	30	Merchant	20,000	100,000	
Urguhart	George	Orleans	LA	45		50,000	10,000	
Waddill	W. W.	Avoyelles	LA	32	Lawyer	340	1,000	

Last Name	First Name	County	State	Age	Occupation	Real Estate ($)	Personal Estate ($)	Slaves (*N*)
Welsh	Michael	Rapides	LA	56	Farmer	12,000	2,300	64
White	George A.	Orleans	LA	30	Customhouse			
White	Maunsel	Plaquemines	LA	77	Planter	60,000	150,000	192
Williams	John R.	Rapides	LA	38	Farmer	330,000	24,000	238
Woodward	J. S.	Orleans	LA	37	Merchant		6,000	2
York	Zebulon	Concordia	LA	33	Lawyer	12,000	5,000	62
Zacharie	J. W.	Orleans	LA	62	Merchant	380,000	20,000	11
Zeigler	F. M.	Orleans	LA	42	Merchant	10,000	8,000	
Austin	Thomas S.	Baltimore	MD	43	Clerk	1,000	300	
Baker	Richard J.	Baltimore	MD	45	Merchant	25,000	600	
Birckhead	James, Jr.	Baltimore	MD	35				
Cannon	James	Baltimore	MD	55	Mariner			
Clebaugh	Edward A.	Baltimore	MD	42	Merchant	10,000	2,500	
Cromer	Thomas W.	Baltimore	MD	41	Merchant	10,000	5,000	
De Ford	Charles	Baltimore	MD	46	Merchant			
Dennis	William R.	Baltimore	MD	62	Cooper		100	
Garther	George O.	Baltimore	MD	38	Agent			5
Gilmor	William	Baltimore	MD		Notary public	110,000	10,000	
Hamilton	M. A.	Baltimore	MD	26	Merchant			
Harvey	Joshua G.	Baltimore	MD	35	Produce dealer		10,000	
Jenkins	Michael	Baltimore	MD		Lawyer	20,000	10,000	
Kirkland	Alexander	Baltimore	MD	76	Merchant	25,000	50,000	
Knabe	William	Baltimore	MD	57	Pianomaker	22,000	50,000	
Lightner	William P.	Baltimore	MD	39	Collector	19,000	4,000	
O'Donnell	Columbus	Baltimore	MD		Manufacturer	300,000	130,000	
Pendergast	James F.	Baltimore	MD	40	Merchant		40,000	
Pennington	William C.	Baltimore	MD	31	Lawyer			
Prestman	George	Baltimore	MD	21	Property agent	20,000	10,000	
Sterling	Archibald	Baltimore	MD	50	Merchant	35,000	80,000	
Taylor	William W.	Baltimore	MD	39	Merchant	20,000	50,000	1
Adams	Wirt	Issaquena	MS	25	Planter			113
Alexander	Amos	Adams	MS	65	Farmer	280,000	20,000	21
Anderson	Edward H.	Madison	MS	42	Physician	22,700	51,550	9
Anderson	John N.	Yazoo	MS	37	Planter		1,200	32
Arthur	Alexander H.	Warren	MS	46	Judge	7,600	500	13
Atchison	R. H.	Adams	MS	49	Physician	18,000	18,000	7
Avery	Edwin M.	Hinds	MS		Merchant	5,000		2
Baine	Alexander C.	Adams	MS	36	Rafterman			
Baker	Edwin Backus	Adams	MS	20	Merchant	16,000	20,000	5
Balfour	W. S.	Issaquena	MS	32	Planter			86
Balfour	William J.	Adams	MS	28	Planter	50,000	150,000	10
Ballard	Lott	Noxubee	MS	62	Planter	26,850	82,362	69
Banks	James	Lowndes	MS	31	Physician	195,000	225,000	128
Barksdale	Ethelbert	Hinds	MS	35	Editor			6
Barksdale	Harrison	Yazoo	MS		Planter	50,000	84,650	56
Barnes	J. M.	Copiah	MS	31	Farmer	10,000	14,000	
Barnett	J. W.	Yazoo	MS	46	Planter	102,000	81,164	58
Battley	W. H.	Madison	MS	46	Planter	21,000	72,000	67
Beck	Thomas W.	Carroll	MS	60	Planter	2,500	17,000	10
Bellamy	Edward	Bolivar	MS	59	Physician	70,000	106,000	27
Blair	James	Lowndes	MS	45	Druggist	14,000	35,000	2
Blanchard	W. A.	Monroe	MS	47	Farmer	49,564	117,050	90
Blanton	Orville Martin	Washington	MS		Physician			
Blewett	Randle	Lowndes	MS	30	Planter	48,000	65,000	1
Blewett	Thomas G.	Lowndes	MS	71	Planter	80,000	190,000	65
Bottens	Sampson	Holmes	MS	41	Farmer	11,000	35,920	7
Boyd	Elijah	Adams	MS	45	Merchant	6,000	11,000	1

Last Name	First Name	County	State	Age	Occupation	Real Estate ($)	Personal Estate ($)	Slaves (*N*)
Boyd	M. W.	Hinds	MS	28	Overseer	10,000	48,000	
Bridewell	L. O.	Claiborne	MS	55	Planter	10,000	25,000	25
Brooke	Walker	Warren	MS	47	Lawyer	10,000	75,000	5
Brown	James	Lafayette	MS	65	Planter	485,110	189,000	74
Buckley	H. D.	Holmes	MS	36	Trader	2,000	7,329	5
Burrus	John R.	Yazoo	MS	45	Planter	72,000	160,820	122
Bynum	Joseph M.	Tishomingo	MS	58	Physician	15,000	80,000	55
Caldwell	J. V.	Yazoo	MS	46	Merchant	2,100		
Cannon	W. R.	Lowndes	MS	40	Planter	38,000	45,000	17
Capshaw	Preston	Holmes	MS	65	Physician	8,000	31,500	36
Cason	J. T.	Holmes	MS	36	Farmer	16,737	38,365	11
Clapp	Jeremiah W.	Marshall	MS	44	Lawyer	139,000	136,600	16
Clayton	Alexander M.	Marshall	MS	58	Lawyer	900,000	150,000	140
Coffield	Horatio D.	Issaquena	MS	40	Planter	52,500	57,000	35
Coker	George M.	Hinds	MS	47	Farmer	15,000	25,000	26
Cooper	William	Warren	MS		Planter	20,000	40,000	41
Cross	Cyprian	Madison	MS	52	Physician	2,500	23,500	18
Crowder	R. D.	Yalobusha	MS	54	Farmer	50,000	100,000	78
Crump	John W.	Lowndes	MS	41	Planter	75,000	50,000	42
Davis	E. M.	Marshall	MS	58	Farmer	300,000	168,000	114
Davis	H. P.	Holmes	MS	29	Physician		320	
Davis	Jefferson	Warren	MS	58	Planter	100,000	225,000	365
Dent	Warren R.	Jefferson	MS	42	Planter	150,000	110,000	76
Duncan	J. H.	Jefferson	MS	68	Physician		9,000	
Edmondson	Robert W	Pontotoc	MS	39	Judge	3,300	29,275	19
Edwards	R. O.	Hinds	MS	47	Farmer	105,000	276,600	124
Elliott	R. T.	Hinds	MS	28	Farmer	44,000	78,880	67
Emannuel	Morris	Warren	MS	56	Physician	65,000	14,500	9
Enloe	Isaac	Neshoba	MS	52	Lawyer	1,200	600	
Farrar	A. K.	Adams	MS	43	Farmer	110,000	300,000	204
Featherston	Edward	Chickasaw	MS		Farmer	15,000		
Foster	James	Adams	MS	45	Physician	6,000	5,000	
Freeman	J. A.	De Soto	MS	28	Planter	9,000	15,050	7
French	S. G.	Warren	MS	40	Farmer	13,000	23,000	
Gaillard	Thomas B.	Adams	MS	36	Planter	10,000	20,000	36
Gale	A. G.	Yazoo	MS	33	Planter	24,980	53,832	49
Garrett	James	Adams	MS	50	Law clerk	1,500	10,000	
Gates	S. P.	Chickasaw	MS	38	Farmer	31,000	50,000	76
Gibbs	A. J.	Warren	MS	29	Physician	30,000	7,000	8
Gibbs	G. W.	Hinds	MS	45	Merchant	85,000	318,000	16
Gibbs	H. D.	Hinds	MS	49	Farmer	9,000	56,320	47
Gibbs	Waits E.	Lowndes	MS	28	Trader	3,000	8,000	4
Gibson	D.	Warren	MS	48	Farmer	10,000	65,000	59
Gladney	James B.	Chickasaw	MS	49	Farmer	45,000	50,000	60
Gordon	Robert	Pontotoc	MS	65	Planter	200,000	180,000	21
Graves	J.	Hinds	MS		Planter	140,000	220,000	39
Hamilton	James	Lowndes	MS	40	Merchant	73,000	20,000	79
Harris	S. H.	Lowndes	MS	31	Physician	7,000	25,000	26
Harris	Wiley Pope	Hinds	MS	40	Lawyer	5,000	34,000	
Harrison	Isham	Lowndes	MS	37	Lawyer	47,000	90,000	69
Harrison	Wiley H.	Noxubee	MS	53	Planter	3,000	80,000	61
Hart	James D.	Madison	MS	57	Planter	100,000	130,000	108
Henry	George W.	Pontotoc	MS	40	Teacher	1,600	5,400	4
Herron	W. E.	Noxubee	MS	30	Minister		1,000	
Hicks	Edward	Jefferson	MS	36	Lawyer	17,870	30,585	
Hill	T. J.	Copiah	MS	30	Overseer		1,500	
Hill	W. R.	Yazoo	MS	60	Planter			86

Last Name	First Name	County	State	Age	Occupation	Real Estate ($)	Personal Estate ($)	Slaves (*N*)
Hodges	J. F.	Holmes	MS	32	Planter	10,800	26,315	18
Hooker	C. M.	Choctaw	MS	28	Farmer	1,920	2,055	
Hooker	Charles Edward	Hinds	MS	35	Lawyer	25,000	30,000	1
Howry	James Moorman	Lafayette	MS	56	Planter	75,000	34,000	18
Hudson	Isaac	Bolivar	MS	50	Farmer	131,000	50,000	44
Hughes	Felix	Warren	MS	35	Planter	10,000	10,000	7
Hull	Isaac	Coohoma	MS	35	Physician	33,600	51,700	47
Humphries	William D.	Lowndes	MS	24	Merchant	20,000	40,000	51
Hunter	Charles M.	Noxubee	MS	27	Planter	6,000	12,000	9
Jackson	Dempsey P.	Adams	MS	65	Planter	12,000	18,000	13
Johnson	N. G.	Holmes	MS	46	Physician		1,850	
Johnson	S. C.	Holmes	MS	56	Planter	480	891	
Johnson	W. H.	Warren	MS	46	Planter	85,000	115,000	83
Latham	H.	Warren	MS	56	Farmer	250,000	150,000	21
Love	William C.	Madison	MS	34	Planter	27,000	36,700	39
Marsh	W. D.	Clarke	MS	51	Physician	30,000	87,000	81
Marshall	C. K.	Warren	MS	47	Minister	100,400	7,000	7
Mason	Eilbeck	Warren	MS		Lawyer	20,000		
McAlpine	E. K.	Claiborne	MS	25	Planter	10,000	80,000	
McGehee	Miles H.	Bolivar	MS	47	Planter	240,000	230,000	234
McQuiston	W. C.	Chickasaw	MS	26	Lawyer	250	20,000	18
Metcalfe	Henry L.	Adams	MS	30	Planter	50,000	125,000	112
Metcalfe	James	Adams	MS	62	Planter	80,000	325,000	304
Metcalfe	Oren	Adams	MS	50	Sheriff	28,000	40,000	2
Miller	Calvin	Panola	MS	50	Lawyer	70,000	20,000	6
Moody	E.	Hinds	MS	45	Farmer	30,000	50,000	41
Moody	E.	Hinds	MS	45	Planter	30,000	50,000	41
Moore	A. T.	Neshoba	MS	23	Farmer	1,200	3,086	1
Morey	J. B.	Madison	MS	35	Druggist	2,500	30,000	1
Mortimer	G. J.	Lawrence	MS	30	Farmer	17,000	25,000	29
Murdock	Abram	Lowndes	MS	49	Merchant	20,000	30,000	4
Nailer	D. B.	Warren	MS	49	Physician	5,000	60,000	17
Napier	J. C.	Hinds	MS	54	Farmer	25,000	14,800	13
Napier	J. C.	Hinds	MS	54	Farmer	25,000	14,800	13
Nelson	J. H.	De Soto	MS		Professor	15,700	2,200	
Orr	H. C.	Pontotoc	MS	26	Physician	28,000	34,750	26
Otley	John K.	Lowndes	MS	40	Merchant	5,000	50,000	
Parker	H. H.	Rankin	MS	41	Physician	16,000	37,200	28
Parks	Willie S.	Tishomingo	MS		House carpenter		1,200	
Paul	John S.	Yazoo	MS	50	Planter	50,000	65,790	61
Penny	J. W.	Yazoo	MS	55	Planter	7,200	3,850	2
Perryman	A.	Clarke	MS	50	Planter	50,000	75,000	58
Phillips	M. A.	Chickasaw	MS		Merchant			
Phillips	Z. A.	Hinds	MS		Factory manager		9,000	
Pickett	R. K.	Yazoo	MS	57	Planter	30,000	89,070	73
Polk	F. M.	Lawrence	MS	40	Farmer	2,000	10,000	9
Pope	H. A.	Noxubee	MS		Planter			66
Potter	G. L.	Hinds	MS	46	Lawyer	10,000	20,000	
Prince	William B.	Carroll	MS	30	Planter	550,000	400,000	150
Proper	Daniel H.	Wilkinson	MS		Planter	1,195	19,158	
Putman	J. D.	Hinds	MS	18				
Roach	J. Wilkins	Adams	MS	46	Planter	16,000	42,000	42
Rucks	James T.	Hinds	MS	37	Lawyer	53,350	30,000	
Shelby	E. W.	Issaquena	MS	42	Planter	37,550	3,000	
Shotwell	Robert	Hinds	MS	54	Farmer	126,000	158,500	108
Shotwell	Robert	Hinds	MS	55	Farmer	126,000	158,500	10
Simms	J. H.	Yazoo	MS	52	Overseer			

Last Name	First Name	County	State	Age	Occupation	Real Estate ($)	Personal Estate ($)	Slaves (*N*)
Smith	F. G.	Yazoo	MS	47	Planter	75,000	85,000	65
Smith	George	Warren	MS	28	Painter	1,000		
Stackhouse	H. W.	Hinds	MS	50	Farmer	57,000	91,900	58
Sykes	G. A.	Monroe	MS	55	Farmer	90,000	150,000	69
Tarpley	C. S.	Hinds	MS					128
Tegarden	W. H.	Harrison	MS	65	Physician	1,000,000	10,000	10
Tinsley	Fredrick	Kemper	MS	35	Farmer	1,600	1,000	
Torrey	J. L.	Holmes	MS	46	Planter	12,000	40,000	40
Townes	E. B.	Yalobusha	MS	37	Physician	29,000	38,250	37
Ussery	John	Lowndes	MS	64	Planter	4,000	75,000	
Vick	H. W.	Warren	MS	50				2
Walker	W. C.	Jefferson	MS	35	Physician		40,000	
Ward	M. S.	Panola	MS	37	Lawyer	1,300	8,000	26
Whaley	Thomas	Warren	MS		Merchant	15,000		
Whitfield	Henry B.	Lowndes	MS	25	Lawyer	2,500	30,000	2
Whitfield	John A.	Lowndes	MS	28	Lawyer	40,000	60,000	54
Whitfield	W. W.	Lowndes	MS	37	Planter	55,000	50,000	59
Wicks	Moses J.	Monroe	MS		Merchant	7,000		
Yerger	William	Hinds	MS	44	Lawyer	150,000	160,000	140
Archer	James	St. Louis	MO		Merchant	3,000	8,000	
Berthold	Pierre A.	St. Louis	MO	46	Merchant	46,000	55,000	2
Block	Henry	St. Louis	MO	43	Merchant	6,000	15,000	
Blossom	Henry M.	St. Louis	MO	27	Bookkeeper	5,000	10,000	
Bogy	Lewis V.	St. Louis	MO	47	Politician	550,000	25,000	3
Boyd	George W.	St. Louis	MO	37	Merchant		15,000	
Buzzard	Milton M.	St. Louis	MO	48	Merchant	3,500	50	
Carson	James B.	St. Louis	MO	39	Merchant	1,500	1,000	
Carter	Walker R.	St. Louis	MO		Merchant	100,000	25,000	15
Chouteau	Charles P	St. Louis	MO	40	Manufacturer	80,000	20,000	4
Clark	Henry L.	St. Louis	MO			163,000	2,000	
Deady	John	St. Louis	MO	32	Merchant			
Dimick	Horace E.	St. Louis	MO	49	Gunsmith	10,000	10,000	
Dodd	Samuel M.	St. Louis	MO		Farmer	1,500	500	
Douglass	John T.	St. Louis	MO	40	Manufacturer		3,000	3
Eaton	Nathaniel J.	St. Louis	MO	53	Insurance	18,000	2,500	
Edgell	Stephen M.	St. Louis	MO	50	Merchant	2,000	10,000	
Elam	Edwin M.	St. Louis	MO	33	Merchant		25	
Gaylord	Erastus H.	St. Louis	MO	64	Collector			
Gordon	William R.	St. Louis	MO		Broker	53,000	300	
Holmes	Nathaniel J.	St. Louis	MO	43	Lawyer			
Horgadan	W. A.	St. Louis	MO	38	Merchant	33,000	10,500	
How	John	St. Louis	MO	49	Merchant	295,000	802,000	2
Jameson	Joseph A.	St. Louis	MO	35	Merchant	3,000	10,000	
Lackland	Rufus J.	St. Louis	MO	41	Merchant	100,000	150,000	1
Langsdorf	Morris	St. Louis	MO		Merchant			
Leggett	John E.	St. Louis	MO	35	Merchant	30,000	14,000	
Lepere	Francis	St. Louis	MO	37	Merchant	13,000	5,000	
Lindsley	Decosa B.	St. Louis	MO	30	Merchant		600	
Lucas	James H.	St. Louis	MO	60	Lawyer	3,500,000	225,000	18
Lynch	Peter	St. Louis	MO	50	Merchant		170	
McConkin	Charles A.	St. Louis	MO	22	Merchant			
McDowell	Augustus	St. Louis	MO	35	Merchant			
Mead	Edward H.	St. Louis	MO	50	Merchant	86,200	50,000	
Miller	John S. J.	St. Louis	MO		Merchant		3,000	
Mitchell	Robert William	St. Louis	MO		Cabinetmaker	100,000	2,000	
Ogilby	Joseph H.	St. Louis	MO		Merchant		4,500	
Orrick	A. C.	St. Louis	MO	38	Merchant	2,500	14,025	

Last Name	First Name	County	State	Age	Occupation	Real Estate ($)	Personal Estate ($)	Slaves (*N*)
Patterson	Robert D.	St. Louis	MO	25	Brickmaker		50	
Perkins	Nathan W.	St. Louis	MO	35	Merchant	5,000	800	
Phelps	John J.	Lafayette	MO	62	Farmer	6,500	750	
Pratt	Elon G.	St. Louis	MO	38	Farmer	3,700	1,000	
Price	William	St. Louis	MO	36	Engineer	1,900	50	
Rhodes	Thomas	St. Louis	MO	27	Merchant		800	
Ridgely	Franklin L.	St. Louis	MO	56	Insurance president	50,000	10,000	
Robinson	George R.	St. Louis	MO		Merchant	30,000	50,000	
Samuels	Moses	St. Louis	MO	30	Merchant		1,000	
Scott	William P.	St. Louis	MO	31	Merchant		4,000	
Shields	John	St. Louis	MO	35	Merchant	7,000	1,000	
Slevin	John F.		MO	35	Merchant		50	
Stinde	Conrad R.	St. Louis	MO	37	Merchant	8,000	25,000	
Suss	Alexander	St. Louis	MO	40	Merchant		5,000	
Taylor	Daniel G.	St. Louis	MO	40	Merchant	50,000	5,000	
Triplett	John R.	St. Louis	MO	35	Merchant	3,000	5,000	
Valle	Jules	St. Louis	MO		Iron merchant	5,000	2,500	
Wells	Charles G.	St. Louis	MO	33	Merchant		3,000	
Wells	Erastus	St. Louis	MO	36	Railroad president	70,000	33,000	
White	David	St. Louis	MO	34	Bookkeeper			
Barry	James	New Hanover	NC	23	Merchant		5,000	
Battle	William Horn	Edgecombe	NC		Farmer	130,000	204,000	10
Bolles	Charles P.	Brunswick	NC	37	US Survey	14,700	4,500	4
Boylan	William M.	Wake	NC	82	Planter	15,000	100,000	24
Broadfoot	William G.	Cumberland	NC	54	Banker	2,500	500	
Busbee	Quinton	Wake	NC	35	Lawyer	5,000	7,000	7
Collins	Josiah, Jr.	Washington	NC	29	Lawyer		16,000	6
Collins	Josiah, Sr.	Washington	NC	52	Planter	200,000	250,000	327
Colton	Harry E.	Buncombe	NC	23	Editor		500	
Donnell	Richard C.	Guilford	NC	35	Farmer	2,500	7,000	
Ellis	C. D.	New Hanover	NC	65	Merchant			12
Flanner	William B.	New Hanover	NC	38	Merchant	1,000	4,000	1
Hall	A. E.	New Hanover	NC	39	Merchant			
Hinton	Chase L.	Wake	NC	67	Farmer	27,500	125,000	120
Kendall	W. P.	Anson	NC	50	Farmer	18,000	54,000	30
Marable	Benjamin F.	Sampson	NC	28	Minister		3,807	
Martin	Alfred	New Hanover	NC	44	Merchant	22,500	6,000	9
Murray	Eli	Alamance	NC	66	Farmer	13,000	20,000	33
Newlin	John R.	Alamance	NC	37	Machinist		100	
Pender	David	Edgecombe	NC	29	Merchant	3,750	40,000	2
Rodman	William Blount	Beufort	NC	43	Lawyer	40,000	100,000	61
Spurell	H. G.	Washington	NC	52	Farmer	3,000	21,500	
Weller	Sidney	Halifax	NC					
Abney	John B.	Edgefield	SC	37	Physician		2,250	
Adams	William W.	Edgefield	SC	40	Lawyer	11,000	41,000	8
Agnew	Samuel White	Abbeville	SC	44	Farmer	6,200	17,200	10
Aiken	James Reid	Fairfield	SC	48	Banker	8,000	71,725	19
Aiken	William	Charleston	SC	54	Planter	290,600	12,000	700
Aimar	George W.	Charleston	SC	33	Druggist			
Allen	J. D.	Barnwell	SC	48	Planter	118,000	198,500	40
Allen	Thomas P.	Charleston	SC	49	Farmer	12,000	17,000	
Allston	R. F. W.	Prince George	SC	59	Planter	150,000	305,000	631
Alston	Charles, Jr.	Georgetown	SC	34	Planter	26,000	19,000	38
Anderson	George F.	Laurens	SC	63	Farmer	26,060	52,583	44
Baggett	James H.	Charleston	SC	28	Banker		2,000	
Bailey	J. R.	Georgetown	SC	28	Physician	3,500	1,600	
Bain	Jonathan C.	Orangeburg	SC		Manufacturer			

Last Name	**First Name**	**County**	**State**	**Age**	**Occupation**	**Real Estate ($)**	**Personal Estate ($)**	**Slaves (*N*)**
Bee	William Cattell	Charleston	SC		Merchant	15,000		6
Bellinger	Edmund E.	Colleton	SC	41	Minister	5,000	15,000	11
Berry	Andrew	Orangeburg	SC	62	Farmer	2,000	10,000	10
Birnie	William	Charleston	SC	77	Gentleman		10,000	
Bland	J. A.	Edgefield	SC	38	Farmer	27,000	55,000	50
Blanding	James Douglass	Sumter	SC	38	Lawyer	11,300	44,500	30
Bonham	Milledge Luke	Edgefield	SC	45	Lawyer	17,000	50,000	60
Bonnell	John	Charleston	SC	47	Merchant	15,000	20,000	5
Boykin	Burwell	Kershaw	SC	46	Planter	75,000	180,000	154
Boykin	L. W.	Kershaw	SC	32	Planter	5,625	24,067	9
Brooks	W. J.	Laurens	SC	25	Farmer	2,208	1,000	
Brown	C. B.	Marion	SC	65	Farmer	6,000	10,000	16
Brown	Scott K.	Charleston	SC	50	Builder			
Bryan	E. B.	Colleton	SC	33	Planter	12,000	30,000	43
Bryce	Robert P.	Richland	SC	62	Merchant	22,000	41,000	6
Budd	Thomas G.	Charleston	SC	35	Merchant		6,000	
Bulwinkle	Henry	Charleston	SC	30	Merchant	14,000	8,000	3
Butler	Loudon	Edgefield	SC	27	Lawyer			
Butler	Matthew C.	Edgefield	SC	24	Lawyer	7,000	17,000	
Butler	William P.	Edgefield	SC		Merchant	4,000		9
Caldwell	Joseph	Newberry	SC	52	Farmer	40,000	139,600	40
Calhoun	A. P.	Pickens	SC	47	Farmer	110,000	184,400	54
Canton	J. K.	Lancaster	SC	28	Planter	36,170	55,000	
Capers	W. G.	Beaufort	SC	30	Planter	12,800	25,000	35
Carr	Charles D.	Charleston	SC		Merchant	13,000		10
Carrere	M. E.	Charleston	SC	35	Physician	31,000	15,000	3
Carroll	James Parsons	Edgefield	SC	51	Chancellor	35,000	100,000	
Chaffe	William H.	Charleston	SC	30	Merchant		7,000	
Charles	E. W.	Darlington	SC	59	Merchant	75,000	110,141	32
Chesnut	James, Jr.	Kershaw	SC	45	Planter	71,000	95,500	16
Claussen	John Christian	Charleston	SC	32	Baker	24,000	40,000	9
Cochrane	John C.	Charleston	SC	54	Banker	10,000	5,000	4
Connor	Henry W.	Charleston	SC	55	Banker	34,000		4
Cook	B.	Kershaw	SC	58	Planter	15,000	60,000	7
Cordes	A. W.	Prince George	SC	30	Planter	10,000	3,000	
Croft	T. H.	Edgefield	SC	47	Lawyer	90,750	133,245	103
Cumins	John C.	Charleston	SC	42	Merchant	1,000		2
Cureton	C. B.	Kershaw	SC	24	Planter	18,000	75,000	45
Dawson	Joseph	Charleston	SC	35		3,000	2,000	3
Depass	H. L.	Kershaw	SC	24	Lawyer	2,000	13,000	4
Desaussure	H. W.	Charleston	SC	44	Physician	8,000	8,000	39
Dickey	M. D.	Greenville	SC	45	Farmer	10,000	6,000	4
Doar	Stephen D.	Charleston	SC	55	Farmer	94,000	200,000	236
Dozier	L.	Prince George	SC	50	Merchant		2,000	15
DuBose	Theodore Samuel	Fairfield	SC	51	Planter	40,000	201,716	204
Dukes	John R.	Charleston	SC	36	Merchant	3,500		1
Dukes	William C.	Charleston	SC		Merchant	37,000		16
Dunbar	B. S.	Edgefield	SC	39	Merchant		50,000	7
Dunlop	James	Kershaw	SC	55	Merchant	50,000	245,000	
Durrant	R. R.	Clarendon	SC	58	Farmer	40,000	136,000	31
Eaves	Nathaniel Ridley	Chester	SC		Lawyer	86,180	118,395	61
Elliott	Thomas A.	Orangeburg	SC	37	Physician	3,500	4,000	9
Evans	Josiah James	Darlington	SC	74	Farmer	4,500		
Evans	Nathan George	Marion	SC	54	Farmer	50,000	60,000	51
Fair	Simeon	Newberry	SC	58	Lawyer	42,000	86,000	63
Farrar	James C.	Charleston	SC	43	Merchant	35,000	10,000	9
Fraser	Thomas Boone	Sumter	SC		Lawyer	13,500	8,000	40

Last Name	First Name	County	State	Age	Occupation	Real Estate ($)	Personal Estate ($)	Slaves (*N*)
Frazier	Marshall	Edgefield	SC	53	Farmer	42,700	136,230	41
Frenholin	E. L.	Charleston	SC	40	Merchant	50,000	5,600	
Fridley	Edward J.	Greenville	SC	65	Stone mason			
Frost	Edward Harry	Charleston	SC	59	Railroad	23,000		45
Frost	Henry Rutledge	Charleston	SC	70	Physician	75,000	25,000	15
Gaillard	Peter C.	Charleston	SC	47	Merchant	6,00	3,000	5
Geiger	William P.	Richland	SC	32	Physician	8,850	6,250	
Gibbes	John B.	Charleston	SC	20	Accountant			1
Gibson	Jesse	Marion	SC	29	Farmer			
Gibson	Samuel Ferdinand	Marion	SC	46	Planter	100,000	200,000	204
Gist	James	Union	SC	26	Farmer	4,000	18,000	33
Glover	G. W.	Orangeburg	SC	63	Judge	26,000	32,000	
Glover	Joseph E.	Colleton	SC	30	Physician	25,000	70,000	74
Godbold	Thomas W.	Marion	SC		Merchant	2,000	35,000	
Goodlet	S. D.	Greenville	SC	29	Lawyer	4,500	9,000	6
Goodwyn	Robert H.	Richland	SC	65	Banker	8,000	10,000	32
Gourdin	Robert N.	Prince George	SC	48	Planter	15,000	60,000	91
Graham	Robert F.	Marion	SC	26	Lawyer	4,500	15,000	6
Gravely	Cowlam	Charleston	SC	35	Merchant	13,500	20,000	6
Gregg	E. A.	Marion	SC	39	Farmer	12,000	32,000	38
Gregg	William	Edgefield	SC	60	Manufacturer	40,000	250,000	14
Guerard	J. D.	Beaufort	SC	67	Planter	6,000	65,000	79
Hampton	Frank	Richland	SC	31	Farmer	40,000	175,000	210
Hampton	Wade	Richland	SC	42	Farmer	25,000	45,000	30
Hanckel	Thomas M.	Charleston	SC	38	Lawyer	8,000	8,000	8
Hanks	Louis B.	Sumter	SC	37	Merchant	18,000	100,000	18
Hart	J. Hartwell	Darlington	SC		Planter	25,000	44,800	1
Hayne	Isaac W.	Charleston	SC	50	Lawyer	22,000	6,000	
Haynesworth	Joseph Cox	Sumter	SC	41	Physician			49
Hear	James O.	Charleston	SC	55	Physician	20,000	5,000	
Heins	Henry S.	Charleston	SC	30	Merchant			
Hertz	Isaac E	Charleston	SC		Merchant			
Heyward	George C.	Charleston	SC	38	Merchant	25,000	15,000	12
Heyward	Thomas J.	Charleston	SC		Merchant	12,000	15,000	20
Hopley	George A.	Charleston	SC		Merchant			
Horlbeck	Edward	Charleston	SC	50	Merchant	21,000	18,000	8
Inglis	John A.	Chesterfield	SC	46		17,000	45,550	13
Johnson	L. B.	Pickens	SC	32	Physician	15,000	7,405	9
Johnson	R. B.	Kershaw	SC	35	Physician	10,000	15,000	14
Jones	Seaton	Kershaw	SC	48	Planter	10,000	27,000	
Keith	Jacob G.	Orangeburg	SC		Farmer	25,000	65,000	59
Kennedy	John D.	Kershaw	SC	40	Law student	16,500	335,000	62
King	M.	Charleston	SC	77		250,000	10,000	19
Kingman	H. W	Charleston	SC		Merchant			6
Kirk	Philip C.	Charleston	SC	47	Planter	10,000	43,500	65
Kirkpatrick	J. D.	Charleston	SC	35	Merchant		5,000	
Kuhtman	H. W.	Pickens	SC	38	Mine owner	50,000	50,000	1
Law	Charles C.	Darlington	SC	48	Planter	10,500	40,500	36
Legare	Isaac S. K.	Orangeburg	SC	50	College president	18,000	22,000	
Lide	Thomas Park	Darlington	SC	50	Planter	51,000	126,245	78
Logan	George W.	Charleston	SC	54	Banker		6,500	14
Lowry	William R.	York	SC	23	Farmer			
Lyler	John V.	Newberry	SC	44	Farmer	12,700	30,000	
MaGill	William Joseph	Georgetown	SC	29	Physician	70,000	100,000	
Magrath	Andrew Gordon	Charleston	SC	47	Lawyer	27,000		10
Marshall	James C.	Charleston	SC	40	Baker	25,000	14,500	20
Matthessen	William	Charleston	SC	50	Merchant			

Last Name	First Name	County	State	Age	Occupation	Real Estate ($)	Personal Estate ($)	Slaves (*N*)
McBee	Vardry	Greenville	SC	85	Farmer	1,850,000	182,350	55
McCants	J. C.	Charleston	SC	42	Planter	6,000	6,000	3
McCants	James C.	Georgetown	SC		Overseer		15,000	
McCrady	John	Charleston	SC	29	Professor		1,200	
McDonald	Arch	Charleston	SC	28	Merchant			
McIntyre	R. C.	Marion	SC	25	Planter	4,000	40,000	32
McLure	James S.	Chester	SC	26	Farmer	39,376	141,645	120
McRae	John	Marion	SC	35	Farmer	1,600	2,500	
Mickle	J. B.	Kershaw	SC	48	Planter	12,000	70,000	91
Middleton	R. J.	Georgetown	SC	46	Planter	15,000	50,000	81
Middleton	Thomas	Charleston	SC	28	Merchant	8,000	17,000	10
Miller	F. C.	Charleston	SC	31	Accountant	3,000		
Mordecai	M. C.	Charleston	SC	53	Merchant	100,000	48,000	12
Morgan	George W.	Edgefield	SC	29	Farmer		2,000	4
Moses	Franklin J.	Sumter	SC	22	Lawyer	55,000	110,000	
Muckinfuss	Benjamin S. D.	Charleston	SC		Dentist	8,500		9
Mure	Robert	Charleston	SC	45	Merchant	10,000	50,000	2
Nelson	S. W.	Fairfield	SC	35	Planter	47,000	16,695	
Nettles	J. R.	Darlington	SC	55	Planter	42,000	106,000	91
Nickerson	Thomas S.	Charleston	SC	38	Proprietor			
Norman	James H.	Horry	SC	30	Physician			19
O'Neal	Lark	Orangeburg	SC	32	Farmer	10,000	45,000	58
O'Neill	Bernard	Charleston	SC	36	Merchant	42,000	15,000	9
Orr	James Lawrence	Anderson	SC	38	Lawyer	35,000	31,200	19
Panknin	Charles H.	Charleston	SC	25	Druggist	30,000		
Parker	Francis Simons	Georgetown	SC	46	Physician	125,000	130,000	220
Patterson	Lewis	Kershaw	SC		Planter	75,000	300,000	70
Paul	Sampson Leith	Colleton	SC		Planter	44,391	81,000	124
Perkins	Benjamin	Kershaw	SC		Planter	27,000	75,000	46
Perry	Josiah B.	Colleton	SC	43	Lawyer	13,500	80,000	89
Poag	James	Chester	SC	52	Farmer	19,500	29,350	22
Porcher	Thomas W.	Charleston	SC	52	Planter	33,000	166,875	181
Pringle	Robert A.	Charleston	SC	23	Merchant		10,000	2
Ravenel	Edmund	Charleston	SC	63	Physician	27,000		4
Ravenel	Henry Edmund	Charleston	SC	70	Planter	15,000	81,560	8
Ravenel	Henry W.	Edgefield	SC	46	Farmer	10,000	55,376	115
Reynolds	James L.	Richland	SC		Professor		8,000	7
Rhett	Robert Barnwell	Charleston	SC	60	Planter	9,000	25,000	59
Rivers	C. M.	Barnwell	SC	45	House carpenter		3,600	5
Robertson	David G.	Fairfield	SC	30	Planter	2,100	24,000	22
Robertson	W. W.	Fairfield	SC		Overseer			
Rogers	E. H.	Charleston	SC		Merchant	19,000		9
Sale	W. W.	Charleston	SC	40	Banker	1,200	15,000	25
Sanders	Benjamin	Colleton	SC	55	Planter	10,000	46,000	23
Sanders	Wilson	Barnwell	SC	63	Planter	7,000	19,400	20
Sass	J. K.	Charleston	SC	43	Bank president			
Seibles	Edwin W.	Edgefield	SC	32	Farmer	5,000	31,500	20
Shannon	T. E.	Kershaw	SC	41	Planter	15,000	75,000	13
Shannon	William M.	Kershaw	SC	37	Lawyer	10,000	35,000	
Simms	William Gilmore	Charleston	SC	56	Historian			4
Singletary	H. M.	Prince George	SC	31	Physician	500	8,000	16
Smith	William B.	Charleston	SC	43	Merchant	33,000	50,000	12
Steinhouse	Adam	Charleston	SC	40	Clerk			
Stoddard	E. B.	Charleston	SC		Merchant	2,500		1
Suder	A. W.	Charleston	SC	22	Engineer			
Taylor	Alexander R.	Richland	SC		Farmer	12,000	50,000	
Taylor	W. R.	Kershaw	SC	28		3,000	26,350	17

Last Name	First Name	County	State	Age	Occupation	Real Estate ($)	Personal Estate ($)	Slaves (*N*)
Tennant	J. K. N.	Marion	SC	38	Bookkeeper		600	
Tharin	Joseph A.	Charleston	SC		Tailor			
Tharin	Marion C.	Charleston	SC	24	Railroad			
Tillman	George Dionysius	Edgefield	SC	33	Lawyer			1
Tompkins	J. W.	Edgefield	SC	32	Farmer		3,500	
Townsend	D. J.	Colleton	SC	53	Planter	187,600	254,000	140
Trenholm	E. L.	Charleston	SC	24	Merchant			1
Trout	Thomas B.	Charleston	SC		Merchant	2,524		2
Wagner	Thomas D.	Charleston	SC	41	Merchant	20,000	100,000	13
Walker	H. P.	Charleston	SC	43	Law clerk	6,000	10,000	
Walker	R. J.	Charleston	SC	39	Merchant			
Walker	William W.	Richland	SC	50	Tailor	4,000	1,000	
Ward	Joshua	Georgetown	SC		Planter	1,200	20,000	1193
Ward	Mayham	Georgetown	SC	22	Planter		3,000	
Wardlaw	Francis Hugh	Edgefield	SC		Judge	6,000	20,000	22
Wells	Thomas J.	Beaufort	SC	42	Teacher		4,000	3
Weston	Francis	Georgetown	SC	49	Planter	90,000	130,000	332
Whaley	Thomas Baynard	Orangeburg	SC	37	Lawyer	30,000	100,000	123
Whaley	William Baynard	Charleston	SC		Lawyer	9,600	10,000	18
Wharley	Ephraim Mikel	St. John's	SC	32				113
Wilbur	William W.	Charleston	SC	63	Broker	10,000	5,000	5
Wilds	Samuel Hugh	Darlington	SC		Planter	48,745	152,711	178
Williams	George Walton	Charleston	SC	40	Merchant	13,000	75,000	12
Willis	Henry	Charleston	SC	68	Broker	10,000	80,000	3
Wilson	Benjamin Huger	Georgetown	SC	41	Lawyer	11,000	30,000	
Wilson	Daniel H.	Chester	SC	26	Merchant		14,812	
Wilson	W. B.	York	SC		Lawyer	22,000	34,100	37
Woodward	Thomas W.	Fairfield	SC	27	Planter	16,800	84,000	79
Adams	Adam Gillespie	Davidson	TN	39	Merchant	40,000	65,000	1
Allison	Alexander	Davidson	TN	60	Merchant	45,000	100,000	12
Anderson	Paulding H.	Wilson	TN	56	Farmer	59,350	82,185	32
Apperson	E. M.	Shelby	TN	47	Merchant	400,000	100,000	96
Barbee	A. J.	Haywood	TN	57	Physician	29,600	67,210	51
Barber	Flavel C.	Giles	TN	30	Teacher	1,000	2,000	1
Bend	William Thomas	Haywood	TN	33	Farmer	7,420	23,000	
Berry	William Wade	Davidson	TN		Druggist	100,000	365,250	10
Bilbo	William N.	Davidson	TN	43	Lawyer	30,000	10,000	12
Blackmore	James A.	Sumner	TN	59	Physician	25,000	25,000	31
Bradford	Hiram S.	Haywood	TN	63	Farmer	49,000	72,775	23
Bransford	T.L.	Davidson	TN	55	Merchant	104,000	60,000	52
Brennan	John M.	Davidson	TN	35	Clerk			
Brinkley	J. H.	Cheatham	TN	40	Constable		100	
Brinkley	Robert C.	Shelby	TN	43	Railroad president	1,520,000	300,000	3
Brown	Aaron Venable	Davidson	TN	64	Politician			
Brown	John S.	Bedford	TN	50	Farmer	16,000	7,400	2
Brown	Milton	Madison	TN	55	Lawyer	154,200	150,000	27
Bullock	Micagah	Madison	TN	51	Lawyer			
Burch	John C.	Davidson	TN	33	Editor			
Burton	William	Fayette	TN	51	Judge	2,900		15
Caldwell	J. S. W.	Haywood	TN	32	Farmer	12,000	30,000	
Callender	John H.	Davidson	TN	28	Physician	20,000	2,000	
Cannon	H. J.	Fayette	TN	48	Farmer			15
Cannon	William J.	Fayette	TN		Physician			29
Caruthers	James P.	Madison	TN	64	Gentleman	100,000	15,000	9
Caruthers	William A.	Madison	TN	32	Lawyer	18,000		
Chase	William	Lauderdale	TN	34	Teacher		1,500	
Cheatham	Felix R.	Davidson	TN	36	Clerk	60,000	20,000	2

Last Name	First Name	County	State	Age	Occupation	Real Estate ($)	Personal Estate ($)	Slaves (*N*)
Cheek	M. C.	Henry	TN	34	Merchant	3,500	4,000	6
Chunn	William Neilson	Fayette	TN	49	Farmer	2,000	7,800	9
Clark	Thomas H.	Madison	TN	38	Clerk	10,800	1,200	
Claybrook	John S.	Williamson	TN	52	Farmer	258,680	85,000	23
Cockrill	James R.	Davidson	TN	27	Farmer	63,600	22,000	
Cockrill	Mark	Davidson	TN	72	Planter	600,000	600,000	99
Coleman	L. L.	Knox	TN	38	Physician		150	
Cooper	W. F.	Davidson	TN	40	Lawyer	170,000	20,000	
Davy	Edward	Haywood	TN	63	Physician	30,000	63,000	58
Dawson	J. S.	Henry	TN	36	Trader	37,550	65,000	9
Degroffinrew	Henry	Fayette	TN	34	Farmer	1,560		
Donelson	Samuel	Blount	TN		Farmer	3,000	2,000	
Dortch	W. B.	Fayette	TN	31	Lawyer	4,840	42,000	25
Dortch	W. B.	Davidson	TN	34	Farmer	43,000	54,860	26
Douglass	Byrd	Davidson	TN	44	Merchant	87,500	159,700	14
Dowdy	William P.	Fayette	TN	43	Farmer	6,000	44,590	38
Dunlap	J. T.	Maury	TN	35	Merchant	1,800	8,000	5
Dupree	Cornelius	Davidson	TN	32	Druggist			
East	Edward H.	Davidson	TN	28	Lawyer	3,000	3,000	
Edmonson	J. H.	Shelby	TN	28	Merchant	21,000	35,000	20
Elder	Joshua	Montgomery	TN	55	Broker	102,180	75,000	30
Elrod	James	Madison	TN	27	Gentleman	3,500	21,500	5
Ewing	John H.	Davidson	TN	44	Druggist	41,000	51,165	
Fall	Alexander	Davidson	TN	45	Insurance president	60,000	124,900	5
Farrow	John J.	Haywood	TN	26	Merchant	350	1,000	
Fenner	Thomas H.	Madison	TN	36	Farmer	1,500	6,000	5
Fulton	W. D.	Hamilton	TN	39	Bank cashier	12,500	20,485	6
Gains	R. H.	Lauderdale	TN	51	Farmer			
Gamewell	Thomas M.	Madison	TN	43	Clerk	15,000	10,000	
Gilmer	John	Montgomery	TN	61	Farmer	18,000	29,500	18
Goodall	J. D.	Fayette	TN	28	Lawyer			29
Greer	John A.	Madison	TN	33	Farmer			
Harding	William G.	Davidson	TN	51	Farmer	275,000	130,500	135
Harrison	Horace H.	Davidson	TN	56	Inspector of boats			1
Hayes	Henry M.	Davidson	TN		Farmer	180,000	24,000	6
Hays	Richard J.	Madison	TN	37	Lawyer	11,000	14,500	
Haywood	James G.	Haywood	TN	33	Physician	4,890	14,500	14
Heron	John	Madison	TN	21	Farmer	11,000	500	
Hillman	Daniel H.	Davidson	TN		Manufacturer			
Holmes	G. L.	Shelby	TN	45	Farmer	60,000	75,000	37
Hummer	Charles W.	Davidson	TN	32	Merchant			
Humphreys	W. H.	Davidson	TN	53	Lawyer	80,000	13,350	14
Hunt	W. C.	Washington	TN	31	Merchant		3,000	
Hunt	William R.	Shelby	TN	42	Broker		500	
Hutchins	Gaston	Fayette	TN	35				
Johnson	C.	Davidson	TN		Farmer	8,350	14,200	
Kerr	Alexander	Davidson	TN	48	Builder	15,000	15,000	3
Klyce	A. J.	Haywood	TN	45	Mechanic	35,360	38,000	5
Lancaster	Samuel C.	Madison	TN	34	Merchant	30,000	35,000	16
Lanier	Buchanan H.	Davidson	TN	32	Merchant		200	
Lyons	James W.	Madison	TN		Planter	60,000	80,000	95
Malone	Thomas H.	Davidson	TN	25	Lawyer	4,000	5,000	
Mason	Joseph D.	Madison	TN	40	Physician	25,000	4,700	
McCamey	S. R.	Hamilton	TN	45	Pork packer	30,000	6,000	4
McCorry	Henry W.	Madison	TN		Planter	150,000	60,000	44
McCutchen	James T.	Dyer	TN	54	Farmer	3,260	15,505	
McFarland	James P.	Wilson	TN	39	Physician	85,000	22,000	13

Last Name	First Name	County	State	Age	Occupation	Real Estate ($)	Personal Estate ($)	Slaves (*N*)
McNairy	R. C.	Davidson	TN	42	Merchant	125,000	25,000	
Miller	Austin	Hardeman	TN	59	Farmer	200,000	110,000	27
Morrill	J. M.	Madison	TN	34	Lawyer			
Mosley	J. R.	Fayette	TN	41	Farmer	74,000	79,000	65
Neilson	W. W.	Fayette	TN	56	Physician	2,940	7,600	
Nichol	Philip L.	Davidson	TN	26	Clerk	9,000	1,000	
Oglesby	John	Franklin	TN	48	Farmer	11,940	12,000	
Parham	R. S.	Davidson	TN	35	Blacksmith		300	
Patterson	W.	Anderson	TN		Farmer	800	900	
Peters	George B.	Hardeman	TN	42	Physician	132,000	80,000	29
Pickett	W. H.	Shelby	TN	33	Physician	88,000	60,000	6
Porter	Alex M.	Davidson	TN	47	Railroad	20,000	7,000	
Rhea	Samuel	Sullivan	TN	65	Merchant	16,500	50,000	3
Ridley	James A.	Rutherford	TN	38	Physician	33,000		
Riva	Alexander	Davidson	TN	33	Merchant		3,000	
Robertson	W. H.	Fayette	TN		Clerk			
Rogers	James A.	Haywood	TN	42	Farmer	35,000	55,000	21
Roseborough	Samuel	Shelby	TN	63	Farmer	63,800	50,000	26
Ross	Horace C.	Davidson	TN	18	Student			
Rutledge	Arthur M.	Franklin	TN	48	Farmer	105,000	35,000	45
Saunders	Thomas G.	Davidson	TN	46	Negro dealer	3,500	5,000	
Sheppard	Thomas	Haywood	TN	39	Farmer	88,000	110,000	51
Sheppard	W. B.	Davidson	TN	30	Merchant		3,000	
Smith	Baxter	Sumner	TN		Lawyer	4,500	5,000	6
Smith	J. R. P.	Davidson	TN		Clerk			
Smith	Robert	Shelby	TN	31		30,000	12,000	
Stanton	J. S.	Shelby	TN	40	Merchant	60,000	20,000	1
Steadman	Enoch	Lincoln	TN	54	Farmer		2,000	
Stevenson	Vernon K.	Davidson	TN	48	Railroad president	597,000	140,000	5
Steward	Joseph C.	Madison	TN		Physician	4,500	1,500	2
Sturdevant	E. C.	Haywood	TN	35	Farmer	11,000	15,000	14
Talliaferro	Lyne S.	Haywood	TN	64	Farmer	12,000	18,600	
Tate	Samuel	Shelby	TN	42	Railroad president	58,000	90,500	4
Taylor	Edward T.	Tipton	TN	45	Agent	16,000	13,840	11
Taylor	John A.	Haywood	TN		Farmer	24,000	64,000	
Taylor	S. A.	Maury	TN	31	Minister	2,600	2,000	3
Taylor	Samuel C.	Fayette	TN	62	Farmer	2,000	3,000	
Topp	Robertson	Shelby	TN	53	Railroad president	520,000	80,000	130
Totten	Archibald W. O.	Madison	TN	47	Lawyer	103,000	100,000	50
Wade	William J.	Davidson	TN	19				
White	F. M.	Shelby	TN	48	Railroad president	100,000	200,000	12
Whitelaw	H. O.	Haywood	TN	52	Merchant	15,000	40,000	53
Williams	J. J.	Madison	TN	36	Engineer	6,000	500	3
Winston	J. D.	Shelby	TN	39	Merchant		9,000	
Wood	James Proudfit	Haywood	TN	39	Railroad	12,000	12,000	5
Woods	James	Davidson	TN	67	Manufacturer	120,000	360,000	9
Yeatman	Henry Clay	Davidson	TN	28	Merchant	60,000	70,000	
Zollikoffer	F. K	Davidson	TN	41	Gentleman	56,000	14,000	3
Alexander	M. T.	Wharton	TX	36	Planter	15,000	10,000	7
Alexander	W. F.	Webb	TX	47	Bookkeeper	1,000	300	
Armstrong	John B.	Washington	TX	61	Farmer	2,500	5,000	7
Atchison	D. D.	Galveston	TX	40	Lawyer	100,000	8,000	6
Baxter	E. G.	Smith	TX	23	Lawyer	5,000	10,000	2
Beeks	William L.	Wharton	TX		Stock raiser	1,240		
Blanch	E. A.	Harrison	TX	45	Farmer	8,000	29,700	16
Bryan	Guy	Galveston	TX	39	Planter	70,000	5,000	8
Burke	James	Harris	TX	54	Merchant	1,000	1,000	11

Last Name	**First Name**	**County**	**State**	**Age**	**Occupation**	**Real Estate ($)**	**Personal Estate ($)**	**Slaves (*N*)**
Burns	W. W.	Fort Bend	TX	40	Physician	40,000	50,000	
Chambers	J. C.	Titus	TX	62	Merchant	8,600	19,595	4
Childress	L. G.	Red River	TX	47	Judge	1,500	5,000	8
Clark	J. C.	Wharton	TX	62	Planter	132,145	104,715	70
Coleman	George	Gonzales	TX	40	Physician	1,600	3,800	
Croom	Jesse	Wharton	TX		Farmer	33,000	28,310	41
Crump	William E.	Bellville	TX	50	Planter	20,000	50,000	20
Cundiff	W. H.	Houston	TX	38	Farmer	205,289	7,835	5
Cureton	M. L.	Wharton	TX	42	Planter		25,000	26
Davidson	A.	Gonzales	TX	49	Merchant	6,400	11,200	15
Denman	G. J.	Gonzales	TX	45	Farmer	20,000	25,000	23
Dickinson	J.	Harris	TX	40	Merchant	150,000	25,000	
Duke	H.	Wharton	TX	23	Overseer		250	
Forbes	R. M.	Lavaca	TX		Merchant	10,000		5
Foster	John	Wharton	TX	58	Collector		1,200	
Franklin	J. R.	Washington	TX	52	Farmer	45,000	40,800	34
Frazier	G. W.	Wharton	TX	38	Farmer			
George	David	Wharton	TX	44	Planter	8,000	2,000	5
Gold	W. A.	Dallas	TX	38	Merchant	20,860	10,020	2
Gordon	J. W.	Lamar	TX	38	Farmer		2,175	
Graham	John G.	Rusk	TX	66	Farmer	15,000	20,250	17
Grigsby	E. O.	Medina	TX	25	Physician			
Groesbeck	Abraham	Harris	TX	41	Railroad president	105,000	54,000	
Hancock	George	Travis	TX	57	Merchant	150,000	200,000	6
Harrison	Charles	Gonzales	TX	52	Farmer	2,800	18,000	27
Herndon	J. H.	Travis	TX	33	Physician	13,500	4,500	1
Herndon	J. H.	Travis	TX	33	Physician	3,500	4,500	1
Horton	A. C.	Matagorda	TX	60	Planter	200,000	119,000	166
Hunt	E. P.	Galveston	TX	46	Insurance agent	35,000	4,000	3
Ireland	John	Guadalupe	TX	33	Lawyer	10,000	20,000	6
James	A. F.	Galveston	TX	47	Real estate agent	150,000	10,000	6
Jarmon	A.	Harris	TX	54	Farmer	5,000	5,000	1
Johnson	Thomas D.	Guadalupe	TX		Farmer	40,000	11,050	11
Law	G. W.	Dallas	TX		Clerk	3,485	3,485	
Lockard	A. H.	Williamson	TX	25	Railroad	1,000	200	
Lubbuck	T. S.	Harris	TX	42	Gentleman	15,000	25,000	
McClarty	John	Rusk	TX	35	Lawyer	1,500	2,500	3
McNeil	J. A.	Gonzales	TX	29	Farmer	5,000	20,000	20
Monroe	H. W.	Gonzales	TX	46	Merchant	9,500	31,350	12
Mooney	John	Gonzales	TX	53	Planter	20,280	44,600	22
Moore	R. D.	Wharton	TX	32	Physician	5,000	10,000	
Myers	J. O.	Wharton	TX	34	Planter	50,000	40,000	40
Nance	E.	Hays	TX	44	Farmer	30,000	40,000	39
Nicholson	E. P.	Dallas	TX	34	Lawyer	12,000	10,150	7
Pelgrens	Thomas J.	Gonzales	TX	52	Broker	12,000	13,000	
Perry	Stephen S.	Brazoria	TX	35	Planter	221,700	51,370	63
Pressler	C. V.	Travis	TX	37	Surveyor	4,500	500	
Pryor	Samuel B.	Dallas	TX	40	Physician	4,258	4,970	
Rice	A. J.	Victoria	TX	46	Farmer	6,000	21,000	12
Ryan	James	Lavaca	TX		Farmer	1,250		
Sears	J. L.	McLennan	TX	34	Merchant	3,500	8,420	6
Shafer	Stephen	Dallas	TX		Merchant		400	
Shaffer	R.	Colorado	TX	42	Physician		2,000	
Shepherd	B. A.	Harris	TX	46	Merchant	125,000	150,000	5
Shepherd	Harvey O.	Dallas	TX	55	Farmer	1,500	6,150	9
Smith	James A.	Dallas	TX	59	Farmer	15,800	15,565	5
Sorley	James	Galveston	TX	45	Merchant			

Last Name	First Name	County	State	Age	Occupation	Real Estate ($)	Personal Estate ($)	Slaves (*N*)
Spivey	Jethro	Wharton	TX		Farmer	1,554		
Stewart	W. A.	Goliad	TX	37	Farmer	2,000	600	
Stith	M. G.	Wharton	TX	46	Planter			118
Thomas	J. L.	Kaufman	TX	40	Merchant		1,500	
Tompkins	A. N. B.	Liberty	TX	51	District surveyor	2,000	600	
Walker	E. M.	Gonzales	TX	35	Physician	3,500	3,500	
Walker	Thomas	Gonzales	TX	34	Merchant	12,000	6,000	
Waters	J. D.	Galveston	TX	37	Stevedore	7,000	1,200	
Waul	T. N.	Gonzales	TX	50	Planter	20,000	35,000	45
Weechler	H.	Bexar	TX	28	Merchant			
Wynn	W. L.	Wharton	TX	48	Farmer	2,000	3,500	
Allen	L. S.	Ritchie	VA	39	Merchant	763	1,700	
Anderson	Joseph Reid	Henrico	VA	47	Iron founder	480,000	275,000	60
Anderson	Thomas Bates	Caroline	VA	68	Physician	18,000	46,230	44
Ayres	Robert	Greenbrier	VA	30	State agent		4,520	
Bacon	John Lyddall	Henrico	VA	48	Merchant	30,000	71,000	5
Barksdale	George Ainsley	Henrico	VA	25	Flour merchant	100,000	5,000	98
Baskerville	Henry E. C.	Henrico	VA	43	Merchant	10,000	219,000	10
Bassett	George W.	Hanover	VA	60	Farmer	139,830	88,729	106
Baylor	Richard	Essex	VA	57	Farmer	390,000	401,630	332
Beale	James	Henrico	VA	57	Physician	20,000	6,000	10
Blanton	Charles	Prince Edward	VA	24	Merchant		3,000	
Bocock	Thomas S.	Appomattox	VA	45	Lawyer	10,000	20,000	
Boyd	Thomas	Wythe	VA	56	Hotel keeper	100,000	7,250	9
Branch	Thomas	Petersburg	VA	57	Merchant	14,000	25,000	16
Brooke	Henry Laurens	Henrico	VA	52	Lawyer			
Brown	Stephen D.	Prince Edward	VA	32	Farmer	5,000	4,500	1
Brummel	Joseph	Henrico	VA	51	Manufacturer	100,000	121,000	4
Burroughs	Henry A.	Campbell	VA	34	Merchant		5,000	
Cabell	David S. G.	Nelson	VA	35	Lawyer	1,800	1,200	
Cabell	Henry Coulter	Henrico	VA	40	Lawyer	195,000	12,000	6
Caskie	John Samuels	Henrico	VA	39	Lawyer	2,500	15,000	2
Chandler	Thomas T.	Caroline	VA	41	Farmer	6,000	12,000	11
Cocke	William Archer	Henrico	VA	38	Lawyer		3,230	
Collier	Robert Ruffin	Prince George	VA	55	Lawyer	22,000	48,000	14
Cox	James Henry	Chesterfield	VA	50	Collier	25,000	126,800	20
Crenshaw	Lewis Dabney	Henrico	VA	43	Merchant	400,000	150,000	10
Crump	William Wood	Henrico	VA	41	Lawyer	85,600	37,000	6
Cuthbert	James E.	Prince George	VA	35	Banker	3,000	1,500	1
Davis	Micajah, Jr.	Campbell	VA	47		10,450		
Dejarnette	John Hampton	Caroline	VA	42	Farmer	76,000	67,500	45
Dill	Adolph	Henrico	VA	68	Manufacturer			
Dimmock	Charles Henry	Henrico	VA	29				
Downey	Mark	Henrico	VA	43	Merchant			
Eiechleberger	George W.	Jefferson	VA		Farmer	27,600	13,000	
Faulkner	Charles James	Berkeley	VA	54	Minister to France	100,000	150,000	13
Fitzhugh	Benjamin F. T.	Spotsylvania	VA	44		10,000	6,000	14
Fitzhugh	George	Caroline	VA	53	Author	3,000	18,000	23
Forbes	John Murray	Fauquier	VA	48	Lawyer	18,000	27,470	22
Fowlkes	James J.	Pittsylvania	VA	64	Farmer	2,700	4,650	3
Fry	Hugh Walker	Henrico	VA	64	Merchant	87,500	58,000	10
Garrett	Alexander	Albemarle	VA	72	Estate	29,000	25,000	17
Gilmer	John Harmer	Henrico	VA	49	Lawyer	70,000	3,500	4
Gilmore	James H.	Smyth	VA	30	Lawyer	7,000	3,000	1
Goddin	Wellington	Henrico	VA	45	Real estate agent			17
Grandy	Cyrus W.	Norfolk	VA	51	Merchant	38,000	30,000	15
Harris	William W.	Nelson	VA	43	Farmer	30,000	50,000	52

Last Name	First Name	County	State	Age	Occupation	Real Estate ($)	Personal Estate ($)	Slaves (*N*)
Haxall	Richard Barton	Henrico	VA	55	Merchant			8
Holmes	George F.	Albemarle	VA		Professor	15,000	16,000	
Inboden	John A. R.	Amelia	VA	27	Teacher		750	
Irby	Richard	Nottoway	VA	35	Farmer	30,000	43,000	64
Johnson	Marmaduke	Henrico	VA	34	Lawyer	1,500		
Jones	J. Ravenscroft	Brunswick	VA	41	Farmer		100	
Kent	Horace Leavitt	Henrico	VA	59	Merchant	85,000	140,000	14
Lancaster	John A.	Henrico	VA	41	Merchant		15,500	
Lee	Robert E.	Alexandria	VA	53	US Army	80,000		40
Lucas	William	Jefferson	VA	60	Planter	126,000	12,100	7
Lynch	George N.	Jefferson	VA		Planter	8,550	2,000	
Lyons	James T.	Henrico	VA	59	Lawyer	100,000	50,000	16
Martin	Nathanial Macon	Henrico	VA	23				
Mason	J. B.	Henrico	VA		Merchant		500	
Mayo	Robert Atkinson	Henrico	VA	61	Merchant			20
McFarland	William Hamilton	Henrico	VA	61	Bank president	90,000	90,000	1
McNutt	James M.	Prince Edward	VA		Farmer	18,000	30,000	22
Meade	R. W.	Prince George	VA		Farmer	1,000	15,000	16
Michie	Thomas J.	Augusta	VA	53	Lawyer	121,000	20,000	13
Morgan	Robert	Jefferson	VA		Overseer			
Morton	John B.	Henrico	VA	30	Banker			
Mosely	W. M.	Pittsylvania	VA	55	Miller			
Munnis	James K.	Petersburg	VA	29	Merchant		4,000	
Myers	Samuel	Henrico	VA		Merchant		1,000	
Myrick	John D.	Norfolk	VA	33	Planter	150,000	160,000	1
Ott	John W.	Jefferson	VA		Farmer	5,000	1,100	
Ott	Thomas Mann	Jefferson	VA		Merchant		750	
Peebles	Lemuel	Prince George	VA		Merchant		4,000	
Peek	Thomas C.	Elizabeth City	VA	56		8,900	7,500	
Pemberton	W. D.	Henrico	VA	48	Clerk	8,000	5,000	
Peyton	Randolph	Caroline	VA	28	Lawyer		7,000	12
Puryear	R. A.	Mecklenburg	VA	63	Farmer	16,000	42,269	44
Quarles	W. R.	Henrico	VA	21	Merchant			
Randolph	John W.	Henrico	VA		Bookbinder	15,000	30,000	
Renner	William P.	Jefferson	VA		Physician	7,000	5,000	
Robinson	Edwin	Henrico	VA	53	Railroad president	100,000	10,000	6
Robinson	L. H.	Essex	VA	25	Physician		3,000	
Rockingbaugh	Thomas	Jefferson	VA		Merchant		750	
Rockingbaugh	W.	Jefferson	VA		Blacksmith	600	300	
Rowland	C. H.	Norfolk	VA	47	Merchant	27,000	15,000	6
Royal	John M.	Henrico	VA		Merchant			
Rucker	A. B.	Campbell	VA	51	Merchant	2,000	6,200	9
Ruffin	Edmund	Prince George	VA	45	Farmer	73,000	160,000	44
Schreak	G.	Jefferson	VA		Railroad		40	
Scott	Francis Woolfolk	Caroline	VA	61	Lawyer	31,500	39,000	21
Scott	Thomas L.	Caroline	VA		Physician	5,000	14,500	5
Shafer	William	Jefferson	VA		Planter	10,000	8,000	6
Sheppard	John M.	Henrico	VA	58	Merchant	30,000	56,000	20
Smith	William	Fauquier	VA	48	Farmer	25,773	35,188	9
Spense	W. A.	Westmoreland	VA	43	Physician	6,000	900	
Spotts	John J.	Henrico	VA	32	Merchant			3
Strider	John	Jefferson	VA		Physician	20,000	7,000	5
Taylor	Fielding L.	Gloucester	VA	35	Farmer	30,000	70,000	66
Taylor	Tazewell	Norfolk	VA	50	Lawyer	45,800	59,450	
Thackston	W. W.	Prince Edward	VA	43	Dentist	5,000	46,400	11
Thomas	James, Jr.	Henrico	VA	56	Merchant	250,000	100,000	94
Thompson	R. S.	Prince George	VA		Merchant	5,000	10,000	
Thornton	William C.	Carroll	VA	36	Hotel keeper	4,000	1,000	1
Tucker	D. M.	Powhatan	VA	57	Merchant	800	4,500	

Last Name	First Name	County	State	Age	Occupation	Real Estate ($)	Personal Estate ($)	Slaves (*N*)
Tucker	St. George	Hanover	VA	32	Lawyer	7,000	10,000	9
Wartham	Charles T.	Henrico	VA	46	Merchant	20,000	40,000	9
Warwick	Abraham	Henrico	VA	65	Flour merchant	400,000	54,000	98
Warwick	William B.	Henrico	VA	23	Merchant	15,000	5,000	
Washington	Lewis W.	Jefferson	VA		Planter	40,000	20,000	12
Watkins	J. B.	Henrico	VA	35	Merchant	5,000	20,000	
Whitlock	N. J. B.	Essex	VA	50	Farmer	20,366	35,800	
Wilson	James H.	Henrico	VA		Tobacco inspector			12
Wilson	Samuel M.	Rockbridge	VA		Farmer	6,000	6,641	4
Womble	John E.	Henrico	VA		Merchant	25,000	20,000	3
Wortham	Charles T.	Henrico	VA	46	Merchant	20,000	40,000	6

Notes

De Bow often changed the title of his journal between January 1846 and February 1867. Although I consistently and uniformly refer to *De Bow's Review* as a singular title—abbreviated throughout the notes as *DR*—the actual titles and date changes were as follows:

Commercial Review of the South and West, January 1846–January 1847;
De Bow's Commercial Review of the South and West, February 1847–June 1850;
De Bow's Review of the Southern and Western States, July 1850–December 1852;
De Bow's Review, January 1853–August 1864;
De Bow's Review, United States Journal of Agricultural, Commercial, Industrial Progress and Resources, January 1866–February 1867.

Readers should also note that US Census Office, *Seventh Census of the United States, 1850* (Washington, DC, 1853), and *Eighth Census of the United States, 1860* (Washington, DC, 1864), are collectively cited as Composite Census Records, 1850–1860, both in the notes and in the tables.

Introduction

1. Ottis C. Skipper, *J. D. B. De Bow: Magazinist of the Old South* (Athens: University of Georgia Press, 1958), 224; Paul Gaston, *The New South Creed: A Study in Southern Mythmaking* (New York: Knopf, 1970), 42–47.

2. William E. Dodd, *The Cotton Kingdom: A Chronicle of the Old South* (New Haven, CT: Yale University Press, 1919); Frank L. Owsley, *Plain Folk of the Old South* (Chicago: Quadrangle, 1949); Ulrich B. Phillips, *Life and Labor in the Old South* (New York: Little, Brown, 1929); Eugene Genovese, *The Political Economy of Slavery: Studies in the Economy and Society of the Slave South* (New York: Pantheon, 1965); Broadus Mitchell, *The Rise of Cotton Mills in the South* (Baltimore: Johns Hopkins University Press, 1921); Philip A. Bruce, *The Rise of the New South,* vol. 17 of *The History of North America* (Philadelphia: George Barrie & Sons, 1905); C. Vann Woodward, *Origins of the New South, 1877–1913* (Baton Rouge: Louisiana State University Press, 1951).

3. Jonathan D. Wells, *The Origins of the Southern Middle Class, 1800–1861* (Chapel

Hill: University of North Carolina Press, 2004); Frank Towers, *The Urban South and the Coming of the Civil War* (Charlottesville: University of Virginia Press, 2004); Tom Downey, *Planting a Capitalist South: Masters, Merchants, and Manufacturers in the Southern Interior, 1790–1860* (Baton Rouge: Louisiana State University Press, 2006); Frank J. Byrne, *Becoming Bourgeois: Merchant Culture in the South, 1820–1865* (Lexington: University Press of Kentucky, 2006); Susanna Delfino and Michele Gillespie, eds., *Global Perspectives on Industrial Transformations in the American South* (Columbia: University of Missouri Press, 2005), and *Southern Society and Its Transformations, 1790–1860* (Columbia: University of Missouri Press, 2011); L. Diane Barnes, Brian Schoen, and Frank Towers, eds., *The Old South's Modern Worlds: Slavery, Region, and Nation in the Age of Progress* (Oxford: Oxford University Press, 2011); Aaron W. Marrs, *Railroads in the Old South: Pursuing Progress in a Slave Society* (Baltimore: Johns Hopkins University Press, 2009); Robert Gudmestad, *Steamboats and the Rise of the Cotton Kingdom* (Baton Rouge: Louisiana State University Press, 2011); Bruce W. Eelman, *Entrepreneurs in the Southern Upcountry: Commercial Culture in Spartanburg, South Carolina, 1845–1880* (Athens: University of Georgia Press, 2008).

1. Learning to Be Southern and American

1. R. C. Nash, "The Organization of Trade and Finance in the Atlantic Economy: Britain and South Carolina, 1670–1775," in *Money, Trade, and Power: The Evolution of Colonial South Carolina's Plantation Society,* ed. Jack P. Greene, Rosemary Brana-Shute, and Randy J. Sparks (Columbia: University of South Carolina Press, 2001), 74–77; Peter Coclanis, "The Sociology of Architecture in Colonial Charleston: Pattern and Process in an Eighteenth-Century Southern City," *Journal of Social History* 18 (Summer 1985): 610–11; Ernest M. Lander Jr., "Charleston: Manufacturing Center of the Old South," *Journal of Southern History* 26 (August 1960): 330–32, 337–48; Richard W. Griffin, "An Origin of the New South: The South Carolina Homespun Company, 1808–1815," *Business History Review* 35 (Autumn 1961): 404–8; George Rogers, *Charleston in the Age of the Pinckneys* (Norman: University of Oklahoma Press, 1969), 3; Robert Mills, *Statistics of South Carolina: A View of the Natural, Civil, and Military History, General and Particular* (Charleston, SC: Hurlbut & Lloyd, 1826), 427–28; US Census Office, *Fourth Census of the United States, 1820* (Washington, DC, 1850); David Moltke-Hansen, "The Expansion of Intellectual Life: A Prospectus," in *Intellectual Life in Antebellum Charleston,* ed. Michael O'Brien and David Moltke-Hansen (Knoxville: University of Tennessee Press, 1986), 4–5, 26–28; Maurie D. McInnis, *The Politics of Taste in Antebellum Charleston* (Chapel Hill: University of North Carolina Press, 2005), 10–13.

2. Samuel M. Derrick, *Centennial History of the South Carolina Railroad* (Columbia, SC: State Co., 1930), 2–8; Murray N. Rothbard, *The Panic of 1819: Reactions and Policies* (New York: Columbia University Press, 1962), 2–15; Lacy K. Ford Jr., *Origins of Southern Radicalism: The South Carolina Upcountry, 1800–1860* (New York: Oxford University Press, 1988), 14–15; Charles Sellers, *The Market Revolution: Jacksonian America,*

1815–1846 (New York: Oxford University Press, 1991), 104, 135–39; Walter B. Edgar, *South Carolina: A History* (Columbia: University of South Carolina Press, 1998), 273–74.

3. John David Miller, *South by Southwest: Planter Emigration and Identity in the Slave South* (Charlottesville: University of Virginia Press, 2002), 30–31, 147; Fletcher M. Green, *Constitutional Development in the South Atlantic States, 1776–1860* (Chapel Hill: University of North Carolina Press, 1930), 147–49; Alfred G. Smith Jr., *Economic Readjustment of an Old Cotton State: South Carolina, 1820–1860* (Columbia: University of South Carolina Press, 1958), 13–14; Downey, *Planting a Capitalist South,* 64–73.

4. Clement Eaton, *A History of the Old South* (New York: Macmillan, 1949), 4–5; Charles S. Sydnor, *The Development of Southern Sectionalism, 1819–1848* (Baton Rouge: Louisiana State University Press, 1948), 32; Glover Moore, *The Missouri Controversy, 1819–1821* (Lexington: University of Kentucky Press, 1953), 13–19, 342; William W. Freehling, *Prelude to Civil War: The Nullification Controversy in South Carolina, 1816–1836* (New York: Harper Torchbooks, 1968), 108–10; Mark D. Kaplanoff, "Charles Pinckney and the American Republican Tradition," in O'Brien and Moltke-Hansen, eds., *Intellectual Life in Antebellum Charleston,* 85–90, 99–102; Rogers, *Charleston in the Age of the Pinckneys,* 141, 162–65; "Founders of the American Union, Charles Pinckney," *DR* 34 (April 1866): 372–78; William R. Taylor, *Cavalier and Yankee: The Old South and American National Character* (New York: George Braziller, 1957), 37–38; Robert P. Forbes, *The Missouri Compromise and Its Aftermath: Slavery and the Meaning of America* (Chapel Hill: University of North Carolina Press, 2007), 96–106; US Congress, House of Representatives, *Annals of Congress,* 16th Cong., 1st Sess., vol. 2 (1819), pp. 1310–29.

5. James W. Hagy, *City Directories for Charleston, South Carolina: From 1819, 1822, 1825, and 1829* (Baltimore: Clearfield, 1996), 38, 76; Skipper, *J. D. B. De Bow,* 2–3; Nicholas M. Butler, *Votaries of Apollo: The St. Cecilia Society and the Patronage of Concert Music in Charleston, South Carolina* (Columbia: University of South Carolina Press, 2007), 7–16.

6. *New York Journal,* March 26, 1767; Louis Cornish, *A National Register of the Society: Sons of the American Revolution* (New York: Press of Andrew Kellogg, 1902), 132.

7. *Charleston (SC) Times,* December 4, 1802; Clara A. Langley, *South Carolina Deed Abstracts, 1719–1772,* vol. 3, *Books QQ-H-3* (Greenville, SC: Southern Historical Press, 1983), 132; Guion G. Johnson, *A Social History of the Sea Islands: With Special Reference to St. Helena Island, South Carolina* (Chapel Hill: University of North Carolina Press, 1930), 11.

8. Robert L. Paquette, "From Rebellion to Revisionism: The Continuing Debate about the Denmark Vesey Affair," *Journal of the Historical Society* 4 (September 2004): 291–334; David Robertson, *Denmark Vesey: The Buried History of America's Largest Slave Rebellion and the Man Who Led It* (New York: Knopf, 1999), 6–9, 35; John Lofton, *Denmark Vesey's Revolt: The Slave Plot That Lit a Fuse to Fort Sumter* (Kent, OH: Kent State University Press, 1964), 211; Rogers, *Charleston in the Age of the Pinckneys,* 3–12, 159,

162. Rogers argues that, by the Nullification Crisis, Charleston's economic and political status had shrunk to the point that "the crucial battle in 1832 and 1833 in Charleston was not so much tariff or no tariff, or slavery or no slavery, as it was whether or not the city should be of the world" (162).

9. James W. Hagy, *City Directories for Charleston, South Carolina: For the Years 1806, 1807, 1808, 1813* (Baltimore: Clearfield, 1996), 64, 101, 144, and *City Directories for Charleston: 1819, 1822, 1825, and 1829*, 7, 38, 76; George K. Bennoitt, *City of Charleston Health Department Death Records: January 1821 to December 1828* (Charleston, SC, n.d.), 31; *Greenville (SC) Republican*, August 19, 1826.

10. "The Light of Other Days," *DR* 6 (September 1848): 236–40; "Editor's Department," *DR* 8 (March 1850): 311–12; "Progress of Our Commerce and Commercial Cities," *DR* 4 (December 1847): 552–60; "Charleston and Savannah," *DR* 8 (March 1850): 243–45.

11. "Fragments of the Past," *DR* 1 (January 1866): 630–32; Lewis E. Atherton, "Mercantile Education in the Ante-Bellum South," *Mississippi Valley Historical Review* 39 (1953): 623–26; J. D. B. De Bow, "Personal Journal," April 28, 1836–August 1, 1836, box 1, De Bow Papers, Special Collections, Perkins Library, Duke University, Durham, NC.

12. Jane H. Pease and William H. Pease, "Intellectual Life in the 1830s: The Institutional Framework and the Charleston Style," in O'Brien and Moltke-Hansen, eds., *Intellectual Life in Antebellum Charleston*, 234–38, 249–50; J. D. B. De Bow, "Personal Journal," box 1, De Bow Papers.

13. Timothy Green to John W. Mitchell, December 4, 1832, John W. Mitchell Papers, Southern Historical Collection, University of North Carolina, Chapel Hill; Freehling, *Prelude to Civil War*, 363; "The Progress of American Commerce," *DR* 2 (December 1846): 412–17; Derrick, *Centennial History of South Carolina Railroad*, 1–6; John McCardell, *The Idea of a Southern Nation: Southern Nationalists and Southern Nationalism, 1830–1860* (New York: Norton, 1979), 4–5, 38–40; "States' Rights and Sovereignty," *DR* 25 (August 1858): 127.

14. J. D. B. De Bow, "Personal Journal," box 5, De Bow Papers.

15. Ibid.

16. Skipper, *J. D. B. De Bow*, 2–3; Walter Fraser, *Charleston! Charleston! The History of a Southern City* (Columbia: University of South Carolina Press, 1989), 189; *Southern Patriot* (Charleston, SC), September 14, 1836; J. D. B. De Bow, "Personal Journal," box 1, De Bow Papers.

17. Lorri Glover, *Southern Sons: Becoming Men in the New Nation* (Baltimore: Johns Hopkins University Press, 2007), 1–5; J. D. B. De Bow, "Personal Journal," box 5, De Bow Papers.

18. J. D. B. De Bow, "Personal Journal," box 1, De Bow Papers.

19. Ibid.; Michael O'Brien, *Conjectures of Order: Intellectual Life and the American South, 1810–1860*, 2 vols. (Chapel Hill: University of North Carolina Press, 2004), 1:498–525.

20. US Census Office, *Fourth Census of the United States, 1820*; "Progress of the South and West," *DR* 11 (September 1850): 307; Richard C. Wade, *Slavery in the Cities:*

The South, 1820–1860 (New York: Oxford University Press, 1964), 20, 91; Robert S. Starobin, *Industrial Slavery in the Old South* (Oxford: Oxford University Press, 1970), 9–11; Leonard P. Curry, *The Free Black in Urban America, 1800–1850* (Chicago: University of Chicago Press, 1981); J. D. B. De Bow, "Random Thoughts on Slavery," box 1, De Bow Papers, and "Address Delivered before the Cliosophic Society—on Education," box 1, De Bow Papers; Phillips, *Life and Labor in the Old South;* Ralph E. Morrow, "The Proslavery Argument Revisited," *Mississippi Valley Historical Review* 47 (June 1961): 79–94.

21. J. D. B. De Bow, "Personal Journal," box 1, De Bow Papers; Fraser, *Charleston! Charleston!* 204; A. B. Meek, "Fires and Firemen," *DR* 4 (October 1847): 199–208. "Fires and Firemen" listed every major fire in Charleston from 1836 to 1846, noting the physical and financial toll of each. Included on this list was the 1838 fire that destroyed De Bow's family home. See also *Newport (SC) Mercury,* May 5, 1838; *Southern Patriot,* May 5, 1838.

22. Willis D. Weatherford, *James Dunwoody Brownson De Bow,* Southern Sketches, no. 3 (Charlottesville, VA: Historical Publishing Co., 1935), 4; J. D. B. De Bow, "Unpublished Papers," box 5, De Bow Papers.

23. Downey, *Planting a Capitalist South,* 20; Edgar K. Knight, *Public Education in the South* (Boston: Ginn, 1922), 102; "Editorial Notes and Miscellany," *DR* 29 (September 1860): 390–93; "Bishop Capers and the Methodist Church," *DR* 26 (February 1859): 179.

24. J. H. Easterby, *A History of the College of Charleston* (New York: Scribner, 1935), 13, 99–100, 138; Skipper, *J. D. B. De Bow,* 7–8.

25. "Bishop Capers and the Methodist Church," *DR* 26 (February 1859): 176–77.

26. R.G.B., "The Late J. D. B. De Bow," *DR* 4 (August 1867): 1–2; "The South Carolina Colleges," *DR* 27 (November 1859): 573; J. D. B. De Bow, "College Days," box 5, De Bow Papers; Easterby, *A History of the College of Charleston,* 138.

27. *Southern Patriot,* March 6, 1843; Moltke-Hansen, "The Expansion of Intellectual Life," 30–33. Moltke-Hansen identifies the generation born in the first decades of the nineteenth century as the impetus for Charleston's sustained cultural growth after 1840. See also J. D. B. De Bow, "The Duel's Effect," *Charleston (SC) Courier,* July 3, 1841, and "Private Journal," April 30, 1836, box 1, De Bow Papers; and Skipper, *J. D. B. De Bow,* 9–10.

28. J. D. B. De Bow, "The Three Philosophers," *Charleston Courier,* October 27–28, 1841.

29. Taylor, *Cavalier and Yankee,* 55–63.

30. *Southern Patriot,* June 27, 1843.

31. "Law and Lawyers, No. 2," *DR* 19 (September 1855): 398; O'Brien, *Conjectures of Order,* 1:508.

32. "Editorial—Book Notices," *DR* 23 (July 1857): 104.

33. *Charleston Courier,* July 22, September 5, 1845; "Editorial Department," *DR* 9 (August 1850): 125; Jane H. Pease and William H. Pease, "The Economics and Politics of Charleston's Nullification Crisis," *Journal of Southern History* 47 (August 1981): 335–62.

34. "A Visit to the High Hills of Santee," *Southern Patriot,* July 8, 1845; "Carolina Manufactures," *Southern Patriot,* July 30, 1845.

35. "Gregg's Essays on Domestic Industry," *Southern Patriot,* August 1, 1845; Tom Downey, "Riparian Rights and Manufacturing in Antebellum South Carolina: William Gregg and the Origins of the 'Industrial Mind,'" *Journal of Southern History* 69 (1999): 77–78; William Gregg, "Domestic Industry—Manufacturers at the South," *DR* 8 (February 1850): 134; "Visit to McBee's Factory," *Southern Patriot,* July 31, 1845.

36. James Gadsden to Dr. Shanks, October 6, 1845, Charleston, South Carolina Historical Society, Charleston; *Southern Patriot,* October 4, 1845; *Charleston Courier,* October 6, 1845. The men nominated to be delegates were John C. Calhoun, James Gadsden, James Petigru, Ker Boyce, J. S. Ashe, James Adger, H. Bailey, William Dearing, Henry Gourdin, William C. Gatewood, William Gregg, Edward Serring, Charles A. Magwood, W. S. King, James Bowie, Alexander Black, John Bryce, S. P. Ripley, Alexander Mazyck, Wade Hampton, Moses Mordecai, William Henry Trescott, S. Y. Tupper, L. A. Edmondson, and De Bow. *Charleston Courier,* July 21, 1845. Fraser refers to Charleston's mercantile class as "entrepreneur-boosters." Fraser, *Charleston! Charleston!* 221–23.

37. Gaston, *The New South Creed.*

38. John Belton O'Neall, *The Annals of Newberry in Two Parts* (Newberry, SC: Aull & Houseal, 1892), 97–101; Derrick, *Centennial History of the South Carolina Railroad,* 11–24; Lander, "Manufacturing Center of the Old South," 347, 350.

39. John G. Van Deusen, *The Ante-bellum Southern Commercial Conventions* (Durham, NC: Duke University Press, 1926), 9–14; Herbert Wender, *Southern Commercial Conventions* (Baltimore: Johns Hopkins University Press, 1930), 17–21; Weymouth T. Jordan, "Cotton Planters' Conventions in the Old South," *Journal of Southern History* 19 (August 1953): 321–45.

40. "The Memphis Convention," *Charleston Courier,* October 9–18, 1845. De Bow's sense of southern identity was similar to what Susan-Mary Grant refers to as *northern nationalism* or the creation of a specific regional identity to influence the evolution of a national one. See Susan-Mary Grant, *North over South: Northern Nationalism and American Identity in the Antebellum Era* (Lawrence: University Press of Kansas, 2000), 39.

41. *Charleston Courier,* October 9, 1845; "Editorial Notes, Etc.," *DR* 35 (July 1866): 109.

42. *Charleston Courier,* November 19, 1845.

2. Leaving an Old South, Entering a New South

1. "New Orleans," *DR* 2 (July 1846): 53–55; "Commerce of American Cities," *DR* 4 (November 1847): 395; "Summer Ramblings," *DR* 9 (September 1850): 347.

2. Robert C. Reinders, "The Free Negro in the New Orleans Economy: 1850–1860," *Louisiana History* 6 (Summer 1965): 273–75; Henry B. Hill and Larry Gara, "A French Traveler's View of Ante-Bellum New Orleans," *Louisiana History* 1 (Fall 1960): 336–38; Benjamin F. Norman, *Norman's New Orleans and Environs* (New York: D. Appleton, 1845), 135. Roger W. Shugg notes that although "Louisiana was as raw and young as

the whole Southwest . . . New Orleans belied its age, and was more like a boom town than a city over a century old." Roger W. Shugg, *Origins of Class Struggle in Louisiana: A Social History of White Farmers and Laborers during Slavery and After, 1840–1875* (Baton Rouge: Louisiana State University Press, 1966), 37. See also "The Moral Advance of New Orleans," *DR* 2 (November 1846): 349–51.

3. William H. Adams, "The Louisiana Whigs," *Louisiana History* 15 (1974): 217–19; Shugg, *Origins of Class Struggle in Louisiana,* 134–35; Joseph G. Tregle, *Louisiana in the Age of Jackson: A Clash of Cultures and Personalities* (Baton Rouge: Louisiana State University Press, 1999).

4. *Charleston Courier,* November 2, 13, 1845.

5. Ulrich B. Phillips, *A History of Transportation in the Eastern Cotton Belt to 1860* (New York: Columbia University Press, 1908), 17–19, 168–69; R. S. Cotterill, "Southern Railroads, 1850–1860," *Mississippi Valley Historical Review* 10 (March 1924): 396–405; Jere W. Roberson, "The South and the Pacific Railroad, 1845–1855," *Western Historical Quarterly* 5 (April 1974): 163–86.

6. *Southern Patriot,* November 15, 1845; Smith, *Economic Readjustment of an Old Cotton State,* 17–19; James Gadsden to John C. Calhoun, Charleston, October 21, 1845, in *The Papers of John C. Calhoun,* vol. 22, *1845–1846,* ed. Clyde N. Wilson (Columbia: University of South Carolina Press, 1995), 236.

7. "Editorial Notes and Miscellany," *DR* 3 (September 1860): 388; *Charleston Courier,* November 13, 1845; *Tri-Weekly Memphis (TN) Enquirer,* January 27, 1846.

8. *Charleston Courier,* November 19, 1845; R.G.B., "The Late J. D. B. De Bow," *DR* 37 (July–August 1867): 2–5.

9. Carolyn Pittman, "Memphis in the Mid-1840s," *West Tennessee Historical Society Papers* 23 (1969): 30–36; James Roper, *The Founding of Memphis: 1818–1820* (Memphis, TN: Memphis Sesquicentennial, 1970), 20, 25; "Cities of the Mississippi and Ohio," *DR* 1 (February 1846): 146.

10. J. P. Young, *Standard History of Memphis, Tennessee: From a Study of the Original Sources* (Knoxville, TN: H. W. Crew, 1912), 78–83, 377–81, 587–88; Forrest Laws, "The Railroad Comes to Tennessee: The Building of the LaGrange and Memphis," *West Tennessee Historical Society Papers* 30 (October 1976): 24–42.

11. William W. Freehling, *The Road to Disunion: Secessionists at Bay, 1776–1854* (New York: Oxford University Press, 1990), 28–29, 36, 164–65. Freehling uses geography and economics to divide the antebellum South into an "Old South" and a "New South." He argues that the South Atlantic seaboard states represented an Old South, dominated by planters resistant to modernity, while the Southwest represented a more economically liberal and commercially vibrant New South. Vernon L. Parrington uses similar divisions in *Main Currents in American Thought: The Romantic Revolution in America* (New York: Harcourt, Brace & World, 1927), 3–4, 8, 104–5. Instead of economics, however, Parrington stresses the philosophical and political divisions between the different regions of the antebellum South. He concludes that those liv-

ing in the antebellum Old South came from an enlightened Jeffersonian tradition that assumed that slavery was a dying institution and that southerners living in the antebellum New South followed the more realistic philosophy espoused by John C. Calhoun in his defense of slavery.

12. *Tri-Weekly Memphis Enquirer,* January 3, 1846; James B. Cook, "The Gayoso Hotel," in *The Tennessee Encyclopedia of History and Culture,* ed. Carroll Van West (Nashville, TN: Rutledge Hill, 1998), 353; *Journal of the Proceedings of the South-Western Convention, Begun and Held at the City of Memphis on the 12th November, 1845* (Memphis, TN, 1845), 3–6.

13. *Journal of the Proceedings of the South-Western Convention,* 7–14; John L. Larson, *Internal Improvement: National Public Works and the Promise of Popular Government in the Early United States* (Chapel Hill: University of North Carolina Press, 2001), 3–7, 19–23, 92, 239; Gerald M. Capers, *John C. Calhoun, Opportunist: A Reappraisal* (Gainesville: University of Florida Press, 1960), 46–52, 229; Charles M. Wiltse, *John C. Calhoun,* vol. 1, *Nationalist, 1782–1828* (Indianapolis: Bobbs-Merrill, 1944), 289–92; Clyde N. Wilson and Shirley Bright Cook, eds., *The Papers of John C. Calhoun,* vol. 23, *1846* (Columbia: University of South Carolina Press, 1996), 574; Freehling, *The Road to Disunion,* 261; Theodore R. Marmor, "Anti-industrialism and the Old South: The Agrarian Perspective of John C. Calhoun," *Comparative Studies in Society and History* 9 (July 1967): 377–78, 399–400.

14. *Young American Magazine,* December 13, 1845; *Cincinnati Weekly Herald and Philanthropist,* November 26, 1845; *Jonesborough (TN) Whig and Independent Journal,* December 31, 1845; "Internal Improvements," *Southern Quarterly Review* 9 (January 1846): 267–69; McCardell, *The Idea of a Southern Nation,* 114–19.

15. "Convention of the South and West," *DR* 1 (January 1846): 7–22; "The Merchant: His Character, Position, Duties," *DR* 3 (February 1847): 98; "American Legislation, Science, Art, and Agriculture," *DR* 2 (September 1846): 87–90; "New Orleans, Her Commerce and Her Duties," *DR* 3 (January 1847): 40–41. William Dodd agrees with De Bow's essential assessment of the Memphis convention and Calhoun's personal motives for attending the meeting. He argues that Calhoun had always been a nationalist at heart and that the convention offered a way for him to create an economically and politically unified South. For Calhoun, this perception of a unified South became increasingly important as political events escalated regional antagonisms. His obsession with political unity became most obvious in South Carolina, according to Lacy Ford. See William E. Dodd, *Statesmen of the Old South: From Radicalism to Conservative Revolt* (New York: Macmillan, 1911), 133–34, 149–51; and Ford, *Origins of Southern Radicalism,* 145–47.

16. *Charleston Courier,* November 24, 1845; *Journal of the Proceedings of the South-Western Convention,* 29–43, 99.

17. Vicki Vaughn Johnson, *The Men and the Vision of the Southern Commercial Conventions: 1845–1871* (Columbia: University of Missouri Press, 1992), 17–18, 26. In

the overall commercial convention movement, 5,716 men served as delegates to at least one commercial convention between 1845 and 1871. Of that number, 648 delegates attended two conventions, 79 attended three, 27 attended four, 7 attended five, and 3 attended six. De Bow attended more conventions than any other southerner.

18. "The Commercial Review," *DR* 1 (January 1846): 2–6.

19. *DR* 1 (January 1846): 1–93.

20. "Mississippi and Atlantic Railroad," *DR* 1 (January 1846): 22–33; "Mobile and Ohio Railroad," *DR* 3 (April 1847): 328–39; "Atlantic and Pacific Railroad," *DR* 3 (June 1847): 475–84; Marshall S. Legan, "Railroad Sentiment in Northern Louisiana in the 1850s," *Louisiana History* 17 (1976): 125–39. For examples of De Bow's interest in individual railroads, see "New Orleans, Her Commerce and Her Duties," *DR* 3 (January 1847): 39–48; and "Railroad Enterprises at the South," *DR* 3 (June 1847): 559–60.

21. "The Progress of American Commerce," *DR* 2 (December 1846): 426; "Cities of the Mississippi and Ohio Rivers," *DR* 1 (February 1846): 146–58; "The City of St. Louis," *DR* 3 (April 1847): 325–28; "Southern Cities," *DR* 6 (September 1848): 226–33; Blaine A. Brownell and David R. Goldfield, eds., *The City in Southern History: The Growth of Urban Civilization in the South* (Port Washington, NY: Kennikat, 1977), 54–55. Brownell and Goldfield argue that southern cities would have been nonexistent without interconnections with railroads and plantations. Planters recognized this reality and often invested heavily in railroad projects that might potentially lead to large profits. Blaine A. Brownell and David R. Goldfield, introduction to *The City in Southern History: The Growth of Urban Civilization in the South,* ed. Blaine A. Brownell and David R. Goldfield (Port Washington, NY: Kennikat, 1977), 5–22.

22. Norman, *New Orleans and Environs,* 70–79; Shugg, *Origins of Class Struggle in Louisiana,* 55; "Southern and Western Statistics, Commerce, Agriculture, Etc.," *DR* 1 (January 1846): 82. C. Vann Woodward touches on the importance of public health and disease prevention in the commercial advancement of the postbellum South. He marks 1906 as the beginning of a new era in public health because of new medical discoveries and increased publicity owing to the work of the Rockefeller Sanitary Commission. See Woodward, *Origins of the New South,* 227–28, 425–26. John Ellis concludes that the commercial elite in postbellum New Orleans, Memphis, and Atlanta set stringent public health policies to minimize the disruption of commerce and trade. These efforts and the support they received from merchants and professional men were similar to those in the antebellum South. See John Ellis, *Yellow Fever and Public Health in the New South* (Lexington: University Press of Kentucky, 1992). See also David R. Goldfield, *Cotton Fields and Skyscrapers: Southern City and Region* (Baton Rouge: Louisiana State University Press, 1982), 41–42.

23. Albert Bly, "On the Revival of Roman Baths," *DR* 2 (October 1846): 228–30; W. P. Hort, "Public Health and the Prevention of Disease in Southern Cities," *DR* 3 (March 1847): 250; Josiah Nott, "Life Insurance at the South," *DR* 3 (May 1847): 367–76.

24. "The Warehousing Policy," *DR* 1 (January 1846): 61–64; "American Legislation,

Science, Art, and Agriculture," *DR* 2 (September 1846): 91–96; "The Origins, Progress, and Influences of Commerce," *DR* 1 (February 1846): 116.

25. "Louisiana Sugar," *DR* 1 (January 1846): 53–56; "Southern and Western Commerce, Statistics, Agriculture, Etc.," *DR* 1 (March 1846): 277–81; "Internal Improvement—Mining, Railroads, Etc.," *DR* 5 (January 1848): 87–95; Richard Abbey, "The Cotton Culture," *DR* 2 (September 1846): 133, 142.

26. Daniel Pratt, "Cotton Gins," *DR* 2 (September 1846): 153–55. Curtis J. Evans agrees with De Bow's initial assessment of Prattville and notes that Pratt's accomplishments became an industrial monument in the agrarian South. By 1860, however, Prattville's cotton factory had added only 485 new spindles in ten years. See Curtis J. Evans, *The Conquest of Labor: Daniel Pratt and Southern Industrialization* (Baton Rouge: Louisiana State University Press, 2001), 28–33, 75–76.

27. John Pope, "Agriculture and Manufactures," *DR* 1 (March 1846): 228–38. For more background on the debate over why planters did not invest more in the industrial and commercial sectors of the antebellum South, see Holland Thompson, "The Civil War and Social and Economic Changes," *Annals of the American Academy of Political and Social Sciences* 154 (January 1931): 11–20; Genovese, *The Political Economy of Slavery;* Gavin Wright, *The Political Economy of the Cotton South: Households, Markets, and Wealth in the Nineteenth Century* (New York: Norton, 1978); Fred Bateman and Thomas Weiss, *A Deplorable Scarcity: The Failure of Industrialization in the Slave Economy* (Chapel Hill: University of North Carolina Press, 1981); and Douglas R. Egerton, "Markets without a Market Revolution: Southern Planters and Capitalism," *Journal of the Early Republic* 16 (Summer 1996): 207–21.

28. James Gadsden, "Commercial Spirit at the South," *DR* 2 (September 1846): 119–32.

29. For representative examples of De Bow's interest in agricultural diversity, see J. S. Duke, "Coffee and the Coffee Trade," *DR* 2 (November 1846): 303–22; "Agriculture of the South and West: Cultivation of the Olive in the Southern States," *DR* 3 (March 1847): 265–68; "The Grain and Flour Trade," *DR* 4 (October 1847): 159–64; and "Agricultural Associations," *DR* 1 (February 1846): 164.

30. "Agricultural Associations," *DR* 1 (February 1846): 161–69; "Southern and Western Agricultural and Mechanic Associations," *DR* 4 (December 1847): 419.

31. "Agriculture and Manufacture in the South and West," *DR* 4 (September 1847): 128–37; C. O. Cathy, "Sidney Weller: Ante-Bellum Promoter of Agricultural Reform," *North Carolina Historical Review* 31 (1954): 6–17; Sidney Weller, "American Native Wines," *DR* 4 (November 1847): 310–18.

32. "The Cotton Plant," *DR* 1 (April 1846): 289–98; A Southwestern Planter, "Remedy for the Cotton Planters," *DR* 1 (May 1846): 434–36; Thomas Affleck, "The Cherokee Rose," *DR* 5 (January 1848): 83–84.

33. "Position of the Commercial Review," *DR* 1 (January 1846): 6; "Some Thoughts on Political Economy and Government," *DR* 9 (September 1850): 257–71.

34. The antiwar contributions of Poinsett, Hodge, and Benjamin give credence to Paul Buck's observation that men of business are often men of peace. See Paul Buck, *The Road to Reunion: 1865–1900* (New York: Vintage, 1937), 165. See also Joel Poinsett, "The Mexican War," *DR* 2 (July 1846): 21–24; William L. Hodge, "New Orleans," *DR* 2 (July 1846): 59–61; Judah Benjamin, "Blockade," *DR* 2 (June 1846): 499–503; and Ernest M. Lander Jr., *Reluctant Imperialists: Calhoun, the South Carolinians, and the Mexican War* (Baton Rouge: Louisiana State University Press, 1979).

35. B. F. Porter, "Slavery, Ancient and Modern," *DR* 2 (November 1846): 351–54; "The Negro: By a Citizen of Mississippi," *DR* 3 (May 1847): 420–22; A Southern Planter, "Prospective Emancipation Examined—the Colonization Society, Etc.," *DR* 21 (September 1856): 265–70.

36. Clement Eaton, *The Mind of the Old South* (Baton Rouge: Louisiana State University Press, 1964), 69–89; "Reminiscences of the West," *DR* 2 (September 1846): 177–79; Maunsel White, "The University of Louisiana," *DR* 3 (March 1847): 263–65. Kenneth R. Johnson explores the relationship between towns and universities in the New South and concludes that many New South boosters saw institutions of higher learning as an important component in attracting new commercial and industrial enterprises to their cities or towns. He specifically examines the development of Florence, Alabama, and links the city's economic growth with efforts to attract a college. Interestingly, three of the men most responsible for promoting Florence and luring colleges to the city were past subscribers to *De Bow's Review.* Although Porter King, Thomas Watts, and John Tyler Morgan became instrumental in the postwar recovery of Alabama, they had been exposed in the so-called Old South to many of the ideas they later initiated. See Kenneth R. Johnson, "Urban Boosterism and Higher Education in the New South: A Case Study," *Alabama Historical Quarterly* 42 (Spring–Summer 1980): 40, 45–54. See also Eaton, *The Mind of the Old South,* 80–81; and *Southern Patriot,* February 24, 1848.

37. J. R. McCormick, "Defective Organization of American Universities," *DR* 5 (March 1848): 241–43.

38. Merl Reed, "Boom or Bust—Louisiana's Economy during the 1830s," *Louisiana History* 4 (Winter 1963): 35–54; Raleigh A. Suarez, "Bargains, Bills, and Bankruptcies: Business Activity in Rural Antebellum Louisiana," *Louisiana History* 6 (Summer 1966): 189–206.

39. "Louisiana Sugar," *DR* 1 (January 1846): 53–56; William Hodge, "New Orleans," *DR* 2 (July 1846): 53–60; "The State of Louisiana," *DR* 1 (May 1846): 383–434.

40. "The Publishing Business," *DR* 1 (March 1846): 286–87; "Late Publications," *DR* 7 (November 1849): 465; "Editor's Arm-Chair," *DR* 6 (December 1848): 458.

41. *Southern Patriot,* November 2, 1846; *Semi-Weekly Natchez (MS) Courier,* July 16, 1847; *Tri-Weekly Memphis Enquirer,* January 24, 1846.

42. "The Cherokee Rose," *DR* 5 (January 1848): 82–83.

43. "Publishing Business," *DR* 6 (August 1848): 159–60; "Editor's Arm Chair," *DR* 6 (October/November 1848): 378.

3. A Busy and Fractured Mind of the South

1. "The Publishing Business," *DR* 7 (July 1849): 101–2; *Charleston (SC) Mercury,* July 7, 1849; "Editorial and Literary Department," *DR* 11 (August 1851): 22; "Editor's Arm Chair," *DR* 6 (October 1848): 378; "Editorial Department," *DR* 9 (July 1850): 125–26.

2. "Editorial Note of Travel and Books," *DR* 7 (August 1849): 189–90.

3. "Gallery of Industry and Enterprise: Hamilton Smith of Kentucky, Manufacturer," *DR* 11 (July 1851): 90–91; Charles T. James, "Facilities for Manufactures in the West," *Merchants' Magazine and Commercial Review* 20 (July 1849): 112–13; Hamilton Smith, "Southern and Western Manufacturers," *DR* 7 (August 1849): 128–34; Barbara Wriston, "Who Was the Architect of the Indiana Cotton Mill, 1849–1850," *Journal of the Society of Architectural Historians* 24 (May 1965): 171–73; Holland Thompson, *From the Cotton Field to the Cotton Mill: A Study of the Industrial Transition in North Carolina* (New York: Macmillan, 1906), 53–54; Starobin, *Industrial Slavery in the Old South,* 11–13; *Louisville (KY) Daily Journal,* June 19, 1849.

4. Skipper, *J. D. B. De Bow,* 23–24; "The Publishing Business," *DR* 7 (July 1849): 101–2.

5. C. Brenden Martin, *Tourism in the Mountain South: A Double-Edged Sword* (Knoxville: University of Tennessee Press, 2007), 1–20; "Summer Ramblings," *DR* 9 (September 1850): 347–50; W. Fitzhugh Brundage, *The Southern Past: A Clash of Race and Memory* (Cambridge, MA: Harvard University Press, 2005), 183–90.

6. "Home Manufactures," *DR* 7 (November 1849): 454–55; "Gallery of Industry and Enterprise: No. 4, Hon. John T. Winter, of Georgia," *DR* 10 (June 1851): 582–86; "Home Manufactures," *DR* 7 (November 1849): 454.

7. Daniel Pratt, "List of Cotton Factories in the State of Alabama," *DR* 9 (August 1850): 214; "Department of Manufactures and Commerce," *DR* 9 (August 1850): 214–15; Hamilton Smith, "Influence of Manufactures on the Growth of Cities," *DR* 9 (October 1850): 436–39; "Progressive Manufacture of Coarse Cottons," *DR* 9 (November 1850): 557; "Gallery of Industry and Enterprise, William Gregg of South Carolina," *DR* 10 (March 1851): 348–52; William Gregg, "Manufactures in South Carolina and the South," *DR* 11 (August 1851): 123–25, 131–33; "Southern Manufacturing Competition," *DR* 9 (November 1850): 558; "Progress of the Cotton Manufacture in the United States," *DR* 8 (March 1850): 272; Mark R. Cockrill, "Manufacture of Cotton by Its Producers," *DR* 7 (December 1849): 484–90; "The Cause of the South," *DR* 8 (July 1850): 120; Mitchell, *The Rise of Cotton Mills in the South,* 48; Broadus Mitchell and George S. Mitchell, *The Industrial Revolution in the South* (Baltimore: Johns Hopkins University Press, 1930), 1–12; Herbert Collins, "The Southern Industrial Gospel before 1860," *Journal of Southern History* 12 (August 1946): 386–402; Starobin, *Industrial Slavery in the Old South,*

12–16; George Stueckrath, "Incidents in the Early Settlement of the State of Tennessee, and Nashville," *DR* 27 (July 1859): 84–94.

8. "Saluda Factory, S.C.—Negro Labor," *DR* 9 (October 1850): 432–33; "Excessive Slave Population—the Remedy," *DR* 12 (February 1852): 182–85; R. G. Morris, "Slave Labor upon Public Works at the South," *DR* 17 (July 1854): 76–82; Starobin, *Industrial Slavery in the Old South,* 221–23.

9. John Majewski, *Modernizing a Slave Economy: The Economic Vision of the Confederate Nation* (Chapel Hill: University of North Carolina Press, 2009), 83–90; Marrs, *Railroads in the Old South,* 7–10; M. Butt Hewson, "Thoughts on a Rail-Road System for New Orleans," *DR* 11 (October/November 1851): 471–74; Legan, "Railroad Sentiment in Northern Louisiana in the 1850s"; "Rail-Road Prospects and Progress," *DR* 12 (May 1852): 492–507; David M. Potter, *The Impending Crisis, 1848–1861* (New York: Harper & Row, 1976), 146–47; *New Orleans Daily Picayune,* October 21, 1849.

10. "Tehuantepec Railroad, Movement in New Orleans," *DR* 10 (January 1851): 94–96; "Internal Improvements," *DR* 9 (August 1850): 218–22; "How Can the Union Be Preserved—Views of Mr. Calhoun, in the Senate Debate on the Compromise of 1850," *DR* 21 (September 1856): 232; Potter, *The Impending Crisis,* 146–49; "Presidential Candidates and Aspirants," *DR* 29 (July 1860): 97–98; G. R. Fairbanks, "Communication between New York, New Orleans, and San Francisco," *DR* 8 (January 1850): 30–32; William Cronon, *Nature's Metropolis: Chicago and the Great West* (New York: Norton, 1991), 68–70; Holman Hamilton, *Prologue to Conflict: The Crisis and Compromise of 1850* (Lexington: University of Kentucky Press, 1964), 119–21, 182–84; "Thoughts on a Rail-Road System for New Orleans," *DR* 10 (February 1851): 175.

11. "Rail-Road Prospects and Progress," *DR* 12 (May 1852): 492–507; "The South and the Union," *DR* 10 (February 1851): 151–62; Gaston, *The New South Creed,* 42–47, 223–24; Robert Darden Little, "The Ideology of the New South: A Study in the Development of Ideas, 1865–1910" (Ph.D. diss., University of Chicago, 1950), 14–18.

12. "Southern and Western Railroad Convention," *DR* 12 (March 1852): 305–32; Johnson, *The Men and the Vision of the Southern Commercial Conventions,* 106; Van Deusen, *The Ante-Bellum Southern Commercial Conventions,* 32–39; "Department of Internal Improvements," *DR* 12 (May 1852), 563–65.

13. "Importance of an Industrial Revolution in the South," *DR* 12 (April 1852): 554–62.

14. "Editorial and Literary Department," *DR* 13 (October 1852): 427; "The Baltimore Southern Commercial Convention," *DR* 14 (April 1853): 373–79; Van Deusen, *The Ante-Bellum Southern Commercial Conventions,* 39–41.

15. Van Deusen, *The Ante-Bellum Southern Commercial Conventions,* 27–30; "The Memphis Convention," *DR* 8 (March 1850): 217–32; "Pacific Railroad," *DR* 9 (December 1850): 601–14; Potter, *The Impending Crisis,* 465–66; James M. McPherson, *Battle Cry of Freedom: The Civil War Era* (New York: Ballantine, 1988), 64–77; Potter, *The Impending Crisis,* 13, 16–17; "The Wilmot Provisos Exclusion," *DR* 4 (December 1847): 557–58;

Thelma Jennings, *The Nashville Convention: Southern Movement for Unity, 1848–1851* (Memphis, TN: Memphis State University Press, 1980), 3–12; Potter, *The Impending Crisis*, 123–30.

16. Eric H. Walther, *William Lowndes Yancey: The Coming of the Civil War* (Chapel Hill: University of North Carolina Press, 2006), 121–27; William C. Davis, *Rhett: The Turbulent Life and Times of a Fire-Eater* (Columbia: University of South Carolina Press, 2001), 274–75; "California, the New El Dorado," *DR* 8 (June 1850): 538–41; Potter, *The Impending Crisis*, 13, 16–17; "The Wilmot Provisos Exclusion," *DR* 4 (December 1847): 557–58; "Slavery in the New Territories," *DR* 7 (July 1849): 62–73; "The Cause of the South," *DR* 9 (July 1850): 121; "Editorial Notes," *DR* 9 (September 1850): 352; "Fugitive Slaves," *DR* 9 (November 1850): 567–68; Henry F. James, *Abolitionism Unveiled! Hypocrisy Unmasked! and Knavery Scourged!* (New York: T. V. Paterson, 1850); "Editor's Department," *DR* 8 (April 1850): 406.

17. "Editorial and Literary Department," *DR* 10 (February 1851): 242; "The Position and Course of the South," *DR* 10 (February 1851): 231–32; "William Chambers on Slavery," *DR* 18 (April 1855): 448–54; "The South and Her Remedies," *DR* 10 (March 1851): 265–68; Solon Robinson, "Negro Slavery at the South: Pts. 1 and 2," *DR* 7 (September 1849): 206–25, 206, and 7 (November 1849): 379–89; Herbert A. Kellar, ed., *Solon Robinson, Pioneer and Agriculturalist*, vol. 2 (Indianapolis: Indiana Historical Bureau, 1936), 253–54.

18. Elizabeth Ammons, *Harriet Beecher Stowe's Uncle Tom's Cabin: A Casebook* (Oxford: Oxford University Press, 2007), 9–11; Stephen C. Crawford, "Quantified Memory: A Study of WPA and Fisk University Slave Narrative Collections" (Ph.D. diss., University of Chicago, 1980); A Small Farmer, "Management of Negroes," *DR* 11 (October/November 1851): 369–72; A Mississippi Planter, "Rules and Regulations for the Government of a Southern Plantation," *DR* 10 (June 1851): 626; "Editorial Miscellany," *DR* 14 (March 1853): 302–3; David A. Copeland, *The Media's Role in Defining the Nation: The Active Voice* (New York: Peter Lang, 2010), 81–83; "Improved Sugar Process," *DR* 9 (December 1850): 665–69; I. T. Danson, "Connection between American Slavery and the British Cotton Manufacture," *DR* 22 (March 1857): 265–88; John Forsyth, "The North and the South," *DR* 17 (October 1854): 361–78.

19. Mark M. Smith, *Mastered by the Clock: Time, Slavery, and Freedom in the American South* (Chapel Hill: University of North Carolina Press, 1997), 91–112; Alfred D. Chandler, *The Visible Hand: The Managerial Revolution in American Business* (Cambridge, MA: Belknap Press of Harvard University Press, 1977), 65–69; "Rules for the Management of Negroes," *DR* 14 (February 1853): 176–78; John A. Calhoun, "Management of Slaves," *DR* 18 (June 1855): 714; Eugene Genovese, *Roll, Jordon, Roll: The World the Slaves Made* (New York: Vintage, 1976), 4, 297–308, and *The Political Economy of Slavery*, 26–31; James Oakes, "'Whom Have I Oppressed?': The Pursuit of Happiness and the Happy Slave," in *The Revolution of 1800: Democracy, Race, and the New Republic*, ed. James Horn, Jan E. Lewis, and Peter S. Onuf (Charlottesville: University of Virginia Press,

2002), 220–39; James O. Breeden, *Advice among Masters: The Ideal in Slave Management in the Old South* (Westport, CT: Greenwood, 1980), 291; Robert Collins, "Essay on the Management of Slaves," *DR* 17 (October 1854): 421–26; William Scarborough, *The Overseer: Plantation Management in the Old South* (Baton Rouge: Louisiana State University Press, 1966); William Wiethoff, *Crafting the Overseers' Image* (Columbia: University of South Carolina Press, 2006), 176–91; "Rules and Regulations for the Government of a Southern Plantation," *DR* 10 (June 1851): 625–27; Thomas Affleck, "The Duties of an Overseer," *DR* 18 (March 1855): 339–45; Genovese, *Roll, Jordon, Roll,* 4–5, 54; Philip D. Morgan, *Slave Counterpoint* (Chapel Hill: University of North Carolina Press, 1998), 284–87; Ira Berlin, *Many Thousands Gone: The First Two Centuries of Slavery in North America* (Cambridge, MA: Belknap Press of Harvard University Press, 1998), 96–98.

20. "Editorial Miscellany," *DR* 14 (March 1853): 300; John R. Gold and Margaret M. Gold, *Cities of Culture: Staging International Festivals and the Urban Agenda, 1851–2000* (Aldershot: Ashgate, 2005), 89–90; "The American Crystal Palace," *DR* 13 (December 1852): 637–40.

21. Skipper, *J. D. B. De Bow,* 69–80; Carroll D. Wright and William C. Hunt, *History and Growth of the United States Census, 1790–1890* (Washington, DC, 1900), 38–39, 45; *New Orleans Daily Picayune,* September 27, October 4–13, November 10, 1849; "Population," *DR* 8 (March 1850): 207–16; "Statistical Bureaus in the States, Etc.," *DR* 8 (May 1850): 422–44; "Census of 1850," *DR* 9 (August 1850): 249; "Our Future," *DR* 14 (May 1853): 524; "Our Future," *DR* 14 (June 1853): 632; "A Work for Every Library," *DR* 14 (June 1853): 631–32.

22. *New York Daily Tribune,* March 28, 1853; *Nashville (TN) Union and American,* August 18, 1853; Margo J. Anderson, *The American Census: A Social History* (New Haven, CT: Yale University Press, 1988), 50–54; LeRoy P. Graf and Ralph W. Haskins, eds., *The Papers of Andrew Johnson,* vol. 5, *1861–1865* (Knoxville: University of Tennessee Press, 1979), 256.

23. "De Bow's Industrial Resources," *DR* 14 (June 1853): 633.

24. Lyman Carrier, "The United States Agricultural Society," *Agricultural History* 11 (1937): 278–88; "National Agricultural Society," *DR* 13 (August 1852), 207–9; Sarah T. Phillips, "Antebellum Agricultural Reform, Republican Ideology, and Sectional Tension," *Agricultural History* 74 (Autumn 2000): 799–822; Avery Craven, "The Agricultural Reforms of the Ante-Bellum South," *American Historical Review* 33 (January 1928): 302–14; Phillips, *Life and Labor in the Old South,* 196–205; Lewis C. Gray, *History of Agriculture in the Southern United States to 1860,* vol. 2, Carnegie Institution Publication no. 430 (Washington, DC: Carnegie Institution of Washington, 1933), 788–89. For examples of typical agricultural contributions, see A Mississippi Planter, "Production and Manufacture of Cotton," *DR* 8 (February 1850): 99–101; M. H. McGehee, "Cotton: Disease of Plant and Remedies," *DR* 11 (July 1851): 7–12; Sidney Weller, "Southern Vines and Vineyards," *DR* 12 (May 1852): 470–75; Leonard Wray, "Culture and Manufacture of Sugar," *DR* 12 (June 1852): 646–55; Edmund Ruffin, "Southern Agricultural Exhaustion

and Its Remedy," *DR* 14 (January 1853): 34–46; Albert W. Ely, "Domestic Poultry," *DR* 15 (November 1853): 496–509; R. F. W. Allston, "Sea-Coast Crops of the South," *DR* 16 (June 1854): 589–615; and "Remarks on Dr. Cartwright's Paper—'Extension of the Sugar Region,'" *DR* 15 (December 1853): 647–48. See also Richard Follett, *The Sugar Masters: Planters and Slaves in Louisiana's Cane World, 1820–1860* (Baton Rouge: Louisiana State University Press, 2005), 17–23.

25. Eric H. Walther, *The Fire-Eaters* (Baton Rouge: Louisiana State University Press, 1992), 232–34; Phillips, *Life and Labor in the Old South,* 131–32; William M. Mathew, *Edmund Ruffin and the Crisis of Slavery in the Old South: The Failure of Agricultural Reform* (Athens: University of Georgia Press, 1989); McCardell, *The Idea of a Southern Nation,* 110–11; William Kauffman Scarborough, *The Diary of Edmund Ruffin,* vol. 1 (Baton Rouge: Louisiana State University Press, 1972), 443; "Editorials, Book Notices, Etc.," *DR* 16 (March 1854), 331–32; Carrier, "The United States Agricultural Society," 278–88.

26. Weymouth T. Jordan, "Noah B. Cloud and the American Cotton Planter," *Agricultural History* 31 (October 1957): 44–49; Noah B. Cloud, "The American Cotton Planter," *American Cotton Planter* 1 (January 1853): 20, 27; Walter Lynwood Fleming, *The South in the Building of the Nation: A History of the Southern States,* vol. 5 (Richmond, VA: Southern Historical Publication Society, 1909), 587–92.

27. Potter, *The Impending Crisis,* 146–76; Van Deusen, *The Ante-Bellum Southern Commercial Conventions,* 44–49; "The Great Southern Convention in Charleston, No. II," *DR* 17 (July 1854): 95–97.

28. Follett, *The Sugar Masters,* 40–45.

29. "Progress of the Great West in Population, Agriculture, Arts, and Commerce," *DR* 4 (September 1847): 40–42; Charles Gayarré, "Influence of the Mechanical Arts on the Human Race," *DR* 17 (September 1854): 229–44; "General Literature," *DR* 3 (April 1847), 353; J.S.W., "Histoire de Louisiane," *Southern Quarterly Review* 9 (April 1846): 361–71. A similar construction of a historical Old South during the antebellum period occurred in Middle Florida. See Edward E. Baptist, *Creating an Old South: Middle Florida's Plantation Frontier before the Civil War* (Chapel Hill: University of North Carolina Press, 2002), 254–57, 283. Baptist identifies social and racial chaos in Middle Florida during the early nineteenth century as the primary reason that planters in the 1850s re-created an idolized version of their past. They used Virginia history and Sir Walter Scott's *Ivanhoe* as historical markers, and Baptist concludes that, by erasing earlier regional crises from public memory, local planters instilled a sense of long-term stability and harmony within their communities. See also Charles Gayarré, *History of Louisiana* (New York: William J. Widdleton, 1867), 632–33.

30. "Editorial and Literary Department," *DR* 11 (December 1851): 687–88; "Editor's Department," *DR* 8 (February 1850): 312; "Editorial and Literary Department," *DR* 10 (May 1851): 599; Richard Hildreth, *Despotism in America; or, An Inquiry into the Nature and Results of the Slave-Holding System in the United States* (Boston: Whipple & Darrell, 1840).

31. Louisiana, vol. 10, p. 331, R. G. Dun & Co. Credit Report Volumes, Historical Collections, Baker Library, Harvard Business School, Cambridge, MA.

4. Embracing Southern Anger and Southern Nationalism

1. James A. Harrison, *Life and Letters of Edgar Allan Poe*, vol. 2 (New York: Thomas P. Crowell, 1903), 14–15, 25, 425–29; Charles Gayarré, "James Dunwoody Brownson De Bow," *DR* 3 (June 1867): 505; Ottis Skipper, "J. D. B. De Bow, the Man," *Journal of Southern History* 10 (November 1944): 414, and *J. D. B. De Bow*, 108–9; *New Orleans Daily Picayune*, August 29, 1854; "Retrospective View—Appeal for the Future," *DR* 17 (December 1854): 643–45.

2. Van Deusen, *The Ante-Bellum Southern Commercial Conventions*, 50–52; "Southern Commercial Convention at New Orleans," *DR* 18 (March 1855): 353–55; "The Southern Commercial Convention," *DR* 18 (February 1855): 240; Roberson, "The South and the Pacific Railroad," 177; Potter, *The Impending Crisis*, 162–64.

3. "Editorial Notices," *DR* 18 (February 1855): 176; Muscoe Garnett, "The South and the Union," *DR* 18 (February 1855): 145.

4. "To Planters and Farmers," *DR* 18 (February 1855): 208; A Farmer, "A Valuable Agricultural Implement," *DR* 18 (June 1855): 736–39; David Myerle, "Bear Grass of Florida," *DR* 19 (September 1855): 363–64; M. W. Philips, "The Southwest," *DR* 19 (November 1855): 613–14.

5. "What Is Thought of the *Review* by Its Subscribers and the Press," *DR* 19 (September 1855): 367–68.

6. David P. Parker, "To the Youth of the Southern Confederacy: Georgia's Confederate Textbooks," in *Breaking the Heartland: The Civil War in Georgia*, ed. John D. Fowler and David B. Parker (Macon, GA: Mercer University Press, 2011), 94–97; "The Publishing Business," *DR* 3 (July 1847): 587; "Literary, Editorial Department," *DR* 9 (November 1850): 573; "Editorial and Literary Department," *DR* 10 (May 1851): 697; "Editorial and Literary Department," *DR* 12 (January 1852): 114–15; "Editorial and Literary Department," *DR* 13 (August 1852): 211; "Editorial, Book Notices, Etc.," *DR* 21 (October 1856): 440–41.

7. C. K. Marshall, "Home Education at the South," *DR* 18 (March 1855): 430–32; Van Deusen, *The Ante-Bellum Southern Commercial Conventions*, 41–44; "Our Department of Education," *DR* 18 (January 1855): 144; Glover, *Southern Sons*, 51–54; "Education in Missouri, Boston, Washington, South Carolina, Arkansas, Germany," *DR* 18 (February 1855): 285–88; "Relation of Education to the Prevention of Crime," *DR* 18 (March 1855): 409–21; Archibald Roane, "Common Schools and Universities North and South," *DR* 18 (April 1855): 520–28; "University of Virginia," *DR* 19 (August 1855): 218; "Events of the Month—Personal Notices—Book Notices, Etc.," *DR* 18 (April 1855): 463.

8. "William Chambers on Slavery," *DR* 18 (April 1855): 448–54; Jesse Chickering,

"The White, Free Colored, and Slave Population of the United States," *DR* 15 (August 1853): 129–43; "Modern Philanthropy and Negro Slavery," *DR* 16 (March 1854): 263–76.

9. "The War against the South," *DR* 21 (September 1856): 271–77; "Kansas, a Slave State," *DR* 20 (June 1856): 741–44; "Kansas Matters—Appeal to the South," *DR* 20 (May 1856): 635–37; "Letter to Kansas Association," *DR* 20 (May 1856): 637–39; "Kansas Meeting in New Orleans," *DR* 20 (May 1856): 639–40; "Sentiments of the South," *DR* 21 (October 1856): 438–40; "Reorganization of Southern Society," *DR* 21 (August 1856): 207–9.

10. "Position of the Commercial Review," *DR* 1 (January 1846): 6; McCardell, *The Idea of a Southern Nation,* 141–76; Muscoe Garnett, "The South and the Union," *DR* 18 (February 1855): 145; Nicole Etcheson, *Bleeding Kansas: Contested Liberty in the Civil War Era* (Lawrence: University Press of Kansas, 2004).

11. John Ashworth, *Slavery, Capitalism, and Politics in the Antebellum Republic,* vol. 1, *Commerce and Compromise, 1820–1850* (New York: Cambridge University Press, 1995), 249–51; "Editorial Miscellany," *DR* 28 (June 1860): 742; "Plantation Life—Duties and Responsibilities," *DR* 29 (September 1860): 361; Eric Foner, *Free Soil, Free Labor, Free Men: The Ideology of the Republican Party before the Civil War* (Oxford: Oxford University Press, 1970), 12–18; "Gallery of Industry and Enterprise, William Gregg of South Carolina," *DR* 10 (March 1851): 348–52; William Gregg, "Manufactures in South Carolina and the South," *DR* 11 (August 1851): 123–25, 131; William J. Grayson, "The Hireling and the Slave," *DR* 18 (February 1855): 185–88, 18 (April 1855): 459–62, 19 (August 1855): 208–18, and 21 (September 1856): 248–56; Parrington, *Main Currents in American Thought,* 98–103.

12. Thomas R. Dew, "Slavery in the Virginia Legislature of 1831–2, Pts. 1 and 2," *DR* 20 (January 1856): 118–40, and 20 (February 1856): 175–89; Drew G. Faust, *The Ideology of Slavery: Proslavery Thought in the Antebellum South, 1830–1860* (Baton Rouge: Louisiana State University Press, 1981), 8–9; Kenneth Stampp, "An Analysis of T. R. Dew's *Review of the Debates in the Virginia Legislatures,*" *Journal of Negro History* 27 (October 1942): 380–87; David Donald, "The Proslavery Argument Reconsidered," *Journal of Southern History* 37 (February 1971): 3–18. Donald suggests that proslavery ideologists felt alienated by the modern world and retreated into historical precedent. He notes that, more than most antebellum southerners, De Bow urged southerners to look toward the future to create "the paradigm of the perfect society" (17).

13. Thomas R. Dew, "Professor Dew's Essays on Slavery: Pts. 1 and 2," *DR* 10 (June 1851): 658; Carol Bleser, ed., *Secret and Sacred: The Diary of James H. Hammond, a Southern Slaveholder* (New York: Oxford University Press, 1988), vii–xvi; Drew G. Faust, *James Henry Hammond and the Old South: A Design for Mastery* (Baton Rouge: Louisiana State University Press, 1982), 2–3, 258, 278–81, 380–81; James H. Hammond, "Negro Slavery at the South, Pts. 1–3," *DR* 17 (October 1849): 289–97, 17 (December 1849): 490–501, and 18 (February 1850): 122–33; Chancellor Harper, "Memoir on Slavery: Pts. 1 and 2," *DR* 8 (March 1850): 232–43, and 8 (April 1850): 339–47; Faust, *The Ideology of*

Slavery, 78–79; Carl L. Becker, *The Declaration of Independence: A Study in the History of Political Ideas* (New York: Knopf, 1922), 247–49.

14. Samuel A. Cartwright, "How to Save the Republic, and the Position of the South in the Union," *DR* 10 (August 1851): 184–97; Paul Finkelman, *Defending Slavery: Proslavery Thought in the Old South: A Brief History with Documents* (Boston: Bedford/St. Martin's, 2003), 157; Faust, *The Ideology of Slavery,* 206–7; "Nott on the Physical History of Man," *DR* 7 (October 1849): 377; "Physical Character of the Negro," *DR* 9 (August 1850): 231–44; Reginald Horsman, *Josiah Nott of Mobile: Southerner, Physician, and Racial Theorist* (Baton Rouge: Louisiana State University Press, 1987); Josiah C. Nott, "Nature and Destiny of the Negro," *DR* 10 (March 1851): 332.

15. George Fitzhugh, "Southern Thought, Pts. 1 and 2," *DR* 23 (October 1857): 338–50, and 23 (November 1857): 449–62; "Cannibals All! or, Slaves without Masters," *DR* 22 (May 1857): 543–49; C. G. Grammer, "Failure of Free Society," *DR* 19 (July 1855): 29–38; Foner, *Free Soil, Free Labor, Free Men,* 66–67; George Fitzhugh, "Family History and the Philosophy of Names," *DR* 29 (September 1860): 257–69; *The Liberator* (Boston), November 23, 1855.

16. William S. White, "The Night Funeral of a Slave," *DR* 20 (February 1856): 218–21.

17. "General Literature," *DR* 3 (April 1847): 353–54; Nathanial Beverly Tucker, "The Path of Disunion—to the North and the South," *DR* 31 (July 1861): 59; "The State of Alabama," *DR* 12 (January 1852): 66; J. Mills Thornton, *Politics and Power in a Slave Society: Alabama, 1800–1860* (Baton Rouge: Louisiana State University Press, 1978), 291–92, 308–11. Pickett's fear of modernity concurs with Thornton's conclusions about how antebellum Alabamians reacted toward urbanization and industrialization.

18. William A. Christian, *Richmond: Her Past and Present* (Spartanburg, SC: Reprint Co., 1912), 140–97; Towers, *The Urban South and the Coming of the Civil War,* 20–21; Central Southern Rights Association of Virginia Records, 1850–1860, Virginia Historical Society, Richmond, VA.

19. Johnson, *The Men and the Vision of the Southern Commercial Conventions,* 95–99; Walther, *The Fire-Eaters,* 216.

20. Van Deusen, *The Ante-Bellum Southern Commercial Conventions,* 58; Wender, *Southern Commercial Conventions,* 17–21; Johnson, *The Men and the Vision of the Southern Commercial Conventions,* 95–99, 146–62; "The Rights, Duties, and Remedies of the South," *DR* 23 (September 1857): 233, 235.

21. "The Times Are Out of Joint," *DR* 23 (December 1857): 652–58; Kenneth M. Stampp, *America in 1857: A Nation on the Brink* (Oxford: Oxford University Press, 1992), 187–89; *Sacramento Daily Union,* December 18, 1857.

22. Edmund Ruffin, "Consequences of Abolition Agitation, Pts. 1–5," *DR* 22 (June 1857): 583–93, 23 (September 1857), 266–72, 23 (October 1857), 385–90, 23 (November 1857), 546–52, and 23 (December 1857), 596–607; George Fitzhugh, "Uniform Postage, Railroads, Telegraphs, Fashions, Etc.," *DR* 26 (June 1859): 657–64.

23. John Tyler Jr., "The Relative Political Status of the North and the South," *DR* 22

(February 1857): 113–32; "Address of the Southern League," *DR* 24 (March 1859): 346–47; Alfred A. Smith, "A Southern Confederacy: Its Prospects, Resources, and Destiny," *DR* 24 (May 1859): 571–78; J. A. Turner, "What Are We to Do?" *DR* 29 (July 1860): 70–77.

24. Edmund Ruffin, "Consequences of Abolition Agitation," *DR* 22 (June 1857): 583–93; "Editorial Notes, Etc.," *DR* 23 (August 1857): 222; R. C. Weightman, "The Union and the Rights of the States," *DR* 23 (October 1857): 391; "The Model Negro Empire of Hayti," *DR* 24 (March 1858): 203–11.

25. "A Vision of a Studious Man," *DR* 23 (November 1857): 522; "Editorial, Book Notices, Etc.," *DR* 23 (October 1857): 446.

26. Charlene M. Boyer-Lewis, *Ladies and Gentlemen on Display: Planter Society at the Virginia Springs, 1790–1860* (Charlottesville: University Press of Virginia, 2001), 3–4, 7; "Editorial Notes, Etc.," *DR* 3 (February 1867): 214; "Editorial Miscellany," *DR* 25 (July 1858): 125; "Southern Travel and Travelers," *DR* 21 (September 1856): 323–29.

27. "Editorial Miscellany," *DR* 25 (September 1858): 371; Skipper, *J. D. B. De Bow*, 108–9, and "J. D. B. De Bow, the Man," 414–15.

28. "Southern Slavery and Its Assailants," *DR* 15 (November 1853): 486–96; "Texas," *DR* 23 (August 1857): 113–14, 117; Frederick Law Olmsted, *A Journey in the Seaboard Slave States: With Remarks on Their Economy* (New York: Six & Edwards, 1856), and *The Cotton Kingdom: A Traveler's Observations on Cotton and Slavery in the American Slave States* (New York: Mason Bros., 1862), 17, 25; David Brown, *Southern Outcast: Hinton Rowan Helper and the Impending Crisis of the South* (Baton Rouge: Louisiana State University Press, 2006), 91–98; Hinton R. Helper, *The Impending Crisis of the South: How to Meet It* (New York: Burdick Bros., 1857), 30; "Editorial Miscellany," *DR* 26 (May 1859): 607; "Editorial, Etc.," *DR* 22 (April 1857): 446.

29. "Southern Manufactures," *DR* 24 (June 1850): 555–59; James Martin, "The Field for Southern Manufactures," *DR* 24 (May 1858): 382–86; George Stueckrath, "Memphis, Tennessee," *DR* 27 (August 1859): 235–39.

30. C. K. Marshall, "We Must Diversify Our Industry," *DR* 24 (March 1858): 261; "Who Profits by Our Commerce?" *DR* 24 (May 1858): 449–50; "Sensible Hints to the South," *DR* 24 (June 1858): 573.

31. "The Yellow Pine Forest of the South," *DR* 23 (November 1857): 536–37; "Agricultural Survey of Mississippi," *DR* 23 (December 1857): 644–50; "Commercial Movements of Mobile," *DR* 23 (November 1857): 485–88.

32. Joseph C. G. Kennedy, *Agriculture of the United States in 1860; Complied from the Original Returns of the Eighth Census* (Washington, DC: US Government Printing Office, 1864), lxiii, lxvi, xciv.

33. Harold D. Woodman, *King Cotton and His Retainers: Financing and Marketing the Cotton Crop of the South, 1800–1925* (Lexington: University of Kentucky Press, 1968), 98–100, 136–42; Bateman and Weiss, *A Deplorable Scarcity*, 158–60; Joseph Segar, "Letters from Lieutenant M. F. Maury and Joseph Segar, on a Line of Steamers from

the Chesapeake to Europe," *DR* 22 (May 1857): 516–17; Edwin Heriott, "Wants of the South," *DR* 29 (August 1860): 215.

34. "Editorial Miscellanies, Book Notices, Etc.," *DR* 22 (May 1857): 555–56; James Montgomery, "Why Southern Factories Fail," *DR* 26 (January 1859): 95–96; William Gregg, "Southern Patronage to Southern Imports and Domestic Industry," *DR* 29 (July 1860): 79; "Development of Southern Industry," *DR* 19 (July 1855): 1–22.

35. "Mississippi Seeking a Gulf Outlet," *DR* 25 (August 1858): 230; A. Dudley Mann, "Southern Direct Trade with Europe," *DR* 24 (May 1858): 352; William M. Burwell, "Overland and Ocean Routes between the Southwest and Europe," *DR* 26 (January 1859): 1–23; Henry A. Wise, "Southern Trade with South America and the West Indies," *DR* 26 (January 1859): 73–76.

36. "Editorial Miscellany," *DR* 27 (July 1859): 112–15.

37. Johnson, *The Men and the Vision of the Southern Commercial Conventions*, 32, 103, 164; Harvey Wish, "The Revival of the African Slave Trade in the United States, 1856–1860," *Mississippi Valley Historical Review* 27 (March 1941): 569–88; Barton J. Bernstein, "Southern Politics and Attempts to Reopen the African Slave Trade," *Journal of Negro History* 51 (January 1966): 16–35; "African Labor Supply Association," *DR* 27 (August 1859): 233; "Excessive Slave Population—the Remedy," *DR* 12 (February 1852): 182–85; Edmund Ruffin, "African Colonization Unveiled," *DR* 29 (November 1860): 638–49; J. J. Pettigrew, "Protest against a Renewal of the Slave Trade," *DR* 25 (August 1858): 166–85; Thomas Walton, "Further Views of the Advocates of the Slave Trade," *DR* 26 (January 1859): 51.

38. J. A. Turner, "What Are We to Do?" *DR* 29 (July 1860): 70–71; Lawrence Huff, "Joseph Addison Turner: Southern Editor during the Civil War," *Journal of Southern History* 29 (November 1963): 469–85. Joseph A. Turner hired Joel Chandler Harris as a typesetter for *The Countryman* in 1862. Harris became one of the postwar South's most popular dialect writers, a group who romanticized black folk tales and stories about plantation life in the Old South. See also J. W. Morgan, "The Conservative Men, and the Union Meetings of the North," *DR* 28 (November 1860): 519; and George Fitzhugh, "Disunion within the Union," *DR* 28 (January 1860): 1–7.

39. "Editorial Miscellany," *DR* 29 (December 1860): 797; "Editorial Miscellany," *DR* 29 (October 1860): 534.

40. "Presidential Candidates and Aspirants," *DR* 29 (July 1860): 92–103.

41. *Charleston Mercury*, November 8, 1860; *Charleston Courier*, November 7, 1860; Mary Boykin Chesnut, *A Diary from Dixie* (New York: D. Appleton, 1905), 1–2; "Memories of the War from Mr. De Bow's Unpublished Papers," *DR* 4 (November 1867): 435–36; "Journal of the War—Entered Up Daily in the Confederacy," *DR* 1 (June 1866): 648.

42. Howard C. Perkins, *Northern Editorials on Secession*, vol. 1 (Gloucester, MA: Peter Smith, 1964), 3–27; Dwight L. Dumond, *Southern Editorials on Secession* (Gloucester, MA: Peter Smith, 1964).

43. George C. Rable, *The Confederate Republic: A Revolution against Politics* (Chapel

Hill: University of North Carolina Press, 1994), 21–22; "Secession Meeting in Charleston," *The Liberator,* November 23, 1860.

44. James L. Huston, "Property Rights in Slavery and the Coming of the Civil War," *Journal of Southern History* 65 (May 1999): 249–86; Freehling, *The Road to Disunion,* 389–94; May Spencer Ringold, "Robert Newman Gourdin and the '1860 Association,'" *Georgia Historical Quarterly* 55 (Winter 1971): 501–9; Jon L. Wakelyn, ed., *Southern Pamphlets on Secession, November 1860–April 1861* (Chapel Hill: University of North Carolina Press, 1996), xxi–xxix.

45. John Hope Franklin, *The Militant South, 1800–1861* (Cambridge, MA: Harvard University Press, 1956), 258; J. D. B. De Bow, *The Interest in Slavery of the Southern Non-Slaveholder: The Right of Peaceful Secession* (Charleston, SC: Evans & Goodwell, 1860), 3–12; Charles Edward Cauthon, *South Carolina Goes to War, 1860–1865* (Columbia: University of South Carolina Press, 2005), 41–42; Wakelyn, *Southern Pamphlets on Secession,* 78; Stephanie McCurry, *Masters of Small Worlds: Yeoman Households, Gender Relations, and the Political Culture of the Antebellum South Carolina Low Country* (New York: Oxford University Press, 1995), 287–88; Brown, *Southern Outcast,* 174–75; "Editorial Miscellany," *DR* 29 (December 1860): 797; Ford, *Origins of Southern Radicalism,* 51, 372.

46. Skipper, "J. D. B. De Bow, the Man," 416; Martha E. De Bow to J. D. B. De Bow, December 30, 1860, box 5, De Bow Papers; "Editorial Notes and Miscellany," *DR* 29 (November 1860): 671–72; Chester G. Hearn, *The Capture of New Orleans, 1862* (Baton Rouge: Louisiana State University Press, 1995), 7–18.

47. "Editorial Miscellany," *DR* 29 (December 1860): 797; "Editorial Miscellany," *DR* 30 (January 1861): 127.

5. Reading and Investing in De Bow's Ideas

1. O'Brien, *Conjectures of Order,* 1:529–29; Eaton, *The Mind of the Old South,* 264–65; Taylor, *Cavalier and Yankee,* 268–69.

2. J. D. B. De Bow, *The Seventh Census of the United States, 1850* (Washington, DC: Robert Armstrong, Public Printer, 1853), lxiv–lxv; O'Brien, *Conjectures of Order,* 1:512–17; Grant, *North over South,* 9–11; Richard Bushman, *The Refinement of America: Persons, Houses, Cities* (New York: Vintage, 1993); Wells, *The Origins of the Southern Middle-Class,* 12–16, 42–56. Grant and Wells stress the interconnectedness of the middle-class experience in the antebellum North and South as being essential to southern cultural development. More than Grant, however, Wells emphasizes the importance of regional periodicals in fostering southern interest in northern culture. Bushman argues that the "mental culture" of the northern middle class had increased the cultural importance of books and periodicals as a way of obtaining middle-class gentility. See also Taylor, *Cavalier and Yankee,* 18–19.

3. O'Brien, *Conjectures of Order,* 1:531, 542–43; "To Our Southern and Western Friends," *DR* 6 (August 1848): 162; Paul F. Paskoff and Daniel J. Wilson, eds., *The Cause*

of the South: Selections from De Bow's Review, *1846–1867* (Baton Rouge: Louisiana State University Press, 1982), 8. All composite readership statistics have been calculated from individual entries in the Composite Census Records, 1850–1860.

4. Composite Census Records, 1850–1860; James Oakes, *The Ruling Race: A History of Slaveowners* (New York: Norton, 1998).

5. Composite Census Records, 1850–1860; David Hackett Fischer and James C. Kelly, *Bound Away: Virginia and the Westward Movement* (Charlottesville: University Press of Virginia, 2000), 135–40, 200–301. Although Fischer and Kelly disagree with Frederick Jackson Turner's frontier thesis and the formation of common American values, they acknowledge cultural similarities between Virginia and places settled predominately by Virginians in the Old Northwest and the Old Southwest.

6. Phillips, *Transportation in the Eastern Cotton Belt,* 1–20; Ford, *Origins of Southern Radicalism,* 44; Charles S. Aiken, *The Cotton Plantation South: Since the Civil War* (Baltimore: Johns Hopkins University Press, 1998), 57–58; Woodman, *King Cotton and His Retainers,* 16–20.

7. Composite Census Records, 1850–1860; Randall Martin Miller, *The Cotton Mill Movement in Antebellum Alabama* (New York: Arno, 1978), 5; Roger L. Ransom and Richard Sutch, *One Kind of Freedom: The Economic Consequences of Emancipation* (New York: Cambridge University Press, 1977), 116. Although Ransom and Sutch focus on the economic development of the postbellum South, they acknowledge the importance of urban cotton centers such as Selma to the antebellum South's economy. See *Acts of Alabama, 1830–1860* (Catawba: Allen & Brickell); Thomas M. Owen and Marie Bankhead Owen, *History of Alabama and Directory of Alabama Biography,* 4 vols. (Chicago: S. J. Clark, 1921), 2:672; Thornton, *Politics and Power in a Slave Society,* 276–77; Composite Census Records, 1850–1860; and Brian Schoen, "The Lower South's Antebellum Pursuit of Sectional Development through Global Interdependence," in Delfino and Gillespie, eds., *Global Perspectives on Industrial Transformation in the American South,* 61. Schoen notes that cotton profits in Alabama and Mississippi forged a relationship between planters and merchants who pursued economic diversification and commercial development as way of maintaining profits.

8. Composite Census Records, 1850–1860; Robert T. McKenzie, *One South or Many? Plantation Belt and Upcountry in Civil War–Era Tennessee* (New York: Cambridge University Press, 1994), 59; A. W. Bradford to J. D. B. De Bow, July 9, 1866, box 5, De Bow Papers.

9. Composite Census Records, 1850–1860.

10. Downey, *Planting a Capitalist South,* 17, 38; George Rogers Taylor, *The Transportation Revolution: 1815–1860,* vol. 4 of *The Economic History of the United States* (New York: Holt, Rinehart & Winston, 1964), 90–91; James M. Russell, *Atlanta, 1847–1890: City Building in the Old South and the New* (Baton Rouge: Louisiana State University Press, 1988), 10–11, 41; Ford, *Origins of Southern Radicalism,* 47; Peter Wallenstein, *From Slave South to New South: Public Policy in Nineteenth-Century Georgia* (Chapel Hill: University of North Carolina Press, 1987), 12–17.

11. Composite Census Records, 1850–1860; “Cities of the Mississippi and Ohio,” *DR* 1 (February 1846): 146; Lawrence H. Larsen, *The Rise of the Urban South* (Lexington: University Press of Kentucky, 1985), 4–5; David R. Goldfield, “Pursuing the American Dream: Cities in the Old South,” in Brownell and Goldfield, eds., *The City in Southern History,* 52–60; Lawrence H. Larsen, *The Urban South: A History* (Lexington: University Press of Kentucky, 1990), 23–48; Taylor, *Cavalier and Yankee,* 33.

12. Charles Dew, *Bond of Iron: Master and Slave at Buffalo Forge* (New York: Norton, 1994), 116–17; Ronald Lewis, *Coal, Iron, and Slaves: Industrial Slavery in Maryland and Virginia, 1715–1865* (Westport, CT: Greenwood, 1979); David R. Goldfield, *Urban Growth in the Age of Sectionalism, 1847–1861* (Baton Rouge: Louisiana State University Press, 1977), 193–94; Virginia, vol. 43, p. 204, R. G. Dun & Co. Credit Report Volumes, Historical Collections, Baker Library.

13. Tennessee, vol. 6, pp. 8, 172–73, R. G. Dun & Co. Credit Report Volumes, Historical Collections, Baker Library; *Acts of Tennessee, Index to Names, 1796–1850,* http://www.tennessee.gov/tsla/history/misc/actsintro.htm.

14. Composite Census Records, 1850–1860; Georgia, vol. 1B, p. 5, and Alabama, vol. 15, p. 115, R. G. Dun & Co. Credit Report Volumes, Historical Collections, Baker Library.

15. Wells, *The Origins of the Southern Middle Class,* 164–66; Composite Census Records, 1850–1860; “Population of Southern States in 1850,” *DR* 19 (September 1855): 328; Fletcher M. Green, *The Role of the Yankee in the Old South* (Athens: University of Georgia Press, 1972), 1–6; Alabama, vol. 2, p. 12, R. G. Dun & Co. Credit Report Volumes, Historical Collections, Baker Library; Ford, *Origins of Southern Radicalism,* 277. Lawrence N. Powell, *New Masters: Northern Planters during the Civil War and Reconstruction* (New Haven, CT: Yale University Press, 1980).

16. In many older monographs such as Owsley’s *Plain Folk of the Old South,* urban “plain folk” are rarely mentioned, and a southern mercantile class is nonexistent. In *Origins of the New South,* Woodward concludes that the emergence of urban, middle-class southerners became significant after the Civil War. See also Byrne, *Becoming Bourgeois,* 17–35; Ford, *Origins of Southern Radicalism,* 88–95; Thornton, *Politics and Power in a Slave Society,* 273, 310–14; and “The Merchant—His Character, Position, and Duties,” *DR* 3 (February 1847): 93.

17. *Cyclopedia of Eminent and Representative Men of the Carolinas of the Nineteenth Century* (Madison, WI: Brant & Fuller, 1892), 372–73; South Carolina, vol. 6, p. 183, R. G. Dun & Co. Credit Report Volumes, Historical Collections, Baker Library.

18. Thornton, *Politics and Power in a Slave Society,* 40–42; Albert Stein, “Mobile River and Bay,” *DR* 16 (March 1854): 225–30; “Gallery of Industry and Enterprise: Charles Le Baron of Mobile, Merchant,” *DR* 10 (June 1851): 694.

19. *Acts of Tennessee, Index to Names, 1796–1850;* Composite Census Records, 1850–1860; Virginia, vol. 53, pp. 603–4, R. G. Dun & Co. Credit Report Volumes, Historical Collections, Baker Library; Kenneth W. Noe, *Southwest Virginia’s Railroad:*

Modernization and the Sectional Crisis in the Civil War Era (Tuscaloosa: University of Alabama Press, 2003), 59, 125–26.

20. Downey, *Planting a Capitalist South,* 222–26; Wells, *The Origins of the Southern Middle Class,* 6–18.

21. Robert A. Sigafoos, *Cotton Row to Beale Street: A Business History of Memphis* (Memphis, TN: Memphis State University Press, 1979), 22–23; Shields McIlwaine, *Memphis: Down in Dixie* (New York: E. P. Dutton, 1948), 85; *Acts of Tennessee, Index to Names, 1796–1850.*

22. "Gallery of Industry and Enterprise, R. C. Brinkley Esq. of Memphis, Tennessee," *DR* 11 (September 1851): 339.

23. Owen and Owen, *History of Alabama,* 1:590–92; Daniel S. Dupre, *Transforming the Cotton Frontier: Madison County, Alabama, 1800–1840* (Baton Rouge: Louisiana State University Press, 1997), 49, 73–82. The evolving relationship between antebellum southerners and modern economic forces has been well documented. The public's negative reaction to the Royal Party's attempt to link Huntsville to larger, outside markets was similar to those in South Carolina's upcountry and in northern Georgia. See Ford, *Origins of Southern Radicalism;* and Steven Hahn, *The Roots of Southern Populism: Yeoman Farmers and the Transformation of the Georgia Upcountry, 1850–1880* (New York: Oxford University Press, 1983).

24. Tennessee, vol. 29, p. 52, R. G. Dun & Co. Credit Report Volumes, Historical Collections, Baker Library; Jesse C. Burt Jr., "The Nashville and Chattanooga Railroad, 1854–1872: The Era of Transition," *East Tennessee Historical Society Publications* 23 (1951): 58–76. The prewar prominence and postwar efforts of Sam Tate, Milton Brown, and Vernon K. Stevenson belie Woodward's contention that a new sort of business leader had emerged in the New South. Tate helped create the New South's most industrialized city, and Stevenson secretly sold his shares in the Nashville and Chattanooga Railroad to the Louisville and Nashville Railroad Co., creating a link between Birmingham's foundries and northern factories. See Woodward, *Origins of the New South,* 126–27.

25. Horace M. Bond, "Social and Economic Forces in Alabama Reconstruction," *Journal of Negro History* 23 (July 1938): 320–22; James F. Doster, "The Shelby Iron Works Collection in the University of Alabama Library," *Bulletin of the Business Historical Society* 26 (December 1952): 215; Robert C. Black III, *The Railroads of the Confederacy* (Chapel Hill: University of North Carolina Press, 1952), 145, 157–58; Marshall Bosher, *Chesterfield County, Virginia: A Collection of Notes Peculiar to Its Early History* (Chesterfield, VA: Chesterfield Historical Society, 1989), 192, 218.

26. "Montgomery, Alabama," *DR* 4 (November 1847): 402–3; Composite Census Records, 1850–1860; Thornton, *Politics and Power in a Slave Society,* 8–12; "Montgomery, Alabama," *DR* 26 (January 1850): 117.

27. Owen and Owen, *History of Alabama,* 4:1373; Thornton, *Politics and Power in a Slave Society,* 271–77; Alabama, vol. 20, p. 259, R. G. Dun & Co. Credit Report

Volumes, Historical Collections, Baker Library; Mildred Beale, "Charles Teed Pollard, Industrialist," *Alabama Historical Quarterly* 2 (Spring 1940): 72–85, and 2 (Summer 1940): 189–202.

28. William Garrett, *Reminiscences of Public Men in Alabama* (Spartanburg, SC: Reprint Co., 1872), 554, 723–25; Owen and Owen, *History of Alabama,* 4:1653; William W. Rogers, *Confederate Home Front: Montgomery during the Civil War* (Tuscaloosa: University of Alabama Press, 1999), 3–5, 15; Frederick Law Olmsted, *Journey in the Seaboard Slave States: With Remarks on Their Economy* (New York: Mason Bros., 1861), 549.

29. Composite Census Records, 1850–1860; Aiken, *The Cotton Plantation South,* 10–11; Oakes, *The Ruling Race,* 65; Wright, *The Political Economy of the Cotton South,* 32; "The Future of the South," *DR* 10 (February 1851): 132.

30. Charles Joyner, *Down by the Riverside: A South Carolina Slave Community* (Urbana: University of Illinois Press, 1984), 23–24; Glenn R. Conrad, *Dictionary of Louisiana Biography,* vol. 1 (Baton Rouge: Louisiana Historical Association, 1988), 146; *Washington Post,* August 31, 1896.

31. William J. Cooper Jr., *The South and the Power of Slavery, 1828–1856* (Baton Rouge: Louisiana State University Press, 1978); Michael F. Holt, *The Rise and Fall of the American Whig Party* (New York: Oxford University Press, 1999); Daniel Walker Howe, *The Political Culture of the American Whigs* (Chicago: University of Chicago Press, 1979); Charles Sellers, "Who Were the Southern Whigs?" *American Historical Review* 59 (1954): 335–46.

32. Composite Census Records, 1850–1860.

33. "To Our Subscribers," *DR* 18 (April 1855): 558; "Notes," *DR* 18 (May 1855): 590; Aaron V. Brown to J. D. B. De Bow, November 9, 1855, Martha Casey De Bow Papers, Tennessee State Archives, Nashville, TN; "Events of the Month, Personal Notices, Book Notices, Etc.," *DR* 18 (March 1855): 316–19; "Address to Subscribers and Others," *DR* 17 (December 1854): 644.

34. "Editorial, Book Notices, Etc.," *DR* 23 (October 1857): 446; "What Is Said of the Review," *DR* 22 (March 1857): 336; "Editorial, Book Notices, Etc.," *DR* 23 (October 1857): 446.

6. War Tests De Bow's Theories and Patience

1. *Charleston Mercury,* December 21, 1860; Ralph A. Wooster, *The Secession Conventions of the South* (Princeton, NJ: Princeton University Press, 1962), 20–25; "Editorial Miscellany," *DR* 30 (January 1861): 124.

2. David Williams, *Bitterly Divided: The South's Inner Civil War* (New York: New Press, 2008), 10–13; Robert R. Russel, *Economic Aspects of Southern Sectionalism, 1840–1861* (Urbana: University of Illinois Press, 1924), 249; Emory Thomas, *The Confederacy as a Revolutionary Experience* (Englewood Cliffs, NJ: Prentice-Hall, 1971), 25–29; Robert M. T. Hunter, "Department of Miscellany," *DR* 30 (January 1861): 114–16;

Henry A. Wise, "Overt Acts of Northern Aggression," *DR* 30 (January 1861): 116–18; Clement Eaton, "Henry A. Wise and the Virginia Fire Eaters of 1856," *Mississippi Valley Historical Review* 21 (March 1935): 495–512; William H. Chase, "The Secession of the Cotton States: Its Status, Its Advantages, and Its Power," *DR* 30 (January 1861): 93–101; *New York Times,* January 15, 1861; *Journal of the Proceedings of the Senate of the General Assembly of the State of Florida* (Tallahassee: Hart & Barefoot, 1859), 230.

3. William W. Freehling, *The South vs. the South: How Anti-Confederate Southerners Shaped the Course of the Civil War* (Oxford: Oxford University Press, 2001), 33–43; Edmund Ruffin, "Fidelity of Slaves to Their Masters," *DR* 30 (January 1861): 118–20; John Townsend, "The Non-slaveholders of the South," *DR* 30 (January 1861): 123–24; "Editorial Miscellany," *DR* 30 (January 1861): 124; Charles B. Dew, *Apostles of Disunion: Southern Secession Commissioners and the Causes of the Civil War* (Charlottesville: University Press of Virginia, 2001), 11–13, 74–83.

4. Potter, *The Impending Crisis,* 448–51; "Editorial Miscellany," *DR* 30 (January 1861): 127–28.

5. Wooster, *The Secession Conventions of the South,* 26–30, 101–4; Donald E. Reynolds, *Editors Make War: Southern Newspapers in the Secession Crisis* (Nashville, TN: Vanderbilt University Press, 1970), 86; Nancy McKenzie Dupont, "Mississippi's Fire-Eating Editor: Ethelbert Barksdale and the Election of 1860," in *The Civil War and the Press,* ed. David B. Sachsman, S. Kittrell Rushing, and Debra Reddin van Tuyll (New Brunswick, NJ: Transaction, 2000), 137–44.

6. Wooster, *The Secession Conventions of the South,* 49–66; Thomas B. Alexander and Peggy J. Duckworth, "Alabama Black Belt Whigs during Secession: A New Viewpoint," *Alabama Review* 17 (July 1964): 181–97; Arthur Charles Cole, *The Whig Party in the South* (Washington, DC: Lord Baltimore, 1913), 72–114.

7. Garrett, *Reminiscences of Public Men in Alabama,* 723–25; *Montgomery (AL) Mail,* March 12, 1855; Walther, *William Lowndes Yancey,* 274–86.

8. *Annual Message of Thomas O. Moore, Governor of the State of Louisiana to the General Assembly* (Baton Rouge: J. M. Taylor, State Printer, January 1861); William T. Sherman, *Memoirs of General William T. Sherman,* ed. William S. McFeely (New York: Da Capo, 1984), 163; Martha De Bow to J. D. B. De Bow, January 2, 1861, box 3, folder 1861, De Bow Papers.

9. Wooster, *The Secession Conventions of the South,* 26–48, 101–20; *Charleston Mercury,* December 15–17, 1860; "Editorial Notes and Miscellany," *DR* 30 (February 1861): 251, 254; Thomas L. Connelly, *Civil War Tennessee: Battles and Leaders* (Knoxville: University of Tennessee Press, 2004), 3–4; Robert T. McKenzie, "Contesting Secession: Parson Brownlow and the Rhetoric of Proslavery Unionism," *Civil War History* 48 (2002): 294–312; Bryan P. McGovern, *John Mitchel: Irish Nationalist, Southern Secessionist* (Knoxville: University of Tennessee Press, 2009), 135, 152–53; Daniel W. Crofts, *Reluctant Confederates: Upper South Unionists in the Secession Crisis* (Chapel Hill: University of North Carolina Press, 1989), 21–30; J. D. B. De Bow to Charles Gayarré,

June 8, 1861, Charles E. A. Gayarré Papers, Grace King Collection, Louisiana State University, Baton Rouge.

10. Thomas, *The Confederacy as a Revolutionary Experience,* 38–42; *New Orleans Daily Picayune,* February 5, 1861; *Alexandria (VA) Gazette,* February 11, 1861; "Editorial Miscellany," *DR* 30 (March 1861): 378–81; Jefferson Davis, *The Rise and Fall of the Confederate Government* (New York: D. Appleton, 1881), 241–46; William C. Davis, *Look Away! A History of the Confederate States of America* (New York: Free Press, 2002), 59–64; "Editorial," *DR* 31 (July 1861): 102.

11. Emma M. Maffitt and John N. Maffitt, *The Life and Services of John Newland Maffitt* (New York: Neale, 1906), 115–19, 219; "Letter from Charleston," *Baltimore Sun,* April 11, 1861; John N. Maffitt, "Harbor of Charleston, S.C.," *DR* 26 (June 1859): 698–701; Orville V. Burton, ed., *The Essential Lincoln: Speeches and Correspondence* (New York: Hill & Wang, 2009), 101–9; "Journal of the War—Entered Up Daily in the Confederacy," *DR* 1 (June 1866): 647; "Editorial," *DR* 32 (March/April 1862): 334–40; "Memories of the War," *DR* 3 (January 1867): 3.

12. "Editorial Notes and Miscellany," *DR* 30 (January 1861): 124–28; Charles G. Leland, "The Southern Review," *Continental Monthly* 2 (October 1862): 467–69; Gary R. Varner, *Charles G. Leland: The Man and the Myth, Journalist, Adventurer, and Folklorist* (Morrisville, NC: Lulu, 2008), 7–8; Charles G. Leland, *Hans Breitmann's Party with Other Ballads* (Philadelphia: T. B. Peterson & Bros., 1869), 49.

13. William Gregg, "Southern Patronage to Southern Imports and Domestic Industry," *DR* 29 (July 1860): 77–83; Wooster, *The Secession Conventions of the South,* 11–25; *Charleston Mercury,* October 11, 1860; *Edgefield (SC) Advertiser,* November 14, 1860; "What Shall the South Carolina Legislature Do?" *Charleston Mercury,* November 3, 1860; "Commerce of the United States," *DR* 30 (March 1861): 364–65; "Editorial Notes and Miscellany," *DR* 30 (February 1861): 252; "Editorial," *DR* 32 (January/February 1862): 163; Chad Morgan, *Planters' Progress: Modernizing Confederate Georgia* (Gainesville: University Press of Florida, 2005), 5–6; "Southern Patronage to Southern Imports and Domestic Industry," *DR* 30 (February 1861): 216–23; Russel, *Economic Aspects of Southern Sectionalism,* 225; Phillips, *Transportation in the Eastern Cotton Belt,* 19–20; H. David Stone Jr., *Vital Rails: The Charleston and Savannah Railroad and the Civil War in Coastal South Carolina* (Columbia: University of South Carolina Press, 2008); William M. Burwell, "The Commercial Future of the South," *DR* 30 (February 1861): 129–56; Frank Owsley, *King Cotton Diplomacy: Foreign Relations of the Confederate States of America* (Chicago: University of Chicago Press, 1931), 15–20; David G. Surdam, "King Cotton: Monarch or Pretender? The State of the Market for Raw Cotton on the Eve of the American Civil War," *Economic History Review* 51 (February 1998): 113–32; "Department of Commerce," *DR* 30 (April 1861): 493.

14. Stanley L. Engerman, "Myths and Realities," in Delfino and Gillespie, eds., *Global Perspectives on Industrial Transformation in the American South,* 18–19; Richard E. Beringer, Herman Hattaway, Archer Jones, and William N. Stills Jr., *Why the South*

Lost the Civil War (Athens: University of Georgia Press, 1986), 215–17; Russel, *Economic Aspects of Southern Sectionalism*, 227; "Editorial," *DR* 32 (January/February 1862): 169; McPherson, *Battle Cry of Freedom*, 94–95; Downey, *Planting a Capitalist South*, 101–3; Black, *The Railroads of the Confederacy*, 1–11; James A. Ward, "A New Look at Antebellum Southern Railroad Development," *Journal of Southern History* 39 (August 1973): 409–20; Sarah Woolfolk Wiggins, *The Journals of Josiah Gorgas, 1857–1878* (Tuscaloosa: University of Alabama Press, 1995), 23.

15. "What We Are Gaining by the War," *DR* 32 (January/February 1862): 158–60; Thomas, *The Confederacy as a Revolutionary Experience*, 98–99; Harold S. Wilson, *Confederate Industry: Manufacturers and Quartermasters in the Civil War* (Jackson: University Press of Mississippi, 2002), xiv–xxii, 12–16.

16. George Fitzhugh, "Conduct of the War," *DR* 32 (January/February 1862): 139–40; "Editorial," *DR* 31 (November/December 1861): 465; "Editorial," *DR* 32 (March/April 1862): 334–40; "A Sinking Fund for the Confederate States Loan," *Charleston Mercury*, April 11, 1861; "The Confederate Currency," *Charleston Mercury*, September 24, 1861; "Forgery," *Charleston Mercury*, September 4, 1862.

17. Wilson, *Confederate Industry*, 17–21; Duff Green, "Commercial Importance and Future of the South," *DR* 32 (January/February 1862): 124–34; Mary A. DeCredico, *Patriotism for Profit: Georgia's Urban Entrepreneurs and the Confederate War Effort* (Chapel Hill: University of North Carolina Press, 1990); Morgan, *Planters' Progress*, 17–45; "Editorial," *DR* 32 (January/February 1862): 161–62; Wilfred Buck Yearns, *The Confederate Congress* (Athens: University of Georgia Press, 1960), 184–96; Richard Cecil Todd, *Confederate Finance* (Athens: University of Georgia Press, 1954), 62–64.

18. "Journal of the War," *DR* 2 (September 1866): 328–30; Emory M. Thomas, *The Confederate Nation, 1861–1865* (New York: Harper & Row, 1979), 137–38; Douglas B. Ball, *Financial Failure and Confederate Defeat* (Urbana: University of Illinois Press, 1991), 80–91; Charles W. Ramsdell, *Behind the Lines in the Southern Confederacy* (Baton Rouge: Louisiana State University Press, 1944), 8–12, 80–82; *Nashville Union and American*, August 10, 1861; *Memphis (TN) Daily Appeal*, September 3, 1861.

19. John B. Jones, *A Rebel War Clerk's Diary at the Confederate States Capital* (Philadelphia: J. B. Lippincott, 1866), 285; *Nashville (TN) Daily Union*, November 14, 1862; *New York Daily Tribune*, February 4, 1862.

20. Martha De Bow to J. D. B. De Bow, September 10, 1861, Robert Norton to J. D. B. De Bow, November 27, 1861, and Joseph Norton to J. D. B. De Bow, September 22, 1860, box 3, De Bow Papers.

21. "Editorial Notes and Miscellany," *DR* 30 (February 1861): 252–53; R. R. Welford, "The Loyalty of the Border States," *DR* 32 (January/February 1862): 87; "Editorial Miscellany," *DR* 30 (March 1861): 380.

22. "Journal of the War—Entered Up Daily in the Confederacy," *DR* 1 (June 1866): 649–50; "Conduct of the War," *DR* 32 (January/February 1862): 140–46.

23. "The Condition of the South," *New York Herald*, January 26, 1862; "Journal of

the War—Entered Up Daily in the Confederacy," *DR* 1 (June 1866): 649–50; James O. Lang, "Gloom Envelops New Orleans: April 24 to May 2, 1862," *Louisiana History* 1 (Autumn 1960): 281–91.

24. "Journal of the War—Entered Up Daily in the Confederacy," *DR* 1 (June 1866): 656.

25. "Journal of the War," *DR* 2 (August 1866): 191, 199; John Elwood Clark, *Railroads in the Civil War: The Impact of Management on Victory and Defeat* (Baton Rouge: Louisiana State University Press, 2001), 5; "What We Are Gaining by the War," *DR* 32 (March/April 1862): 327–28; Robert G. Angevine, *The Railroad and the State: War, Politics, and Technology in Nineteenth-Century America* (Stanford, CA: Stanford University Press, 2004), 141–46; "Journal of the War," *DR* 2 (November 1866): 553–55.

26. "Journal of the War—Entered Up Daily in the Confederacy," *DR* 2 (July 1866): 63–65; "Journal of the War," *DR* 2 (November 1866): 553–55.

27. "Journal of the War—Entered Up Daily in the Confederacy, No. 3," *DR* 2 (August 1866): 193–99.

28. "Journal of the War—Entered Up Daily in the Confederacy," *DR* 2 (July 1866): 60.

29. Jennifer L. Weber, *Copperheads: The Rise and Fall of Lincoln's Opponents in the North* (Oxford: Oxford University Press, 2006), 9–10; Beringer, Hattaway, Jones, and Stills, *Why the South Lost the Civil War,* 64–80; "Journal of the War—Entered Up Daily in the Confederacy, No. 3," *DR* 2 (August 1866): 197–98; "Journal of the War," *DR* 3 (March 1867): 320; "Journal of the War," *DR* 2 (October 1866): 439–45.

30. "Editorial," *DR* 33 (May/August 1862): 90–96.

31. "Editorial," *DR* 31 (August 1861): 208; Martha De Bow to J. D. B. De Bow, September 10, 12, December 28, 1861, and Robert Norton to J. D. B. De Bow, November 27, 1861, box 3, De Bow Papers; Stephen V. Ash, *When the Yankees Came: Conflict and Chaos in the Occupied South, 1861–1865* (Chapel Hill: University of North Carolina Press, 1999), 16–17; Skipper, *J. D. B. De Bow,* 136–37; "Editorial," *DR* 32 (January/February 1862): 168; "Editorial," *DR* 32 (March/April 1862): 338–39; "Journal of the War—Entered Up Daily in the Confederacy," *DR* 1 (June 1866): 646; Skipper, *J. D. B. De Bow,* 170–72.

32. Robert W. Dubay, *Mississippi Fire-Eater: His Life and Times, 1813–1867* (Oxford: University Press of Mississippi, 1975), 145–63; "Journal of the War," *DR* 2 (November 1866): 540–43; "A Dark Day for Jackson," *Jackson Weekly Mississippian,* November 6, 1862; Thomas, *The Confederacy as a Revolutionary Experience,* 88; "Journal of the War," *DR* 2 (December 1866): 649–50.

33. "Memories of the War," *DR* 5 (February 1868): 160–62; "Journal of the War," *DR* 3 (February 1867): 207–8; "Journal of the War," *DR* 3 (March 1867): 326–27.

34. McPherson, *Battle Cry of Freedom,* 334–36; Herman Hattaway and Archer Jones, *How the North Won the War: A Military History of the Civil War* (Urbana: University of Illinois Press, 1991), 82, 288; Owsley, *King Cotton Diplomacy,* 73; "Manufacturers: The

South's True Remedy," *DR* 3 (February 1867): 174; Walther, *William Lowndes Yancey,* 297–304; "Editorial," *DR* 31 (August 1861): 203–4; "The Mason-Slidell Federal Diplomacy Burlesqued," *DR* 32 (March/April 1862): 339–40; J. D. B. De Bow to Frank De Bow, November 25, 1861, box 3, De Bow Papers; "Journal of the War," *DR* 2 (November 1866): 546.

35. Gray, *History of Agriculture in the Southern United States,* 811–30; Roger L. Ransom, *The Confederate States of America* (New York: Norton, 2005), 188; Ramsdell, *Behind the Lines in the Southern Confederacy,* 34–35; "Editorial," *DR* 31 (August 1861): 203–4; William Hume, "The Grape—Its Culture and Manufacture at the South," *DR* 30 (March 1861): 335–51; Mary E. Massey, *Ersatz in the Confederacy* (Columbia: University of South Carolina Press, 1952), 55–77.

36. "Journal of the War," *DR* 3 (February 1867): 200–203; "Journal of the War," *DR* 3 (March 1867): 330.

37. "Editorial," *DR* 33 (May/August 1862): 84; "Journal of the War," *DR* 3 (January 1867): 104–5; "Times in the Confederacy," *DR* 2 (December 1866): 570–76; "Editorial," *DR* 33 (January/February 1862): 168.

38. "Journal of the War," *DR* 3 (March 1867): 321–29.

39. John Tyler Jr., "Our Present Confederate Status, Foreign and Domestic," *DR* 34 (July/August 1864): 1–32; Carl V. Harris, "Right Fork or Left Fork? The Section-Party Alignments of Southern Democrats in Congress, 1873–1897," *Journal of Southern History* 42 (November 1976): 471–506.

40. "The War—Independence—Watchman, What of the Night?" *DR* 34 (July/August 1864): 47–58.

41. *Nashville Daily Union,* March 29, 1863, January 28, 1864; *Daily National Republican* (Washington, DC), January 28, 1864; *Union County Star and Lewisburg (PA) Chronicle,* February 9, 1864; *Western Reserve Chronicle* (Warren, OH), February 10, 1864.

42. "Manufacturers: The South's True Remedy," *DR* 3 (February 1867): 174; "Southern Patronage to Southern Imports and Domestic Industry," *DR* 30 (February 1861): 218; R. Thomassy, "The New Sea Salt Manufacture of the Confederate States," *DR* 31 (October/November 1861): 442.

43. "Memories of the War," *DR* 4 (March 1867): 229; "Memories of the War," *DR* 3 (January 1867): 8–11; "Journal of the War," *DR* 3 (January 1867): 104–5; "Memories of the War," *DR* 4 (February 1867): 141–43.

44. "Journal of the War," *DR* 3 (January 1867): 95.

45. *Charleston (SC) Daily News,* August 21, 1865; J. D. B. De Bow, "History of the War," n.d., box 5, De Bow Papers; US War Department, *The War of the Rebellion: A Compilation of the Official Records of the Union and Confederate Armies,* ser. 1, vol. 7 (Washington, DC: US Government Printing Office, 1882), 430–31; Burt, "The Nashville and Chattanooga Railroad"; *Weekly Vincennes (IN) Western Sun,* December 13, 1862.

7. The Reformulation of De Bow's Old New South

1. See the J. D. B. De Bow file in *Case Files of Applications from Former Confederates for Presidential Pardons ("Amnesty Papers"), 1865–67,* Records of the Adjutant General's Office, 1780s–1917, Record Group 94, Publication M1003, National Archives, Washington, DC; *Washington Standard* (Olympia, WA), November 15, 1865.

2. Virginia, vol. 43, p. 313, R. G. Dun & Co. Credit Report Volumes, Historical Collections, Baker Library; William Thomson, *Thomson's Mercantile and Professional Directory* (Baltimore: William Thomson, 1851), 141; Wilson, *Confederate Industry,* 164; *Richmond (VA) Dispatch,* May 16, 1863. David Goldfield identifies Richmond's prewar urban leaders and groups them by level of activism. Among the city's most active business leaders were the following *Review* readers: Joseph R. Anderson, Hugh W. Fry, Richard B. Haxall, William H. Macfarland. See Goldfield, *Urban Growth in the Age of Sectionalism,* 191–96, 309. See also John C. Waugh, *Surviving the Confederacy: Rebellion, Ruin, and Recovery—Roger and Sara Pryor during the Civil War* (New York: Harcourt, 2002).

3. Virginia, vol. 43, pp. 112, 204, 259, R. G. Dun & Co. Credit Report Volumes, Historical Collections, Baker Library; Virginius Dabney, *Richmond: The Story of a City* (Richmond: University Press of Virginia, 1976), 201; *Richmond (VA) Whig,* April 15, 1865; *Richmond (VA) Times,* August 30, 1865; "Editorial and Miscellanies," *DR* 1 (February 1866): 217–19; *The Liberator,* September 8, 1865.

4. Kenneth R. Johnson, "N. H. R. Dawson: United States Commissioner of Education," *History of Education Quarterly* 11 (Summer 1971): 174–83; Wiley Sword, *Southern Invincibility: A History of the Confederate Heart* (New York: St. Martin's, 1999), 41–60; Alabama, vol. 20, p. 61, R. G. Dun & Co. Credit Report Volumes, Historical Collections, Baker Library; Owen and Owen, *History of Alabama,* 3:851, 4:1022; T. A. De Land and A. Davis Smith, *Northern Alabama: Historical and Biographical Illustrated* (Chicago: Donohue & Henneberry, 1888), 538.

5. Owen and Owen, *History of Alabama,* 3:724–25, 4:1749; Ezra J. Warner and W. Buck Yearns, *Biographical Register of the Confederate Congress* (Baton Rouge: Louisiana State University Press, 1975), 108; Garrett, *Reminiscences of Public Men in Alabama,* 542–45.

6. "Editorial Notes and Miscellany," *DR* 1 (February 1866): 217–20; "Profits of Cotton-Growing," *DR* 1 (February 1866): 197; "Editorial Notes and Miscellany," *DR* 1 (February 1866): 219.

7. James M. Edmunds, *Manufactures of the United States in 1860: Compiled from the Original Returns of the Eighth Census, Under the Direction of the Secretary of the Interior* (Washington, DC: US Government Printing Office, 1865), ix–xiii.

8. Ibid., xxiv–cxcv.

9. "Department of Commerce," *DR* 1 (January 1866): 94–100; "Estimate for Cultivating 500 Acres of Cotton Land," *DR* 2 (July 1866): 74–75; "The Cotton Interests of the South," *DR* 1 (January 1866): 303–5; "The Coming Cotton Crop," *DR* 1 (April 1866): 435–36; "Cost of Growing Cotton by Free Labor," *DR* 2 (September 1866): 300–301; "The

Cotton Supply for 1866," *DR* 2 (September 1866): 302; "Sources of the British Cotton Supply," *DR* 2 (July 1866): 81–82; Fred A. Conkling, "Production and Consumption of Cotton in the World," *DR* 1 (April 1866): 378–98.

10. Kennedy, *Agriculture of the United States in 1860,* xiii–cxxviii.

11. *Rochester (NY) Republican,* December 21, 1865; *New York Times,* September 1, 1865; *Canton (MS) Daily Mail,* December 28, 1865.

12. "Future of the United States," *DR* 1 (January 1866): 3–5; *Philadelphia Inquirer,* September 2, 1865; "The Future of the South," *DR* 1 (January 1866): 6–16.

13. "Editorial and Miscellanies," *DR* 1 (March 1866): 331–32; Potter, *The Impending Crisis,* 482–83.

14. "Times in the Confederacy," *DR* 2 (December 1866): 570–73; George Fitzhugh, "Shall the Spartan Virtues of the South Survive the War?" *DR* 2 (August 1866): 145–50.

15. "Memories of the War: From Mr. De Bow's Unpublished Papers," *DR* 4 (December 1867): 530–32; Edward A. Pollard, *The Lost Cause: A New Southern History of the War of the Confederates* (New York: E. B. Treat, 1866); Jubal A. Early, *A Memoir of the Last Year of the War for Independence in the Confederate States of America* (Lynchburg, VA: Charles W. Button, 1867), iv–ix; William J. Cooper Jr., *Jefferson Davis and the Civil War Era* (Baton Rouge: Louisiana State University Press, 2008), 3–15; David M. Potter, "Jefferson Davis and the Political Factors in Confederate Defeat," in *Why the North Won the Civil War,* ed. David Herbert Donald (Baton Rouge: Louisiana State University Press, 1960), 23–48; Paul D. Escott, *After Secession: Jefferson Davis and the Failure of Confederate Nationalism* (Baton Rouge: Louisiana State University Press, 1978), 19–53.

16. "Memories of the War," *DR* 3 (January 1867): 7–12.

17. "Shall Southerners Emigrate to Brazil?" *DR* 2 (July 1866): 30–38; "Editorial and Miscellanies," *DR* 1 (March 1866): 331; Cyrus B. Dawsey and James M. Dawsey, *The Confederados: Old South Immigrants in Brazil* (Tuscaloosa: University of Alabama Press, 1995), 74; "Editorial Notes and Miscellany," *DR* 1 (January 1866): 108.

18. "Editorial and Miscellanies," *DR* 1 (May 1866): 555–60; Benjamin B. Kendrick, *The Journal of the Joint Committee of Fifteen on Reconstruction* (New York, 1914); *Report of the Joint Committee on Reconstruction at the First Session of the Thirty-Ninth Congress* (Washington, DC: US Government Printing Office, 1866), 132–36; Eric L. McKitrick, *Andrew Johnson and Reconstruction* (Chicago: University of Chicago Press, 1960), 209–10. McKitrick notes that a small minority of white southerners supported black suffrage immediately after the war. Two *Review* readers, Alexander Stephens and Edward Frost, became prominent supporters of granting limited voting rights to ex-slaves.

19. "Editorial Notes and Miscellanies," *DR* 1 (January 1866): 217, 220.

20. "A Talk with Radical Leaders," *DR* 2 (October 1866): 334; "The Future of the Negro Population," *DR* 1 (January 1866): 58; Josiah C. Nott, "The Problem of the Black Races," *DR* 1 (March 1866): 266–83; Heather Cox Richardson, *The Death of Reconstruction: Race, Labor, and Politics in the Post–Civil War South* (Cambridge, MA: Harvard University Press, 2001), ix–xv.

21. Julie Saville, *The Work of Reconstruction: From Slave to Wage Laborer in South Carolina, 1860–1870* (New York: Cambridge University Press, 1994), 102–10; Steven Hahn, *A Nation under Our Feet: Black Political Struggles in the Rural South from Slavery to the Great Migration* (Cambridge, MA: Harvard University Press, 2003), 2–10; "Editorial and Miscellanies," *DR* 2 (February 1866): 217–24; "The Future of the South," *DR* 1 (January 1866): 6–12; Isaac I. Henderson, "The Future of the Negro Population," *DR* 1 (January 1866): 58–67; "The Freedmen in Georgia," *DR* 1 (May 1866): 550; "The Freedmen of North Carolina," *DR* 1 (March 1866): 328; "Department of the Freedmen," *DR* 2 (July 1866): 91–92; W. Archer Cocke, "The South and Direct Foreign Trade," *DR* 2 (September 1866): 285–88.

22. Eric Foner, *Reconstruction: America's Unfinished Revolution, 1863–1877* (New York: Perennial Classics, 1988), 214–15; "The Future of South Carolina—Her Inviting Resources," *DR* 2 (July 1866): 41; "Justice to the Negro," *DR* 2 (July 1866): 91–92; "The National Freedmen's Bureau," *DR* 1 (February 1866): 215–16; "Education of the Freedmen," *DR* 2 (July 1866): 94–95; William H. Trescott, "The Freedmen on the Sea Islands of South Carolina," *DR* 1 (April 1866): 440–41; "Atrocities of the Freedmen's Bureau," *DR* 2 (July 1866): 92–94; "Editorial Notes, Etc.," *DR* 2 (July 1866): 111.

23. Starobin, *Industrial Slavery in the Old South*, 116–28; "The Future of the South," *DR* 1 (January 1866): 6–12; "Profits of Cotton Growing," *DR* 1 (February 1866): 197–98; E. C. Cabell, "White Immigration to the South," *DR* 1 (January 1866): 91–94; Foner, *Reconstruction*, 68–70, 81–88; C. L. Fleishman, "Opening of New Fields to Immigration," *DR* 1 (January 1866): 87–91; "Immigration to the United States," *DR* 1 (March 1866): 329; "Coolies as a Substitute for Negroes," *DR* 2 (August 1866): 215–17; "Vast Resources of Tennessee," *DR* 1 (May 1866): 553–54.

24. Foner, *Reconstruction*, 214–15; "French Enterprise in Virginia," *DR* 1 (May 1866): 554; "The Cotton Crop of the South, and What It Costs to Produce Cotton, and How Great a Field Is Opened to Enterprise and Capital," *DR* 1 (May 1866): 542–47; F. A. Conkling, "Production and Consumption of Cotton in the World," *DR* 1 (April 1866): 378–95; Edward Atkinson, "The Cotton Resources of the South, Present and Future," *DR* 2 (August 1866): 132–44; "Editorials, Book Notices, Etc.," *DR* 2 (December 1866): 667.

25. "Sugar Beet and Beet Sugar, No. 1," *DR* 1 (February 1866): 194–96; "The Grain Products of the United States," *DR* 2 (July 1866): 79–80; "Crops in the Prairie Lands of Mississippi," *DR* 2 (November 1866): 532; "Agricultural Machinery," *DR* 1 (April 1866): 432–33; "Profits of Cotton Growing," *DR* 1 (February 1866): 197; "Department of Agriculture," *DR* 1 (May 1866): 542–46.

26. Percy Roberts, "The Southern Cotton Crops—Mississippi," *DR* 2 (August 1866): 210–12; "Manufacturing in Mississippi," *DR* 2 (August 1866): 218.

27. "Manufactures: The South's True Remedy," *DR* 3 (February 1867): 174; "The Future of South Carolina—Her Inviting Resources," *DR* 2 (July 1866): 41–49; "The Lumber Business of the South," *DR* 2 (August 1866): 201–2; Starobin, *Industrial Slavery in the Old South*, 24–25; Victor S. Clark, *History of Manufactures in the United States*, vol.

2, *1860–1893* (Washington, DC: Carnegie Institution of Washington, 1929), 126–27; Woodward, *Origins of the New South,* 116–17. Woodward considers the development of the southern lumber industry essential to attracting outside investors from the North and Europe during the 1880s and 1890s.

28. "Editorial Notes and Miscellany," *DR* 1 (January 1866): 106; W. A. Van Benthuysen, "Petroleum," *DR* 1 (February 1866): 173–78; "Petroleum as an Element of National Wealth," *DR* 2 (August 1866): 203.

29. Sean P. Adams, *Old Dominion, Industrial Commonwealth: Coal, Politics, and Economy in Antebellum America* (Baltimore: Johns Hopkins University Press, 2004), 1–6; "The Iron and Coal of Alabama," *DR* 1 (January 1866): 84; Albert Stein, "Alabama and Her Resources," *DR* 2 (October 1866): 362–72.

30. Evans, *The Conquest of Labor,* 200–237; Alabama, vol. 2, p. 5, R. G. Dun & Co. Credit Report Volumes, Historical Collections, Baker Library; Daniel Pratt to J. D. B. De Bow, May 14, 1866, box 4, De Bow Papers; Henry Martin Caldwell, *History of the Elyton Land Company and Birmingham, Alabama* (Birmingham: Caldwell-Garber, 1892), 3–8.

31. "The Future of South Carolina—Her Inviting Resources," *DR* 2 (July 1866): 38–49; J. B. Robinson, "The Vast Resources of Louisiana," *DR* 2 (September 1866): 274–85; "Virginia—Her Spirit and Development," *DR* 2 (July 1866): 53–56; Dan H. Doyle, *New Men, New Cities, New South: Atlanta, Nashville, Charleston, Mobile, 1860–1910* (Chapel Hill: University of North Carolina Press, 1990), 27–31; "Nashville and Its Projected Railroad Improvements," *DR* 2 (July 1866): 97–100.

32. For examples of postwar statistical reports, see "Commerce of Mobile," *DR* 1 (February 1866): 199–200; "Trade of Memphis," *DR* 1 (April 1866): 425–26; "The City of Nashville," *DR* 2 (October 1866): 427–28; "Sources of the British Cotton Supply," *DR* 2 (July 1866): 82; and "Commerce of Charleston, S.C.," *DR* 1 (February 1866): 199. Despite De Bow's positive forecast for complete economic recovery, the city of Charleston languished in ruin for decades. More than any southern city it remained a symbol of the destruction and loss of an older South. See Woodward, *Origins of the New South,* 107.

33. "Nashville and Its Projected Railroad Improvements," *DR* 2 (July 1866): 97–100; Henry M. McKiven Jr., *Iron and Steel: Class, Race, and Community in Birmingham, Alabama, 1875–1920* (Chapel Hill: University of North Carolina Press, 1995), 8–12; Bruce, *The Rise of the New South,* 213–14. Despite Birmingham's industrial success, Bruce noted that in the early twentieth century most pig iron still traveled to northern factories and that southerners only extracted and manufactured raw iron and did not create finished products. This had been De Bow's main concern when confronted by the lack of an antebellum industrial sector. Northerners would sell finished goods that had been built with southern raw materials and then ship them back to southern markets. Woodward confronts this unbalanced commercial relationship by noting that, like their antebellum counterparts, postwar southerners served mostly as agents or retainers for northern businessmen. See Woodward, *Origins of the New South,* 292.

34. "Tennessee Pacific Railroad for Knoxville to Memphis," *DR* 2 (September

1866): 318–19; *New York Times,* October 19, 1866; "Railroad History and Results," *DR* 2 (December 1866): 609–39; John F. Stover, *The Railroads of the South, 1865–1900: A Study of Finance and Control* (Chapel Hill: University of North Carolina Press, 1955), 27; "Editorial Notes, Etc.," *DR* 3 (January 1867): 109–12; Richard Prince, *Nashville, Chattanooga, and St. Louis Railway: History and Steam Locomotives* (Bloomington: Indiana University Press, 2001), 28.

35. "The Future of the South," *DR* 1 (January 1866): 14.

36. "Manufactures: The South's True Remedy," *DR* 3 (February 1867): 172–73.

37. "Editorial Notes, Etc.," *DR* 3 (February 1867): 213–17.

38. Skipper, *J. D. B. De Bow,* 223–24.

39. *Boston Daily Advertiser,* March 2, 1867; *North American and United States Gazette* (Philadelphia), March 1, 1867; Charles Gayarré, "James Dunwoody Brownson De Bow," *DR* 3 (June 1867): 497–506.

40. Susanna Delfino, "Southern Economic Backwardness: A Comparative View," in Delfino and Gillespie, eds., *Global Perspectives on Industrial Transformation in the American South,* 107–8.

41. Harold E. Davis, *Henry Grady's New South: Atlanta, a Brave and Beautiful City* (Tuscaloosa: University of Alabama Press, 1990), 15–18; Raymond B. Nixon, *Henry W. Grady, Spokesman of the New South* (New York: Knopf, 1943); "Commerce of Savannah," *DR* 3 (June 1847): 404; "Iron Rolling Mills at the South," *DR* 25 (October 1858): 474–75; C. Vann Woodward, *Tom Watson: Agrarian Rebel* (New York: Macmillan, 1938), 113–15.

42. Woodward, *Origins of the New South,* 134; Doyle, *New Men, New Cities, New South,* 169–71; George W. Williams and George Sherwood Dickerman, *History of Banking in South Carolina from 1712 to 1900* (Charleston, SC: Walker, Evans, & Cogswell, 1903), 95–103.

43. *Atlanta Constitution,* March 12, 1899; *Nashville (TN) American,* November 17, 1903, September 22, 1904.

44. *Minutes of the Third Semi-annual Convention of the Southern Industrial Association* (New Orleans: E. S. Upton, 1901), 8; *Publications of the Southern History Association,* vol. 5 (Washington, DC: Southern History Association, 1901), 87.

Bibliography

Manuscript Collections

ALABAMA STATE ARCHIVES, MONTGOMERY, AL

George Goldthwaite Papers.
Bolling Hall Papers.
Charles T. Pollard Papers.

BIRMINGHAM PUBLIC LIBRARY, BIRMINGHAM, AL

Elyton Land Company Business Records.

HISTORICAL COLLECTIONS, BAKER LIBRARY, HARVARD BUSINESS SCHOOL, CAMBRIDGE, MA

R. G. Dun & Co. Credit Report Volumes.

W. S. HOOLE SPECIAL COLLECTIONS LIBRARY, UNIVERSITY OF ALABAMA, TUSCALOOSA

Robert Jemison Papers.
Montgomery Tax Records.
Northeast and Southwest Railroad Company Records.
Daniel C. Smyly Papers.

GRACE KING COLLECTION, LOUISIANA STATE UNIVERSITY, BATON ROUGE

Charles E. A. Gayarré Papers.

SOUTHERN HISTORICAL COLLECTION, UNIVERSITY OF NORTH CAROLINA, CHAPEL HILL

Nathaniel Henry Rhodes Dawson Papers.
John W. Mitchell Papers.
Maunsel White Papers.

SPECIAL COLLECTIONS, JAMES D. HOSKINS LIBRARY, UNIVERSITY OF TENNESSEE, KNOXVILLE

The Land We Love.

SPECIAL COLLECTIONS, PERKINS LIBRARY, DUKE UNIVERSITY, DURHAM, NC

James Dunwoody Brownson De Bow Papers.

SPECIAL COLLECTIONS, WASHINGTON AND LEE UNIVERSITY, LEXINGTON, VA

Franklin Subscription Library Collection.

TENNESSEE STATE ARCHIVES, NASHVILLE, TN

Martha Casey De Bow Papers.

VIRGINIA STATE HISTORICAL SOCIETY, RICHMOND, VA

George Barksdale Scrapbook.
Cabell Family Papers.
Central Southern Rights Association of Virginia, Records, 1850–1860.
Crump Family Papers.
Bolling Walker Haxall, Account Book, 1851–1883.
Proceedings of the First Annual Meeting of the Stockholders of the Richmond and Danville Railroad Company, President's Report, Chief Engineers Report, Financial Statement, and By-Laws.

Newspapers and Periodicals

Alexandria (VA) Gazette.
American Cotton Planter.
Atlanta Constitution.
Baltimore Sun.
Boston Daily Advertiser.
Canton (MS) Daily Mail.
Canton (MS) Times.
Charleston (SC) Courier.
Charleston (SC) Daily News.
Charleston (SC) Mercury.
Charleston (SC) Times.
Cincinnati Weekly Herald and Philanthropist.

Continental Monthly.
Daily National Republican (Washington, DC).
De Bow's Review.
Edgefield (SC) Advertiser.
Greenville (SC) Republican.
Jackson Weekly Mississippian.
Jonesborough (TN) Whig and Independent Journal.
The Liberator (Boston).
Louisville (KY) Daily Journal.
Memphis (TN) Daily Appeal.
Merchants' Magazine and Commercial Review.
Montgomery (AL) Mail.
Nashville (TN) American.
Nashville (TN) Daily Union.
Nashville (TN) Union and American.
New Orleans Daily Picayune.
Newport (SC) Mercury.
New York Daily Tribune.
New York Herald.
New York Journal.
New York Times.
North American and United States Gazette (Philadelphia).
Philadelphia Inquirer.
Richmond (VA) Dispatch.
Richmond (VA) Times.
Richmond (VA) Whig.
Rochester (NY) Republican.
Sacramento Daily Union.
Semi-Weekly Natchez (MS) Courier.
Southern Patriot (Charleston, SC).
Southern Quarterly Review.
Tri-Weekly Memphis (TN) Enquirer.
Union County Star and Lewisburg (PA) Chronicle.
Washington Post.
Washington Standard (Olympia, WA).
Weekly Mississippian (Jackson, MS).
Weekly Vincennes (IN) Western Sun.
Western Reserve Chronicle (Warren, OH).
Young American Magazine.

Primary Sources

Acts of Alabama, 1830–1860. Catawba: Allen & Brickell, 1860.

Acts of Tennessee, Index to Names, 1796–1850. http://www.tennessee.gov/tsla/history/misc/actsintro.htm.

Annual Message of Thomas O. Moore, Governor of the State of Louisiana to the General Assembly. Baton Rouge: J. M. Taylor, State Printer, 1861.

Bennoitt, George K. *City of Charleston Health Department Death Records: January 1821 to December 1828.* Charleston, SC, n.d.

Case Files of Applications from Former Confederates for Presidential Pardons ("Amnesty Papers"), 1865–67. Records of the Adjutant General's Office, 1780s–1917, Record Group 94, Publication M1003, National Archives, Washington, DC.

Chesnut, Mary Boykin. *A Diary from Dixie.* New York: D. Appleton, 1905.

Composite Census Records, 1850–1860. *See* US Census Office, *Seventh Census of the United States, 1850,* and *Eighth Census of the United States, 1860.*

Cornish, Louis. *A National Register of the Society: Sons of the American Revolution.* New York: Press of Andrew Kellogg, 1902.

Davis, Jefferson. *The Rise and Fall of the Confederate Government.* New York: D. Appleton, 1881.

De Bow, J. D. B. *The Industrial Resources, etc., of the Southern and Western States: Embracing a View of Their Commerce, Agriculture, Manufactures, Internal Improvements, Slave and Free Labor, Slavery Institutions, Products, etc., of the South: Together with Historical and Statistical Sketches of the Different States and Cities of the Union: Statistics of the United States Commerce and Manufactures, from the Earliest Periods, Compared with Other Leading Powers: The Results of the Different Census Returns since 1790, and Returns of the Census of 1850, on Population, Agriculture and General Industry, etc.: With an Appendix.* 3 vols. New Orleans: Office of *De Bow's Review,* 1852.

———. *The Interest in Slavery of the Southern Non-Slaveholder: The Right of Peaceful Secession.* Charleston, SC: Evans & Goodwell, 1860.

Early, Jubal A. *A Memoir of the Last Year of the War for Independence in the Confederate States of America.* Lynchburg, VA: Charles W. Button, 1867.

Edmunds, James M. *Manufactures of the United States in 1860: Compiled from the Original Returns of the Eighth Census, under the Direction of the Secretary of the Interior.* Washington, DC: US Government Printing Office, 1865.

Gadsden, James. James Gadsden to Dr. Shanks, October 6, 1845, Charleston. South Carolina Historical Society, Charleston, SC.

Gayarre, Charles. *History of Louisiana.* New York: William J. Widdleton, 1867.

Gorgas, Josiah. *The Journals of Josiah Gorgas, 1857–1878.* Edited by Sarah Woolfolk Wiggins. Tuscaloosa: University of Alabama Press, 1995.

Hagy, James W. *City Directories for Charleston, South Carolina: For the Years 1806, 1807, 1808, 1813.* Baltimore: Clearfield, 1996.

———. *City Directories for Charleston, South Carolina: From 1819, 1822, 1825, and 1829.* Baltimore: Clearfield, 1996.

Helper, Hinton R. *The Impending Crisis of the South: How to Meet It.* New York: Burdick Bros., 1857.

Hildreth, Richard. *Despotism in America; or, An Inquiry into the Nature and Results of the Slave-Holding System in the United States.* Boston: Whipple & Darrell, 1840.

James, Henry F. *Abolitionism Unveiled! Hypocrisy Unmasked! and Knavery Scourged!* New York: T. V. Paterson, 1850.

Johnson, Andrew. *The Papers of Andrew Johnson.* Vol. 5, *1861–1862,* ed. Leroy P. Graf and Ralph W. Haskins. Knoxville: University of Tennessee Press, 1979.

Jones, John B. *A Rebel War Clerk's Diary at the Confederate States Capital.* Philadelphia: J. B. Lippincott, 1866.

Journal of the Proceedings of the Senate of the General Assembly of the State of Florida. Tallahassee: Hart & Barefoot, 1859.

Journal of the Proceedings of the South-Western Convention, Began and Held at the City of Memphis, on the 12th November, 1845. Memphis, TN, 1845.

Kennedy, Joseph C. G. *Agriculture of the United States in 1860; Compiled from the Original Returns of the Eighth Census, under the Direction of the Secretary of the Interior.* Washington, DC: US Government Printing Office, 1864.

Langley, Clara A. *South Carolina Deed Abstracts, 1719–1772.* Vol. 3, *Books QQ-H-3.* Greenville, SC: Southern Historical Press, 1983.

Leland, Charles G. *Hans Breitmann's Party with Other Ballads.* Philadelphia: T. B. Peterson and Bros., 1869.

Lincoln, Abraham. *The Essential Lincoln: Speeches and Correspondence.* Edited by Orville V. Burton. New York: Hill & Wang, 2009.

Mills, Robert. *Statistics of South Carolina: A View of the Natural, Civil, and Military History, General and Particular.* Charleston, SC: Hurlbut & Lloyd, 1826.

Minutes of the Third Semi-Annual Convention of the Southern Industrial Association. New Orleans: E. S. Upton, 1901.

Norman, Benjamin M. *Norman's New Orleans and Environs: Containing a Brief Historical Sketch of the Territory and State of Louisiana and the City of New Orleans.* New Orleans: B. M. Norman, 1845.

Olmsted, Frederick Law. *A Journey in the Back Country.* New York: Mason Bros., 1860.

———. *Journey in the Seaboard Slave States: With Remarks on Their Economy.* New York: Mason Bros., 1861.

———. *The Cotton Kingdom: A Traveler's Observations on Cotton and Slavery in the American Slave States.* New York: Mason Bros., 1862.

Pollard, Edward A. *The Lost Cause: A New Southern History of the War of the Confederates.* New York: E. B. Treat, 1866.

Publications of the Southern History Association. Vol. 5. Washington, DC: Southern History Association, 1901.

Report of the Joint Committee on Reconstruction at the First Session of the Thirty-Ninth Congress. Washington, DC: US Government Printing Office, 1866.

Sherman, William T. *Memoirs of General William T. Sherman.* Edited by William S. McFeely. New York: Da Capo, 1984.

Thomson, William. *Thomson's Mercantile and Professional Directory.* Baltimore: William Thomson, 1851.

US Adjutant General's Office. J. D. B. De Bow File. In *Case Files of Applications from Former Confederates for Presidential Pardons ("Amnesty Papers"), 1865–67.* Records of the Adjutant General's Office, 1780s–1917, Record Group 94, Publication M1003, National Archives, Washington, DC.

US Census Office. *Fourth Census of the United States, 1820.* Washington, DC, 1850.

———. *Seventh Census of the United States, 1850.* Washington, DC, 1853.

———. *Eighth Census of the United States, 1860.* Washington, DC, 1864.

US Congress. House of Representatives. *Annals of Congress.* 16th Cong., 1st sess., vol. 2 (1819).

US War Department. *The War of the Rebellion: A Compilation of the Official Records of the Union and Confederate Armies.* Ser. 1, vol. 7. Washington, DC: US Government Printing Office, 1882.

White, George. *Statistics of the State of Georgia: Including an Account of Its Natural, Civil, and Ecclesiastical History: Together with a Particular Description of Each County.* Savannah: W. Thorne Williams, 1849.

Secondary Sources

Adams, Sean P. *Old Dominion, Industrial Commonwealth: Coal, Politics, and Economy in Antebellum America.* Baltimore: Johns Hopkins University Press, 2004.

Adams, William H. "The Louisiana Whigs." *Louisiana History* 15 (Summer 1974): 213–28.

Aiken, Charles S. *The Cotton Plantation South: Since the Civil War.* Baltimore: Johns Hopkins University Press, 1998.

Alexander, Thomas B., and Peggy J. Duckworth. "Alabama Black Belt Whigs during Secession: A New Viewpoint." *Alabama Review* 17 (July 1964): 181–97.

Ammons, Elizabeth. *Harriet Beecher Stowe's Uncle Tom's Cabin: A Casebook.* Oxford: Oxford University Press, 2007.

Anderson, Margo J. *The American Census: A Social History.* New Haven, CT: Yale University Press, 1988.

Angevine, Robert G. *The Railroad and the State: War, Politics, and Technology in Nineteenth-Century America.* Stanford, CA: Stanford University Press, 2004.

Ash, Stephen V. *When the Yankees Came: Conflict and Chaos in the Occupied South, 1861–1865.* Chapel Hill: University of North Carolina Press, 1999.

Ashworth, John. *Slavery, Capitalism, and Politics in the Antebellum Republic.* Vol. 1, *Commerce and Compromise, 1820–1850.* New York: Cambridge University Press, 1995.

Atherton, Lewis E. "Mercantile Education in the Ante-Bellum South." *Mississippi Valley Historical Review* 39 (1953): 623–64.

Ball, Douglas B. *Financial Failure and Confederate Defeat.* Urbana: University of Illinois Press, 1991.

Baptist, Edward E. *Creating an Old South: Middle Florida's Plantation Frontier before the Civil War.* Chapel Hill: University of North Carolina Press, 2002.

Bateman, Fred, and Thomas Joseph Weiss. *A Deplorable Scarcity: The Failure of Industrialization in the Slave Economy.* Chapel Hill: University of North Carolina Press, 1981.

Beale, Mildred. "Charles Teed Pollard, Industrialist." *Alabama Historical Quarterly* 2 (Spring 1940): 72–85, 2 (Summer 1940): 189–202.

Beard, Charles A., and Mary R. Beard. *The Rise of American Civilization.* Vol. 2. New York: Macmillan, 1927.

Becker, Carl L. *The Declaration of Independence: A Study in the History of Political Ideas.* New York: Knopf, 1922.

Beringer, Richard E., Herman Hattaway, Archer Jones, and William N. Stills Jr. *Why the South Lost the Civil War.* Athens: University of Georgia Press, 1986.

Berlin, Ira. *Many Thousands Gone: The First Two Centuries of Slavery in North America.* Cambridge, MA: Belknap Press of Harvard University Press, 1998.

Bernstein, Barton J. "Southern Politics and Attempts to Reopen the African Slave Trade." *Journal of Negro History* 51 (January 1966): 16–35.

Black, Robert C., III. *The Railroads of the Confederacy.* Chapel Hill: University of North Carolina Press, 1952.

Blackson, Robert M. "Pennsylvania Banks and the Panic of 1819: A Reinterpretation." *Journal of the Early Republic* 9 (Autumn 1989): 335–58.

Bleser, Carol, ed. *Secret and Sacred: The Diary of James H. Hammond, a Southern Slaveholder.* New York: Oxford University Press, 1988.

Bond, Horace M. "Social and Economic Forces in Alabama Reconstruction." *Journal of Negro History* 23 (July 1938): 363–77.

Bosher, Marshall. *Chesterfield County, Virginia: A Collection of Notes Peculiar to Its Early History.* Chesterfield, VA: Chesterfield Historical Society, 1989.

Boyer-Lewis, Charlene M. *Ladies and Gentlemen on Display: Planter Society at the Virginia Springs, 1790–1860.* Charlottesville: University Press of Virginia, 2001.

Breeden, James O. *Advice among Masters: The Ideal in Slave Management in the Old South.* Westport, CT: Greenwood, 1980.

Brown, David. *Southern Outcast: Hinton Rowan Helper and the Impending Crisis of the South.* Baton Rouge: Louisiana State University Press, 2006.

Brownell, Blaine A., and David R. Goldfield, eds. *The City in Southern History: The Growth of Urban Civilization in the South.* Port Washington, NY: Kennikat, 1977.

Bruce, Philip A. *The Rise of the New South.* Vol. 17 of *The History of North America.* Philadelphia: George Barrie & Sons, 1905.

Brundage, W. Fitzhugh. *The Southern Past: A Clash of Race and Memory.* Cambridge, MA: Harvard University Press, 2005.

Buck, Paul. *The Road to Reunion: 1865–1900.* New York: Vintage, 1937.

Burt, Jesse C., Jr. "The Nashville and Chattanooga Railroad, 1854–1872: The Era of Transition." *East Tennessee Historical Society Publications* 23 (1951): 58–76.

Burton, Orville V., ed. *The Essential Lincoln: Speeches and Correspondence.* New York: Hill & Wang, 2009.

Bushman, Richard. *The Refinement of America: Persons, Houses, Cities.* New York: Vintage, 1993.

Butler, Nicholas M. *Votaries of Apollo: The St. Cecilia Society and the Patronage of Concert Music in Charleston, South Carolina.* Columbia: University of South Carolina Press, 2007.

Byrne, Frank J. *Becoming Bourgeois: Merchant Culture in the South, 1820–1865.* Lexington: University Press of Kentucky, 2006.

Caldwell, Henry Martin. *History of the Elyton Land Company and Birmingham, Alabama.* Birmingham: Caldwell-Garber, 1892.

Capers, Gerald M. *John C. Calhoun, Opportunist: A Reappraisal.* Gainesville: University of Florida Press, 1960.

Carrier, Lyman. "The United States Agricultural Society." *Agricultural History* 11 (1937): 278–88.

Cathy, C. O. "Sidney Weller: Ante-Bellum Promoter of Agricultural Reform." *North Carolina Historical Review* 31 (1954): 1–17.

Cauthon, Charles E. *South Carolina Goes to War, 1860–1865.* Columbia: University of South Carolina Press, 2005.

Chandler, Alfred D. *The Visible Hand: The Managerial Revolution in American Business.* Cambridge, MA: Belknap Press of Harvard University Press, 1977.

Chandler, Walter. "The Memphis Navy Yard: An Adventure in Internal Improvement." *Western Tennessee Historical Society Papers* 1 (1947): 68–72.

Christian, William A. *Richmond: Her Past and Present.* Spartanburg, SC: Reprint Co., 1912.

Clark, John Elwood. *Railroads in the Civil War: The Impact of Management on Victory and Defeat.* Baton Rouge: Louisiana State University Press, 2001.

Clark, Victor S. *History of Manufactures in the United States.* Vol. 2, *1860–1893.* Washington, DC: Carnegie Institution, 1929.

Coclanis, Peter. "The Sociology of Architecture in Colonial Charleston: Pattern and Process in an Eighteenth-Century Southern City." *Journal of Social History* 18 (Summer 1985): 607–23.

Cole, Arthur C. *The Whig Party in the South.* Washington, DC: Lord Baltimore, 1913.

Collins, Herbert. "The Southern Industrial Gospel before 1860." *Journal of Southern History* 12 (August 1946): 386–402.

Connelly, Thomas L. *Civil War Tennessee: Battles and Leaders.* Knoxville: University of Tennessee Press, 2004.

Conrad, Glenn R., ed. *A Dictionary of Louisiana Biography.* Vol. 1. New Orleans: Louisiana Historical Association, 1988.

Cook, James B. "The Gayoso Hotel." In *The Tennessee Encyclopedia of History and Culture,* ed. Carroll Van West, 353. Nashville, TN: Rutledge Hill, 1998.

Cooper, William J., Jr. *The South and the Power of Slavery, 1828–1856.* Baton Rouge: Louisiana State University Press, 1978.

———. *Jefferson Davis and the Civil War Era.* Baton Rouge: Louisiana State University Press, 2008.

Copeland, David A. *The Media's Role in Defining the Nation: The Active Voice.* New York: Peter Lang, 2010.

Cotterill, R. S. "Southern Railroads, 1850–1860." *Mississippi Valley Historical Review* 10 (March 1924): 396–405.

Craven, Avery. "The Agricultural Reforms of the Ante-Bellum South." *American Historical Review* 33 (January 1928): 302–14.

Crawford, Stephen C. "Quantified Memory: A Study of WPA and Fisk University Slave Narrative Collections." Ph.D. diss., University of Chicago, 1980.

Crofts, Daniel W. *Reluctant Confederates: Upper South Unionists in the Secession Crisis.* Chapel Hill: University of North Carolina Press, 1989.

Cronon, William. *Nature's Metropolis: Chicago and the Great West.* New York: Norton, 1991.

Curry, Leonard P. *The Free Black in Urban America, 1800–1850.* Chicago: University of Chicago Press, 1981.

Cyclopedia of Eminent and Representative Men of the Carolinas of the Nineteenth Century. Madison, WI: Brant & Fuller, 1892.

Dabney, Virginius. *Richmond: The Story of a City.* Richmond: University Press of Virginia, 1976.

Davis, Harold E. *Henry Grady's New South: Atlanta, a Brave and Beautiful City.* Tuscaloosa: University of Alabama Press, 1990.

Davis, William C. *Rhett: The Turbulent Life and Times of a Fire-Eater.* Columbia: University of South Carolina Press, 2001.

———. *Look Away! A History of the Confederate States of America.* New York: Free Press, 2002.

Dawsey, Cyrus B., and James M. Dawsey. *The Confederados: Old South Immigrants in Brazil.* Tuscaloosa: University of Alabama Press, 1995.

DeCredico, Mary A. *Patriotism for Profit: Georgia's Urban Entrepreneurs and the Confederate War Effort.* Chapel Hill: University of North Carolina Press, 1990.

De Land, T. A., and A. Davis Smith. *Northern Alabama: Historical and Biographical Illustrated.* Chicago: Donohue & Henneberry, 1888.

Delfino, Susanna. "Southern Economic Backwardness: A Comparative View." In *Global Perspectives on Industrial Transformation in the American South,* ed. Susanna Delfino and Michele Gillespie, 105–30. Columbia: University of Missouri Press, 2005.

Derrick, Samuel M. *Centennial History of South Carolina Railroad.* Columbia, SC: State Co., 1930.

Dew, Charles B. *Bond of Iron: Master and Slave at Buffalo Forge.* New York: Norton, 1994.

———. *Apostles of Disunion: Southern Secession Commissioners and the Causes of the Civil War.* Charlottesville: University Press of Virginia, 2001.

Dodd, William E. *Statesmen of the Old South: From Radicalism to Conservative Revolt.* New York: Macmillan, 1927.

Donald, David. "The Proslavery Argument Reconsidered." *Journal of Southern History* 37 (February 1971): 3–18.

Doster, James F. "The Shelby Iron Works Collection in the University of Alabama Library." *Bulletin of the Business Historical Society* 26 (December 1952): 214–17.

Downey, Tom. "Riparian Rights and Manufacturing in Antebellum South Carolina: William Gregg and the Origins of the 'Industrial Mind.'" *Journal of Southern History* 69 (February 1999): 77–108.

———. *Planting a Capitalist South: Masters, Merchants, and Manufacturers in the Southern Interior, 1790–1860.* Baton Rouge: Louisiana State University Press, 2006.

Doyle, Don Harrison. *New Men, New Cities, New South: Atlanta, Nashville, Charleston, Mobile, 1860–1910.* Chapel Hill: University of North Carolina Press, 1990.

Dubay, Robert W. *Mississippi Fire-Eater: His Life and Times, 1813–1867.* Oxford: University Press of Mississippi, 1975.

Dumond, Dwight L. *Southern Editorials on Secession.* Gloucester, MA: Peter Smith, 1964.

Dupont, Nancy McKenzie. "Mississippi's Fire-Eating Editor: Ethelbert Barksdale and the Election of 1860." In *The Civil War and the Press,* ed. David B. Sachsman, S. Kittrell Rushing, and Debra Reddin van Tuyll, 137–46. New Brunswick, NJ: Transaction, 2000.

Dupre, Daniel S. *Transforming the Cotton Frontier: Madison County, Alabama, 1800–1840.* Baton Rouge: Louisiana State University Press, 1997.

Easterby, J. H. *A History of the College of Charleston.* New York: Scribner, 1935.

Eaton, Clement. "Henry A. Wise and the Virginia Fire Eaters of 1856." *Mississippi Valley Historical Review* 21 (March 1935): 495–512.

———. *A History of the Old South.* New York: Macmillan, 1949.

———. *The Mind of the Old South.* Baton Rouge: Louisiana State University Press, 1964.

Edgar, Walter B. *South Carolina: A History.* Columbia: University of South Carolina Press, 1998.

Egerton, Douglas R. "Markets without a Market Revolution: Southern Planters and Capitalism." *Journal of the Early Republic* 16 (Summer 1996): 207–21.

Ellis, John H. *Yellow Fever and Public Health in the New South.* Lexington: University Press of Kentucky, 1992.

Engerman, Stanley L. "Myths and Realities." In *Global Perspectives on Industrial Transformation in the American South,* ed. Susanna Delfino and Michele Gillespie, 14–25. Columbia: University of Missouri Press, 2005.

Escott, Paul D. *After Secession: Jefferson Davis and the Failure of Confederate Nationalism.* Baton Rouge: Louisiana State University Press, 1978.

Etcheson, Nicole. *Bleeding Kansas: Contested Liberty in the Civil War Era.* Lawrence: University Press of Kansas, 2004.

Evans, Curtis J. *The Conquest of Labor: Daniel Pratt and Southern Industrialization.* Baton Rouge: Louisiana State University Press, 2001.

Faust, Drew G., ed. *The Ideology of Slavery: Proslavery Thought in the Antebellum South, 1830–1860.* Baton Rouge: Louisiana State University Press, 1981.

———. *James Henry Hammond and the Old South: A Design for Mastery.* Baton Rouge: Louisiana State University Press, 1982.

Finkelman, Paul. *Defending Slavery: Proslavery Thought in the Old South: A Brief History with Documents.* Boston: Bedford/St. Martin's, 2003.

Fischer, David Hackett, and James C. Kelly. *Bound Away: Virginia and the Westward Movement.* Charlottesville: University Press of Virginia, 2000.

Fleming, Walter L. *The South in the Building of the Nation: A History of the Southern States.* Vol. 5. Richmond, VA: Southern Historical Publication Society, 1909.

Follet, Richard. *The Sugar Masters: Planters and Slaves in Louisiana's Cane World, 1820–1860.* Baton Rouge: Louisiana State University Press, 2005.

Foner, Eric. *Free Soil, Free Labor, Free Men: The Ideology of the Republican Party before the Civil War.* Oxford: Oxford University Press, 1970.

———. *Reconstruction: America's Unfinished Revolution, 1863–1877.* New York: Perennial Classics, 1988.

Forbes, Robert P. *The Missouri Compromise and Its Aftermath: Slavery and the Meaning of America.* Chapel Hill: University of North Carolina Press, 2007.

Ford, Lacy K., Jr. *Origins of Southern Radicalism: The South Carolina Upcountry, 1800–1860.* New York: Oxford University Press, 1988.

Franklin, John Hope. *The Militant South, 1800–1861.* Cambridge, MA: Harvard University Press, 1956.

Fraser, Walter J. *Charleston! Charleston! The History of a Southern City.* Columbia: University of South Carolina Press, 1989.

Freehling, William W. *Prelude to Civil War: The Nullification Controversy in South Carolina, 1816–1836.* New York: Harper Torchbooks, 1968.

———. *The Road to Disunion: Secessionists at Bay, 1776–1854.* Vol. 1. New York: Oxford University Press, 1990.
———. *The South vs. the South: How Anti-Confederate Southerners Shaped the Course of the Civil War.* New York: Oxford University Press, 2001.
———. *The Road to Disunion: Secessionists Triumphant, 1854–1861.* Vol. 2. New York: Oxford University Press, 2007.
Garrett, William. *Reminiscences of Public Men in Alabama.* Spartanburg, SC: Reprint Co., 1872.
Gaston, Paul. *The New South Creed: A Study in Southern Mythmaking.* New York: Knopf, 1970.
Genovese, Eugene D. *Roll, Jordon, Roll: The World the Slaves Made.* New York: Vintage, 1976.
———. *The Political Economy of Slavery: Studies in the Economy and Society of the Slave South.* 2nd ed. Middletown, CT: Wesleyan University Press, 1989.
———. *The Southern Front: History and Politics in the Cultural War.* Columbia: University of Missouri Press, 1995.
Glover, Lorri. *Southern Sons: Becoming Men in the New Nation.* Baltimore: Johns Hopkins University Press, 2007.
Gold, John R., and Margaret M. Gold. *Cities of Culture: Staging International Festivals and the Urban Agenda, 1851–2000.* Aldershot: Ashgate, 2005.
Goldfield, David R. "Pursuing the American Dream: Cities in the Old South." In *The City in Southern History: The Growth of Urban Civilization in the South,* ed. Blaine A. Brownwell and David R. Goldfield, 52–91. Port Washington, NY: Kennikat, 1977.
———. *Urban Growth in the Age of Sectionalism: Virginia, 1847–1861.* Baton Rouge: Louisiana State University Press, 1977.
———. *Cotton Fields and Skyscrapers: Southern City and Region.* Baton Rouge: Louisiana State University Press, 1982.
Grant, Susan-Mary. *North over South: Northern Nationalism and American Identity in the Antebellum Era.* Lawrence: University Press of Kansas, 2000.
Gray, Lewis C. *History of Agriculture in the Southern United States to 1860.* Vol. 2. Carnegie Institution Publication no. 430. Washington, DC: Carnegie Institution of Washington, 1933.
Green, Fletcher M. *Constitutional Development in the South Atlantic States, 1776–1860.* Chapel Hill: University of North Carolina Press, 1930.
———. *The Role of the Yankee in the Old South.* Athens: University of Georgia Press, 1972.
Griffin, Richard W. "An Origin of the New South: The South Carolina Homespun Company, 1808–1815." *Business History Review* 35 (Autumn 1961): 402–14.
Hahn, Steven. *The Roots of Southern Populism: Yeoman Farmers and the Transformation of the Georgia Upcountry, 1850–1880.* New York: Oxford University Press, 1983.

———. *A Nation under Our Feet: Black Political Struggles in the Rural South from Slavery to the Great Migration.* Cambridge, MA: Harvard University Press, 2003.

Hamilton, Holman. *Prologue to Conflict: The Crisis and Compromise of 1850.* Lexington: University of Kentucky Press, 1964.

Harris, Carl V. "Right Fork or Left Fork? The Section-Party Alignments of Southern Democrats in Congress, 1873–1897." *Journal of Southern History* 42 (November 1976): 471–506.

Harrison, James A. *Life and Letters of Edgar Allan Poe.* Vol. 2. New York: Thomas P. Crowell, 1903.

Hattaway, Herman, and Archer Jones. *How the North Won the War: A Military History of the Civil War.* Urbana: University of Illinois Press, 1991.

Hearn, Chester G. *The Capture of New Orleans, 1862.* Baton Rouge: Louisiana State University Press, 1995.

Hill, Henry B., and Larry Gara. "A French Traveler's View of Ante-Bellum New Orleans." *Louisiana History* 1 (Fall 1960): 336–38.

Holt, Michael F. *The Rise and Fall of the American Whig Party.* New York: Oxford University Press, 1999.

Horsman, Reginald. *Josiah Nott of Mobile: Southerner, Physician, and Racial Theorist.* Baton Rouge: Louisiana State University Press, 1987.

Howe, Daniel Walker. *The Political Culture of the American Whigs.* Chicago: University of Chicago Press, 1979.

Huff, Lawrence. "Joseph Addison Turner: Southern Editor during the Civil War." *Journal of Southern History* 29 (November 1963): 469–85.

Huston, James L. "Property Rights in Slavery and the Coming of the Civil War." *Journal of Southern History* 65 (May 1999): 249–86.

Jennings, Thelma. *The Nashville Convention: Southern Movement for Unity, 1848–1851.* Memphis, TN: Memphis State University Press, 1980.

Johnson, Guion G. *A Social History of the Sea Islands: With Special Reference to St. Helena Island, South Carolina.* Chapel Hill: University of North Carolina Press, 1930.

Johnson, Kenneth R. "N. H. R. Dawson: United States Commissioner of Education." *History of Education Quarterly* 11 (Summer 1971): 174–83.

———. "Urban Boosterism and Higher Education in the New South: A Case Study." *Alabama Historical Quarterly* 42 (Spring–Summer 1980): 40–58.

Johnson, Vicki Vaughn. *The Men and the Vision of the Southern Commercial Conventions, 1845–1871.* Columbia: University of Missouri Press, 1992.

Jordan, Weymouth T. "Cotton Planters' Conventions in the Old South." *Journal of Southern History* 19 (August 1953): 321–45.

———. "Noah B. Cloud and the American Cotton Planter." *Agricultural History* 31 (October 1957): 553–69.

Joyner, Charles. *Down by the Riverside: A South Carolina Slave Community.* Urbana: University of Illinois Press, 1984.

Kaplanoff, Mark D. "Charles Pinckney and the American Republican Tradition." In *Intellectual Life in Antebellum Charleston,* ed. Michael O'Brien and David Moltke-Hansen, 85–122. Knoxville: University of Tennessee Press, 1986.

Kellar, Herbert A., ed. *Solon Robinson, Pioneer and Agriculturalist.* Vol. 2. Indianapolis: Indiana Historical Bureau, 1936.

Kendrick, Benjamin B. *The Journal of the Joint Committee of Fifteen on Reconstruction.* New York, 1914.

Knight, Edgar K. *Public Education in the South.* Boston: Ginn, 1922.

Lander, Ernest M., Jr. "Charleston: Manufacturing Center of the Old South." *Journal of Southern History* 26 (August 1960): 330–51.

———. *Reluctant Imperialists: Calhoun, the South Carolinians, and the Mexican War.* Baton Rouge: Louisiana State University Press, 1979.

Lang, James O. "Gloom Envelops New Orleans: April 24 to May 2, 1862." *Louisiana History* 1 (Autumn 1960): 281–91.

Larsen, Lawrence H. *The Rise of the Urban South.* Lexington: University Press of Kentucky, 1985.

———. *The Urban South: A History.* Lexington: University Press of Kentucky, 1990.

Larson, John L. *Internal Improvements: National Public Works and the Promise of Popular Government in the Early United States.* Chapel Hill: University of North Carolina Press, 2001.

Laws, Forrest. "The Railroad Comes to Tennessee: The Building of the LaGrange and Memphis." *West Tennessee Historical Society Papers* 30 (1976): 24–42.

Legan, Marshall S. "Railroad Sentiment in Northern Louisiana in the 1850s." *Louisiana History* 17 (1976): 125–42.

Lewis, Ronald. *Coal, Iron, and Slaves: Industrial Slavery in Maryland and Virginia, 1715–1865.* Westport, CT: Greenwood, 1979.

Little, Robert D. "The Ideology of the New South: A Study in the Development of Ideas, 1865–1910." Ph.D. diss., University of Chicago, 1950.

Lofton, John. *Denmark Vesey's Revolt: The Slave Plot That Lit a Fuse to Fort Sumter.* Kent, OH: Kent State University Press, 1964.

Maffitt, Emma M., and John N. Maffitt. *The Life and Services of John Newland Maffitt.* New York: Neale, 1906.

Majewski, John. *Modernizing a Slave Economy: The Economic Vision of the Confederate Nation.* Chapel Hill: University of North Carolina Press, 2009.

Marmor, Theodore R. "Anti-Industrialism and the Old South: The Agrarian Perspective of John C. Calhoun." *Comparative Studies in Society and History* 9 (July 1967): 377–406.

Marrs, Aaron W. *Railroads in the Old South: Pursuing Progress in a Slave Society.* Baltimore: Johns Hopkins University Press, 2009.

Martin, C. Brenden. *Tourism in the Mountain South: A Double-Edged Sword.* Knoxville: University of Tennessee Press, 2007.

Massey, Mary E. *Ersatz in the Confederacy.* Columbia: University of South Carolina Press, 1952.

Mathew, William M. *Edmund Ruffin and the Crisis of Slavery in the Old South: The Failure of Agricultural Reform.* Athens: University of Georgia Press, 1989.

McCardell, John. *The Idea of a Southern Nation: Southern Nationalists and Southern Nationalism, 1830–1860.* New York: Norton, 1979.

McCurry, Stephanie. *Masters of Small Worlds: Yeoman Households, Gender Relations, and the Political Culture of the Antebellum South Carolina Low Country.* New York: Oxford University Press, 1995.

McGovern, Bryan P. *John Mitchel: Irish Nationalist, Southern Secessionist.* Knoxville: University of Tennessee Press, 2009.

McIlwaine, Shields. *Memphis, Down in Dixie.* New York: E. P. Dutton, 1948.

McInnis, Maurie D. *The Politics of Taste in Antebellum Charleston.* Chapel Hill: University of North Carolina Press, 2005.

McKenzie, Robert T. *One South or Many? Plantation Belt and Upcountry in Civil War–Era Tennessee.* New York: Cambridge University Press, 1994.

———. "Contesting Secession: Parson Brownlow and the Rhetoric of Proslavery Unionism." *Civil War History* 48 (2002): 294–312.

McKitrick, Erik L. *Andrew Johnson and Reconstruction.* Chicago: University of Chicago Press, 1960.

McKiven, Henry M., Jr. *Iron and Steel: Class, Race, and Community in Birmingham, Alabama, 1875–1920.* Chapel Hill: University of North Carolina Press, 1995.

McPherson, James M. *Battle Cry of Freedom: The Civil War Era.* New York: Ballantine, 1988.

Miller, John David. *South by Southwest: Planter Emigration and Identity in the Slave South.* Charlottesville: University of Virginia Press, 2002.

Miller, Randall M. *The Cotton Mill Movement in Antebellum Alabama.* New York: Arno, 1978.

Milton, George F. *The Eve of Conflict: Stephen A. Douglas and the Needless War.* Boston: Houghton Mifflin, 1934.

Mitchell, Broadus. *The Rise of Cotton Mills in the South.* Baltimore: Johns Hopkins University Press, 1921.

Mitchell, Broadus, and George S. Mitchell. *The Industrial Revolution in the South.* Baltimore: Johns Hopkins University Press, 1930.

Moltke-Hansen, David. "The Expansion of Intellectual Life: A Prospectus." In *Intellectual Life in Antebellum Charleston,* ed. Michael O'Brien and David Moltke-Hansen, 1–44. Knoxville: University of Tennessee Press, 1986.

Moore, Glover. *The Missouri Controversy, 1819–1821.* Lexington: University of Kentucky Press, 1953.

Morgan, Chad. *Planters' Progress: Modernizing Confederate Georgia.* Gainesville: University Press of Florida, 2005.

Morgan, Philip D. *Slave Counterpoint.* Chapel Hill: University of North Carolina Press, 1998.

Morrow, Ralph E. "The Proslavery Argument Revisited." *Mississippi Valley Historical Review* 47 (June 1961): 79–94.

Nash, R. C. "The Organization of Trade and Finance in the Atlantic Economy: Britain and South Carolina, 1670–1775." In *Money, Trade, and Power: The Evolution of Colonial South Carolina's Plantation Society,* ed. Jack P. Greene, Rosemary Brana-Shute, and Randy J. Sparks, 95–151. Columbia: University of South Carolina Press, 2001.

Nixon, Raymond B. *Henry W. Grady, Spokesman of the New South.* New York: Knopf, 1943.

Noe, Kenneth W. *Southwest Virginia's Railroad: Modernization and the Sectional Crisis in the Civil War Era.* Tuscaloosa: University of Alabama Press, 2003.

Oakes, James. *The Ruling Race: A History of American Slaveholders.* New York: Knopf, 1982.

———. "'Whom Have I Oppressed?': The Pursuit of Happiness and the Happy Slave." In *The Revolution of 1800: Democracy, Race, and the New Republic,* ed. James Horn, Jan E. Lewis, and Peter S. Onuf, 220–39. Charlottesville: University of Virginia Press, 2002.

O'Brien, Michael. *Conjectures of Order: Intellectual Life and the American South, 1810–1860.* 2 vols. Chapel Hill: University of North Carolina Press, 2004.

O'Neall, John Belton. *The Annals of Newberry in Two Parts.* Newberry: Aull & Houseal, 1892.

Owen, Thomas M., and Marie Bankhead Owen. *History of Alabama and Directory of Alabama Biography.* 4 vols. Chicago: S. J. Clark, 1921.

Owsley, Frank. *King Cotton Diplomacy: Foreign Relations of the Confederate States of America.* Chicago: University of Chicago Press, 1931.

———. *Plain Folk of the Old South.* Baton Rouge: Louisiana State University Press, 1949.

Paquette, Robert L. "From Rebellion to Revisionism: The Continuing Debate about the Denmark Vesey Affair." *Journal of the Historical Society* 4 (September 2004): 291–334.

Parker, David B. "To the Youth of the Southern Confederacy: Georgia's Confederate Textbooks." In *Breaking the Heartland: The Civil War in Georgia,* ed. John D. Fowler and David B. Parker, 94–109. Macon, GA: Mercer University Press, 2011.

Parrington, Vernon L. *Main Currents in American Thought: The Romantic Revolution in America.* New York: Harcourt, Brace, & World, 1927.

Paskoff, Paul F., and Daniel J. Wilson, eds. *The Cause of the South: Selections from* De Bow's Review, *1846–1867.* Baton Rouge: Louisiana State University Press, 1982.

Pease, Jane H., and William H. Pease. "The Economics and Politics of Charleston's Nullification Crisis." *Journal of Southern History* 47 (August 1981): 335–62.

———. "Intellectual Life in the 1830s: The Institutional Framework and the Charleston Style." In *Intellectual Life in Antebellum Charleston*, ed. Michael O'Brien and David Moltke-Hansen, 231–54. Knoxville: University of Tennessee Press, 1986.

Perkins, Howard C. *Northern Editorials on Secession*. Vol. 1. Gloucester, MA: Peter Smith, 1964.

Phillips, Sarah T. "Antebellum Agricultural Reform, Republican Ideology, and Sectional Tension." *Agricultural History* 74 (Autumn 2000): 799–822.

Phillips, Ulrich B. *A History of Transportation in the Eastern Cotton Belt to 1860*. New York: Columbia University Press, 1908.

———. *Life and Labor in the Old South*. New York: Little, Brown, 1929.

Pittman, Carolyn. "Memphis in the Mid-1840s: Memphis before the Mexican War." *Western Tennessee Historical Society Papers* 23 (1969): 30–44.

Potter, David M. "Jefferson Davis and the Political Factors in Confederate Defeat." In *Why the North Won the Civil War*, ed. David Herbert Donald, 23–48. Baton Rouge: Louisiana State University Press, 1960.

———. *The Impending Crisis, 1848–1861*. New York: Harper & Row, 1976.

Powell, Lawrence N. *New Masters: Northern Planters during the Civil War and Reconstruction*. New Haven, CT: Yale University Press, 1980.

Prince, Richard. *Nashville, Chattanooga, and St. Louis Railway: History and Steam Locomotives*. Bloomington: Indiana University Press, 2001.

Rable, George C. *The Confederate Republic: A Revolution against Politics*. Chapel Hill: University of North Carolina Press, 1994.

Ramsdell, Charles W. *Behind the Lines in the Southern Confederacy*. Baton Rouge: Louisiana State University Press, 1944.

Ransom, Roger L. *The Confederate States of America*. New York: Norton, 2005.

Ransom, Roger L., and Richard Sutch. *One Kind of Freedom: The Economic Consequences of Emancipation*. New York: Cambridge University Press, 1977.

Rawley, James A. *Race and Politics: "Bleeding Kansas" and the Coming of the Civil War*. Philadelphia: J. B. Lippincott, 1969.

Ray, P. Orman. *The Repeal of the Missouri Compromise*. Cleveland: Arthur H. Clark, 1909.

Reed, Merl. "Boom or Bust—Louisiana's Economy during the 1830s." *Louisiana History* 4 (Winter 1963): 35–54.

Reinders, Robert C. "The Free Negro in the New Orleans Economy: 1850–1860." *Louisiana History* 6 (Summer 1965): 273–85.

Reynolds, Donald E. *Editors Make War: Southern Newspapers in the Secession Crisis*. Nashville, TN: Vanderbilt University Press, 1970.

Richardson, Heather Cox. *The Death of Reconstruction: Race, Labor, and Politics in the Post–Civil War South*. Cambridge, MA: Harvard University Press, 2001.

Ringold, May Spencer. "Robert Newman Gourdin and the '1860 Association.'" *Georgia Historical Quarterly* 55 (Winter 1971): 501–9.

Roberson, Jere W. "The South and the Pacific Railroad, 1845–1855." *Western Historical Quarterly* 5 (April 1974): 163–86.

Robertson, David. *Denmark Vesey: The Buried History of America's Largest Slave Rebellion and the Man Who Led It.* New York: Knopf, 1999.

Rogers, George. *Charleston in the Age of the Pinckneys.* Norman: University of Oklahoma Press, 1969.

Rogers, William W. *Confederate Home Front: Montgomery during the Civil War.* Tuscaloosa: University of Alabama Press, 1999.

Roper, James E. "Marcus B. Winchester, First Mayor of Memphis: His Later Years." *Western Tennessee Historical Society Papers* 8 (1959): 5–38.

———. *The Founding of Memphis, 1818–1820.* Memphis, TN: Memphis Sesquicentennial, 1970.

Rothbard, Murray N. *The Panic of 1819: Reactions and Policies.* New York: Columbia University Press, 1962.

Russel, Robert R. *Economic Aspects of Southern Sectionalism, 1840–1861.* Urbana: University of Illinois Press, 1924.

Russell, James M. *Atlanta, 1847–1890: City Building in the Old South and the New.* Baton Rouge: Louisiana State University Press, 1988.

Saville, Julie. *The Work of Reconstruction: From Slave to Wage Laborer in South Carolina, 1860–1870.* New York: Cambridge University Press, 1994.

Scarborough, William K. *The Overseer: Plantation Management in the Old South.* Baton Rouge: Louisiana State University Press, 1966.

———. *The Diary of Edmund Ruffin.* Vol. 1. Baton Rouge: Louisiana State University Press, 1972.

Schoen, Brian. "The Lower South's Antebellum Pursuit of Sectional Development through Global Interdependence." In *Global Perspectives on Industrial Transformation in the American South,* ed. Susanna Delfino and Michele Gillespie, 50–75. Columbia: University of Missouri Press, 2005.

Sellers, Charles. "Who Were the Southern Whigs?" *American Historical Review* 59 (1954): 335–46.

———. *The Market Revolution: Jacksonian America, 1815–1846.* New York: Oxford University Press, 1991.

Shugg, Roger W. *Origins of Class Struggle in Louisiana: A Social History of White Farmers and Laborers during Slavery and After, 1840–1875.* Baton Rouge: Louisiana State University Press, 1966.

Sigafoos, Robert A. *Cotton Row to Beale Street: A Business History of Memphis.* Memphis, TN: Memphis State University Press, 1979.

Skipper, Ottis C. "J. D. B. De Bow, the Man." *Journal of Southern History* 10 (November 1944): 404–23.

———. *J. D. B. De Bow: Magazinist of the Old South.* Athens: University of Georgia Press, 1958.

Smith, Alfred G., Jr. *Economic Readjustment of an Old Cotton State: South Carolina, 1820–1860.* Columbia: University of South Carolina Press, 1958.

Smith, Mark M. *Mastered by the Clock: Time, Slavery, and Freedom in the American South.* Chapel Hill: University of North Carolina Press, 1997.

Stampp, Kenneth M. "An Analysis of T. R. Dew's *Review of the Debates in the Virginia Legislatures.*" *Journal of Negro History* 27 (October 1942): 380–87.

———. *America in 1857: A Nation on the Brink.* Oxford: Oxford University Press, 1992.

Starobin, Robert S. *Industrial Slavery in the Old South.* Oxford: Oxford University Press, 1970.

Stone, H. David, Jr. *Vital Rails: The Charleston and Savannah Railroad and the Civil War in Coastal South Carolina.* Columbia: University of South Carolina Press, 2008.

Stover, John F. *The Railroads of the South, 1865–1900: A Study of Finance and Control.* Chapel Hill: University of North Carolina Press, 1955.

Suarez, Raleigh A. "Bargains, Bills, and Bankruptcies: Business Activity in Rural Antebellum Louisiana." *Louisiana History* 6 (Summer 1966): 189–206.

Surdam, David G. "King Cotton: Monarch or Pretender? The State of the Market for Raw Cotton on the Eve of the American Civil War." *Economic History Review* 51 (February 1998): 113–32.

Sword, Wiley. *Southern Invincibility: A History of the Confederate Heart.* New York: St. Martin's, 1999.

Sydnor, Charles S. *The Development of Southern Sectionalism, 1819–1848.* Baton Rouge: Louisiana State University Press, 1948.

Taylor, George Rogers. *The Transportation Revolution: 1815–1860.* Vol. 4 of *The Economic History of the United States.* New York: Holt, Rinehart & Winston, 1964.

Taylor, William R. *Cavalier and Yankee: The Old South and American National Character.* New York: George Braziller, 1957.

Thomas, Emory M. *The Confederacy as a Revolutionary Experience.* Columbia: University of South Carolina Press, 1971.

———. *The Confederate Nation, 1861–1865.* New York: Harper & Row, 1979.

Thompson, Holland. *From the Cotton Field to the Cotton Mill: A Study of the Industrial Transition in North Carolina.* New York: Macmillan, 1906.

———. "The Civil War and Social and Economic Changes." *Annals of the American Academy of Political and Social Sciences* 154 (January 1931): 11–20.

Thornton, J. Mills, III. *Politics and Power in a Slave Society: Alabama, 1800–1860.* Baton Rouge: Louisiana State University Press, 1978.

Todd, Richard Cecil. *Confederate Finance.* Athens: University of Georgia Press, 1954.

Towers, Frank. *The Urban South and the Coming of the Civil War.* Charlottesville: University of Virginia Press, 2004.

Tregle, Joseph G. *Louisiana in the Age of Jackson: A Clash of Cultures and Personalities.* Baton Rouge: Louisiana State University Press, 1999.

Van Deusen, John G. *The Ante-Bellum Southern Commercial Conventions.* Durham, NC: Duke University Press, 1926.

Varner, Gary R. *Charles G. Leland: The Man and the Myth, Journalist, Adventurer, and Folklorist.* Morrisville, NC: Lulu, 2008.

Vedder, O. F. *History of the City of Memphis.* Vol. 2. Syracuse, NY: D. Mason, 1888.

Wade, Richard C. *Slavery in the Cities: The South, 1820–1860.* New York: Oxford University Press, 1964.

Wakelyn, Jon L. *Southern Pamphlets on Secession: November 1860–April 1861.* Chapel Hill: University of North Carolina Press, 1996.

Wallenstein, Peter. *From Slave South to New South: Public Policy in Nineteenth-Century Georgia.* Chapel Hill: University of North Carolina Press, 1987.

Walther, Eric H. *The Fire-Eaters.* Baton Rouge: Louisiana State University Press, 1992.

———. *William Lowndes Yancey: The Coming of the Civil War.* Chapel Hill: University of North Carolina Press, 2006.

Ward, James A. "A New Look at Antebellum Southern Railroad Development." *Journal of Southern History* 39 (August 1973): 409–20.

Warner, Ezra J., and W. Buck Yearns. *Biographical Register of the Confederate Congress.* Baton Rouge: Louisiana State University Press, 1975.

Waugh, John C. *Surviving the Confederacy: Rebellion, Ruin, and Recovery—Roger and Sara Pryor during the Civil War.* New York: Harcourt, 2002.

Weatherford, Willis D. *James Dunwoody Brownson De Bow.* Southern Sketches, no. 3. Charlottesville, VA: Historical Publishing Co., 1935.

Weber, Jennifer L. *Copperheads: The Rise and Fall of Lincoln's Opponents in the North.* Oxford: Oxford University Press, 2006.

Wells, Jonathan D. *The Origins of the Southern Middle Class, 1800–1861.* Chapel Hill: University of North Carolina Press, 2004.

Wender, Herbert. *Southern Commercial Conventions.* Baltimore: Johns Hopkins University Press, 1930.

Wiethoff, William. *Crafting the Overseers' Image.* Columbia: University of South Carolina Press, 2006.

Williams, David. *Bitterly Divided: The South's Inner Civil War.* New York: New Press, 2008.

Williams, George W., and George Sherwood Dickerman. *History of Banking in South Carolina from 1712 to 1900.* Charleston, SC: Walker, Evans, & Cogswell, 1903.

Wilson, Clyde N., ed. *The Papers of John C. Calhoun.* Vol. 22, *1845–1846.* Columbia: University of South Carolina Press, 1995.

Wilson, Clyde N., and Shirley Bright Cook, eds. *The Papers of John C. Calhoun*. Vol. 23, *1846*. Columbia: University of South Carolina Press, 1996.

Wilson, Harold S. *Confederate Industry: Manufacturers and Quartermasters in the Civil War*. Jackson: University Press of Mississippi, 2002.

Wiltse, Charles M. *John C. Calhoun*. Vol. 1, *Nationalist, 1782–1828*. Indianapolis: Bobbs-Merrill, 1944.

Wish, Harvey. "The Revival of the African Slave Trade in the United States, 1856–1860." *Mississippi Valley Historical Review* 27 (March 1941): 569–88.

Woodman, Harold D. *King Cotton and His Retainers: Financing and Marketing the Cotton Crop of the South, 1800–1925*. Lexington: University of Kentucky Press, 1968.

Woodward, C. Vann. *Tom Watson: Agrarian Rebel*. New York: Macmillan, 1938.

———. *Origins of the New South, 1877–1913*. Baton Rouge: Louisiana State University Press, 1951.

Wooster, Ralph A. *The Secession Conventions of the South*. Princeton, NJ: Princeton University Press, 1962.

Wright, Carroll D., and William C. Hunt. *History and Growth of the United States Census, 1790–1890*. Washington, DC, 1900.

Wright, Gavin. *The Political Economy of the Cotton South: Households, Markets, and Wealth in the Nineteenth Century*. New York: Norton, 1978.

———. *Old South, New South: Revolutions in the Southern Economy since the Civil War*. Baton Rouge: Louisiana State University Press, 1996.

Wriston, Barbara. "Who Was the Architect of the Indiana Cotton Mill, 1849–1850." *Journal of the Society of Architectural Historians* 24 (May 1965): 171–73.

Yearns, Wilfred Buck. *The Confederate Congress*. Athens: University of Georgia Press, 1960.

Young, J. P. *Standard History of Memphis, Tennessee: From a Study of the Original Sources*. Knoxville, TN: H. W. Crew, 1912.

Index

Page numbers that refer to tables are denoted by the letter *t*.

New Directions in Southern History

Series editors

Michele Gillespie, Wake Forest University

William A. Link, University of Florida

The Lost State of Franklin: America's First Secession
Kevin T. Barksdale

Bluecoats and Tar Heels: Soldiers and Civilians in Reconstruction North Carolina
Mark L. Bradley

Becoming Bourgeois: Merchant Culture in the South, 1820–1865
Frank J. Byrne

Cowboy Conservatism: Texas and the Rise of the Modern Right
Sean P. Cunningham

A Tour of Reconstruction: Travel Letters of 1875
Anna Dickinson (J. Matthew Gallman, ed.)

Raising Racists: The Socialization of White Children in the Jim Crow South
Kristina DuRocher

Lum and Abner: Rural America and the Golden Age of Radio
Randal L. Hall

Mountains on the Market: Industry, the Environment, and the South
Randal L. Hall

The New Southern University: Academic Freedom and Liberalism at UNC
Charles J. Holden

Entangled by White Supremacy: Reform in World War I–era South Carolina
Janet G. Hudson

Bloody Breathitt: Politics and Violence in the Appalachian South
T. R. C. Hutton

Cultivating Race: The Expansion of Slavery in Georgia, 1750–1860
Watson W. Jennison

De Bow's Review: *The Antebellum Vision of a New South*
John F. Kvach

Remembering The Battle of the Crater: War as Murder
Kevin M. Levin

The View from the Ground: Experiences of Civil War Soldiers
edited by Aaron Sheehan-Dean

Reconstructing Appalachia: The Civil War's Aftermath
edited by Andrew L. Slap

Blood in the Hills: A History of Violence in Appalachia
edited by Bruce E. Stewart

Moonshiners and Prohibitionists: The Battle over Alcohol in Southern Appalachia
Bruce E. Stewart

The U.S. South and Europe: Transatlantic Relations in the Nineteenth and Twentieth Centuries
edited by Cornelis A. van Minnen and Manfred Berg

Southern Farmers and Their Stories: Memory and Meaning in Oral History
Melissa Walker

Law and Society in the South: A History of North Carolina Court Cases
John W. Wertheimer

Family or Freedom: People of Color in the Antebellum South
Emily West

www.ingramcontent.com/pod-product-compliance
Lightning Source LLC
LaVergne TN
LVHW040154080826
844660LV00014B/961/J

* 9 7 8 0 8 1 3 1 4 4 2 0 7 *